Healing your Heart
of Painful Emotions

Healing your Heart of Painful Emotions

Healing For Damaged Emotions

Putting Away Childish Things

Healing of Memories

Freedom From the Performance Trap

Four Bestselling Books Complete in One Volume

David A. Seamands

INSPIRATIONAL PRESS

First Inspirational Press edition published in 1993.

Inspirational Press
A division of BBS Publishing Corporation
450 Raritan Center Parkway
Edison, NJ 08837

Inspirational Press is a registered trademark of BBS Publishing Corporation.

Published by arrangement with Chariot Victor Publishing, a division of Cook Communications Ministries.

Distributed by World Publishing
Nashville, TN 37214
www.worldpublishing.com

Library of Congress Control Number: 92-76131

ISBN: 0-88486-363-8

Printed in the United States of America.

Scripture Quotation Sources

Contents

HEALING
FOR
DAMAGED
EMOTIONS

Contents

Foreword

WHEN THE HEALING of memories became a popular topic several years ago, a psychologist friend gave me some good advice: "Listen to the tape by David Seamands. It's concise, biblical, and the clearest statement that anyone has given on this topic."

Now Dr. Seamands has expanded his earlier ideas into a book which blends clear biblical theology, solid psychology, and practical common sense. The author writes about anger, guilt, depression, inferiority, and perfectionism—that constant and all pervading feeling that we are never "good enough." Then he takes us to the heart of lingering emotional pain and shows how we can find permanent freedom from our inner turmoil and damaged feelings.

This book avoids simplistic answers, pious condemnation, and confusing jargon. Instead, Dr. Seamands writes with compassion, graciousness, and understanding, all interspersed with bright humor and warm anecdotes about real people. Here is the gentle sharing of a sensitive pastor who is equally at ease in imparting biblical truths and in counseling troubled and searching people.

Because I deeply respect David Seamands' many abilities, I approached his book with high expectations. I did not come away disappointed. His book proved to be interesting, informative, and personally helpful. I am grateful to have the privilege of enthusiastically recommending the following pages.

Gary R. Collins, Ph.D.
Professor and Chairman,
Division of Pastoral Counseling and Psychology
Trinity Evangelical Divinity School

Preface

EARLY IN MY pastoral experience, I discovered that I was failing to help two groups of people through the regular ministries of the church. Their problems were not being solved by the preaching of the Word, commitment to Christ, the filling of the Spirit, prayer, or the Sacraments.

I saw one group being driven into futility and loss of confidence in God's power. While they desperately prayed, their prayers about personal problems didn't seem to be answered. They tried every Christian discipline, but with no result. As they played the same old cracked record of their defeats, the needle would get stuck in repetitive emotional patterns. While they kept up the outward observances of praying and paying and professing, they were going deeper and deeper into disillusionment and despair.

I saw the other group moving toward phoniness. These people were repressing their inner feelings and denying to themselves that anything was seriously wrong, because "Christians can't have such problems." Instead of facing their problems, they covered them with a veneer of Scripture verses, theological terms, and unrealistic platitudes.

The denied problems went underground, only to later reappear in all manner of illnesses, eccentricities, terribly unhappy marriages, and sometimes even in the emotional destruction of their children.

During this time of discovery, God showed me that the ordinary ways of ministering would never help some problems. And He began to enable me to open up my own heart to personal self-discovery, and to new depths of healing love through my marriage, my children, and intimate friends.

God then led me to enlarge my pastoral ministry to include special care and prayer for damaged emotions and unhealed memories.

In the twenty years that I have been preaching, teaching, counseling, and distributing tapes on this subject, I have heard from thousands of formerly defeated Christians who have found release from emotional hangups and who have experienced the healing of crippling memories of the past.

In this book, you will meet some of those people. You will read of attitudes and feelings that are familiar to you or to someone dear to you.

Any resemblance to real persons is completely intentional. All of the people in this book are very much alive; their stories are used with permission. Names and locations have been changed to protect their confidence.

Any resemblance to your life may seem coincidental, but it is also intentional. For most of us have the same needs and longings.

I pray that these chapters will be helpful in picturing God's ways of repairing damaged emotions, of recycling hangups into wholeness, and of transforming crippled Christians into healed helpers.

David A. Seamands
The Methodist Parsonage
Wilmore, Kentucky

1

Damaged Emotions

vonovonovonovonovonovonovonovonovonovonovonovonovonovon

He Himself took our infirmities.

Matthew 8:17, NASB

Likewise the Spirit also helpeth our infirmities; for we know not what we should pray for as we ought; but the Spirit itself maketh intercession for us . . . according to the will of God.

Romans 8:26–27

vonovonovonovonovonovonovonovonovonovonovonovonovonovon

ONE SUNDAY EVENING in 1966, I preached a sermon called "The Holy Spirit and the Healing of Our Damaged Emotions." It was my first venture into this area, and I was convinced that God had given me that message, or I would never have had the courage to preach it. What I said that evening about the healing of the memories and damaged emotions is now old hat. You will find it in a lot of books. But it wasn't old then.

When I got up to preach I looked down at the congregation and saw dear old Dr. Smith. Now Dr. Smith had been a very real part of my boyhood. When my wife, Helen, and I first heard that we were appointed to our present pastorate, a few elderly faces appeared in our minds to trouble us. Dr. Smith was one of them, for I wondered how I could ever minister to him. He had nearly scared the life out of me with his preaching when I was young, and I was still uneasy in his presence.

When I saw him in the congregation that evening, my heart sank. But I went ahead and preached the message that I felt God had given me. After the service, which was followed by a very wonderful time for many at the prayer altar, Dr. Smith remained seated in the congregation. I was busy praying with people at the altar; somewhere back in my mind, I was also praying that he would leave. He didn't. Finally, he came up to the altar; and in his own inimitably gruff way, he said, "David, may I see you in your office?"

All those images from the past arose and the frightened little boy inside of me followed the old man. As I sat down in my office, I felt somewhat like Moses must have before the fire and smoke of Sinai. But I was so wrong about him—I hadn't allowed for change. I had frozen him at one stage and hadn't let him grow.

Very kindly, Dr. Smith said to me, "David, I've never heard a sermon quite like that before, but I want to tell you something." His eyes got moist. He had been an outstanding evangelist and preacher for many years, and had won thousands to Christ. He was a truly great man; but as he looked back over his own ministry he said, "You know, there was always a group of people I could never help. They were sincere people. I believe many of them were Spirit-filled Christians. But they had problems. They brought these things to me and I tried to help. But no amount of advice, no amount of Scripture or prayer on their part ever seemed to bring them lasting deliverance."

Then he said, "I always felt guilty in my ministry, David. But I think you are onto something. Work on it, develop it. Please keep preaching it, for I believe what you have found is the answer."

When he rose to leave, *my* eyes were wet as I said, "Thank you, Doctor." But most of all, I was inwardly saying, "Thank You, God, for Your affirmation through this dear man."

The Problem

Through fifteen years, as tapes have gone out all over the world, letters and testimonies have confirmed my belief that there is another realm of problems which requires a special kind of prayer and a deeper level of healing by the Spirit. Somewhere between our sins, on the one hand, and our sicknesses, on the other, lies an area the Scripture calls "infirmities."

We can explain this by an illustration from nature. If you visit the far West, you will see those beautiful giant sequoia and redwood trees. In most of the parks the naturalists can show you a cross section of a great tree they have cut, and point out that the rings of the tree reveal the developmental history, year by year. Here's a ring that represents a year when there was a terrible drought. Here are a couple of rings from years when there was too much rain. Here's where the tree was struck by lightning. Here are some normal years of growth. This ring shows a forest fire that almost destroyed the tree. Here's another of savage blight and disease. All of this lies embedded in the heart of the tree, representing the autobiography of its growth.

And that's the way it is with us. Just a few minutes beneath the protective bark, the concealing, protective mask, are the recorded rings of our lives.

There are scars of ancient, painful hurts . . . as when a little boy rushed downstairs one Christmas dawn and discovered in his Christmas stocking a dirty old rock, put there to punish him for some trivial boyhood naughtiness. This scar has eaten away in him, causing all kinds of interpersonal difficulties.

Here is the discoloration of a tragic stain that muddied all of life . . . as years ago behind the barn, or in the haystack, or out in the woods, a big brother took a little sister and introduced her into the mysteries—no, the miseries of sex.

And here we see the pressure of a painful, repressed memory . . . of running after an alcoholic father who was about to kill the mother, and then of rushing for the butcher knife. Such scars have been buried in pain for so long that they are causing hurt and rage that are inexplicable. And these scars are not touched by conversion and sanctifying grace, or by the ordinary benefits of prayer.

In the rings of our thoughts and emotions, the record is there; the memories are recorded, and all are alive. And they directly and deeply affect our concepts, our feelings, our relationships. They affect the way we look at life and God, at others and ourselves.

We preachers have often given people the mistaken idea that the new birth and being "filled with the Spirit" are going to automatically take care of these emotional hangups. But this just isn't true. A great crisis experience of Jesus Christ, as important and eternally valuable as this is, is not a shortcut to emotional health. It is not a quickie cure for personality problems.

It is necessary that we understand this, first of all, so that we can compassionately live with ourselves and allow the Holy Spirit to work with special healing in our own hurts and confusions. We also need to understand this in order to not judge other people too harshly, but to have patience with their confusing and contradictory behavior. In so doing, we will be kept from unfairly criticizing and judging fellow Christians. They're not fakes, phonies, or hypocrites. They are people, like you and me, with hurts and scars and wrong programming that interfere with their present behavior.

Understanding that salvation does not give instant emotional health offers us an important insight into the doctrine of sanctification. It is impossible to know how Christian a person is, merely on the basis of his outward behavior.

Isn't it true that by their fruits ye shall know them? (Matt. 7:16) Yes, but it is also true that by their roots you shall understand, and not judge them. Over here is John who may appear to be more spiritual and responsible as a Christian than Bill. But actually, considering John's roots and the good kind of soil he had to grow in and out of, Bill may be a saint by comparison. He may have made much more progress than John in really being conformed to the image of Jesus Christ. How wrong, how unchristian to superficially judge people!

Some may object: "What are you doing? Lowering standards? Are you denying the power of the Holy Spirit to heal our hangups? Are you trying to give us a copout for responsibility, so that we can blame life, or heredity, or parents, or teachers, or sweethearts or mates for our defeats and failures? In the words of St. Paul: 'Shall we continue in sin, that grace may abound?'" (Rom. 6:1)

And I would answer as Paul answered that question, "God forbid!" What I am saying is that certain areas of our lives need special healing by the Holy Spirit. Because they are not subject to ordinary prayer, discipline, and willpower, they need a special kind of understanding, an unlearning of past wrong programming, and a relearning and reprogramming transformation by the renewal of our minds. And this is not done overnight by a crisis experience.

Two Extremes

Understanding these things will protect us from two extremes. Some Christians see anything that wiggles as the devil. Let me say a kind but firm word to young or immature Christians. Throughout the centuries the church has been very careful about declaring a person demon-possessed. There *is* such a thing as demon possession. On rare occasions, during my many years of ministry, I have felt led to take the authority of the name of Jesus to cast out what I believed was an evil spirit, and I have seen deliverance and healing.

But only careful, prayerful, mature, Spirit-filled Christians should ever attempt anything in the nature of exorcism. I spend a lot of time in the counseling room, picking up the pieces of people who have been utterly disillusioned and devastated, because immature Christians tried to cast imaginary demons out of them.

The other extreme is an overly simplistic pat-answer syndrome, which says, "Read your Bible. Pray. Have more faith. If you were spiritually OK, you wouldn't have this hangup. You would never get depressed. You would never have any sexual compulsions or problems."

However, people who say such things are being very cruel. They are only piling more weights on a person who is in pain and unsuccessfully struggling with an emotionally rooted problem. He already feels guilty about it; when people make him feel worse for even having the problem, they double the weight of his guilt and despair.

Perhaps you have heard about the man who was traveling on a dinner flight. When he opened his prepackaged meal, right on top of the salad he saw an enormous roach. When he got home he wrote an indignant letter to the president of that airline. A few days later, a special delivery letter came from the president. He was all apologies. "This was very unusual, but don't worry. I want to assure you that that particular airplane has been completely fumigated. In fact, all the seats and the upholstery have been stripped out. We have taken disciplinary action against the stewardess who served you that meal, and she may even be fired. It is highly probable that this particular aircraft will be taken out of service. I can assure you that it will never happen again. And I trust you will continue to fly with us."

Well, the man was terrifically impressed by such a letter, until he noticed something. Quite by accident the letter he had written had stuck to the back of the president's letter. When he looked at his own letter, he saw a note at the bottom that said, "Reply with the regular roach letter."

So often we reply with the regular roach letter to people suffering with emotional problems. We give pat, oversimplified answers, which drive them to deeper despair and disillusionment.

The Evidence

What are some of these damaged emotions? One of the most common is a deep *sense of unworthiness,* a continuous feeling of anxiety, inadequacy, and inferiority, an inner nagging that says, "I'm no good. I'll never amount to anything. No one could ever possibly love me. Everything I do is wrong."

What happens to this kind of person, when he becomes a Christian? Part of his mind believes in God's love, accepts God's forgiveness, and feels at peace for a while. Then, all of a sudden, everything within him rises up to cry out, "It's a lie! Don't believe it! Don't pray! There's no one up there to hear you. No one really cares. There's no one to relieve your anxiety. How could God possibly love you and forgive someone like you? You're too bad!"

What has happened? The good news of the Gospel has not penetrated down into his damaged inner self, which also needs to be evangelized. His deep inner scars must be touched and healed by the Balm of Gilead.

Then there's another kind, that for want of a better term, I call the *perfectionist complex*. This is the inner feeling that says, "I can never quite achieve. I never do anything well enough. I can't please myself, others, or God." This kind of a person is always groping, striving, usually feeling guilty, driven by inner oughts and shoulds. "I ought to be able to do this. I should be able to do that. I must be a little bit better." He's ever climbing, but never reaching.

What happens to this person, when he becomes a Christian? Tragically enough, he usually transfers his perfectionism onto his relationship with God, who is seen now as a figure on top of a tall ladder. He says to himself, "I'm going to climb up to God now. I'm His child, and I want to please Him, more than I want anything else."

So he starts climbing, rung by rung, working so hard, until his knuckles are bleeding and his shins are bruised. Finally, he reaches the top, only to find that his God has moved up three rungs; so he puts on his Avis button and determines to try a little harder. He climbs and struggles, but when he gets up there, his God has gone up another three rungs.

Some years ago I received a telephone call from the wife of a minister friend of mine, asking me to counsel her husband who had just suffered a complete nervous breakdown. As we were driving to the hospital, she began to talk about him. "I just don't understand Bill. It's almost as if he has a built-in slave driver that won't let him go. He can't relax, can't let down. He's always overworking. His people just love him; and they would do anything for him, but he can't let them. He's gone on and on like this for so many years that finally he has broken completely."

I began to visit with Bill, and after he was well enough to talk, he shared with me about his home and his childhood. As Bill grew up he wanted very much to please his parents. He tried to win his mother's approval by occasionally helping her set the table. But she'd say, "Bill, you've got the knives in the wrong place." So he would put the knives in the right place. "Now you've got the forks wrong." After that it would be the salad plates. He could never please her. Try as hard as he might, he could never please his father either. He brought home his report card with B's and C's. His dad looked at the card and said, "Bill, I think if you try, you could surely get all B's, couldn't you?" So he studied harder and harder, until one day he brought home all B's. Dad said, "But surely, you know, if you just put a little more effort into it, you could get all A's." So he worked and struggled through a semester or two, until finally he got all A's. He was so excited—now Mother and Dad would surely be pleased with him. He ran home, for he could hardly wait. Dad looked at the report card and said, "Well, I know those teachers. They always give A's."

When Bill became a minister, all he did was exchange one mother and one father for several hundred of them: his congregation became his unpleaseable parents. He could never satisfy them, no matter what he did. Finally, he just collapsed under the sheer weight of struggling for approval and trying to prove himself.

A famous God-is-dead theologian was being interviewed. The reporter asked, "What do you mean by *God?*"

"God? God, to me, is that little inner voice that always says, 'That's not quite good enough.'"

He didn't tell us much about God, but he did say a lot about his own damaged personality. And I presume that such sick people produce sick theologies. Oh how the perfectionist complex defeats people in the Christian life! And how it even keeps people out of the kingdom!

Then there is another kind of damaged emotion that we can call *supersensitivity*. The supersensitive person has usually been hurt deeply. He reached out for love and approval and affection, but instead he got the opposite, and he has scars deep inside of him. Sometimes he sees things other people don't see, and tends to feel things other people don't feel.

One day I was walking down the street and saw supersensitive Charlie coming toward me. I usually give him a lot of attention, but that morning I was very busy so I just said, "Hi, Charlie. How are you?" and passed on by. When I got back to the office, a church member called me on the phone and asked, "Are you mad at Charlie?"

"Charlie who?"

"Well, you know, Charlie Olson."

"Why, no. I just saw him down the street." Then I suddenly realized that I hadn't given Charlie the appreciation and the affirmation I usually do, knowing he is supersensitive.

Did you ever hear about the man who was so supersensitive he had to stop going to football games? You see, every time the team got into a huddle, he thought they were talking about him.

Supersensitive people need a lot of approval. You can never quite give them enough. And sometimes they seem very insensitive. They have been hurt so badly that instead of becoming sensitive, they cover it by being hard, tough. They want to get even and hurt others. So quite unbeknown to them, they spend their lives pushing people around, hurting and dominating them. They use money or authority or position or sex or even sermons to hurt people. Does all this affect their Christian experience? Yes, very deeply.

Then there are the people who are filled with *fears*. Perhaps the greatest of them all is the fear of failure. These damaged persons are so afraid of losing the game of life that they have a simple way out— never get into the game; just sit on the sidelines. They say, "I don't like the rules," or, "I don't care for the referee." "The ball isn't quite round." "The goals are not right."

I remember some years ago talking with a salesman in a used car lot. As we looked out the showroom window, we saw a man who was going around kicking tires on the cars. He was also raising the hoods and banging the fenders. The salesman said disgustedly, "Look at that guy out there. He's a wheel-kicker. They are the bane of our existence. They come in here all the time, but never buy cars because they can't make up their minds. Now watch him out there. He's kicking the tires. He'll say the wheels are out of line. He'll listen to the motor and say, 'Hear that knock?' Nobody else can hear the knock, but he can hear it. Something is always wrong. He is afraid to choose; he can never make up his mind, so he always finds an excuse."

Life is filled with wheel-kickers, people who fear failure, fear making the wrong decision. What happens to such people as they approach the Christian life? Believing is a great risk; it's very hard. Decisions tear them up. Faith comes hard. Witnessing is difficult. Launching out in the Holy Spirit and really surrendering to God is almost a trauma. Discipline is difficult. The fearful people live on *if onlys*: "If only this or if only that, then I would be OK." But since the *if only* never comes to pass, they usually never accomplish what they would like to. The fearful are the defeated and the indecisive.

The whole area of *sex* is intricately mixed in with all these others, but needs a special word said about it.

When the Apostle Paul wrote his first epistle to the Corinthians, he dealt with every imaginable kind of human problem, and some which are almost unimaginable. He talked about quarrels, party splits, court cases, property disputes, and various kinds of sexual difficulty, from incest to prostitution. He talked about premarital relations and marital relations and postmarital relations. He wrote about widowhood, divorce, vegetarianism, getting drunk at the Communion table, speaking in tongues, death and funerals, taking up offerings, and conducting an every-member canvass in the church!

But he began his letter by saying he was not going to know anything among them except "Jesus Christ, and Him crucified" (1 Cor. 2:2). This means our Gospel is most practical, and gets right down to where we live. Much of Paul's letter had to do with sexual problems.

Because we Americans have been weaned on indiscipline, indecency, and sensuality, we are living in a modern Corinth. In our society, it is very difficult for anyone to grow to young adulthood without suffering some damage in the sex department of his personality.

I'm thinking of scores of people who have come to me for help. I remember a lady who had heard me speak in her church and then drove 1,200 miles to talk with me. I remember a man who finally came into the office and said that he had driven eleven times around the church, getting up enough nerve to come and see me. Both of these people were genuine Christians, and both were struggling with problems of homosexuality.

I am thinking of a young lady in a distant university where I held a preaching mission. To this day I don't know what she looks like, for she kept her back turned to me and her coat pulled up around her face, as she sat in a corner, sobbing. Finally, she said, "I've got to share this with someone before I explode." Then, still facing the corner, she told me the sad story which we hear more and more often these days, about a father who had treated her not as a daughter, but as a wife.

I am thinking of scores of young men and women who were fed a lot of false and harmful ideas by well-meaning but ignorant parents and preachers. Now they are unfit for marriage, unable to be husbands and wives who can live without fear, guilt, and shame. Damaged? Yes, badly damaged.

Does the Gospel have a message for these various kinds of emotionally damaged persons? For if it doesn't offer healing for all of them, then we had better put a padlock on our church doors, quit playing Christianity, and shut up about our "good news."

Divine Repairs

Does God have some repairs for us? Yes, He does! Paul wrote to the Roman Christians about the Holy Spirit who *helps our infirmities* (Rom. 8:26). Many of the modern translations use *weaknesses* or *cripplings* in place of the word *infirmities*. One meaning of the word *help* has a medical connotation, suggesting the way a nurse helps in the healing process. So it is not simply "to take hold of on the other side," which is the literal meaning of the verb, but that the Holy Spirit becomes our partner and helper, who works along with us in a mutual participation, for our healing.

What is our part in the healing of our damaged emotions? The Holy Spirit is, indeed, the divine counselor, the divine psychiatrist, who gets ahold of our problem on the other end. But we're on this end of it. Just what are you and I supposed to do in this healing process?

That is the very purpose of this book and you will find many suggestions as you read further. However, at this point let me suggest the general, biblical principles which must be followed throughout in order for you to find healing for damaged emotions.

1. *Face your problem squarely.* With ruthless moral honesty, and with God's grace, confront that awful, hidden childhood memory, however deep the feelings within you. Acknowledge it to yourself, and acknowledge it to another human being. Some problems can never be solved until you confess them to others. "Confess your faults one to another, and pray one for another, that you may be healed" (James 5:16). Some people miss deep inner healing because they lack the courage to share deeply with another person.

2. *Accept your responsibility in the matter.* "But," you say, "I was sinned against. I was a victim. You don't know what happened to me."

True enough. But what about your response? What about the fact that you learned to hate or resent, or to escape into an unreal world?

You may say, "My folks never told me anything about sex, and I grew up and I went out into this evil world, innocent and ignorant, and got into trouble." That's the way it happened the first time. But what about the second time or the third time—whose fault was it then? Life is like a complicated tapestry, woven with a loom and shuttle. Heredity, environment, all the things experienced in childhood, from parents, teachers, playmates, all of life's handicaps—all of these things are on one side of the loom, and they pass the shuttle to you. But remember, you pass the shuttle back through the loom. And this action, together with your responses, weaves the design in the tapestry of your life. You are responsible for your actions. You will never receive healing for your damaged emotions until you stop blaming everyone else and accept your responsibility.

3. *Ask yourself if you want to be healed.* This is what Jesus asked the sick man who had lain ill for thirty-eight years (John 5:6). Do you really want to be healed, or do you just want to talk about your problem? Do you want to use your problem to get sympathy from others? Do you just want it for a crutch, so that you can walk with a limp?

The lame man said to Jesus, "But, Lord, nobody puts me into the pool. I try, but they all get there ahead of me." He would not look deep within his heart to find out whether he really wanted to be healed.

We live in an age that some call the "goof-off" era, where each person wants to blame someone else instead of facing his own responsibilities. I have been working with college students for many years, and sometimes I wonder what the B.A. degree really means: Bachelor of Arts or Builder of Alibis. Ask yourself: "Do I really want to be healed? Am I willing to face my responsibility in the matter?"

4. *Forgive everyone who is involved in your problem.* Facing responsibility and forgiving people are really two sides of the same coin. The reason some people have never been able to forgive is that if they forgave, the last rug would be pulled out from under them and they would have no one to blame. Facing responsibility and forgiving are almost the same action; in some instances you need to do them simultaneously. Jesus made it very plain that no healing occurs until there is deep forgiveness.

5 . *Forgive yourself.* So many Christians say, "Yes, I know that God

has forgiven me, but I can never forgive myself." This statement is a contradiction in terms. How can you really believe that God has forgiven you, and then not forgive yourself? When God forgives, He buries your sins in the sea of His forgiveness and His forgetfulness. As Corrie Ten Boom says, "He then puts a sign on the bank which says: 'No fishing allowed.'" You have no right to dredge up anything that God has forgiven and forgotten. He has put it behind His back. Through an inscrutable mystery, divine omniscience has somehow forgotten your sins. You *can* forgive yourself.

6. *Ask the Holy Spirit to show you what your real problem is, and how you need to pray.* Paul said that often we do not know how to pray as we ought (Rom. 8:26). But the Holy Spirit prays in and through us, and makes intercession for us. Sometimes the Holy Spirit uses a temporary assistant in the form of a human counselor, who can help us to perceive what the real problem is. Sometimes the Spirit is able to do this through God's Word or through some incident in life that suddenly makes us aware of our real problem. For it is important that we realize the true problem and know how we should pray. James reminded us that we sometimes do not receive because we pray for the wrong things (James 4:3). It may be essential for you to get help from a counselor or a pastor or a friend; then together with this person, you can ask the Holy Spirit to show you where your real need is.

Do you remember the story of Henry Ford and Charlie Steinmetz? Steinmetz was a dwarf, ugly and deformed, but he had one of the greatest minds in the field of electricity that the world has ever known. Steinmetz built the great generators for Henry Ford in his first plant in Dearborn, Michigan. One day those generators broke down and the plant came to a halt. They brought in ordinary mechanics and helpers who couldn't get the generators going again. They were losing money. Then Ford called Steinmetz. The genius came, seemed to just putter around for a few hours, and then threw the switch that put the great Ford plant back into operation.

A few days later Henry Ford received a bill from Steinmetz for $10,000. Although Ford was a very rich man, he returned the bill with a note, "Charlie, isn't this bill just a little high for a few hours of tinkering around on those motors?"

Steinmetz returned the bill to Ford. This time it read: "For tinkering around on the motors: $10. For knowing where to tinker: $9,990. Total: $10,000." Henry Ford paid the bill.

The Holy Spirit knows where to tinker. We do not know what we ought to be praying for. We often do not receive, because we ask for the wrong things. As you read these chapters, ask the Holy Spirit to show you what you need to know about yourself, and then to guide you in your prayers.

2

Guilt, Grace, and Debt-Collecting

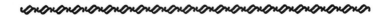

Therefore is the kingdom of heaven likened unto a certain king, which would take account of his servants. . . . One was brought unto him, which owed him ten thousand talents. But forasmuch as he had not to pay, his lord commanded him to be sold . . . he fell down, and worshiped him saying, "Lord, have patience with me, and I will pay thee all." Then the lord of that servant was moved with compassion and loosed him, and forgave him the debt.

But the same servant went out, and found one of his fellow servants, which owed him an hundred pence; and he . . . took him by the throat, saying, "Pay me that thou owest" . . . and cast him into prison, till he should pay the debt.

And his lord was wroth, and delivered him to the tormentors, till he should pay all that was due unto him. So likewise shall My heavenly Father do also unto you, if ye from your hearts forgive not every one his brother their trespasses.

Matthew 18:23–35

Forgive us our debts, as we forgive our debtors.

Matthew 6:12

WITH THIS PARABLE, Jesus put into living color and stereophonic sound His teachings about forgiveness. The parable is filled with profound insights about spiritual and emotional healing. We shouldn't be surprised at this. Jesus was the only normal and perfectly sane Person who has ever lived We are told that He knew what was in man, and at the deepest levels. So we should expect His truths, His teachings, to contain the most penetrating psychological truths.

The Parable

When the king decided to settle his accounts, he found that one servant owed him the fantastic sum of ten million dollars. Jesus used an impossible sum of money in this parable. The annual taxes from the provinces of Judea, Idumea, Samaria, Galilee, and Perea all put together only amounted to $800,000. But the exaggerated size of the debt is the whole point. A person's debt to God and to others is so great that it can never be paid back, any more than a servant working for a few cents a day could ever save up enough money to repay a debt of ten million dollars.

The servant fell on his knees and begged for mercy. He was asking for a special kind of mercy, *makrothumason*. Every time this word is used in the New Testament. it means "an extension of time, a delay." "Lord, have patience with me. Please delay and I'll pay you back everything. Give me more time."

We see that the servant's idea of forgiveness was one thing, but the lord's idea was another. The lord in his mercy forgave him all his debt and released him.

But that same servant as he went out saw a fellow servant, a co-worker, who owed him a measly twenty bucks. He seized him by the throat and said, "Pay me what you owe me." When the co-worker couldn't do it, the servant showed no mercy on him but put him into the debtor's prison until he paid in full.

Then the lord summoned the servant and said, "Look, I forgave you all your debts and now you treat your fellow servant this way." So in anger the lord delivered him to prison until he should pay all.

Now, that's bad enough, but Jesus' next statement is the real shocker. "So also My heavenly Father will do to every one of you if you do not forgive your brother from your heart."

Wait a minute, Jesus. What are you trying to tell us? What kind of picture of the heavenly Father is this? Is it a mistranslation? No, the inference is clear. To the unforgiven and the unforgiving, God will be like a harsh and stern debt-collector.

Is this an exaggeration, like the inflated sum of money? Or does it refer to the future life, to the punishment of the wicked? It may include those, but we don't have to wait until the next life to see Jesus' words come true. For here and now, the unforgiven and unforgiving person is plagued with guilt and resentment. He lives in a prison house where he finds himself tortured by all manner of inner emotional conflicts.

Oughts and Debts

Woven into Jesus' parable is a picture of human relationships. The world is made for forgiveness; it is made for grace; it is made for love in all of life.

The need for these has been built into the structure of nature, of persons. It is in every cell of our bodies, in every interpersonal relationship. We are made for grace and love and acceptance.

One of the biblical descriptions of sin is "violation of God's laws." When we break those laws we are, in a sense, in debt to them. The words *ought* and *owe* come from the same root. To say, "I ought to do this," or "I ought not to do this," is like saying, "I owe it to God," or "I owe it to this person" to do this or not to do this.

What is true about God's laws is also true in the realm of interpersonal relationships. We feel *oughts* and *debts* to one another. When we sin against a person, we often say, "Somehow I feel as if I'm in debt to him," or "I feel as if she owes me an apology." When a person is released from prison, we say he has paid his *debt* to society.

Jesus put this concept at the very heart of the Lord's Prayer when He taught us to pray, "Forgive us our debts as we forgive those who owe us debts." A pastor, counselor, or anyone who works closely with human beings knows that this whole debt system has been built into the human personality in a most incredible fashion. There is a sense of *oughtness*, of *owing* a debt, an automatic mechanism by which the built-in debt collectors go to work. We seek to atone for those wrongs, to pay the debt we owe, or to collect the debt that someone else owes us. If we feel anger at ourselves, we say, "I must pay in full." Or if we feel anger at someone else, he or she must pay. In this way the whole inexorable process is set in motion as the personality is turned over to the inner tormentors. They are the jailers who work as debt-collectors in this awful prison.

Some of us remember the defensive lineup of the Los Angeles Rams of a few years ago. Half a ton of human flesh simply buried the opposition. They were called the Fearsome Foursome. Jesus is saying that the unforgiven and the unforgiving get turned over to a Fearsome Foursome of guilt, resentment, striving, and anxiety. These four produce stress, conflict, and all sorts of emotional problems.

Dr. David Belgum, commenting on the claim that up to seventy-five percent of the people in hospitals today with physical illnesses have sicknesses rooted in emotional causes, says that these patients are punishing themselves with their illnesses; and that their physical symptoms and breakdowns may be their involuntary confessions of guilt (*Guilt: Where Psychology and Religion Meet*, Prentice-Hall, p. 54).

Causes for Emotional Problems

Many years ago I was driven to the conclusion that the two major causes of most emotional problems among evangelical Christians are these: the failure to understand, receive, and live out God's unconditional grace and forgiveness; and the failure to give out that unconditional love, forgiveness, and grace to other people.

1. *Failure to receive forgiveness.* So many of us are like that servant in the parable. Because he misunderstood the offer the lord gave him, he pled for an extension of time. And what happened? The lord in his mercy gave him far more than he asked for, more than he could dream about or pray for; he released him and forgave him all his debts.

But the servant never heard what the lord said to him. He thought that his master had given him what he asked for. And what did he ask for? Patience and extension of time. "Lord, please don't foreclose on my debt. Extend my promissory note a little longer and I assure you I'll pay you everything l owe you." And in his pride and moral stupidity, he thought he could pay back $10 million, if he was only given enough time. But the master in his mercy wiped out the whole debt. He didn't extend the note. He tore it up. He canceled it, and set the man free from his debts, free from the threat of imprisonment.

The poor servant really couldn't believe the wonderful news. He couldn't receive it. He couldn't live it. He couldn't enjoy it. He thought he was still under sentence as a debtor and he'd simply been given more time to work and skimp, and to save and then pay what he owed.

Because he didn't realize the debt had been canceled, the hidden tormentors of resentment, guilt, striving, and anxiety went to work in him. Because he thought he still owed, he thought he still had to pay, and also to collect debts from others.

Many of us are like that. We read, we hear, we believe a good theology of grace. But that's not the way we live. We believe grace in our heads but not in our gut level feelings or in our relationships. There's no other word we throw around more piously. We affirm grace in our creeds and sing about it in our hymns. We proclaim it as distinctive of the Christian faith—that we are saved by grace alone through faith. But it's all on a head level. The good news of the Gospel of grace has not penetrated the level of our emotions. It hasn't worked its way into our interpersonal relationships. We rattle off the definition: "Grace is God's undeserved favor." But it's not in our feelings. It's not in our living. We don't go far enough.

Grace is not only God's undeserved mercy and favor. It is also unearned and can never be repaid. The failure to see and know and feel grace drives many Christians to the tragic treadmill of performing, achieving, and striving. They try to get rid of their guilt. They try to atone and pay the debt. They read an extra chapter in the Bible and extend their prayertime for another ten minutes, and then go out and do some guilty witnessing. And what they have is salvation by promissory note.

Many Christians are like the young minister who once came to see me. He was having a lot of problems getting along with other people, especially his wife and family. I had already talked privately with his wife; she was a very fine person—attractive, warm, affectionate, loving—and totally supported him in his ministry. But he was continually criticizing her, scapegoating her. Everything she did was wrong. He was sarcastic and demanding, and withdrew from her advances, rejecting her love and affection. Slowly but surely it began to dawn on him: he was destroying their marriage.

Then he realized that in his weekend pastorate he was hurting people through sermons which were excessively harsh and judgmental. You can do that, you know. He was working out all of his unhappiness on other people.

Finally, in his desperation, he came to see me. At the beginning of our interview, he met trouble like a real man: he blamed it on his wife!

But after a while, when he became honest, the painful root of the matter came to light.

While he was in the armed forces in Korea, he had spent two weeks of R and R in Japan. During that leave, walking the streets of Tokyo, feeling empty, lonely, and terribly homesick, he fell into temptation and went three or four times to a prostitute.

He had never been able to forgive himself. He had sought God's forgiveness, and with his head, believed he had it. But the guilt still plagued him and he hated himself. Every time he looked in the mirror, he couldn't stand what he was seeing. He had never shared this with anyone and the burden was becoming intolerable.

When he returned home to marry his fiancee, who had faithfully waited for him all those years, his emotional conflicts increased because he still could not accept complete forgiveness. He couldn't forgive himself for what he had done to himself and to her; so he couldn't accept her freely offered affection and love. He felt he had no right to be happy. He said to himself, "I have no right to enjoy my wife. I have no right to enjoy my life. I've got to pay back the debt."

The terrible tormentors were at work within him and he was trying to punish himself, to suffer, to atone for all of his guilt. All those years he lived in a prison house, with the debt-collectors doing their deadly work. As A. W. Tozer put it, the young minister was living in "the perpetual penance of regret."

How beautiful it was to see him receive full, free forgiveness from God, then from his wife, and perhaps best of all, from himself. Sure he was a Christian. He believed and even preached grace, but he had never completely accepted God's forgiveness. He was trying to repay by promissory note. He was doing a self-atonement job, with the guilt disposal unit going inside him.

There is no forgiveness from God unless you freely forgive your brother from your heart. And I wonder if we have been too narrow in thinking that *brother* only applies to someone else. What if *you* are the brother or sister who needs to be forgiven, and you need to forgive *yourself*? Does it not apply to *you* too? The Lord says to forgive your enemies. What if *you* are the worst enemy? Does that exclude *you*? This serviceman-minister had to realize that to forgive the other meant to forgive himself also. Anger and resentment against yourself, a refusal to forgive yourself—these are just as damaging when directed at yourself as when they are directed against other people.

2. *Failure to give forgiveness.* When we fail to accept and receive God's grace and forgiveness, we also fail to give unconditional love, forgiveness, and grace to other people. And this results in a breakdown of our interpersonal relationships. It results in emotional conflicts between us and other people. The unforgiven are the unforgiving, and the unforgiving complete the vicious circle because they cannot be forgiven.

How tragic is this parable! The servant, not realizing he was completely forgiven, thought he still had to go around collecting money from the servants who owed him, so that he could pay the lord a debt—that had been canceled. He went home, checked his ledger, and said, "I've got to get all this money because I told the master I would pay him back." And what happened? He grabbed hold of the first fellow servant he found, seized him by the throat, and said. "Pay me what you owe me. Give me that twenty bucks."

Think of it. He thought he had at least been given an extension on his promissory note. He wouldn't even give this guy more time, but said, "Pay me right now or I'll throw you in prison." When the poor fellow didn't have the money, he was sent to jail. Not a very healthy way to maintain good interpersonal relations!

The vicious circle becomes more vicious. The unaccepted are the unaccepting. The unforgiven are the unforgiving. The ungraced are the ungracious. In fact, their behavior is sometimes positively disgraceful. And emotional conflicts and broken relationships are the result.

Think of how you apply this to the Significant Others in your life: *parents* who hurt you when you were growing up; *brothers and sisters* who failed you when you needed help, who teased you, and put you down; a *friend* who betrayed you; a *sweetheart* who rejected you; your *marriage partner*, who promised to love, honor, comfort, and care for you, but instead has nagged or scapegoated or caused you pain. They all owe you a debt, don't they?

They owe you affection and love, security and affirmation, but since you feel indebted and guilty, resentful, insecure, and anxious, since you see yourself as unforgiven and unacceptable, you in turn become unforgiving and unaccepting. You have not received grace, so how can you give it to others? And as you feel tormented, you hurt others.

You've got to collect on the grievances, collect on your hurts. You must make all these people who have hurt you pay the debts they owe you. You are a grievance collector.

Marriage in Debt

Many married people fail to allow God to do for them what only God can do. Then they ask other human beings, their spouses, to do what they cannot possibly do. If they work at it, men make good husbands, and women make good wives. But they make lousy gods. They're not meant for that. And all those wonderful promises that people make on their wedding day—"I promise to love, care for you, cherish you, through all the circumstances and vicissitudes of life"—these are possible only when a heart is secure in God's love, grace, and care. Only a forgiven and graced soul can keep such promises. What the person often really means when he says those beautiful words is, "I have a lot of terrific inner needs and inner emptiness and debts to pay and I'm going to give you a marvelous opportunity to fill my Grand Canyon and take care of me. Aren't I wonderful?"

Psychologist Larry Crabbe compares this behavior to a tick on a dog. The tick isn't really interested in a good life for the dog; he's simply taking all the time. You see, the tragedy with some marriages is that both partners are takers, and the marriage is like two ticks and no dog! Two collectors and nothing to collect.

Many years ago a couple came to see me. They'd been married fifteen years. Fifteen years of marital Ping-Pong. Every time he pinged, she ponged, or vice versa. Offensive and defensive play alternated. As we slowly and painfully counseled together, we first had to remove some theological wrappings to uncover the terrible disappointment, hurt, and real resentment they felt against one another. She had married *him* for his spiritual leadership—he had been a VIP on campus. He seemed disciplined, firm, and hard-working—a young man who would really go places for the Lord.

You can imagine her shock when he turned out to be indecisive, and undisciplined, lazy and procrastinating. In her anger she, like the servant of old, was seizing him by the throat and saying, "You cheated me. You owe me all those expectations I had when I married you." She saw him as a person in debt to her. With her nagging words she had spent fifteen years saying, "Pay me what you owe me, old man."

But, you see, he had married *her* for her good looks and her neatness and orderliness. You can imagine his terrible disappointment when he discovered she was sloppy about the housework, careless about her hair and dress and appearance. He felt she had cheated him. "You owe me these things because this is the promise you gave me in courtship; this is who I thought you were. You made me these promises." And so he was seizing her by the throat, and with his sarcasm and cutting remarks, was saying, "Pay me what you owe me. You didn't come through on your promissory note."

Each one had been waiting fifteen years for the other one to change. Oh, the tragedy of interpersonal relationships among professing Christians. We are debt-collectors. We are grievance collectors. Why? Because we don't realize our debt has been fully canceled, that it's over. Although God has torn up the note at Calvary, we're still trying so hard.

After I preached about debt-collecting at a counseling conference, I was going up the aisle when a mother grabbed ahold of me. She said, "I never realized it. That's what I've been doing to my kids for the last eighteen years—collecting debts, asking them to pay me what they owed me, instead of giving them unconditional love." And what a lot of hangups it caused.

Three Tests

Will you take three tests with me, to see if there is someone you need to forgive, including yourself?

1. *First of all, there's the resentment test.* Is there someone you resent, you've never let off the hook? A parent, brother, sister, sweetheart, marriage partner, friend, co-worker, someone who wronged you in childhood, some teacher in grade school, or someone who misused you sexually as you grew up?

2. *The responsibility test is a little trickier.* It goes something like this: "Oh, if only Mary, Joe, or Pete, my parents, my wife, my children, life, God—if only they had given me what they owed me, I wouldn't be in this mess today. I wouldn't have all these personality problems. If they had paid me, then I could have paid off my debts to the master."

For many years I was guilty of passing the buck. Every time I failed or fell or blew it, I heard a comforting voice within me that said, "Don't worry, David. That wasn't your fault. You would have been OK if only . . ."

Do you take responsibility for your own faults and failures, or is there a recording that goes on every time: "They made me what I am. He did it, she did it"? In many instances, extending forgiveness to someone else and assuming responsibility for yourself are two sides of the same coin, and can only be done together.

3. *The reminder and reaction test is really subtle.* Do you find yourself reacting against a person because he reminds you of someone else? Maybe you don't like the way your husband disciplines your children because he reminds you of your father who overdid it. So that causes a clash. You don't like your neighbor, or you respond to a co-worker with a bit of anger, a bit of resentment. Why? Because you have never really forgiven someone else. And your reaction to reminders of that unforgiven person from the past triggers resentment against this person.

How to Deal with Your Debts

There is a scriptural way to deal with all these hurts from our past. God's way goes far beyond forgiving and surrendering resentment. God takes sins, failures, and hurts that happened earlier in your life and wraps His loving purposes around them to change them.

The greatest illustration of this is the Cross. There God took what, from a human standpoint, was the worst injustice and the deepest tragedy that ever happened and turned it into the most sublime gift man has ever known; the gift of salvation.

We see a human illustration of this in the life of Joseph who had been so brutally wronged by his older brothers. When his brothers later groveled before Joseph the ruler, there was no debt-collecting on his part; no leaning heavily on them. He wasn't concerned about collecting the debt. Instead, because he knew they were going to have a hard time forgiving themselves, he said, "Have no fear; for am I in God's place? True enough you planned evil against me, but God planned it for good, to bring about what today is fact, the keeping alive of much people" (Gen. 50:19–20, BERK.).

Are you part of a debt-free community of Christians? Is your marriage free of debt-collecting? Your family? Every church should be a debt-free society, where we love each other because we are loved. Where we accept because we are accepted. Where we grace one another and are gracious because we have been graced, because we know the joy of having seen the Master tear up the charge card that we have spent beyond paying. It's been canceled. He's torn it up. He doesn't add something more to it and say, "Well, I'll give you a little more time to repay."

And so because He has set us free, we can set others free and thereby set in motion grace and love. The Apostle Paul summed it up in nine words: "Owe no man anything, but to love one another" (Rom. 13:8).

In Jesus' words, "Freely you have received, freely give," the root word for *gift is* used four times, so that it literally says, "Giftwise you have been given, giftwise give!" (Matt. 10:8)

3

The Wounded Healer

Seeing then that we have a great High Priest, that is passed into the heavens, Jesus the Son of God, let us hold fast our profession. For we have not an High Priest which cannot be touched with the feeling of our infirmities; but was in all points tempted like as we are, yet without sin. Let us therefore come boldly unto the throne of grace, that we may obtain mercy, and find grace to help in time of need.

In the days of His flesh, when He had offered up prayers and supplications with strong crying and tears unto Him that was able to save Him from death, and was heard in that He feared; though He were a Son, yet learned He obedience by the things which He suffered; and being made perfect, He became the author of eternal salvation unto all them that obey Him.

Hebrews 4:14–16; 5:7–9

IF WE WERE to rephrase Hebrews 4:15 to a positive statement, it would read: "For we have a High Priest who is touched with the feeling of our infirmities." In the Old Testament, the word *infirmity* is connected with the sacrifices offered by the priests. An infirmity was primarily a physical spot, a blemish. It was a defect or a deformity either in a man or in an animal. If a man had an infirmity, even though he was a member of the priestly family of Aaron, he could not function as a priest. His infirmity disqualified him from entering the presence of the holiness of God (Lev. 21:16–24). In the same way, offerings and sacrifices had to be "without spot or blemish." Scores of references in the Book of Leviticus make plain that no infirm animal could be offered to God. Both the offering and the offerer had to be free from infirmities.

In the New Testament we begin to see a figurative use of the word *infirmity*. It is a metaphor, a figure of speech. The common New Testament word for *infirmity* is the negative form of *sthenos* which means "strength." Now, when you put the letter *a* in front of something, that negates it. A *theist* is one who believes in God; you put an *a* in front of the word and it becomes *atheist*, one who does not believe in God. If you put an *a* in front of *sthenos*, which means "strength," you get the root word for infirmity, *astheneia*, "a want of strength, a lack of strength, a weakness, an infirmity, a crippling."

The word is hardly ever used in a purely physical sense in the New Testament. Rather, it refers to mental, moral, and emotional weaknesses, to lack of strength. Infirmities in themselves are not sins, but they do undermine our resistance to temptation. In the New Testament, infirmities are qualities in human nature which may predispose or incline us to sin, sometimes without any conscious choice on our part.

The Book of Hebrews is more like the Book of Leviticus than any other book in the New Testament, and shows that the sacrificial system outlined in Leviticus finds its fulfillment in Jesus Christ, our High Priest. This fulfillment also applies to the matter of infirmities in the priests. The Old Testament priest had infirmities because he shared in the common lot of all human beings. Therefore, when he made his sacrifices, he was also sacrificing for himself to cover all his imperfection, as well as presenting an offering for his people. However, because he had infirmities, he could understand the infirmities of his people and deal more gently with them. He could be more understanding as a priest. For he too was subjected to the inner infirmities which predispose all of us to temptation and sin.

The writer to the Hebrews applied this picture to our great High Priest and Mediator, our Lord Jesus Christ. Because He never sinned, because He never yielded to the temptations unlike the Old Testament priest, He never had to make a sacrifice on His own behalf. But since He was tempted, since He was tested at every point as we are, we have a great High Priest who understands *the feeling of our infirmities*.

If He merely understood the *fact* of our infirmities, that would be good enough. But I've got better news for you. He even understands the *feeling* of our infirmities—not just the cripplings, not just the weaknesses, not just the emotional hangups and the inner conflicts, but the pain that comes from them. He understands the frustration, the anxiety, the depression, the hurts, the feelings of abandonment and loneliness and isolation and rejection. He who is touched with the feeling of our infirmities experiences the whole ghastly gamut of emotions which goes along with our weaknesses and our cripplings.

And what's the proof of this? To what does the writer to the Hebrews turn to show that Jesus understands how we feel as a result of our infirmities? "In the days of His flesh," while Jesus was human, He "offered up prayers and supplications" (Heb. 5:7). In a beautiful, soft quiet time? Oh no. He "offered up prayers and supplications with strong crying and tears unto Him that was able to save Him from death, and was heard in that He feared. Though He were a Son, yet learned He obedience by the things which He suffered" (Heb. 5:7–8).

This points to Gethsemane, to the passion and suffering, to the cross of our Lord, as if to say, "There, He has experienced it all. He knows what it is to cry out with tears. He knows what it is to pray to God with loud sobs. He wrestled with feelings that nearly tore Him to pieces. He knows. He's been through it, and can feel with you. He hurts along with you."

Of all the words for the Incarnation, the greatest title is *Emmanuel,* "God with us." God is in it with us. Better still, God having gone through it Himself knows how to be in it and feel it with us. That is why we can come boldly; we can draw near with confidence. God doesn't say, "You can come guiltily," or "You can come shamefacedly." You never need to feel, *There's something wrong with me because I'm having this depression. I'm not spiritual.* These are cruelties we Christians often inflict on one another, and they are not biblical.

We are not coming into the presence of a neurotic parent who has to hear only good things from his children. We're not coming into the presence of a father who says, "Shhh, don't feel that way; that's wrong. Don't cry. If you keep crying I'll really give you something to cry about."

We are coming to a heavenly Father who understands our feelings and invites us to share them with Him. So we can draw near with confidence unto the throne of grace knowing that we will obtain mercy and find grace in the time of need. We can come when we need forgiveness and when we feel guilty for our sins. And we can also come when we are being racked and tormented by the feelings of our infirmities.

The Garden

To understand what it cost the Saviour to be our Healer, we need to walk with Him through His passion and suffering, as shown in the Gospels, in the Psalms, and in the Book of Isaiah.

Come with me now into the Garden of Gethsemane. Discover what it cost our Saviour to be Emmanuel, God with us. Listen to His prayers. Can you hear them, as if for the first time? He "began to be sorrowful and very heavy. Then saith He unto them, 'My soul is exceeding sorrowful, even unto death'" (Matt. 26:37–38).

Wait a minute, Jesus. What did You say? "My soul is exceeding *sorrowful, even unto death*"? Do You mean to say that You experienced such feelings, such emotions and pain in that wretched hour, that You even wanted to die? Do You mean to say, Lord, You understand when I am so depressed that I no longer want to live?

Look at Psalm 22, one of the so-called Psalms of Dereliction: "I am poured out like water, and all my bones are out of joint: my heart is like wax; it is melted. . . . My strength is dried up like a potsherd [clay in the baking]; and my tongue cleaveth to my jaws; and Thou hast brought me into the dust of death" (vv. 14–15).

Psalm 69 is another: "Save me, O God; for the waters are come in unto my soul" (v. 1). "I am come into deep waters, where the floods overflow me" (v. 2). "I am weary of my crying" (v. 3). "Reproach hath broken my heart; and I am full of heaviness: and I looked for some to take pity, but there was none; and for comforters, but I found none" (v. 20).

"Peter, what, could ye not watch with Me for one hour?" (Matt. 26:40) Three times He implored His friends, but to no avail. Finally, "all the disciples forsook Him, and fled" (Matt. 26:56).

If you have battled terrible loneliness, or pathological emptiness, if you have experienced the blackest bouts of depression, you know that when you are in the pits, the hardest thing to do is to pray, because you do not feel God's presence. I want to assure you that He knows, He understands, He feels your infirmity. He shares all your feelings because He has been through them.

The Trial

Follow Him into the trial, where He listened to false testimony. Have you been falsely accused? Do you know the hurt of that? "They spit in His face and buffeted Him; and others smote Him" (Matt. 26:67). "They mocked Him. . . . they struck Him on the face" (Luke 22:63).

So often when I counsel people who are filled with deep hurt, rage, or pain, they will look at me like the great stone face, without even a flicker of emotion. But when I probe more deeply, asking, "Tell me, what's the worst picture in all of your memory? The one that comes most often to bring you pain?" a change comes about. In the beginning only a trace, then the eyes start to fill with tears; soon the overflow comes down the cheeks, and before long, even strong, strapping men are shaking with pain and anger.

"Oh, I know what it is. I remember. It was when Dad would lash out and hit me on the head. It was when Mother would slap me." Nothing is more destructive to a human personality than a slap in the face. It is so humiliating, so demeaning, so deeply dehumanizing. It destroys something very basic to our personhood.

But our wounded Healer understands. He knows what it is to be struck on the head, to be slapped in the face. He is touched with the feelings, the feelings that arise in you from that hurt. He feels the problems that touch you. He wants to heal. He wants you to know that He is not angry with you about your feelings. He understands.

The Cross

Let us go even farther until we come to the cross itself. They derided Him, wagging their heads and saying, "If Thou be the Son of God, come down from the cross" (Matt. 27:40). They mocked Him, railed Him, scoffed at Him. *Deriding, wagging their heads, mocking, railing, scoffing*—these words bring to mind the growing pains and humiliating hurts of the teen years. One man believes high school is often such a traumatic experience that he' s written a book called *Is There Life after High School?*

I am amazed at the painful sights and sounds grownups share with me from their adolescent memories. The sounds that so often come to people's memories are those of derision, like "Na-na-na-na-*na-na*." Or names like "Smarty," "Fatty," "Clumsy," "Pimple-face," and "Acne."

Or was it being reminded of those big horn-rimmed glasses, or those ugly braces for buck teeth? You fill it in. The cruelty of children to one another is a part of life.

Jesus knows how you feel when you are rejected by a friend, cast off by a lover, made fun of by the gang. In the words of Isaiah, "He hath no form nor comeliness; and when we shall see Him, there is no beauty that we should desire Him. He is despised and rejected of men; a Man of sorrows, and acquainted with grief: and we hid as it were our faces from Him, He was despised, and we esteemed Him not" (Isa. 53:2–3).

Yes, He was a Man of sorrows and acquainted with grief. If you are grieving, He can feel it with you. For the lonely one—the widow or widower, the divorcee—He understands what it is to be alone, to feel that a part of yourself has been literally torn away.

Studies show that the two greatest stress-producing factors to body, mind, and emotions are the death of a spouse and divorce. In some ways, divorce can be worse. The death of a spouse, though painful, can be a clean wound. Divorce often leaves a dirty, infected wound, throbbing with pain. Jesus understands when a single parent is trying to be husband and wife, mother and father, all in one.

But does He know the worst feeling of all our infirmities—when we can't even pray? When we feel abandoned and forsaken by God Himself? The Apostles' Creed says, "He descended into hell." When Christ was hanging on the cross, the very heavens became brassy, not brotherly. They became frighteningly deaf as He was cut off from the land of the living. He cried for help in His final anguish but there was no answer. "My God, My God, why hast Thou forsaken Me? Why art Thou so far off from helping Me, and from the words of My roaring? O My God, I cry in the daytime, but Thou hearest not" (Ps. 22:1–2). God understands the cry of dereliction. He knows the feelings of our infirmities.

To say, as do the ancient creeds, that Christ descended into hell, means that Jesus Christ has entered into every one of the fears, terrors, and anxious feelings that you and I can experience at our lowest moments of rejection, forsakenness, and depression. It means there is not a single feeling that we cannot bring to Him.

We do not need to come guiltily, or shamefacedly. We are to approach boldly, with confidence, knowing He not only feels with us, but wants to heal us. And He has not left us alone, for the Holy Spirit helps us with our infirmities (Rom. 8:26). The human experience of Jesus Christ is now with us in the presence of the Holy Spirit who will aid us with our infirmities, in a mutual participation for their healing.

Young, beautiful, vivacious, athletic Joni Eareckson struck a rock one day when she dived into a lake. Paralysis resulted and she is now a quadraplegic. She paints pictures with a brush in her teeth. Her witness has become worldwide through her books and the movie of her life.

Joni realized how really helpless she was one desperate night when she begged a friend to give her some pills so she could die. When her friend refused, she thought, *I can't even die on my own!* At first life was hell for Joni. Pain, rage, bitterness, and emotional pain shook her spirit. Although she couldn't really feel physical pain, piercing sensations racked her nerves and ran through her body. This went on for three years.

Then one night a dramatic change began in Joni that now makes her the beautiful, radiant Christian she is. Her best friend, Cindy, was at her bedside searching desperately for some way to encourage her. It must have come from the Holy Spirit, for she suddenly blurted it out, "Joni, Jesus knows how you feel. You're not the only one who's been paralyzed. He was paralyzed too."

Joni glared at her. "Cindy, what are you talking about?"

"It's true. It's true, Joni. Remember, He was nailed to the cross. His back was raw from beatings like your back sometimes gets raw. Oh, He must have longed to move. To change His position, to redistribute His weight somehow, but He couldn't move. Joni, He knows how you feel."

That was the beginning, as Cindy's words gripped Joni. She had never thought of it before. God's Son had felt the piercing sensations that racked her body. God's Son knew the helplessness she suffered.

Joni later said, "God became incredibly close to me. I had seen what a difference the love shown me by friends and family had made. I began to realize that God also loved me." (*Where Is God When It Hurts*, Phillip Yancey, Zondervan, pp. 118–119)

As Christians we often thank God that Jesus bore our sins in His body on the tree. We need to remember something else. In His full identification with our humanity, and especially on that cross, He took unto Himself the entire range of our feelings. And He bore the feeling of our infirmities, that we would not have to bear them alone.

Most of us are familiar with the words of the traditional folk spiritual, "Lonesome Valley."

> Jesus walked this lonesome valley,
> He had to walk it by Himself;
> O nobody else could walk it for Him,
> He had to walk it by Himself.

> You must go and stand your trial,
> You have to stand it by yourself;
> O nobody else can stand it for you,
> You have to stand it by yourself.

But I was delighted that recently Erna Moorman added another stanza which has brought the song much more in line with the message of the Scriptures.

> As we walk our lonesome valley,
> We do not walk it by ourselves;
> For God sent His Son to walk it with us,
> We do not walk it by ourselves"

(*Hymns for the Family of God*, Paragon Associates, p. 217).

"We have no superhuman High Priest to whom our weaknesses are unintelligible—He Himself has shared fully in all our experience" (Heb. 4:15, PH). It is this assurance which gives us the grounds for our hope and our healing. The fact that God not only knows and cares, *but fully understands* is the most therapeutic factor in the healing of our damaged emotions.

4

Satan's Deadliest Weapon

Finally, my brethren, be strong in the Lord, and in the power of His might. Put on the whole armor of God, that ye may be able to stand against the wiles of the devil. For we wrestle not against flesh and blood, but against principalities, against powers, against the rulers of the darkness of this world, against spiritual wickedness in high places . . . Praying always with all prayer and supplication in the Spirit, and watching thereunto with all perseverance.

Ephesians 6:10–12, 18

Lest Satan should get an advantage of us; for we are not ignorant of his devices.

2 Corinthians 2:11

THE BIBLICAL PICTURE of Satan is quite different from the popular one. In the Bible he is not the comical creature of the cartoons, with horns, tail, and pitchfork, and ludicrously dressed in long red underwear. Rather, Satan is an adversary, who is clever, wily, and dangerous (1 Peter 5:8).

Because he is of the spirit world, Satan knows your weaknesses; he understands your infirmities and uses them to great advantage against you. The Bible doesn't speak as much of the power of Satan as of his extreme *subtlety*, *trickery*, and *deceptiveness*. He uses clever wiles and devices, stratagems and designs. He knows how to exploit your weaknesses in the direction of discouragement, disappointment, failure, and abdication of the Christian life. He is spoken of as a roaring lion, prowling about trying to find somebody to devour (1 Peter 5:8). Paul wrote of the evil powers of darkness against which we fight (Eph. 6:12). And it is in the dark that we are easily attacked or deceived.

Low Self-Esteem

Some of the most powerful weapons in Satan's arsenal are psychological. Fear is one of these. Doubt is another. Anger, hostility, worry, and of course, guilt. Long-standing guilt is hard to shake off; it seems to hang on even after a Christian claims forgiveness and accepts pardoning grace.

An uneasy sense of self-condemnation hangs over many Christians, like a Los Angeles smog. They find themselves defeated by the most powerful psychological weapon that Satan uses against Christians. This weapon has the effectiveness of a deadly missile. Its name? Low self-esteem.

Satan's greatest psychological weapon is a gut-level feeling of inferiority, inadequacy, and low self-worth. This feeling shackles many Christians, in spite of wonderful spiritual experiences, in spite of their faith and knowledge of God's Word. Although they understand their position as sons and daughters of God, they are tied up in knots, bound by a terrible feeling of inferiority, and chained to a deep sense of worthlessness.

There are four ways that Satan uses this deadliest of all of his emotional and psychological weapons, to bring defeat and failure into your life.

1. *Low self-esteem paralyzes your potential.* In the places I have ministered, I have seen the awful impact of the feeling of inferiority. I have witnessed the tragic loss in human potential, the watered-down living, the wasted gifts, the leakage of a veritable gold mine of human power and possibility. And inwardly I have wept.

Do you know that God also weeps over it? He is not so much angry as He is grieved. He weeps over the paralysis of your potential through low self-esteem. The cost is so great, for it seems all of us have to struggle against this. Very few people have fully overcome the haunting self-doubts, the dragging disappointments about who they are, and what they can be. Low self-esteem begins even in the crib, follows to the kindergarten, and worsens during the teen years. In adult life, it seems to settle in like a great fog that covers many people day by day. Sometimes it lifts a little but always returns, trying to engulf, to drown.

Unfortunately, this is a plague among Christians. In a tape entitled "Satan's Psychological Warfare," Christian psychologist Jim Dobson tells about a poll he took among a large group of women. Most of them were married, in excellent health, and happy. According to their own statements, they had happy children and financial security. On the test Dr. Dobson listed ten sources of depression. He asked the women to number them in the order of how the ten affected their lives. This is the list he gave them:

absence of romantic love in your marriage,
in-law conflicts,
low self-esteem,
problems with children,
financial difficulties,
loneliness, isolation, boredom,
sexual problems in marriage,
health problems,
fatigue and time pressure,
aging.

The women rated these by the amount of depression each produced. What came out way ahead of all the others? Low self-esteem. Fifty percent of these Christian women rated it first; eighty percent of them rated it in the top two or three. Can you see the wasted emotional and spiritual potential? These women were battling depression which came chiefly from the downward pull of feelings of low self-worth.

Jesus told a parable about the talents. The man with the one talent was immobilized by fear and feelings of inadequacy. Because he was so afraid of failure he didn't invest his talent, but buried it in the ground and tried to play it safe. His life was a frozen asset—frozen by fear of rejection by the master, fear of failure, fear of comparison to the other two who were making their investments, fear of taking a risk. He did what a lot of people with low self-esteem do—nothing. And that's exactly what Satan wants for you as a Christian—that you will be so tied up that you are tied down, frozen, paralyzed, settling into a job and a life far below your potential.

2. *Low self-esteem destroys your dreams.* You've probably heard the old

definition, "Neurotics are people who build castles in the air; psychotics are those who move into them; and psychiatrists are the ones who collect the rent!"

However, I'm not talking about daydreams or unrealistic fantasies. We can't live *in* our dreams, we can't live *on* our dreams, but we do live *by* our dreams. One of the characteristics of Pentecost, as prophesied by Joel and fulfilled in the Book of Acts, was that when the Holy Spirit was poured out, the young would see visions and the old would dream dreams (Acts 2:17). The Holy Spirit helps us to dream bold dreams, to see visions of what God wants to do for us and in us, and especially through us.

"Where there is no vision, the people perish" (Prov. 29:18). Yes, and with the wrong kind of vision about yourself, with a low-esteeming picture of yourself as inferior and unable, you will surely self-destruct. Your dreams will be destroyed and God's great plan for your life will not be fulfilled.

The greatest illustration of this is in the Old Testament, in the Book of Numbers, chapters 13 and 14. God had a vision for His people, a bold, beautiful dream. He implanted into their hearts and minds the picture of a Promised Land, flowing with milk and honey, a land which they would possess.

God brought them up to the edge of the Promised Land, to the bold plan He had for them. Moses got his orders from the Lord and then sent a military reconnoitering party into the land to look it over. That's the first historical mention of the CIA—the Canaan Information Agency. Moses sent the cream of the crop, the best man from each tribe. And he fully expected that the realities of Canaan would confirm God's dreams and God's promise. And in a sense they did, for all of the scouts agreed: "It's a fantastic land. Look at the fruit—we never saw grapes and pomegranates like that. And the honey—it is the sweetest you have ever tasted!" (See Num. 13:23.)

"But the people are giants of incredible strength. And the cities are not really cities; they're forts. And those descendants of Anak, the Naphtaliim—why in their sight we were as grasshoppers." (See Num. 13:31–33.)

Now, you can't have a much lower self-concept than to see yourself as a grasshopper. The envoys began to weep and to be filled with fear. Only Caleb and Joshua had a different story. Oh, they agreed on all the facts. Their *observations* were the same; but because their *perceptions* were different, so their *conclusions* were different. Why? Because Caleb was a man of a different spirit (Num. 14:24). There's your answer. Caleb had no worm theology. He and Joshua had no grasshopper esteem of themselves. They said, "Of course the people are big, but don't fear them. The Lord is with us."

I like the Hebrew slang Caleb and Joshua used. "They are as bread for us. We don't care how big they are; we can eat them up just like bread, and we can do this because it is God's will for us. It is God's dream, and He delights to do it in us and through us. He'll give us our dream and give us our land." (See Num. 14:8–10.)

God's great dream, the whole purpose for which He had saved and delivered them from Egypt's slavery was detoured and delayed for forty wretched years in the wilderness. God's dream wasn't a neurotic air castle; it was reality—fruit and honey, land and cities—everything God wanted to give them, all within their reach. The *dream* was ready and *God* was ready, but the people weren't because of their low self-esteem. "We are as grasshoppers." They forgot they were the children of God. They forgot *who* they were and *what* they were.

How we need this message today. We wrap a lot of our fears in morbidly sanctified self-belittling. We piously cover this self-despising and call it consecration and self-crucifixion. It's time we have some bold dreams. It's time we get into the world with our witness, in a far greater way. What holds us back? Fear of criticism, fear of taking a risk, fear of tradition, fear of constituency. In our low self-esteem, we destroy God's dream for us as a community of believers—we who are His very own body.

What happened to your dream? Where is the vision God put before you? What wrecked it? Your sins and transgressions and bad habits? I doubt it. Probably your dream has been delayed or destroyed because Satan tricked you into thinking of yourself as a grasshopper or a worm. And as a result, you never have realized your full potential as a son or a daughter of God. You've filled up with fears and doubts, inferiority, and inadequacy.

How far do you think William Carey, the first great Protestant missionary to India, would have gotten without a dream? He expressed it this way: "Expect great things from God, attempt great things for God." That's the kind of divine dream that is destroyed by low self-esteem. Lack of faith in God is often fed by underestimating what He wants to do through you.

3. *Low self-esteem ruins your relationships.* Think about your relationship with God Himself. It follows quite naturally that if you consider yourself inferior or worthless, you will think that God really must not love and care for you. Such thinking often leads to those inner questions and resentments which begin to foul up your relationship with God. After all, isn't it somewhat His fault that you are this way? He made you as you are. He could have and probably should have done it differently. But He didn't. So it probably means that though He cares for others and gives them a lot of things, He isn't really concerned about you. They're OK, but you're not.

However, once you become critical of the *design*, it isn't long until you feel resentful toward the *Designer*. This is how your concept of God becomes contaminated and your perception of how He feels about you gets all mixed-up, finally ruining your relationship with Him.

Low self-esteem also spoils your relationships with other people. Satan uses your nagging sense of inferiority and inadequacy to isolate you. For the commonest way to cope with feelings of inferiority is to pull within yourself, to have as little contact with other people as you possibly can, and just occasionally to peek out as the rest of the world goes by.

Christ commanded us to love our neighbors as we love ourselves. This implies that it is basic to Christian ethics and to interpersonal relationships for a Christian to have a healthy self-image.

You are able to give to others only when you have a proper and healthy opinion of yourself. When you devaluate yourself, you become overly absorbed *in* and *with* yourself, and you don't have anything left over to give to others.

Who are the hardest people to get along with? Those who don't like themselves. Because they don't like themselves, they don't like others, and they're hard to get along with. Low self-esteem wrecks interpersonal relationships more than anything else I know.

If you have low self-esteem, you ask another human being to do for you what no other person can do—to make you feel adequate and able—when you are already convinced that you are inadequate and unable. That puts too heavy a demand on husband or wife, on children, friends, neighbors, or church. You may become either suspicious and hostile, or cringing and clinging. God wants you to bloom with your own individual beauty, to do your part in making His garden colorful and beautiful.

4. Low self-esteem sabotages your Christian service. What's the greatest obstacle that prevents members of the body of Christ from functioning as parts of the body? What's the first thing people say when you ask them to do something in the body of Christ?

- Teach a Sunday School class? I can't stand up in front of people.
- "Share at the women's meeting, or at the men's meeting? Oh, I couldn't do that.
- "Go knocking on doors? That would scare me to death.
- "Sing in the choir? Why don't you ask Mary? She has a much better voice."

We pastors are nearly drowned in the torrent of downgrading that pours over us in excuses for not doing God's work. I'm not talking about trying to put a square peg in a round hole. Not everybody can do everything. I know people in the church who say, "Pastor, I'm tongue-tied. Public speaking is not my gift, but I can do something else." Everybody can do something and function as a giver of his gift in the body of Christ.

Did you ever notice that God doesn't choose superstars to do His work? Check it out, all the way from Moses—who lost no time in telling God about his stuttering, to Mama's boy Mark—who ran out on Paul and Barnabas. Paul was right when he said that not many wise and noble and terrific are chosen. It seems that God takes people with shortcomings and infirmities, gives them work to do, and then supplies them with sufficient grace to do it. Not many wise, not many noble, not many supermen, not many wonderwomen are on this team (1 Cor. 1:26–31).

The trouble is that your low self-esteem robs God of marvelous opportunities to show off His power and ability through your weaknesses. Paul said, "Therefore, will I rather glory in my infirmities." Why? Because they gave God such a wonderful chance to show off His perfection (2 Cor. 12:9–10). Nothing sabotages Christian service more than thinking so little of yourself that you never really give God a chance.

Do you remember the story about bazaar day in an Indian village? Everybody brought his wares to trade and sell. One farmer brought in a whole covey of quail. And he had tied a string around one foot of each bird. The other ends of all the strings were tied to a ring on a central stick. And the quail were dolefully walking in a circle, around and around, like mules at a sorghum mill. Nobody seemed interested in buying any quail, until along came a devout Brahman. He believed in the Hindu idea of respect for all life and his heart of compassion went out to these poor little creatures. The Brahman inquired the price of the quail and then said to the merchant, "I want to buy them all." The merchant was elated. After he received his money, he was surprised to hear the Brahman say, "Now I want you to set them all free."

"What's that, sir?"

"You heard me. Cut the strings off their feet and turn them loose. Set them all free."

"Well, all right, sir. If that will please you." With his knife the farmer cut the strings off the legs of the quail and set them free. What happened? The quail simply continued marching around and around in a circle. Finally, he had to shoo them off. Even when they landed some distance away, they resumed marching. Free, unbound, released, yet going around in circles as if still tied.

Are you in that picture? Freed, forgiven, a son, a daughter of God, a member of His family, but thinking of yourself as a worm or a grasshopper? Low self-esteem is Satan's deadliest psychological weapon, and it can keep you marching around in vicious circles of fear and uselessness.

5

Healing Our Low Self-Esteem Part 1

Consider the incredible love that the Father has shown us in allowing us to be called "children of God"—and that is not just what we are called, but what we are. Our heredity on the Godward side is no mere figure of speech—which explains why the world will no more recognize us than it recognized Christ. Oh, dear children of mine (forgive the affection of an old man), have you realized it?

Here and now we are God's children. We don't know what we shall become in the future. We only know that, if reality were to break through, we should reflect His likeness, for we should see Him as He really is.

1 John 3:1–2, PHILLIPS

MANY YEARS AGO, a famous plastic surgeon, Dr. Maxwell Maltz, wrote a best-selling book, *New Faces—New Futures*. It was a collection of case histories of people for whom facial plastic surgery had opened the door to a new life. The author's theme was that amazing personality changes can take place when a person's face is changed.

However, as the years went by, Dr. Maltz began to learn something else, not from his successes but from his failures. He began to see patient after patient who, even after facial plastic surgery, did not change. People who were made not simply acceptable, but actually beautiful, kept on thinking and acting the part of the ugly duckling. They acquired new faces but went on wearing the same old personalities. Worse than that, when they looked in a mirror, they would angrily exclaim to the doctor, "I look the same as before. You didn't change a thing." This, in spite of the fact that their friends and their family members could hardly recognize them. Although before-and-after photographs were drastically different, Dr. Maltz's patients kept insisting, "My nose is the same," "My cheekbones are the same," "You didn't help at all."

In 1960 Dr. Maltz wrote his best-seller, *Psycho-Cybernetics* (Prentice-Hall). He was still trying to change people, not by correcting jutting jawbones, or smoothing out scars, but by helping them change the pictures they had of themselves.

Dr. Maltz says it is as if every personality has a face. This emotional face of personality seems to be the real key to change. If it remains scarred and distorted, ugly and inferior, then the person continues to act out a role, regardless of the change in his physical appearance. But if the face of his personality can be reconstructed, if the old emotional scars can be removed, the person can be changed.

All of us could confirm this by our experiences with people as well as our knowledge of ourselves. It is absolutely amazing the way self-image influences our actions and attitudes, and especially our relationships with other people.

Take Marie, for example. Marie's husband, Jim, thought his wife was beautiful. He told me so before they ever came to talk things over. When I saw her, I agreed with him. Jim liked to brag on her to others, and never tired of lovingly telling Marie that she was beautiful. He enjoyed buying her pretty clothes, little love gifts to make her look even more attractive. Now deep down, every wife wants this from her husband. But in Marie's case, her husband's admiration was causing problems, for Marie's picture of herself was diametrically opposite to what Jim saw.

"You're only saying that to flatter me," she'd say. "You don't really mean it."

Jim would feel hurt and frustrated. The more ways he tried to convince Marie that he really thought she was beautiful, the bigger the barrier became.

"I know what I look like," she said. "I can see myself in the mirror. You don't have to make up things like that. Why don't you love me for what I am?" And round and round it went.

Marie's self-concept kept her from thanking God for the gift of beauty. It prevented her from seeing reality. Worst of all, it hindered her from developing a beautiful love-gift relationship with her very devoted husband.

What is self-image or self-concept? Your self-image is based on a whole system of pictures and feelings you have put together about yourself. To express this combination of imagery and emotions, I often use the compound words *feeling-concepts* or *concept-feelings*. For self-concept includes both mental pictures and emotional feelings. You have a whole system of feeling-concepts and concept-feelings about yourself. This is at the very core of your personality. And nowhere is the biblical statement about the heart and mind more appropriate than here: "As he thinketh in his heart, so is he" (Prov. 23:7). The way you *look at* yourself and *feel about* yourself, way down deep in the heart of your personality—so you will be and so you will become. What you see and feel will determine your relationships both with other people and with God.

This fact is vitally important for teenagers, for nothing is more necessary to their Christian growth and their nurture in the Lord than developing a good, healthy Christian self-image.

Dr. Maurice Wagner, a professional Christian counselor, in his excellent book *The Sensation of Being Somebody* (Zondervan, pp. 32–37), explains the three essential components of a healthy self-image:

The first is *a sense of belongingness*, of being loved. This is simply the awareness of being wanted, accepted, cared for, enjoyed, and loved. I personally believe that this sense begins before birth. I've counseled people with such deep wounds that I am convinced their sense of rejection traces back to their parents' attitudes before birth. If a child is unwanted, rarely will he have a sense of belonging.

The second component is *a sense of worth and value*. This is the inner belief and feeling: "I count. I am of value. I have something to offer."

The third is *a sense of being competent*. It is the feeling-concept: "I can do this task; I can cope with that situation; I am able to meet life." Put them all together, Dr. Wagner says, and you have a triad of self-concept feelings: belongingness, worthwhileness, and competence.

Sources of Self-Image

There are four sources of self-image, four factors which help a person construct self-image: the outer world, the inner world, Satan with all the forces of evil, and God and His Word. In this chapter we will look at the outer world since this is the primary source, the basic soil out of which our self-image grows.

Your outer world includes all the factors that have gone into your makeup—your inheritance and birth, your infancy, childhood, and teen years. Your outer world is your experience of life right up to the present time. Your experience with the outer world tells you how you were treated, how you were trained, and how you related to people in the early years of your life. It primarily reflects your parents and family members and the messages they sent to you about yourself through their facial expressions, tones, attitudes, words and actions.

George Herbert Mead, a great social psychologist, uses an interesting phrase to describe a person's relationship to the outer world. He calls it the "looking-glass self." A baby has little concept of the self. But as he grows, he gradually comes to distinguish differences and to gain a picture of himself. Where does he get it? From the reflection of the reactions of the important other people in his life.

Saint Paul was centuries ahead of Dr. Mead. At the heart of the Love Chapter, 1 Corinthians 13 (vv. 9–12), Paul used the same idea when he spoke of growing up:

> My knowledge is imperfect, including my knowledge about myself. When I was a child, I spoke and thought and reasoned like a child. When I grew up I put away my childish ways, and yet even so I still see as in a mirror that offers me only reflections. But one day I'll have perfect knowledge. Then I'll see God and reality face-to-face. Now I know in part, but I will then understand myself fully, even as I have been fully understood. My present partial understanding comes because I see myself in a mirror darkly and dimly. (Author's paraphrase)

One of the characteristics of the child is that he knows and understands things partially. Part of growing up into mature love is to reach a fuller, face-to-face understanding. Our pictures and our feelings about ourselves come largely from the pictures and the feelings we see reflected in our family members—what we watch in their expressions, hear from the tone in their voices, and see from their actions. These reflections tell us not only who we are, but also what we are going to become. As the reflections gradually become part of us, we take on the shape of the person we see in the family looking glass.

Do you remember the last time you went into the house of mirrors in an amusement park? You looked in one mirror and saw yourself as tall and skeletal, with foot-long hands. In the next one, you were round like a big balloon. Another mirror combined both, so that from the waist up you looked like a giraffe, while from the waist down you looked like a hippopotamus.

Looking into the mirrors was a hilarious experience, especially for the person standing next to you. He was just knocked out at how funny you looked. What was happening? The mirrors were so constructed that you saw yourself according to the curvature of the glass.

Now, move those mirrors over into the family. What if somehow your mother, your dad, your brother, your sister, your grandparents, the important others in your early life—what if they had taken every mirror in the house and curved them a certain way, so that in every mirror you saw a distorted reflection of yourself? What would have happened? It wouldn't have taken you long to develop an image of yourself just like the one you were seeing in the family mirrors. After a while you would have begun talking and acting and relating to people in a way that would have fit the picture you kept seeing in those mirrors.

At our Ashram retreats we have a session called "The Hour of the Open Heart," when people openly share their deepest needs. The question of the hour is, "What is it in your life that keeps you from being your best for Jesus Christ?" One evening a minister got up to share. He was in his early forties, handsome, successful, in the prime of life. He was pastor of a large and growing church. But he confessed with deep emotion his nagging fears of inadequacy, his constant battle with inferiority. He was too sensitive to what people said about him and found himself freezing up at the slightest criticism. His fear kept him from launching out in creative ministries to which he felt God was leading him.

After that open-heart session, a church leader said to me, "You know, that minister is the last person in the world I ever expected to hear say that. Why, he is so handsome and so successful. He's got a great family and a marvelous church. I would never have guessed that such torment would go on in that man's heart."

I happened to know the minister's family. I knew the way he had been neglected by his father—and that "mirror" tells a kid a lot. If a dad doesn't have time for his child, he reflects an important message: "You're not worth my time; I've got more important things to do." I knew of the constant put-downs from his father, and the honeyed, syrupy, spiritual way his mother was always trying to help him. Her way of helping was to remind him of what was expected of him, or to compare him with a very bright, and attractive older sister. I knew the destructively curved mirrors of neglect and lack of affection, criticism and comparison in which his self-esteem had been badly distorted. Those hurts and those wounds were infecting his personality thirty years later, paralyzing his potential, and sabotaging his service for God.

In case this sounds as if I am looking for someone on whom to place the blame, let me say that indeed I am not. In this fallen and imperfect world, all parents are imperfect in parenting. Most parents I know do the very best they can. Unfortunately, the role models they had weren't so hot either, all the way back to Adam and Eve. Cain and Abel must have seen a lot of conflict and tension: theirs must have been an unhappy home, for one brother to end up killing the other.

Though all of us are guilty, I am not trying to assess blame. Rather, I am trying to help us gain insight and understanding so we can find where we need healing, where we need to reconstruct a proper self-esteem.

Do you need a new set of mirrors for yourself? So many teenagers do, and so do young couples as they bring up their children. Someone has said, "Your childhood is the time of life when God desires to build the rooms of the temple in which He wants to live when you are an adult." What a beautiful thought! Parents have the great privilege, *and* heavy responsibility, of giving the basic design to the temple—the child's self-image.

If he is convinced he is of low worth, a child will place little value on what he says or does. If he is programmed for incompetence, he will be incompetent. One man told me that the thing he remembers more than anything else is the way his father always said to him, "I tell you, if there's a wrong way to do it, you'll find it."

If this kind of low self-esteem has been programmed into a person, it is difficult, and in some cases almost impossible, for that person to feel beloved of God, accepted by Him, and of worth to Him in His kingdom and service. A great many seemingly spiritual struggles are not spiritual at all in their origin. Although they sound and act and feel like God's judgment on a guilty conscience, they actually come from damning and damaging feeling-concepts that cause low self-esteem.

Shirley

That was the case with Shirley, the wife of a seminarian. She was about twenty-five when she came for help. When Shirley began to pour out her pain, it came in a torrent. She had marriage problems by the bucketful and tensions in her work. She'd already changed jobs several times because of difficulties in getting along with people. In spite of the sincerest attempts at devotions, witnessing, Christian work, and prayer, she was not at all happy with her relationship with God and was sure that God was not at all happy with her.

She had been given many good things by her parents in their rural home—security, hard work, discipline, strong Christian commitment, and high standards of morality. Shirley's parents were salt-of-the-earth folks, and from them she had gained a sincere though dutiful love for God and His Word and the church.

But gradually Shirley and I began to see that though her parents had done their best, they'd gone at it the wrong way, by giving compliments that made comparisons or set conditions.

- "Shirley, you're so nice when . . ."
- "Shirley, I hope you'll never be like Sally down the road."
- "That's fine, Shirley, but . . ."
- "We love you when . . . if . . . but . . ."

So many conditions! And Shirley grew up outdoing herself, performing, working, striving, and achieving. And she did remarkably well, except in one area. You know how some girls during adolescence go through an "ugly duckling" stage. Shirley was one of these, and her dad tried to help her accept herself. He really did love her, but again and again he said to her, "You know, you just can't make a peach out of a potato." While he thought he was helping her, he was really scarring and cutting at the very heart of her self-esteem. She grew up with a potato self, thinking of herself as misshapen, ugly, as something that grew under the ground.

Shirley and I began to see that the potato image had affected everything in her life, had made her as sensitive as an open wound. She took everything wrong that was said to her by her friends, her boss, her fellow workers, her neighbors, and her loving husband. And, of course, her God. How could she believe God loved her if He had made her a potato? It wasn't very nice of Him to do that, was it? Neither could she accept her husband's love. We like potatoes to eat, but their appearance leaves something to be desired.

The hurts Shirley suffered were deep. We had to walk through those painful memories with our Lord, turning them over to Him for healing. All during the long time we counseled together, I rarely used Shirley's name. I often called her "God's Peach" or "My Peach."

I went out of my way to reprogram her self-image. And she responded to the grace of God in such a marvelous way. When she discovered she was a daughter of God, she let love and grace pour in and wash away all those potato feelings and potato images. It was one of the most remarkable changes I have ever seen. Her very appearance changed. As Shirley began caring for herself, she started to look more attractive. Better still, she became an attractive person and began to relate better to people. She became a human being with proper Christian self-worth.

Some years later when I was a guest speaker in another state, Shirley came up to me after the service, holding the most precious baby—a real beauty. I looked at that little girl and said, "Shirley, no potato ever produced that." She looked at me with a mischievous smile and laughingly said, "Pretty peachy, huh?"

6

Healing Our Low Self-Esteem Part 2

In human experience it is a rare thing for one man to give his life for another, even if the latter be a good man, though there have been a few who have had the courage to do it. Yet the proof of God's amazing love is this: that it was while we were sinners that Christ died for us. Moreover, if He did that for us while we were sinners, now that we are men justified by the shedding of His blood, what reason have we to fear the wrath of God?

If while we were His enemies, Christ reconciled us to God by dying for us, surely now that we are reconciled we may be perfectly certain of our salvation through His living in us. "Nor, I am sure, is this a matter of bare salvation—we may hold our heads high in the light of God's love because of the reconciliation which Christ has made.

Romans 5:7–11, PHILLIPS

Thou shalt love the Lord thy God with all thy heart, and with all thy soul, and with all thy mind. This is the first and great commandment. And the second is like unto it, "Thou shalt love thy neighbor as thyself." On these two commandments hang all the Law and Prophets.

Matthew 22:37–40

A PERSON'S SELF-CONCEPT is a system of feelings and concepts he has constructed about himself. There are four sources from which we get our self-concepts.

• The *first* is the *outer world,* that we looked at in chapter 5. From this outer world we see pictures and feelings about ourselves reflected in the mirrors of family members. We decide who we are from our earliest system of relationships—by how we are treated and loved and cared for, and the language of relationships that we learn as we are growing up.

• The second source is the *world within us,* the physical, emotional, and spiritual equipment that we bring into the world. This includes our senses, our nerves, our capacity to learn, to register, to respond. For some of us, the world within includes handicaps, deformities, and defects.

No two children are alike. They are as marvelously different as snowflakes. And what a mistake parents make in going by any book to raise their children as if they were all alike. You parents know what I'm talking about. You've got one child who's so much like the proverbial mule that you may have to use a two-by-four just to get his attention, let alone discipline him. And then you have another child who is as sensitive as a touch-me-not plant—you don't have to raise a hand or a voice to get response. How ridiculous to think that one set of child-rearing principles is enough. These differences exist because of who we are and because of our psychophysical equipment.

However, there is also a spiritual factor. And it is at this point that we differ with all secular, humanistic, and pagan psychology, which looks at human nature as essentially good or morally neutral. We Christians do not do that. God has revealed to us in His Word that we do not enter this life morally neutral. Rather, we are victims of a basic tendency toward evil, a proclivity toward the wrong. We call it original sin.

The truth is that sin is the one thing about all of us that is not very original. The laws and the principles which govern all personal relationships and human development guaranteed sin's transmission, when our first set of parents got out of sorts with God and began living in self-centeredness and pride. Beginning with the first sin of Adam and Eve, there was set in motion a chain reaction of imperfect parenting, through failures and ignorance and misguided actions and, worst of all, through conditional love.

This parental inheritance makes every human being a victim of corporate sinfulness. We do not come into this world perfectly neutral, but imperfectly weighted in the direction of the wrong. We are out of balance in our motives, desires, and drives. We are out of proportion, with a bent toward the wrong. And because of this defect in our natures, our responses are off-center.

Years ago I found a saying that is extremely helpful in counseling people: "Children are the world's greatest recorders, but they are the world's worst interpreters." Kids pick up many of the imperfections around them and, because of the self-centeredness which is in all of us, they misinterpret much of what they take in, and this greatly affects their self-image. Regardless of how well parents do by their children, it seems that most people reach young adulthood feeling, "You're OK but I'm not OK." It is almost a part of our human equipment.

The Bible makes it clear that we are not merely victims. We all are sinners and share in the responsibility of who we are and what we are becoming. I have never seen anyone truly healed until, along with forgiving all those who hurt and wronged him, he also received God's forgiveness for his own wrong responses.

• *Satan* is a third source, and we have already considered him as a source of our low self-esteem. Satan uses our feelings of self-despising as a terrible weapon in three roles that he plays. Satan is a liar (John 8:44), the accuser (Rev. 12:10), and the one who blinds our minds (2 Cor. 4:4). In all three roles he uses inferiority, inadequacy and self-belittling to defeat Christians and prevent them from realizing their full potential as God's own children.

• The fourth source for our self-concept is *God. We* now move from the problem of low self-image to the power for a new Christian self-image. We now turn away from the disease to its cure, for there are practical steps you can take toward the healing of your low self-esteem.

Correct Your Faulty Theology

Let God and His Word straighten out your false beliefs. Many Christians have adopted an idea which is really a sin in God's sight, and have wrapped it in pious theological garb. You too may have made a virtue out of a vice. Now you cannot at the same time think wrongly and live rightly. You cannot believe error and practice truth.

This false belief suggests that a self-belittling attitude is pleasing to

God, that it is a part of Christian humility, and necessary to sanctification and holiness.

The truth is that self-belittling is not true Christian humility and runs counter to some very basic teachings of the Christian faith. The great commandment is that you love God with all your being. The second commandment is an extension of the first—that you love your neighbor as you love yourself. We do not have two commandments here, but three: to love God, to love yourself, and to love others. I put *self* second, because Jesus plainly made a proper self-love the basis of a proper love for neighbor. The term *self-love* has a wrong connotation for some people. Whether you call it self-esteem or self-worth, it is plainly the foundation of Christian love for others. And this is the opposite of what many Christians believe.

Years ago, after I preached a sermon about these two great commandments of Jesus, a man came up to me. He said, "As old as I am, I have never before actually heard Jesus' Word correctly."

I said, "What do you mean?"

"Well," he said, "while you were preaching, I suddenly realized that with my lips I have said, 'Love thy neighbor as thyself,' but deep down in my inner self I have really been hearing, 'Love thy neighbor but hate thyself.' I'm afraid I have been scrupulously living up to the commandment as I translated it."

After a revival meeting when I preached about proper self-love, a woman came to me and said that she had been in the church all her life, but that I was the first evangelist she had ever heard say that she was supposed to love herself. "All this time I thought that God wanted me to dislike myself in order to stay humble."

Do you need to get your theology straightened out? When you love God and yourself and others, you are fulfilling the whole law of God (Matt. 5:43–48). As Jesus proclaimed the law, He was not endorsing or glorifying it, as some rabbis of His day used to do. Rather He was authoritatively restating the principle of the eternal triangle—proper love for God, for ourselves, and for other people. This basic law of God is written into the nature of the entire universe. It operates in every cell of your body. The person who has proper self-esteem is healthier in every way than the person with low self-esteem. This is the way God has made you, and if you go against this, you are not only following wrong theology, but bargaining with your own destruction.

Although many Scriptures suggest the importance of high self–
esteem, the Apostle Paul directly declared it to be the basis of one of
the most intimate and important relationships of life—that of husband
and wife in marriage: "Husbands ought also to love their own wives
as their own bodies. He who loves his own wife loves himself; for
no one ever hated his own flesh, but nourishes and cherishes it"
(Eph. 5:28, 29, TLB).

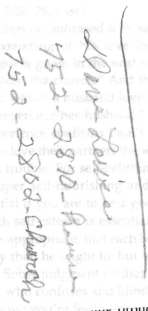

Phillips paraphrased this saying, "The love a man gives his wife is
the extending of his love for himself to enfold her." The divine
example is given in the next verse: "And that is what Christ does for
His body, the church." And then Paul stated it again: "Let every one
of you in particular so love his wife as he loves himself, and let the
wife reverence her husband."

Experience confirms Paul's psychological accuracy. Because some
people love themselves in the wrong way they love themselves their marriages
are in hot water. For self-belittling works its way out through marriage.
A proper self-nourishing and a realization of your own worth are
essential if you are to be a good wife or husband.

Such self-esteem is essential to being a good neighbor. Paul's caution is appropriate, that each believer would not think of himself more
highly than he ought to, but would think with sober judgment (Rom
12:3). Sober judgment neither overestimates nor underestimates. It is
satan who confuses and blinds us at this point, as he accuses, "Look
out now, you're feeling proud."

But really the opposite is true. For the person with low self-esteem
is always trying to prove himself. He has a need to be right in every
situation, to verify himself. He gets all wrapped up in constantly looking at himself.

A person with low self-esteem becomes extremely self-centered. This
doesn't necessarily mean he is selfish. He may be a doormat, and this
is part of his problem. But he is self-centered in that he is always looking at himself and wondering about himself. He may even become
a praise-aholic, constantly maneuvering others into reassuring him.

You cannot really unconditionally love others when you need to
prove your own self-worth. It may look as if you are loving them, when
actually you are just using them to reassure yourself that you're OK.

Self-negation is not a part of humility or holiness or sanctification. Self-
crucifixion and self-surrender do not mean the downgrading of self.

Take Your Self-Estimate from God

Develop the picture of your worth and value from God, not from the false reflections that come out of your past. The healing of low self-esteem really hinges on a choice you must make: Will you listen to Satan as he employs all the lies, the distortions, the put-downs, and the hurts of your past to keep you bound by unhealthy, unchristian feelings and concepts about yourself? Or will you receive your self-esteem from God and His Word?

Here are some very important questions to ask yourself.

• What right have you to belittle or despise someone whom God *loves* so deeply? Don't say, "Well, I know God loves me, but I just can't stand myself." That's a travesty of faith, an insult to God and His love. It is the expression of a subtly hidden resentment against your Creator. When you despise His creation, you are really saying that you don't like the design or care much for the Designer. You are calling unclean what God calls clean. You are failing to realize how much God loves you and how much you mean to Him.

• What right have you to belittle or despise someone whom God has *honored* so highly? "Consider the incredible love that the Father has shown us in allowing us to be called 'children of God'" (1 John 3:1, PH). And that's not just what we're called. It's what we are. "Oh, dear children of mine . . . have you realized it? Here and now we are God's children" (v. 2, PH).

Do you think that when you consider God's son or daughter worthless or inferior, He is pleased by your so-called humility?

• What right have you to belittle or despise someone whom God *values* so highly? How much does God value you? "In human experience it is a rare thing for one man to give his life for another, even if the latter be a good man. . . . Yet the proof of God's amazing love is this: that it was while we were sinners that Christ died for us. . . . We may hold our heads high in the light of God's love" (Rom. 5:7–8, 11, PH). God has declared your value. You are someone whom God values so highly as to give the life of His own dear Son to redeem you.

• What right have you to belittle or despise someone whom God has *provided* for so fully? "How much more shall your Father which is in heaven give good things?" (Matt. 7:11) "God shall supply all your need" (Phil. 4:19). This doesn't sound as if He wants you to be self-loathing or to feel inadequate.

• What right have you to belittle or despise someone whom God has *planned* for so carefully?

Praise be to God . . . for giving us through Christ every spiritual benefit. . . . Consider what He has done—before the foundation of the world He chose us to become in Christ, His holy and blameless children, living within His constant care. He planned, in His purposeful love, that we should be adopted as His own children (Eph. 1:3–5, PH).

• What right have you to belittle or despise someone in whom God *delights?* The Apostle Paul said that we are "accepted in the beloved" (Eph. 1:6). Do you remember the Father's words at the baptism of Jesus? "This is My beloved Son in whom I am well pleased" (Matt. 3:17). Paul gives us a daring thought: we are "in Christ." He used this phrase some ninety times. You are in Christ, therefore you are in the Beloved. God looks at you in Christ and says to you, "You are My beloved son, you are My beloved daughter, in whom I am well pleased."

From where will you get your idea of yourself? From distortions of your childhood? From past hurts and false ideas that have been programmed into you? Or will you say, "No, I will not listen to those lies from the past any longer. I will not listen to Satan, the liar, the confuser, the blinder, who twists and distorts. I am going to listen to God's opinion of me, and let Him reprogram me until His loving estimate of me becomes a part of my life, right down to my innermost feelings."

Cooperate with the Holy Spirit

You must become a partner with God in this reprogramming and renewal process. Such work is a continuous process, not a sudden crisis. I don't know of any single Christian experience that will change your self-image overnight. You are to be "transformed by the renewing of your mind" (Rom. 12:2). The verbs in this verse represent continuous action, and the word *mind* describes the way you think, the way you look at life as a daily process.

How can you cooperate with the Holy Spirit in doing this?

• Ask God to check you every time you belittle yourself. When you start doing this, you're in for a surprise. For you may find that your whole lifestyle is a direct or indirect put-down of yourself. Here are few hints. What do you do when someone compliments you? Can you say, "Thank you"? "I'm glad you liked that"? "I appreciate that"? Or do you go into a long song and dance of cutting yourself down? If you have been belittling yourself, it'll tear you up for a while to stop, because you'll want to go through the whole routine. Don't do it.

I think the spiritualizing is the worst; it must be nauseating to God. Someone says, "I heard you sing today and I enjoyed your song." Then do you become very spiritual and say, "Well, it really wasn't me; it was the Lord"? Sure, it was the Lord; you are dependent on Him. But you don't need to say that every time.

• Let God love you, and let Him teach you how to love yourself and how to love others. You want love. You want God to affirm and accept you, and that's what He does. But because of wretched programming from the other sources, it is difficult to accept love. In fact, it is so hard that you may think it is more comfortable to go on the way you are.

I challenge you to enter the healing process, so that you can lift your head high as a son or a daughter of God Himself.

7

Symptoms of Perfectionism

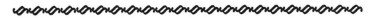

Come unto Me, all ye that labor and are heavy laden, and I will give you rest. Take My yoke upon you, and learn of Me; for I am meek and lowly in heart; and ye shall find rest unto your souls. For My yoke is easy, and My burden is light.

Matthew 11:28–30

There remaineth therefore a rest to the people of God. For he that is entered into his rest, he also hath ceased from his own works, as God did from His. Let us labor therefore to enter into that rest.

Hebrews 4:9–11

THERE ARE MANY different kinds of depression, and they vary greatly in degree. I am going to focus on a kind of depression caused by damaged emotions, and specifically by a spiritual distortion known as *perfectionism*.

Now the moment I mention that word, some red flags of defense go up. Isn't it a fact that we believe in Christian perfection? Indeed, we do. But there is a great difference between true Christian perfection and perfectionism. While on the surface they may look alike, there is a great gulf fixed between the two.

Perfectionism is a counterfeit for Christian perfection, holiness, sanctification, or the Spirit-filled life. Instead of making us holy persons and integrated personalities—that is, whole persons in Christ—perfectionism leaves us spiritual Pharisees and emotional neurotics.

You think I'm exaggerating the picture? That this is some new-fangled discovery by psychologists or the pastor? I want to assure you that throughout the centuries, sensitive pastors observed these kinds of suffering Christians, and were deeply concerned, long before the word *psychology* was ever in popular use. Although they didn't know what to do about it, they recognized the problem.

John Fletcher, a contemporary of John Wesley, described certain of his parishioners:

> Some bind heavy burdens on themselves of their own making and when they cannot bear them, they are tormented in their consciences with imaginary guilt. Others go distracted through groundless fears of having committed the unpardonable sin. In a word, do we not see hundreds who, when they have reason to think well of their state, instead think there is no hope for them whatever?

The itinerant pastor, John Wesley, recorded it this way:

> Sometimes this excellent quality, tenderness of conscience, is carried to an extreme. We find some who fear where no fear is, who are continually condemning themselves without cause, imagining something to be sinful where Scripture nowhere condemns it, supposing other things to be their duty where Scripture nowhere enjoins it. This is properly termed a scrupulous conscience, and is a sore evil. It is highly expedient to yield to it as little as possible, rather it is a matter of prayer that you may be delivered from this sore evil and may recover a sound mind. (Arthur C. Zepp, *Conscience Alone Not a Safe Guide,* Chicago: The Christian Witness Company, 1913, p. 103)

One ancient minister actually wrote a book about perfectionism, called *The Spiritual Treatment of Sufferers from Nerves and Scruples.* An amazingly accurate title!

Symptoms

Perfectionism is the most disturbing emotional problem among evangelical Christians. It walks into my office more often than any other single Christian hangup.

What is perfectionism? Since it is a lot easier to describe than to define, I want you to see some of its symptoms.

1. *Tyranny of the oughts.* Its chief characteristic is a constant, overall feeling of never doing well enough or being good enough. This feeling permeates all of life, but especially affects our spiritual lives. Psychologist Karen Horney's classic phrase describes it perfectly, "The tyranny of the *oughts.*" Here are its typical statements:

- "I ought to do better,"
- "I ought to have done better,"
- "I ought to be able to do better."

All the way from preparing a meal to praying or witnessing—"I didn't do it quite well enough."

The three favorite phrases of the perfectionist are: "could have," "should have," "would have." If you are living in this emotional state, the official state song is "If Only." Always standing on tiptoe, always reaching, stretching, trying, but never quite making it.

2. *Self-depreciation.* The connection between perfectionism and low self-esteem is obvious. If you are never quite good enough, you feel a continuous sense of self-depreciation. If you are never quite satisfied with yourself and your achievements, then the next step is quite natural: God is never really pleased with you either. He's always saying, "Come on now, you can do better than that!" And if you are a perfectionist and never pleased with yourself anyway, you reply, "Of course."

Try as you will, you always remain in second, not first place. And since you and God always demand first place, that's not quite good enough. So, back to the spiritual salt mines you go, with increased efforts to please yourself and an increasingly demanding God who is never quite satisfied. But you always fall short, you are inadequate, you never arrive but you must never stop trying.

3. *Anxiety.* The oughts and self-depreciation produce an oversensitive conscience under a giant umbrella of guilt, anxiety, and condemnation. Like a great cloud, the umbrella hangs over your head. Once in a while it lifts and the sun shines through, particularly during revivals, deeper life conferences, and retreats, when you go forward for prayer or "make a deeper surrender."

Unfortunately, the sunshine lasts about as long as it did the last time you made the same trip, went through the same process, and claimed the same blessing. Soon you fall off spiritual cloud nine with a sickening thud. Those same dreaded feelings settle in again. The general sense of divine disapproval, and comprehensive condemnation return, nagging and knocking at the back door of your soul.

4. Legalism. The oversensitive conscience and comprehensive guilt of the perfectionist are usually accompanied by a great scrupulosity and legalism which rigidly overemphasize externals, do's and don'ts, rules and regulations. Let's see why this almost inevitably follows the first three symptoms.

The perfectionist with his fragile conscience, his low self-esteem, and his almost built-in sense of automatic guilt is very sensitive to what other people think about him. Since he cannot accept himself, and is quite unsure of God's approval, he desperately needs the approval of other people. Thus he is easy prey to the opinions and evaluations of other Christians. Every sermon gets to him. He introspects: *Ah-h, maybe that's what's wrong with me. Maybe if I give this up . . . add that to my life . . . Maybe if I stop doing this or I start doing that, I will experience peace, joy, and power. Maybe then God will accept me, and I will please Him.*

All the while, the do's and don'ts are piling up; they keep adding up because more and more people have to be pleased. The halo has to be adjusted for this person and readjusted for that one. So the perfectionist keeps fitting it this way and that way and, before he realizes what is happening, the halo has turned into what Paul called "the yoke of bondage" (Gal. 5:1). The yoke was a very familiar farm implement in those days, put upon an animal to pull the plow or to join two oxen together. But the word was used in another way, and this is the meaning Paul had in mind. In the Old Testament the yoke was a symbol of the despotic authority laid upon the necks of a conquered people as a symbol of their enslavement. It was something humiliating and destructive.

The Good News of grace had broken into the lives of the Galatians, freeing them from that kind of spiritual yoke. The Good News is that the way to God is not the path of perfect performance. No matter how much you try, you can never *win* God's favor. Why? Because His favor, His being pleased with you, is a love-gift of His grace through Jesus Christ.

After a while, grace seemed *too good* to be true, and the Galatians began to listen to other voices in the marketplace; "another gospel" as Paul termed it (Gal. 1:6). Maybe they listened to *the Jerusalem legalists,* who said you had to keep all the law, including the ceremonial law. Maybe they listened to *the Colossian ascetics* who majored in giving up things in order to please God. They also majored in observing special days, new moons, and Sabbaths. They insisted on "self-abasement," and deliberate low self-esteem (Col. 2–18, NASB). They stressed what Paul called *regulations*. "Do not handle, do not taste, do not touch." Paul said they had "the appearance of wisdom in self-made religion and self-abasement" which was "of no value against fleshly indulgence" (Col. 2:21, 23, NASB). How accurate!

And so, the Jerusalem legalists and the Colossian ascetics produced *the Galatian diluters, the Galatian reversionists*. They reverted to a diluted mixture of faith and works, law and grace. And the result was the same then as it is today when we mix law and grace. Immature and sensitive believers can become neurotic perfectionists who are guilt-ridden, tight-haloed, unhappy, and uncomfortable. They are rigid in their outlook, frigid in their lovelessness, conforming to the approval and disapproval of others. Yet, in a strange paradox, they critically judge, blame, and bind those same others.

5. *Anger*. But the worst is yet to come. For you see, something terrible is beginning to happen to the perfectionist. He may not realize it but deep in his heart a kind of anger is developing. A resentment against the oughts, against the Christian faith, against other Christians, against himself, but saddest of all, against God.

Oh, not that it's really against the true God. That's the sadness of it; that's what breaks my heart. The perfectionist is not against the gracious, loving, self-giving God who has come to us, who in Jesus Christ went all the way to the Cross at such cost. No, his resentment is against a caricature of a god who is never satisfied. A god whom he can never please no matter how hard he tries, no matter what he gives up or holds on to. This cruel god always ups the ante a little, always demands a bit more and says, "Sorry, that wasn't quite good enough."

Anger against this kind of god seethes up in the perfectionist. Sometimes his anger is recognized and the whole wretched ought-tyranny is seen for what it is: a desperate satanic substitute for true Christian perfection. And sometimes the perfectionist can work through all this, find grace, and marvelously be set free.

6. *Denial*. But too often the anger is not faced but denied. Because anger is considered a terrible sin, it is pushed down. And the whole mixture of bad theology, legalism, and salvation by performance becomes a frozen Niagara. This is when deep emotional problems set in. Mood changes are so great and so terrible that such a person seems to be two different people at the same time.

Under the stress and the strain of trying to live with a self he can't like, a God he can't love, and other people he can't get along with, the strain can become too much. And one of two things can happen: either there is a breakaway or a breakdown.

The *breakaway* is so sad. Much of my time is spent in counseling people who used to be active Christians but who have now broken away. The breakaway just throws the whole thing over. He doesn't become an unbeliever. He believes with his head but he can't believe with his heart. Perfectionism is impossible to live up to. He's tried so many times and it made him so miserable that he just left it behind.

Others suffer a *breakdown*. The load is too heavy to bear, and they break under the weight. That's exactly what happened to Dr. Joseph R. Cooke, professor of anthropology at the University of Washington in Seattle. A brilliant Ph.D. and well trained in biblical theology, he became a missionary teacher to Thailand. But after a few years he left the mission field a broken man. A nervous breakdown left him no longer able to preach or teach or even to read his Bible. And as he put it, "I was a burden to my wife and useless to God and to others" (*Free for the Taking*, Fleming Revell, 1975).

How did this happen? "I invented an impossible God, and I had a nervous breakdown." Oh, he believed in grace, he even taught it. But his real feelings about the god he lived with day by day didn't correspond with his teaching. His god was ungracious and unpleasable.

> God's demands of me were so high, and His opinion of me was so low, there was no way for me to live except under His frown.
> . . . All day long He nagged me: "Why don't you pray more? Why don't you witness more? When will you ever learn self-discipline? How can you allow yourself to indulge in such wicked thoughts? Do this. Don't do that. Yield, confess, work harder." . . . God was always using His love against me. He'd show me His nail-pierced hands, and then He would look at me glaringly and say, "Well, why aren't you a better Christian? Get busy and live the way you ought to."
>
> Most of all, I had a God who down underneath considered me to be less than dirt. Oh, He made a great ado about loving me, but I believed that the day-to-day love and acceptance I longed for could only be mine if I let Him crush nearly everything that was really me. When I came down to it, there was scarcely a word or a feeling or a thought or a decision of mine that God really liked.

Can you understand why a sincere Christian who feels this way would have a total breakdown? And my years of preaching and counseling and praying with evangelical Christians lead me to believe that this disease of perfectionism is very common among church people.

Cure

There is only one ultimate cure for perfectionism: it is as profound and yet as simple as the word *grace*. Grace is simply our anglicized form of the Greek word *charis* which means "gracefulness, graciousness, kindness, a favor." But in the New Testament this word has a special meaning: "freely given, undeserved, unmerited, unearnable, and unrepayable favor." God's loving acceptance of us has nothing to do with our worthiness. As Dr. Cooke reminds us, grace is the face God wears when He meets our imperfection, sin, weakness, and failure. Grace is what God is and what God does when He meets the sinful and undeserving. Grace is a pure gift, free for the taking. The healing of perfectionism does not begin with some initial experience of grace in salvation or sanctification, and then move into a life lived by effort and perfect performance. The healing of perfectionism takes place in day-by-day believing, living, and realizing this grace relationship with a loving, caring heavenly Father.

But that's the rub, for sometimes this cannot happen by itself. The realization of grace cannot be maintained in some people without an inner healing of the past. God's care cannot be felt without a deep, inner reprogramming of all the bad conditioning that has been put into them by parents and family and teachers and preachers and the church.

These perfectionists have been programmed to unrealistic expectations, impossible performance, conditional love, and a subtle theology of works. They can't get rid of this pattern overnight. The change requires time, process, understanding, healing, and above all, reprogramming—the renewal of the mind that brings transformation.

I want to tell you how it happened in one young man's life. Don was raised in a strict evangelical home, where everything they believed in their heads was right, but where everything they practiced in everyday interpersonal relationships was wrong. Is that possible? Oh, yes! Very possible. And parents need to remember that it is not only what is taught to a child that matters, but also what is caught. Don was taught one thing, but he caught an opposite message, and was thus in great conflict.

Don grew up with unpredictable and conditional love. From his earliest childhood he was given to understand: "You will be loved IF . . ." "We will accept and approve of you WHEN . . ." "You will be loved BECAUSE OF . . . IF YOU . . ." He grew up feeling that he never pleased his parents.

Don came to see me as a young adult in his thirties because his depressions were becoming more frequent, lasting longer, and were more frightening. Some well-meaning Christian friends told him that his problem was entirely spiritual. "Truly Spirit-filled Christians shouldn't have such feelings. They should always feel joyful." This left Don with a double burden: his problem, and his guilt because he had the problem.

Don and I spent many hours together. It wasn't easy for him to understand and accept God's love and grace, let alone to feel it at the gut level. Because every experience of interpersonal relationships from childhood to adulthood contradicted grace and love, it was very difficult for him to believe and feel God's grace.

And Don had added to his problem. During those down times, he had entered into wrong relationships with the opposite sex. Oh, never all the way, but far enough that he would use this girl, and then that one, to help him pull out of his depression. That was sin and he knew it. Such misuse of another person added to his guilt, so that there was real guilt on top of his pseudoguilt. Again and again he had gone through the whole cycle of tears, repentance, salvation, and renewed promises, only to break them later.

Our process together took more than a year. But during this time there was healing of many painful memories and reprogramming of wrong ways of coping. He did his homework well, kept an honest journal of his feelings, read good books and listened to tapes, memorized many Scripture passages, and spent time in specific and positive prayer.

Some of the relearning took place in our relationship. He tried many, many times to maneuver me into rejecting him, and withdrawing my loving acceptance of him. Don was trying to get me to behave the way his mom and dad did and the way he thought God did.

Healing didn't happen overnight, but thank God, it happened! Slowly, but surely, Don discovered grace in God's incredible and unconditional acceptance of him as a person. His down times began to come less frequently. He didn't work at getting rid of them, they just left—like dead leaves fall off the tree in the springtime when the new leaves come. He gained more control over his thoughts and his actions. His depressions began to lift, until now he has the normal ups and downs that we all have.

Whenever I see Don alone he smiles and says, "Doc, it's still too good to be true, but it's true!" That's the message. The trouble with the perfectionist is that he has been programmed to think it is too good to be true. You too may think: *Of course, I believe in grace, but. . .*

"Come unto Me," said Jesus, "all ye that labor and are heavy laden, and I will give you rest" (Matt. 11:28). Isn't that good news? You don't have to live the way you do, for there's a better way to live! "I will give you rest. Take *My* yoke upon you . . . for My yoke is easy, and My burden is light" (11:28–30).

"My yoke is easy." What does that mean? His yoke is comfortable, because it is tailor-made to your personality, your individuality, and your humanity. "My burden is light," means that the Christ who fits you with a yoke will never leave you alone, but will always be yoked with you in the form of the Paraclete, the One who comes alongside to help you carry that comfortable burden and yoke.

Notice the words of Charles Wesley's hymn as he traced the progression of God's healing grace in a guilt-ridden, perfectionist's heart.

Arise, My Soul, Arise

Arise, my soul, arise; shake off thy guilty fears;
The bleeding Sacrifice in my behalf appears:
Before the throne my surety stands,
before the throne my surety stands,
My name is written on His hands.

He ever lives above, for me to intercede;
His all-redeeming love, His precious blood, to plead:
His blood atoned for all our race,
His blood atoned for all our race,
And sprinkles now the throne of grace.

Five bleeding wounds he bears, received on Calvary;
They pour effectual prayers; they strongly plead for me:

"Forgive him, O forgive," they cry,
"forgive him, O forgive," they cry,
"Nor let that ransomed sinner die!"
The Father hears Him pray, His dear anointed One;
He cannot turn away the presence of His Son:
His Spirit answers to the blood,
His Spirit answers to the blood,
And tells me I am born of God.

My God is reconciled; His pardoning voice I hear;
He owns me for His child; I can no longer fear:
With confidence I now draw nigh,
with confidence I now draw nigh,
And "Father, Abba, Father," cry.

8

The Process of Healing for Perfectionism

Surely He hath borne our griefs, and carried our sorrows; yet we did esteem Him stricken, smitten of God, and afflicted. But He was wounded for our transgressions, He was bruised for our iniquities; the chastisement of our peace was upon Him; and with His stripes we are healed. All we like sheep have gone astray; we have turned every one to his own way; and the Lord hath laid on Him the iniquity of us all.

He hath poured out His soul unto death; and He was numbered with the transgressors; and He bore the sin of many, and made intercession for the transgressors.

Isaiah 53:4–6, 12

PERFECTIONISM IS A constant and all-pervading feeling of never quite measuring up, never quite being or doing enough to please. To please whom? Everyone—yourself, others, and God. Naturally, a lot of self-belittling and self-contempt goes along with it, together with a supersensitivity to the opinions, to the approval, and the disapproval of others. And all of this is accompanied by a cloud of guilt. The perfectionist almost *has* to feel guilty, if for nothing else, not feeling guilty about something!

Perfectionism produces a distorted picture of God with feelings of doubt, rebellion, and anger against a God you can never please.

There is a cure for perfectionism in the graciousness of God who comes to us in Jesus Christ. But to experience this cure you need to accept the prescription for the process of healing.

Healing Is a Process

The first step is to abandon all ideas of a quick cure. Don't let anyone delude you with the idea that a crisis cure will instantaneously heal you. In fact, part of the disease itself is to be always looking for a solution just around the corner. For perfectionism specializes in *if-onlys:* "If only I could _____ , I would be OK." How did you fill in the blank? With a *positive?* "If only I could . . . read, pray, give, witness, serve"? Or with a *negative?*

- "If only I could give up . . .
- "If only I could stop . . .
- "If only I could quit . . .
- "If only I could follow the four laws, or the three steps, or receive the two blessings, or get the one gift; surely that would do it!"

Every such desperate grasp for quick solutions is a search for magic, not miracle. Healing is a process; you didn't get to be a perfectionist overnight, and you will not be healed overnight either. It will involve a process of growth in grace, of reprogramming, and of healing in every level of your life. You will need healing of your mind with its distorted concepts, healing of your feelings with their damaged emotions, healing of your perception with its downgrading evaluations, and healing of your relationships with all of their disruptive contradictions. You also need a deep, inner healing of your memories to blot out the destructive, slow-motion video replays that interfere with the way you live.

You may think this sounds like a pretty thorough overhauling. It is, and your submission to this process is the beginning of healing for perfectionism.

God Will Be Pleased with You

Not only will God and His grace *be with you* in every step of the healing process, but God will *be pleased with you* at every step of the process. In the Bible the word *grace is* always woven into the presence of the Giver of grace. We should never use the word *grace* as if we were describing some kind of commodity that God dispenses. Grace means a gracious God coming to you. "My grace is sufficient" (2 Cor. 12:9). Not *grace* but "My grace." One of Paul's favorite phrases was "the grace of our Lord Jesus Christ" (1 Cor. 16:23; Gal. 6:18; Phil. 4:23; 1 Thes. 5:28; 2 Thes. 3:18). Grace is not a commodity but our Lord Himself, coming to us in His graciousness. A loving, gracious God accepts us as we are, offers Himself lovingly to us right here and now, not when we shape up.

God is as pleased with you when you are in this healing process as loving parents are when their child starts learning to walk. Those are exciting days in a home, especially with the first child—the child stumbles, knocks over the furniture, may even bend the lamp a bit. But do the parents scold him, tell him how displeased they are because he isn't doing a perfect job? Does Dad shout, "You ought to do better than that, kid"? Does Mother chime in with, "That sure was a stupid step you took. No wonder you fell and hurt yourself"? Do you see how we so often have made God into a neurotic parent? If Jesus were preaching His Sermon on the Mount, He might paraphrase this idea: "If you being evil know how to do that well when teaching your child to walk, how much more will the heavenly Father be pleased with every step in your healing process." (See Matt. 7:11.) God will be pleased with you, every step of the way.

Let me suggest a prayer to go along with this, a prescription, to take as often as needed. "Thank You, Lord, that You are healing me according to Your perfect schedule." In this way you turn the process not into another form of irritation for your perfectionism, or anger at your slow progress, but into a prayer of thanksgiving for His graciousness every step of the way.

Root Causes

Emotional problems often result from the kind of a god, the kind of people, the kind of life we saw, as we looked through the relational windows of our childhood. Most of us developed our concept/feelings about our heavenly Father from our earthly mothers and fathers, and these feelings become so intertwined and confused. But the guilty and contradictory feelings are not the voice of God. They are often

the continuing voice of Mother or Dad or Brother or Sister, or something internalized that puts pressure on us. Remember, most of our
basic patterns for relating to other people come from the patterns of
the relationships of our family.

1. *Unpleaseable parents.* One of the most common parental family
situations which produces perfectionism and depression is unple35e-
able parents. Such parents give only conditional love which demands
that certain standards are lived up to, top grades achieved, or the
highest kind of performance met in athletics or in spiritual life. There
is little or no affirmation and plenty of criticism. Even approval is
conditional. Encouragement is given but only to stress the fact that
"you should have and could have done better." The three A's on the
report card aren't mentioned, but the B—"I think you can pull the
B up to an A if you try harder." And then when you do try harder
and you get that B pulled up to an A and you show the report card to
Mother, sure she is going to be pleased, she looks at you for a moment
and all of a sudden frowns and says, "My goodness! Where did you
get that stain on your jacket! You must have spilled catsup on yourself at the cafeteria. Have you been going around all day looking like
that?" Which really translated means, "You lousy ungrateful kid. What
kind of a parent are you making me look like before the community?"

Unpleaseable parents and conditional love produce unreachable
goals and unattainable standards. Some years ago a lady told me that
every time I used the word *obey* or *obedience* in a sermon, she would
feel uneasy and guilty. Her mother used to dress her up in the morning for play, in very fancy clothing. And then she would say, "Now,
when you go out, don't get any dirt on that pretty dress of yours. I
worked hard to iron all those ruffles." You can well imagine what
the dress looked like by afternoon and evening. And when the little
girl came in, her mother would scold her angrily: "You naughty girl,
you never obey me." Absurd, unrealistic, unattainable demands were
made. And when they weren't achieved, guilt and punishment were
meted out. Since this was a deeply religious home, are you surprised
that the child, now a grown woman, struggles with wretched concepts
of God, with low self-esteem, and a cloud of guilt?

2. *Unpredictable home situations.* In one of his works, Charles Dickens
said, "In the world of little children, the greatest hurt of all is injustice." Unpredictable home situations produce injustice. If parents
cannot control their own emotions, a child never knows what kind
of response he is going to get from them.

Beth had a terribly up-and-down Christian life. She tried hard, but faith and trust were so difficult. Her feelings of condemnation and guilt were so strong at times that she couldn't bear to come to church. Finally, we made a deal—she would sit way back, close to one of the exits, so that if she couldn't bear something from my sermon, she could walk out. And many, many times in the midst of a sermon when I wasn't talking about anything that *I* thought was heavy, I would see Beth get up and walk out.

What a home she had! It was like living on eggshells day and night. Her father was an alcoholic. Her mother was one of those quiet, gentle people—quiet and gentle like a dormant volcano which can erupt at any time. I'll never forget Beth's statement: "I never knew if I would get hugged or slugged. And I could never figure out the reason for either one." So, of course, she thought God was as unpredictable, irrational, and unreliable as her parents were.

Besides those emotional scars, there were some literal scars. Surgery once was required on a dislocated jaw. And those scars had left deeply painful memories which needed healing before she could believe in the God from whom every good and perfect gift comes, the God in whom there is light without the slightest shadow of variation or change (James 1:17).

It's not hard to see how such home situations are the breeding grounds for emotional cripples and perfectionists. Unpleaseable parents, unacceptable selfhood, unrealistic, unattainable standards, unclear signals, unendurable conflicts—all program people to the wrong kind of responses.

Do you understand why healing is a process that needs time, effort, ofttimes the help of a counselor, and always the supportive, loving fellowship of the body of Christ? How we need the affirmation, the support, and the ministry from fellow members of the body of Christ! James implies that in many cases the reprogramming, renewing, and healing process comes about only as we share with and pray for one another (James 5:16).

Cower Power

Countless hurts that come to us are hard to classify. They are part and parcel of living in a fallen world. Ben was one of the most timid souls I have ever counseled. I couldn't even hear him. "What did you say, Ben?" We began practicing to raise Ben's voice. I would have him read things to me. "A little louder, Ben. Assert yourself. Speak up!" He was so afraid to be a burden to people. It could make a person uncomfortable to be around him. You might look to see if he was wearing sandwich board that read, "Excuse me for living."

Have you ever heard of the "Dependent Order of Really Meek and Timid Souls"? When you make an acrostic of its first letters, you have "Doormats." The Doormats have an official insignia—a yellow caution light. Their official motto is: "The meek shall inherit the earth, if that's OK with everybody!" The society was founded by Upton Dickson who wrote a pamphlet called "Cower Power." Well, Ben could have been a charter member of the Doormats.

Improvement for Ben began in the process of talking things over, but the real healing opened up at a marriage enrichment weekend. Surrounded by a loving, accepting, affirming group of couples, Ben began to recall a series of painful memories. He remembered hearing the neighbors talk about his family. You see, his mother was a frail, hysterical woman. She'd had a nervous breakdown and had spent many years as a semi-invalid. And he remembered the neighbors whispering that she had had the breakdown because her little boy just followed her around, clinging to her apron strings, and never letting her out of his sight. A pretty heavy burden to lay on a toddler or even on a teenager—"*You* are the cause of your mother's breakdown, of her being an invalid." Now Ben sobbed with release, and how beautifully the group loved and accepted him. There was lifted from him a great burden, for he could stop the inner penance he had done all these years for an unjust accusation.

How much hurt and damage have been done from chance remarks like this one we'll never know. Seeds of hurt, humiliation, hate are sown into a little mind, to fester, to become gangrenous, and someday to infect an adult personality.

Remarks like this one: "I'm afraid he'll grow up to be just like his Uncle Ed." And who is Uncle Ed? Well, Uncle Ed just happened to have spent ten years in the pen; he died in a mental institution.

Or this one: "Boy, that kid, that face. Isn't it a shame he couldn't have gotten just a little bit of his brother's good looks?"

Or the little girl, with the more beautiful sister, who overheard the relatives whispering at the family reunion, "That's the homely one."

And what can we possibly say about all the hurts and agonies, the guilts and fears and the hates that are intertwined with the American obsession—sex? All the way from those childish curiosities where children explore each other's bodies, to older brothers and sisters with threats or bribes taking advantage of younger ones, arousing powerful feelings—that are destructive at that age—like running 800 volts through 110 wire. Move on to fathers and stepfathers who treat their daughters not as daughters, but as wives and mistresses. Sex, being what it is, can produce the deadliest of all emotional conflicts: dread and desire, fear and pleasure, love and hate, all combined into a violent emotional earthquake which can tear a person's guts out.

Rage

Speaking of hate—that's the real problem, isn't it? The anger, the resentment, the hate that gets buried deep down inside. Sometimes I ask people when I'm counseling with them, "Would the word *rage* be too strong?" They often hang their heads and say, "No. That's right." Don't let an external doormat meekness fool you. I have yet to deal with a person troubled by perfectionistic emotional problems who was not very angry about something. The anger may be buried underneath layers of timdity, meekness, and spiritual piety, but it's there.

The healing process must include the courage to unmask the anger, bring it out before God, and put it on the Cross where it belongs. There will be no healing until it is acknowledged, confronted, and resolved. Resolution means forgiving every person involved in that hurt and humiliation; it means surrendering every desire for a vindictive triumph over that person; it means allowing God's forgiving love to wash over your guilt-plagued soul.

I was surprised to get a phone call many years ago from a professor in a Christian college. He remembered a statement I had made, while preaching a revival at his school. He said. "I remember you saying, 'Whenever you experience a response on your part that is way out of proportion to the stimulus, then look out. You have probably tapped into some deeply hidden emotional hurt.' I guess that is what has happened to me." So he came to our town, and we spent almost a week together. He was a learned man, and highly spiritual, with a deep knowledge of Scripture. But there had been a confrontation on that college campus, and all of a sudden this controlled, Christian scholar was reacting in violent anger. *Rage* was really the word for it. He was shocked at himself, and felt so guilty. He didn't know what to do, and no amount of Scripture reading or praying or trying to leave the whole situation with God seemed to help. He was really on the brink and in agony confessed to me: "I can't believe it, but when this happened, I actually felt as if I wanted to go out and kill somebody."

It wasn't hard to find the roots of the problem, but he had trouble accepting them. As he told me about it he kept saying, "Oh, but that's so silly . . . it can't be that!"

I said, "Nothing is silly. Tell me about it."

He had been a bright, precocious child, an egghead almost from birth. You know the kind—six years old, going on fifteen. He was so bright that it wasn't easy for him to live with the ones who weren't as smart. He was always first in the classroom but last on the playground. Every recess was a hell for him. There were those unforgettable scenes, as the intelligent but uncoordinated little boy was teased and made fun of. The rougher and tougher boys and girls bullied him, tortured him, knocked him down, hurt him physically. But more than that, they made an emotional cripple out of him. He was amazed at the sensitivity of his memory. He remembered all the children by name, and even what they wore. It was all there, though years had elapsed, and he tapped into this fountain of rage. As we went through every incident, he called each youngster by name. We put every one under his forgiveness. "Will you forgive Dan? Will you forgive Sally? And will you forgive . . ." Does this sound trivial? Quite the contrary, it was incredibly painful. But in prayer he found grace to forgive each one of those kids who had made life so intolerable for him. The Holy Spirit took the sting out of those memories and defused their compulsive power. That was the beginning of an in-depth change, and it took time until the healing power of God filled in those torturous, hurtful holes in his heart.

The Justification of God

Such basic inner resentment is really an anger against injustice and it cries out, "I was a victim. I had no choice. I didn't choose to be born. I didn't choose my parents. I didn't choose my brothers and sisters. I didn't choose my handicaps and my illness. I was a victim, and my hurts and my humiliations and my scars are unjust." And we often see this hidden anger coming out in perfectionists who want to correct every mistake they see and set right all the wrongs of the world.

The place of healing for this damaged person is the Cross—the very peak of all injustice. In P.T. Forsythe's profound book, he calls the Cross "the justification of God" (*The Justification of God*, London, Independent Press). In the Cross God demonstrated His total identification with us in *our undeserved suffering*, as well as in *our deserved punishment*. Never was there more injustice than in that Cross. No one ever received more rejection than our Lord. His accusations, His trial, His crucifixion were all vastly unjust.

Never say, "God doesn't know what it is like to suffer" and never think that God allows us to suffer things that He has not been willing to bear Himself. He was led as a Lamb to the slaughter; all His rights were taken from Him; all His powers were suspended. The support of His friends was removed, as they forsook Him and fled, while He was humiliated, stripped, mocked, ridiculed. "So you're the Son of God, huh? Well, come down and prove it if You are so great."

As we look at the Cross, we begin to see how deeply Christ is the *truth*, and not just the bright, shiny, beautiful truth of God *for* all of us. His Cross is the ghastly, revolting truth *about* all of us—the truth about the envy and the hate and the lust and the selfishness and the rage that permeate this fallen, sinful world of human beings. The truth of life in this world came out in the crucifixion of the Son of God. Now we know that God understands what it is like to live in this kind of a world. He is the Wounded Healer, He is our High Priest who is touched with the feelings of our infirmities.

Here is the unbelievable, too-good-to-be-true good news for every perfectionist—for you who cannot face all those conflicting feelings inside you which you think you can't possibly share with God. I've heard a thousand times in my office, "How can I tell these things to God? How can I express my hurt, my humiliation, my anger, my resentment against people; yes, against Him? How can I share *that* with Him?" Don't you understand? On the Cross He has already experienced all of that and far more.

On the Cross, God in Christ has absorbed all these kinds of painful feelings into His love. They have entered into His heart, pierced His soul, and been dissolved in the ocean of His forgiveness and the sea of His forgetfulness.

The Apostle Paul, formerly the bitterest enemy of the Christian faith, was the one who hated Jesus Christ, the one who hurled insults at Him, the one who vented his rage by being at the killing of the first martyr, Stephen. When Paul discovered that all that rage had been absorbed into the gracious heart of God, he wrote, "God was in Christ, reconciling (let's make it personal), reconciling *me* to Himself, not counting *my* trespasses against me." (See 2 Cor. 5:19).

There is *nothing* you can share out of the agonizing hurts and depths and hates and rages of your soul that God has not heard. There is *nothing* you take to Him that He will not understand. He will receive you with love and grace.

Because Jesus knew that we would all think this was too good to be true, on the night before He went to the Cross, He instituted the Communion Supper. Taking bread and wine, simple things we could feel and touch and taste and smell and receive into ourselves, He said, "Eat and drink this to remind you of it all." (See Matt. 26:26–28.)

As we take and eat of the body, from His brokenness we receive healing and wholeness for our brokenness. As we partake of the cup, we receive His forgiving and healing love into our souls and bodies.

"Oh Wounded Healer, Broken One, we give You all the broken pieces of our lives, and ask that You put them all together and make us whole. Amen."

9

*Super You
or Real You?*

ರೊಞೕೞೕೞೕೞೕೞೕೞೕೞೕೞೕೞೕೞೕೞ

*For we dare not make ourselves of the number, or compare our-
selves with some that commend themselves; but they measuring
themselves by themselves, and comparing themselves among themselves, are not wise. But we will not boast of things without our
measure, but according to the measure of the rule which God hath
distributed to us.*

*He that glorieth, let him glory in the Lord. For not he that com-
mendeth himself is approved, but whom the Lord commendeth.*

2 Corinthians 10:12–13, 17–18

*Behold, Thou desirest truth in the inward parts; and in the hidden
part Thou shalt make me to know wisdom.*

Psalm 51:6

ರೊಞೕೞೕೞೕೞೕೞೕೞೕೞೕೞೕೞೕೞೕೞ

THE PERFECTIONIST NEEDS to learn to be his true self in Christ.
Yet it's in being his real self that the perfectionist runs into his biggest
snags, and needs his deepest healing and most drastic reprogramming.
Perhaps the most terrible consequence of perfectionism is alienation
from the true self. Let's see where this tragic loss begins and how it
takes place.

Somewhere in the process of growing up, the child receives messages about himself, about God, about other people, and about relationships. These messages can be taught or caught. They can come
through what is directly said or done, or what is *not* said and *not* done.

Usually it is a combination of many factors. Slowly but surely, and quite unconsciously to the youngster, the messages come through. The child who has received negative messages then knows: "I am not accepted and loved as I am. I've tried every way to get this approval by being the way I am. Now I can only be accepted and loved *if* I become something else and someone else."

This youngster doesn't sit down and figure this all out. He doesn't know what is happening in his life—that he is not receiving fulfillment of deep, God-given needs which are basic to the development of a human being. Some very necessary feelings never come across to him, feelings like security, acceptance, belongingness, and value. His need to be loved and to learn to give love is not met. Instead there develops a growing deep anxiety, and feelings of insecurity, unworthiness, and undesirableness. And the youngster begins to climb the long, torturous trail of trying to become someone else.

The tragedy is that the person's God-designed selfhood doesn't ever get a chance to grow. His unique talents are not developed. His true self is denied or squelched, and a kind of pseudo-self takes its place. All the emotional and spiritual energies which ought to go into the development of his God-intended self are used to create a false and idealized picture of himself.

Unfortunately, when this person becomes a Christian, this self-destructive process is not automatically stopped. Forgiveness, loving acceptance and God's grace penetrate some outer layers of his unreal self, bringing a new spirit of honesty to his life.

But if the distortion is serious and the emotions are badly damaged, a deeper kind of healing is needed. For all too often, the pseudo-self transfers over into the Christian life itself, and reorganizes around the new religious experience.

Super You vs. Real You

What are *Super You* and *Real You?* Super You is a false idealized image you think you have to be in order to be loved and accepted. Super You is an imaginary picture of yourself. Since you have been programmed to believe that no one will love you if he gets to know the real you, you strive to become Super You, to gain love and acceptance.

This distortion extends even to God who is Absolute Perfection, who demands perfection, and to whom you must somehow present only your good side. You must let God see only Super You, not Real You.

Let me ask you a very personal question. When you come into the presence of God in meditation or prayer, which of the two do you present to Him? I asked that once of a successful evangelist who had come seeking help for some emotional and spiritual problems. I said to him, "In your dealings with God, when you go to Him in prayer, which self do you present to Him? What's the picture of yourself, in your imagination, that you are bringing to God?" I said, "Don't answer quickly. Take your time. We'll just sit and you think about it."

Well, he was silent for an unusually long time. Then he said to me, "You know, I've never really thought of it that way before. But I've got to be honest with you. I'm afraid that I always go into the presence of God with my best spiritual foot forward and my finest halo on. I would have to, in honesty, admit that when I imagine myself in the presence of God, I'm always Super Me. I don't think I have ever gone as Real Me, just as I am." And then he shook his head and said, "And I've sung that song a thousand times, 'Just As I Am,' but I have never lived it out when I came to God."

He's not alone in this. There are subtle ways of presenting Super Self to God and hiding Real Self. One is the *futuristic* way. "Well, God, of course, I haven't achieved Super Me yet. You know that and I know that. I'm not the picture of Super Me yet, but someday I will be. Someday I'm going to be that perfect Christian. Someday I'll pray enough, read enough, witness enough, do enough sensational things for You. Someday I will be the idealized picture of myself. I'll be Super Me. So don't pay any attention to Real Me now, God—that's just temporary. Get Your eyes on what I am going to be."

Then there's the *penitential* way. And this is where so much low self-esteem and even self-contempt comes into the perfectionist's life. "Well, God, don't look at Real Me, with all my sins and failures and my shortcomings. Don't look at that because You can see how much I despise Real Me, can't You? And I presume, of course, that You too hate Real Me with all my failures and shortcomings. But You know what my goals are, Lord. Since You hate Real Me and I hate Real Me, You can see I'm really on Your side, so I'm really Super Me."

In these subtle ways, self-belittling becomes a perpetual inner penance to impress God. You hope He doesn't see your Real Self, but only

looks at your Super Self. Since God can't stand that ugly, unacceptable Real You and since you keep telling Him you can't stand it
either, He must be impressed with your very high standards, realize
what you really are, and therefore, accept and love you.

The tragedy of this is that Real You got stuck emotionally at some
childhood level. And this explains some of the utterly childish things
that come out of your personality. You stayed in the past somewhere;
you never grew. You obviously have the chronological body of a man
or a woman, but spiritually and emotionally you live on an immature
level.

Super You and Feelings

It's in the area of feelings that the perfectionist has his biggest problems, because the image of Super Self is a person who never admits to
experiencing certain kinds of feelings. Usually he has an unbiblical
mental picture of Jesus as "gentle Jesus, meek and mild." This Jesus is
sissified, passive, a stoic person whose emotions are never expressed.
He's under the tightest emotional control; and usually doesn't express
emotions at all.

However, there are no such things as bad feelings and good feelings. Feelings are *just* feelings. They are consequences of a whole range
of things that come out of your personality. No emotions are in themselves sinful. What you do with them will determine whether they are
wrong or right. How you handle them will determine whether they
lead you to righteousness or to sinfulness. The emotions themselves
are a very important part of your God-given personality equipment.

One emotion that Super You generally considers bad is *anger*. I grew
up on some unbiblical, inhuman, and destructive preaching about
anger always being an unsanctified emotion. It took me years to get
over these attitudes. They almost destroyed my Christian life and
nearly wrecked my marriage, because I had to learn how to properly
express my anger to my wife. Every good husband or wife has to learn
how to do that in acceptable ways.

In Mark 3:5 we read that Jesus looked around at them in anger.
While this is the only place in the New Testament that actually says
Jesus got angry, I think we can safely presume that Jesus was angry
when He whipped the moneychangers out of the temple and when
He called certain people "blind fools," "whitewashed tombs," "mur-
derers," "serpents," and "miserable frauds." (See Matt. 23, PH.) Never

was Jesus more divine than at those moments when He was expressing white-hot anger. Many times, perfect love and anger go hand in hand; indeed, the anger is the result of perfect love.

We Christians have a semantic trick that sounds good but confuses people. "Oh, that's not anger; it's 'righteous indignation.'" Why don't we just come out and say that there is a right use of anger, and that anger in itself is not a sinful emotion? It would be a lot less confusing.

What matters is your use of anger—how you express it and how you resolve it. But when you have this unreal, false image of Super You who must never experience or never express any feelings of anger, you become a perfect setup for emotional wreckage and depression.

Don't confuse anger and resentment, for they are entirely different. Anger, controlled and properly expressed, is one thing; out-of-control anger, improperly expressed, is another. The Apostle Paul made a plain distinction between the right kind of anger and resentment. He carefully contrasted anger with hate, malice, bitterness, and all the rest of it. Interestingly enough, his statement, "Be ye angry and sin not" (Eph. 4:26), is in the imperative. Paul didn't say, "It's all right, I will allow you to get angry once in a while as a concession." Paul said, "Get angry! Be angry!" He was quick to add, "But be careful." Paul knew that anger can lead to resentment, malice, bitterness, if it is not handled very carefully. Paul was saying, "Express your anger, but be sure that it doesn't lead you into any form of bitterness, resentment, or hatred." Now the strange fact of the matter is that unless you and I learn proper ways of expressing and resolving anger, we will become resentful and bitter. Many marriages are being destroyed because partners have not learned how to properly express their anger. They are keeping the lid on a lot of deep feelings, doing a slow burn, and getting even in a thousand and one subtle ways.

Be angry, but be careful. Anger becomes resentful and bitter when you don't know proper ways to express it. This is exactly what happens to the perfectionist who can never even allow himself to express anger; who won't even allow himself to be aware that he is angry. He denies it and pushes it down deep into his inner self where it simmers and festers and comes out in various kinds of disguised emotional problems, marital conflicts, and even in forms of physical illness.

Anger is a divinely implanted emotion, part of God's image in the human personality, and is to be used for constructive purposes.

Super You and Conflict

Super You has the notion that you ought to always get along with everybody, be liked by everybody, and that there should never be any conflict between Christians.

A brief visit to a mission station is a shock for the perfectionist, because it doesn't take him long to realize that the missionaries often have more problems in getting along with one another than with the unbelievers they are trying to minister to. We see this in our own churches. But still the perfectionistic myth persists: "This is what I ought to be."

Does such an idea come from Scripture? Not even two greats like Paul and Barnabas could work together. Very wisely they parted company, and very wisely the early church laid hands on them both, blessed them both, and sent them in opposite directions.

God used their humanness to establish two mission works instead of one. God also used their disagreement to help John Mark to mature and become the great writer of the Gospel of Mark.

While you cannot work with everybody, that doesn't mean you have the right to resent anyone. That doesn't mean you have the right to hate or to be bitter. It *does* mean you may not necessarily like or feel comfortable around everybody. And don't let Super You become your Screwtape who says, "Well now, if you're not getting along, *you* are the one at fault. The problem is *you*, and if only you would take care of something, you'd get along OK." Paul never said, "If you are filled with the Holy Spirit, you will live peacefully and smoothly with all people." What he did say is, "If possible, so far as it depends on you, be at peace with all men" (Rom. 12:18, NASB). The problem may lie in the other person. Paul did not add, as Super You does, "Yes, and that problem is also your problem and you are responsible for fixing the other guy up too." There is a little rhyme that says it well:

> To live above with saints in heaven,
> Oh, that will be glory;
> But to live below with saints on earth—
> Now that's a different story.

Real You faces real differences, real conflicts, and loves and cares enough to confront persons in a spirit of love. But Real You also knows that sometimes the best solution and the only solution is, to use Stanley Jones' great phrase, "to agree to disagree agreeably."

Super You and Happiness

Super You believes the myth: "I've always got to be superhappy." But are you always happy? Never depressed? Bubbling over with "Praise the Lord"? Is there never a time of struggle? Is there never a time when the heavens seem brass? When you do things out of sheer duty, without happy feelings?

In the Garden of Gethsemane, our Lord said to His disciples, "My soul is exceedingly troubled, even unto death." He was writhing on the ground; He was sweating profusely and undergoing a terrific struggle between His emotions and His will. His emotions were saying, "Father, You can do everything; take the cup away from Me if it's possible." But His will was as fixed as the magnet to the North Pole, and His will kept saying, "Not My will, but Yours." And sometimes that same kind of struggle gives us an exceedingly troubled soul.

The word *happiness* has its roots in the word *happenings*. Happiness depends on happenings, on what happens to us, externals that we can't control. *Joy* is the right word for what we Christians are to expect. For *joy* is an internal word which has to do with relationships, not circumstances, not happenings. Joy is the inner calm at the eye of the storm; feelings can be stormy, but there can also be an inner sense of rightness to the will of God. But this does not mean that we have to go about with Super Self masks on, with smiling lips, sparkling teeth, and a "Praise the Lord!"

Real-You Realism

As a Christian, you can be a realist. This means you don't need to be afraid to face the worst, the ugliest, the most painful. You don't have to be afraid to express your feelings of grief, sorrow, hurt, loneliness, struggle, even depression. Sometimes you may even experience depressive feelings like Elijah had after his greatest moment of triumph: "Oh, Lord, it is enough. Let me die."

There is a rugged honesty about the life of Jesus—every kind of emotion was so clearly recorded and freely expressed, without any sense of shame or guilt or imperfection. Take your pattern from Jesus, not from some mythical Super Self. You need never be afraid to express your real feelings and be your real self in Jesus Christ.

When you waste time and energy trying to be Super Self, you rob yourself of growth and the friendship of God. And you never let God accept and love the Real You for whom Christ died. This is the *only you* that God really knows and sees. Super You is an illusion of your imagination, a false image, an idol. I'm not sure that God even sees Super You. You can be yourself in Jesus, and you need not compare yourself to anyone else. He wants to heal *you* and to change *you* in order that Real You can grow up to be the person He intended you to be.

Super Self dies very hard, and the religious super self dies the hardest of all. If you find that you cling to it tenaciously, I hope you will hear the Holy Spirit saying, "Abandon it! Give it up! Then you and I can start the whole healing process of making the Real You."

When you stop wasting your spiritual energies to maintain this false Super You and start using those energies in cooperating with the Holy Spirit for true growth, you will find yourself free in Jesus Christ, liberated from false oughts and shoulds, freed from the approval and disapproval of other people, freed from that awful condemnation of the performance gap between what you're trying to be and what you really are.

What is it that fills in the performance gap? I have good news for you: From the cross of Jesus Christ, all the perfections of Jesus, God's true Superman, are given to you as a free gift of His grace, and these more than fill in the gaps of your life.

Paul said it so well, "But of Him are ye in Christ Jesus, who of God *is made unto us* wisdom, and righteousness, and sanctification, and redemption" (1 Cor. 1:30).

10

Myths and Truths About Depression

∽✕∽✕∽✕∽✕∽✕∽✕∽✕∽✕∽✕∽✕∽✕∽✕∽✕∽✕∽✕∽✕∽

*Why art thou cast down, O my soul? And why art thou disquieted
in me? Hope thou in God: for I shall yet praise Him for the help of
His countenance. O my God, my soul is cast down within me. . . .
Deep calleth unto deep at the noise of Thy waterspouts: all Thy waves
and Thy billows are gone over me.*

*My tears have been my meat day and night, while they continu-
ally say unto me, "Where is thy God?"*

Psalm 42:5–7, 3

∽✕∽✕∽✕∽✕∽✕∽✕∽✕∽✕∽✕∽✕∽✕∽✕∽✕∽✕∽✕∽✕∽

DEPRESSION IS A common experience among Christians. You may
ask, "How can that be? A depressed Christian? The very words are
contradictory; they are incompatible. If a person has been truly born
of the Spirit, and certainly if he has been filled with the Spirit, then
shouldn't it be impossible for him to be depressed? Surely, the fact
that a Christian would be suffering from depression at all should be a
sign that something is wrong, that something needs to be straightened
out with the Lord. It must be a sign of sin in that person's life."

Now all of that may sound very good and very simple, but it does
not stand the test of Scripture, the facts of Christian experience, or the
truths about psychology. And it certainly does not square with the
biographies of the saints.

Christians Can Be Depressed

Have you read some of David's psalms recently?

"Why art thou cast down, oh my soul?" (Ps. 42:5)

"O my God, my soul is cast down within me" (Ps. 42:6).

"Why art thou cast down? Hope in God; for I shall yet praise Him, who is the health of my countenance" (Ps. 43:5).

Or listened to Elijah? "O Lord, take away my life" (1 Kings 19:4).

Or Jonah? "It is better for me to die than to live" (Jonah 4:3).

Or heard Jesus' words in the Garden, as He was in pain and in prayer? "My soul is exceeding sorrowful, even unto death" (Matt. 26:38). Can you find better descriptions of depression—a depression in which the person almost despaired of life itself? Many of the depressive psalms speak of the countenance, the person's face, and how accurate those psalms are! The person who is depressed and dejected has a miserable countenance. He looks troubled, worried, unhappy, as if he is bearing the weight of the world on his shoulders.

Another very common symptom of depression is tears. "My tears have been my meat day and night" (Ps. 42:3), says the psalmist. This is an amazingly accurate psychological statement! Depression often brings a loss of appetite. You just don't feel like eating. Because food seems repulsive, you begin to live on tears instead of food. "My tears have been my meat," and some of us could add, "Yes, and my vegetable, salad, dessert, and drink too." What's wrong? Unable to stop crying, you feed on despair, and that of course increases the depression.

The Scriptures are much more realistic and kind to us than some Christians are, as they clearly show that it is possible for Christians to be very depressed. The biographies of the saints also deal with this. We often quote from John Wesley's great Aldersgate conversion experience, but I could show you several quotations that follow which almost seem to nullify it, as Wesley spoke out in depression, doubt, and dejection.

Samuel Logan Brengle, Portrait of a Prophet is the story of a great saint of the Salvation Army (Clarence W. Hall, The Salvation Army, Inc.). Brengle's classic works on holiness have been translated into scores of languages, and have been the means of leading millions of believers into a deeper life in Christ.

Speaking of Brengle, Hall wrote, "Then would come a battle with his feelings with the descent upon his mind of a constitutional melancholia" (p. 213). In a letter, Brengle wrote: "'My nerves were ragged, frazzled, exhausted. And such gloom and depression fell upon me as I have never known, although depression is an old acquaintance of mine'" (p. 214). In later life he suffered an injury to his head, when at a street meeting a drunk threw a brick at Brengle and hit him on the head. Complications from this injury increased the depression that had been a lifelong struggle, an "old acquaintance," as he called it. Yet was there ever a more sanctified saint than Samuel Logan Brengle?

Before a person can deal with depression, he must acknowledge it. And many a Christian, if he were completely honest about his emotions, would have to admit: "Yes, depression is an acquaintance of mine too. I know what you are talking about."

By denying their depression, many Christians add to their troubles. They add guilt on top of the depression and thereby double the problem. Let's say that a severe depression is equal to carrying one ton of emotional weight. That's about what it feels like, doesn't it? To carry a ton on your back is bad, but you may have the strength for it. However, when you then add guilt by saying, "There's something wrong with me because I have this depression," you have then doubled the weight, and that's an impossible load for anyone to carry.

Depression is not necessarily a sign of spiritual failure. In the Scripture stories, some of the greatest depressions came as emotional letdowns following the greatest spiritual successes. This was true in the life of Elijah. After that greatest moment in his life, the triumph over the prophets of Baal on Mt. Carmel, what happened? The next time we see him he is sitting alone under the juniper tree, asking God to take his life. Abraham had a similar experience (Gen. 15). And many of us have too. Depression seems to be nature's emotional kickback. It is a reaction like the wallop from firing a gun of heavy caliber. It is nature's recoil, or perhaps the balance wheel in what C.S. Lewis calls "the law of undulation" in the human personality.

Unfortunately, some of our Christian friends can be our worst enemies at this point, offering us false and unrealistic advice. There are Christians who have little understanding about depression. Because their own personalities are not very subject to it, they fail to understand people who suffer depression. This can be especially cruel when two such people are married to one another. If a husband does not suffer much from depression but his wife does, he may have a difficult time appreciating her emotions and her moods. It can be a doubly cruel situation if he uses her depressed time to put a spiritual heavy on her. Or the wife on the husband, if the situation is reversed.

You can't assume that because you never suffer from depression, you are therefore more spiritual. C.S. Lewis once said that about half the times when we credit ourselves with virtue, it's really just a matter of temperament and constitution, and not of spirituality.

Depression and Guilt

There is a depression that can come from the guilt of sin, from known disobedience and transgression. However, that kind is not what I am writing about. You may wonder, "How do I recognize the depression that comes from sin?" And that's a good question, especially if you are a perfectionist who suffers from an oversensitive conscience, from the tyranny of the oughts and the shoulds, or from a constant feeling of uneasiness, anxiety, and condemnation. Let me give you a general principle that I think can be very helpful. A concrete, specific feeling of guilt which can be related to a particular, precise act or attitude is generally a true and reliable feeling of guilt. And the emotions that follow can be real guilt and real depression for a real transgression.

However, a vague, all-inclusive umbrella of systematic self-accusation, general overall feelings of anxiety and condemnation which cannot be pinpointed—these are generally signs of pseudo-guilt or just plain depression that has come from emotional sources. Sin may lead to depression, but all depression does not come from sin. The roots of depression often run deep and are very complicated, as complicated as many of the child-hood hurts and scars that people carry into adulthood.

Depression and Personality

Depression is related to personality structure, physical makeup, body chemistry, glandular functions, emotional patterns, and learned feeling-concepts. As Christians we must realize and accept this. If all of us had the good common sense found in one of our most ancient nursery rhymes, we would be better off.

> Jack Sprat could eat no fat,
> His wife could eat no lean;
> And so between them both,
> They licked the platter clean.

Now this is an amazingly profound analysis of personality structure, believe it or not. Constitutionally, Jack Sprat and Mrs. Sprat are entirely different. Don't try to make them both eat the same way, or live the same way. That would be a violation of their personalities. They are both valuable human beings, and we presume that they love each other very much even though they are totally different in their makeup. I wish more preachers, teachers, evangelists, and especially parents would master the sound good sense of that nursery rhyme.

"Wait a minute," someone says. "You've forgotten that when we are in Christ, we are new creatures, and old things pass away. Don't regeneration and sanctification do away with old differences?" To this I must say, "No! Thank God, they do not!"

The new birth does not change your basic temperament. It can put within you, as Oswald Chambers loves to say, "the disposition of Jesus Christ," but it does not change your basic temperament. The fact that you have become a Christian does not mean that from now on you cease to live with yourself as yourself. Paul was still very much Paul after his conversion. Peter was still very much Peter, and John was John. They did not become other people. In God's plan, no two things are ever identical. No two snowflakes are alike. Through great variety within unity, God shows the wonder of His ways. We are each different, in temperament and personality structure. We see and feel, react to and interpret things individually.

The Apostle Paul reminded us: "We have this treasure in earthen vessels" (2 Cor. 4:7). By nature and temperament, some people are nervous, apprehensive, or easily frightened. They are oversensitive and their feelings are easily touched and changed. I sometimes wonder if Paul wasn't one of these. As strong as he was, he went to Corinth in "weakness and fear, with much trembling" (1 Cor. 2:3). He was a highstrung young man, "without were fightings, within were fears" (2 Cor. 7:5). Certainly this was true of young pastor Timothy. The entire Second Epistle to Timothy seems to have been written by Paul to pull Timothy out of depression. Brengle's biographer called him a "constitutional melancholic." People who are extremely introspective and sensitive often have the worst problems with depression.

Our failure to deal realistically with ourselves regarding depression is the root cause of much of our depression. If we have the idea that there is no connection between the *natural* (our temperament and personality structure) and the *supernatural* (our spiritual lives), we are seriously mistaken. Both our feelings and our faith operate through the same personality equipment. God does not come to us in special ways which bypass or short-circuit or sidetrack our personality equipment. He doesn't drill a hole in the tops of our skulls and with some magical, mystical funnel pour His grace into us. The mechanisms of our personalities which we use in faith are the same instruments through which our feelings operate.

Maybe we can understand it if we can think of one of these great, big, expensive, combination centers with a TV in the middle, and a stereo record player, and radio. It's a beautiful piece of furniture. But if something goes wrong with some of the transistors in that vast assemblage, the audio system goes out. Why? All the components are all working through the same mechanism. If a connection burns out over here, or a condenser and some transistors go wrong over there, all three of the operations are going to be affected. Why? They are operating through the same system.

Depressions can come from sources outside the purely spiritual. They come because something has gone wrong with the equipment—perhaps in the physical, or in the balance of emotions and personality. Transistors have been affected, a connection has burned out, and it has affected even the spiritual life.

Let's return to Brengle, that very saintly man, as he writes about himself: "'Such gloom and depression fell upon me as I have never known. . . . God *seemed* nonexistent. The grave *seemed* my endless goal. Life lost all of its glory, charm, and meaning. . . . Prayer brought me no relief; indeed, I seemed to have lost the spirit of prayer and the power to pray'" (Hall, *Portrait of a Prophet*, p. 214).

To apply our previous illustration, there was nothing wrong with the sender; the love of God was still coming through. The radio station was sending out beautiful music, the TV transmitter was sending out the right images, but the only sound was static and the sight was TV "snow." Why? Because something had gone wrong with the receiving set.

That's what happened to Brengle. And notice how wise he was. In spite of his feelings, he realized God was still there. In every sentence he used the word *seemed*. "It *seemed* like God was nonexistent. . . . It *seemed* like the grave was my goal." And Brengle himself underlined the word *seemed*.

Have you ever experienced a complete change in your feelings? You go to bed one night and everything's fine. You wake up the next morning, and nothing's fine. Nothing you can think of accounts for it. Yesterday you were happy. You were looking forward to a great day. But something happened, and your responses are different. Your feelings, actions, interpretations of the very same things that took place yesterday are very different today. And you are not alone. God is there, but so is Screwtape. Satan is sitting there on the side of the bed, for he sees an opening to ride right into your personality. Why? Because Satan is of the spirit world, he already knows what you and I need to learn—that the same equipment which affects the natural also affects the spiritual. So Satan tries to turn temperamental depression into spiritual depression. Satan always wants to turn emotional depression into spiritual defeat. He wants to take a burned-out emotion in your receiving set and turn it into a burned-out trust. He's aware of your infirmities; and he knows the depths of your spirit and he comes riding that monorail right into the heart of your personality.

Do you know how Satan wants to win? He tries to get you to foul yourself out of the game. He wants to turn the natural mood of depression into spiritual defeat, doubt, and despondency.

Acceptance of Your Personality

I urge you to accept your personality and acknowledge your temperament. Having truth in the inward parts means you no longer resist who you are. You stop fighting your temperament as an enemy and begin to accept it as a gift from God.

I personally spent many years fighting myself, trying to be someone else, battling my nervous, high-strung temperament, always feeling a bit angry about that, and trying to be someone else. The turning point came when I could accept myself as I am. For one day the Lord said, "Hey, this is all you've got! You're not going to get another personality. You'd better settle down and live with it and learn to do something with it."

"And, furthermore, if you'll just give the Real You into My hands—not Super You, which you are not—if you'll turn that over to Me, then you and I are going to get along fine, and I'll be able to use you as you are."

The first step in learning to live above depression is to accept yourself as you are. This does not mean you are to be controlled by your temperament. After conversion, the Holy Spirit is to be in control. But the Holy Spirit can only fill and control that which you acknowledge and surrender to Him. While you cannot change your temperament, you can allow it to be controlled by the Holy Spirit.

We left Brengle in deep depression, and I don't want to leave him there—or you either. He said,

Prayer brought no relief. Indeed, I seem to have lost the spirit of prayer and the power to pray. Then I remembered to give thanks and to praise God, though I felt no spirit of praise and thanksgiving. Feeling, except that of utter depression and gloom, was gone. But as I thanked God for the trial, it began to turn to blessing, light glimmered, grew very slowly, and then broke through the gloom. The depression passed away, and life was beautiful and desirable again, and full of gracious incomings once more (Hall, *Portrait of a Prophet*, p. 214).

That's it! Brengle said, "I remembered." Paul wrote to Timothy, "I put you in remembrance." Tomorrow morning, remember that the love of God is not grounded in your feelings, nor in your performance, and not even in your love for Him. His love is grounded in His own faithfulness. The steadfast love of the Lord never ceases; His mercies never come to an end. They are new every morning: "Great is Thy faithfulness. The Lord is my portion. . . . Therefore will I hope in Him" (Lam. 3:23–24).

11

Dealing with Depression

*This priceless treasure we hold, so to speak, in a common earthen-
ware jar—to show that the splendid power of it belongs to God and
not to us. We are handicapped on all sides, but we are never frustrated; we are puzzled, but never in despair. We are persecuted, but
we never have to stand it alone: we may be knocked down but we
are never knocked out!*

*This is the reason why we never collapse. The outward man does
indeed suffer wear and tear, but every day the inward man receives
fresh strength.*

2 Corinthians 4:7–9, 16, PHILLIPS

BY HONESTLY ACKNOWLEDGING your feelings about depression,
you are not adding to God's information about you. He knows those
feelings. Through His Son He experienced them as He walked in your
moccasins, and He is with you to understand and to help. As you admit
and examine your depression, you can go on to take positive steps
toward healing.

Are You Living Beyond Your Means?

You have physical, emotional, and spiritual limitations, and you need
to stay within them. Have you been getting enough sleep? Occasionally, we all are called upon to go without sufficient rest; we have
reserves on which we can draw. But to make the exception the rule

means you will live regularly with fatigue. If you do so, I can guarantee that you will suffer from chronic, and perhaps even clinical and pathological depression. You will feel like the man who said he not only had an identity crisis, but also an energy crisis. He didn't know who he was and he was just too tired to find out!

Let me answer one question before you ask it—no, it makes no difference if you are in the Lord's service! God does not suspend His laws and make cosmic pets of preachers, missionaries, high achievers and overcommitted church workers. They still come under the laws He has built into our bodies and emotions. And you cannot regularly violate those laws and expect to get by with it. What kind of load are you carrying? Who do you think you are, anyhow? God? That is one of the perfectionist's problems, you know.

Are you eating properly and regularly? My niece, who is a doctor, at one time specialized in emergency-room treatment. I asked her, "What do you do when depressed people who have attempted suicide are brought into the emergency room?"

She surprised me when she said, "Well, sometimes the first thing we do is to feed them, often a steak dinner. They are generally low in protein. We often discover that they have not eaten properly for two or three days. Their protein level is very low; therefore, their energy level is low, and their depression level is high." There are Christians who consistently neglect the physical area of their lives and then wonder why they are depressed.

Did you ever think that perhaps your depression is God's built-in cruise control for your life? Trying to slow you down, trying to balance out your emotions, because you regularly try to live above realistic possibilities? When the slave-driver of perfectionism propels you with that sense of "ought," you overstrain your emotional motor, and pay the price for it in chronic depression.

What About Your Reactions?

The things that happen to you are not as important as the ways you respond to those events. And there are certain responses that can produce a chain reaction leading to emotional and spiritual depression.

Has something happened which has been a blow to your ego? Has someone disappointed you badly? When you tried so hard, did you get a B+ instead of an A? You may have had a deep experience of hurt or loss, a home broken by death or divorce. Or, on a lesser level, but just as hurtful at a youthful stage in life, is a breakup with a boyfriend or a girlfriend. I've had many a depressed young person come to me and say, "My friends are all jumping on me, saying, 'You shouldn't feel this way if you are a real Christian.'" How cruel we can be to our young people with such unrealistic standards! Leaving familiar, safe, comfortable places, roots and faces, coming into strangeness and newness—these are blows which can lead to depression.

Sometimes it is an unusual blow to our selfhood that catches us off guard! We won the major battle; we took on the tanks, the heavy artillery, but then we got picked off by some little sniper in the bushes. That's the way it was with the Prophet Elijah. He confronted 400 priests in one of the most dramatic showdown battles in all of history. And then, a caustic, snippy remark by Jezebel, Ahab's wife, got to him: "You go tell that prophet that I'll make his life so miserable that by sunset he will wish he were dead!" (See 1 Kings 19:2.)

That's where it all began: "If you're not out of town by sunset . . ." Elijah was feeling so good that the sniper's bullet caught him off guard. He was drained from hours of prayer, struggle, and fatigue. When Jezebel's sniping hit him, he went into suicidal depression. Then God used the emergency room technique on him. First, He sent the ravens to feed Elijah some protein; this was followed by some much needed sleep. Then God reoriented Elijah's perception: "You're not the only one, my friend; there are 7,500 who are with you. You forgot that." Before long, Elijah's emotions and spirit had been restored to normal.

I see three primary reactions that lead to depression. They are indecision, anger, and a sense of unfairness or injustice.

1. *Indecision.* When a decision is needed, do you consistently put off making it? Is this your standard way of coping? If it is, you have a built-in depressor that will destroy your peace of mind and increase your feeling of being trapped. Many depressed people feel a sense of powerlessness: "I'm trapped. I don't see any way out." You could be using the same energy, not to postpone the decision, but to make it and carry it out. Using your energy to make a constructive decision is a good way to avoid depression.

Do you postpone decisions because you are afraid to say No? Because you are afraid to hurt someone? There are some situations you can never get out of without hurting someone. When you postpone dealing with them, you end up hurting people twice as much, and become depressed yourself. Are you afraid to say Yes? Afraid of responsibility or of risk? If you sit and look at the two roads and go back and forth, you literally end up being double-minded. And the double-minded person, said James, is unstable in all his ways. (See James 1:8.) Indecision is often the precursor of depression.

2. *Anger.* The most concise definition of depression I know is this: "Depression is frozen rage." If you have a consistently serious problem with depression, you have not resolved some area of anger in your life. As surely as the night follows the day, depression follows unresolved, repressed, or improperly expressed anger.

3. *Injustice.* Perfectionists have a very disproportionate sense of justice and injustice. They feel a deep need to right the wrongs of the world, to correct things, to pull up the weeds that are growing with the wheat. Now, that feeling is valuable; it exists in every reformer, in every preacher and missionary; and to some degree it should be in every Christian. That sense of injustice surrendered, cleansed, and controlled by the Holy Spirit can be a useful instrument in the hands of God "for spreading scriptural holiness and reforming the nation," as John Wesley said. But out of hand, out of balance, with the basic anger problem behind it unresolved, the sense of injustice is very destructive, producing depression and disrupting good personal relationships.

I have rarely met a depressive perfectionist who didn't have a terrific sense of injustice and unfairness. The only answer to this deep anger against the injustices of life is forgiveness. Who most often needs to be forgiven? Parents and family members. So often, the roots of depression are buried in the subsoil of early family life. And unless you learn to deal honestly with those angry roots, to face your resentment and forgive, you'll be living in a greenhouse where depression is sure to flourish.

A Story of Forgiveness

Two sisters, Mary and Martha, were opposites. Mary was an outgoing and vivacious blonde. Martha was a quiet and very talented brunette. Martha came to talk because a dating relationship, the best in her life so far, was developing. It was also bringing out a whole parcel of emotional problems, a lot of depression, and an angry, faultfindingness toward the young man. She wanted to love him and was learning to, but was shocked to realize she also wanted to pick him to pieces and hurt him. As she looked back, she realized that this was her dating pattern from years past, and it scared her.

As we talked, a lot of deep resentments came to the surface and she began to deal with them. Some were feelings toward Mother and Dad, and those were forgiven so that love could replace the anger.

But one day it became very obvious that Martha's real problem was Mary. And all of a sudden the angry memories marched across the screen of her imagination. As far back as she could remember, life was comparisons—comparisons by parents, teachers, friends, preachers, and neighbors.

As we began praying for the healing of those memories, and as she told God she was willing to forgive and to be forgiven and to let God change her feelings, it was as if the Holy Spirit pulled back a curtain, revealing to Martha a whole chain of insights. And in her praying she began to cry out, "Oh, Lord! I realize that everything I have ever said or thought or done or aimed at has been in reference to Mary. She has ruled my life; she has been my obsession; she's almost taken over Your place in my life!"

Martha had never chosen a dress or a course in college or a boy-friend or set a goal, or made any choice without feeling that she was in competition with Mary. And all the hidden hurts and anger had emotionally enslaved her to her older sister. What a struggle it was to let go, to forgive what she felt were the injustices of the comparisons, and the favoritisms which may or may not have been shown. Martha had a prayer battle that went on for well over an hour. At the end, she was exhausted; and so was I. But after that time of struggling prayer, Martha was able to truly forgive; she was released and set free from the hateful, competitive, angry little girl inside of her who had never grown because she had been frozen.

The best part of the story came months later when she said, "You know, I've literally been born all over again. My depressions are just normal mood changes now; none of those black pits I used to have. And best of all, I've discovered myself to be a totally different person than I thought I was. I'm free! I've got my own ideas, my own tastes. I make my own choices now, and set my own goals. I'm just so happy being me!"

Even her facial expression had changed, and in time Martha became a whole person, free to love. Why? Because she had faced her hurt and her anger and her sense of unfairness, and had let God's love wash them all out.

Is there frozen anger somewhere in your life? Toward parents? Family members? Are you angry at God? So many people need to forgive God, not because He has ever done anything wrong, but because they have held Him responsible. It is time to face up to your true feelings and resolve them in an understanding of His love.

You may need to forgive your marriage partner for past mistakes. But to forgive is also a present extension of grace to the person himself. Forgive your partner for just being the way he or she is—unable to meet some of your needs. Some of the most serious marital depressions arise when a husband or a wife thinks, *But, God, I have a right to feel this way! I ought to feel this way because she/he* . . . And when we say we have a *right* to feel cheated and resentful and betrayed, we are on the road to depression!

You may be depressed because you hold on to anger and refuse to forgive people who have authority over you. Granted, they may have misused their authority. They may have done wrong. But you need to forgive those whom God in His providence has allowed to have authority over you. If you refuse, don't be surprised if you and depression become close companions.

When Paul wrote to the church at Rome, he said, "Never take vengeance into your own hands, my dear friends: stand back and let God punish if He will. For it is written: 'Vengeance belongeth unto Me: I will recompense. . . . If thine enemy hunger, feed him; if he thirst, give him to drink.' . . . Don't allow yourselves to be overpowered with evil. Take the offensive—overpower evil with good!" (Rom. 12:19–21, PH.) The correcting of the injustices and the unfairnesses and the hurts of this world is God's business, and He warns, "Keep out of MY business!"

However, He does invite you to join Him in His work of forgiving and loving. "Be kind, tender hearted one to another, forgiving one another," as God would say it—"even as *I* for Christ's sake have forgiven you" (Eph. 4:32). Get out of the setting right and getting even business, and into the forgiving and the loving business.

When you surrender your anger and oversensitivity to injustice and unfairness, you won't have trouble with self-pity, and your depressions will lessen immediately.

Luther and Seamands

It may surprise you to know that Martin Luther wrote a great deal about depression. Because of his unhappy childhood, because of an overbearingly strict, religious upbringing, Martin Luther had a constant battle with low self-esteem and depression. He offered a lot of wonderfully up-to-date suggestions about meeting this problem. Let me share a few of his, and some of my own, which I have found to be most helpful.

1. *Avoid being alone.* When you are depressed you don't want to be around people. You want to withdraw. But withdrawing means isolation, and isolation during depression means alienation. Force yourself to be with people. This is one of the major areas where you have a definite choice in your depressions.

2. *Seek help from others.* During depression your perceptions change. A little hill becomes a great mountain. But real friends can help you see its true height in perspective. You can no more pull yourself out of depression than you can get yourself out of quicksand by pulling at your own hair. Seek out people and situations which generate joy. Here again your choice is definitive.

3. *Sing! Make music.* This was the only cure for King Saul's moods of depression. The harmony and beauty of David's music lifted King Saul's spirit of depression (1 Sam. 16:14–23).

4. *Praise and give thanks.* All the saints of the centuries agree on this one. It was Brengle's way out. When he couldn't feel God's presence or really pray, he would thank God for the leaf on the tree or the beautiful wing of a bird. For simple, everyday things. In essence Paul told Timothy: "Remember, and be thankful" (2 Tim. 1). To the Thessalonians he didn't say, "*Feel* thankful for everything," but "*In* everything *give* thanks" (1 Thes. 5:18).

5. *Lean heavily on the power of God's Word.* God can use any portion of the Scriptures to minister to you during times of depression, but throughout the centuries His people have found the psalms to be the most beneficial. This is because the psalmist is the one most familiar with and open to the whole range of depressive emotions. Out of the 150 Psalms, there are 48 which can speak to your condition. Here is a list I often give out: 6, 13, 18, 23, 25, 27, 31, 32, 34, 37, 38, 39, 40, 42, 43, 46, 51, 55, 57, 62, 63, 69, 71, 73, 77, 84, 86, 90, 91, 94, 95, 103, 104,

107, 110, 116, 118, 121, 123, 124, 130, 138, 139, 141, 142, 143, 146, and 147.

The most profitable procedure is to read them out loud. This allows the psalmist to become your contemporary expressing both his and your feelings of abandonment, despair, and melancholy, and his (and I trust, your) affirmation of faith and hope in God.

6. *Rest confidently in the presence of God's Spirit.* The psalmist repeatedly affirmed the secret of deliverance from depression. He encouraged himself, "Hope thou in God; for I shall yet praise Him for the *help of His countenance*" (Ps. 42:5, italics mine). It is the assurance of God's "countenance"—His face, that is the guarantee of His personal presence.

Jesus used this same basic concept when comforting His deeply depressed disciples on the eve of His departure. "I shall ask the Father to give you Someone else to stand by you, to be with you always. . . . I am not going to leave you alone in the world,—I am coming to you. In a very little while . . . you will see Me, because I am really alive" (John 14:16, 18–19, PH).

I read the experience of a man who underwent open heart surgery. He said:

> The day before the surgery an attractive nurse came into my room to visit. She took hold of my hand, and told me to feel it and hold it. I thought that was a great idea!
>
> "Now," she said, "during the surgery tomorrow you will be disconnected from your heart and you will be kept alive only by virtue of certain machines. And when your heart is finally restored and the operation is over and you are reconnected, you will eventually awaken in a special recovery room. But you will be immobile for as long as six hours. You may be unable to move, or speak, or to even open your eyes, but you will be perfectly conscious and you will hear and you will know everything that is going on around you. During those six hours I will be at your side and I will hold your hand exactly as I am doing now. I will stay with you until you are fully recovered. Although you may feel absolutely helpless, when you feel my hand, you will *know* that I will not leave you."
>
> It happened exactly as the nurse told me. I awoke, and could do nothing. But I could feel the nurse's hand in my hand for hours. And that made the difference!

Jesus' favorite word for His promised presence in the Holy Spirit is *Paraclete*—"the One called alongside." Engrave the words of Jesus on your mind until they will be such a part of you that during the lowest depression you will know, regardless of how you feel, that He is with you.

Jesus knew that [His disciples] wanted to ask Him what He meant, so He said to them: "Are you trying to find out from each other what I meant when I said, 'In a little while you will not see Me, and again, in a little while you will see Me'? I tell you truly that you are going to be both sad and sorry while the world is glad. Yes, you will be deeply distressed, but your pain will turn into joy. . . . Now you are going through pain, but I shall see you again and your hearts will thrill with joy—the joy that no one can take away from you—and on that day you will not ask Me any questions" (John 16:19–20, 22–23, PH.).

12

Healed Helpers

For we know that the whole creation groans and suffers the pains of childbirth together until now. And not only this, but also we ourselves, having the first fruits of the Spirit, even we ourselves groan within ourselves, waiting eagerly for our adoption as sons, the redemption of our body.

And in the same way the Spirit also helps our weakness; for we do not know how to pray as we should, but the Spirit Himself intercedes for us with groanings too deep for words; and He who searches the hearts knows what the mind of the Spirit is, because He intercedes for the saints according to the will of God. And we know that God causes all things to work together for good to those who love God, to those who are called according to His purpose.

Romans 8:22–23, 26–28 NASB

WE COME NOW to an important part of the healing process, perhaps the most important of all, because it reveals God's healing power at its greatest triumph—His ability to take the human hurts and turn them to our good and His glory.

We have dealt with various kinds of grace. Let us now look at what I like to call *recycling grace.* I once visited a city where they had a great recycling plant for garbage. In this recycling plant the garbage was turned into useful fuel for energy. In a similar way God's recycling grace takes our infirmities, our damaged emotions, and the garbage of our lives and turns them from curses that cripple into means for growth and instruments to be used in His service.

There is no place in Scripture that deals with this more profoundly or beautifully than Romans 8:18–28. While this passage certainly has a wider application, I want to apply it particularly to the way God can change people who are hurting into healed helpers.

Paul began by recognizing the fact that we live in a fallen, imperfect, and suffering world. Immediately, someone may object: "I get tired of you preachers always falling back on this. Why does there have to be so much pain and suffering in this world?"

The important words in that protest are *this world*, and they are precisely Paul's point. We suffer because it is *this world*, not some dream world that we would like to have, some utopia that we may fantasize about and wish to live in. We live in *this world*—after the Fall, this side of Eden, this paradise-lost world where sin entered by the choices of God's children. In *this world* where evil spoiled God's original perfect blueprint: marred it, scarred it, defaced and disfigured it. In *this world*, where now, instead of God's perfect and intentional will, we often—perhaps always—have to settle for His permissive and conditional will. Paul was really saying, "Face reality! You cannot push history back before the Fall; you cannot live in a dream world." He then said that *all* of this world, the total creation from the inanimate to the human, is defective. The world is suffering, hoping for a new birth, a final redemption for nature and humanity, in which we will be new persons with new bodies and minds, and everything set right.

Paul was not saying that God *needs* our sins and our infirmities, our failures and our blunders, to work out His designs and His will in this world. But in this fallen world, these are just about the only materials through which He can work out His providential and permissive will. If we were able to trace all human damages and hurts, we would find that ultimately they are the result of someone's sin, perhaps even generations back. If we could trace a hurt far enough, we would see that what comes through as infirmities and damaged emotions was passed along through imperfect genes and imperfect parenting and imperfect performance.

So often when someone in my office has been pouring out a fearful story of hurts, he will stop and say, "But one of the things that helped is that later I got to know his or her parents or grandparents, the family. I found out what had happened to him and how damaged and destroyed he was. Then I began to understand and even to feel compassion." I am always glad to hear that, for I know that compassion can bring acceptance, and acceptance can give birth to love.

The One Alongside

Paul applied this profound theology to a very practical area—the place where we live with our damaged emotions and hangups. "The Holy Spirit helps us in our infirmities," in our weaknesses (Rom. 8:26). Thank God! He doesn't leave us alone; we are not abandoned to our paltry resources to somehow struggle through all this mess, to live defeated lives. No! For our Wounded Healer, our High Priest, Jesus Christ, is "touched with the feelings of our infirmities." Jesus, the Son of God, identified with us humans when He became the Son of Man. He not only knows our infirmities, but also our feelings. He understands the pain of rejection, the anxiety of separation, the terror of loneliness and abandonment, the dark clouds of depression. These infirmities, these cripplings and weaknesses, He knows, He understands, He feels. He is our Wounded Healer, the One "wounded for our transgressions," who "bore our iniquities and our infirmities."

Because Christ is the Wounded Healer, because He does fully understand, when He got ready to leave this world, He promised that He would not leave His friends alone, but would come to them by sending the Comforter, the Paraclete. (See John 14:16–18.) *Para* means "alongside," and *kaleo* means "to call." "I will send you One whom you can call upon who will come alongside and *help* you with your infirmities."

We must take a look at the Greek word for *help*. It's a combination of three words: sun—"along with, together"; *anti*—"on the opposite side"; and *lambano*—"to take hold of." When you put them together, *sunantilambanotai* means "to take hold of together with us over on the other side." Did you ever get excited over a Greek word? You should when you think of this one! "I will send you a Paraclete who comes alongside when you call, who will take hold of, together with you, on the other side."

It helps to get even more technical in our word analysis, for this word is in the indicative mood and represents a fact. It is in the middle voice, indicating that the Holy Spirit is doing the action; it is in the present tense, that speaks of habitual, continuous action. He is always there!

Here is one of the great works of the comforting, counseling Paraclete—He is always available to take hold on the other side of our crippling infirmity, our damaged emotion, our painful hangup. He doesn't leave us because we are damaged or imperfect in our performance. He is exactly the opposite from the misconceived caricature of the God which the perfectionist imagines—the God who is always whispering, "Come on now! Try a little harder! You can do better than that! Measure up and I will love you!" The Paraclete is the God who understands, who sees we are carrying a burden too heavy for us, who realizes we cannot make it on our own, who comes alongside and takes hold of the heavy burden and its pain and helps us to lift it, enabling us to carry our crippling infirmity. What a beautiful picture!

This verb is found in only one other place in the New Testament, in Luke 10:40. Mary was sitting at the feet of Jesus, enjoying His love and His teachings. Martha was scurrying about in the kitchen, doing all the work by herself. She was also doing a slow burn, getting madder by the minute. Finally, she burst through the door onto the front porch where Jesus and Mary were sitting and blurted out, "Jesus, will You please speak to Mary and tell her to come in here and *sunantilambano* me? Tell her to come in here and do her share and get hold of the other side. I can't do it all myself." That's the picture in this word: the Holy Spirit helping us, taking hold of the other side.

Here is the good news of the Gospel for people with damaged emotions:

• God loves us, not because we are good, but because we need His love in order to be good.

• Christ, our High Priest, bore our sins and our infirmities, not because we are good, but because we need His love and acceptance in order to be good.

• The Holy Spirit offers us His continuous enabling presence and power, not because we are good, but because we need Him in order to be good. What good news!

Here is the complete provision of the grace of God. The *Father's* unconditional and accepting love, the *Son's* complete identification as our High Priest and Wounded Healer with our sins and our infirmities, and the *Spirit's* daily loving, lifting help.

And how does the Holy Spirit help us with these crippling infirmities? "For we do not know how to pray as we should, but the Spirit Himself intercedes for us" (Rom. 8:26, NASB). Only the Holy Spirit truly knows the mind of God. And only the Holy Spirit truly understands us. Because He understands the inside of us and understands the inside of the heart of God, He knows how to get these two together. And so the Spirit Himself intercedes for us with groanings too deep to be uttered. He intercedes for us in agreement with the will of God.

"He who searches the hearts knows what the mind of the Spirit is" (v. 27, NASB). If you will take the word *hearts* and roughly translate it "subconscious minds," I think you will understand what Paul was saying. In this deep inner self—this great storehouse of our memories where our hurts and pains lie buried too deep for ordinary prayer, sometimes too deep for any audible prayer—this is where emotional healing takes place by the work of the Holy Spirit. This is where the soothing Balm of Gilead cleans out old wounds, brings forgiveness, repairs damages, and pours in the love of God to bring healing. The Paraclete not only comes alongside, but He also comes inside.

The best is yet to be! Too often we quote Romans 8:28, out of context. It is the final step in this whole corrective sequence: "And we know that God causes all things to work together for good to those who love God" (NASB). The older version of this verse can be misleading: "All things work together for good . . ." Unfortunately the *things* do not; they may even work against us. But *God* works in and through the things, causing circumstances to work out for our good. That's different, for it turns the emphasis from fate to a Father! From things and happenstance to God, a Person of love and design. That God causes all things to work together for good is the greatest part of the entire healing process; that He can change hurtful insights to helpful outreach is the greatest miracle of all.

Without this, the healing could not be considered total, for total healing is more than soothing painful memories, more than forgiving and being forgiven of harmful resentments, even more than the reprogramming of our minds. Healing is the miracle of God's recycling grace, where He takes it all and makes good come out of it, where He actually recycles our hangups into wholeness and usefulness.

This doesn't mean that all of the harmful things we've been describing were God's intentional will for our lives. God is not the *Author* of all events, but He is the *Master* of all events. This means that nothing has ever happened to you that God cannot and will not use for good if you will surrender it into His hands and allow Him to work.

God does not change the actual, factual nature of the evil which occurs. Humanly speaking, nothing can change this; it is still evil, tragic, senseless, and perhaps unjust and absurd. But God can change the *meaning* of it for your total life. God can weave it into the design and purpose of your life, so that it all lies within the circle of His redeeming and recycling activity.

God is the great Alchemist who, if you will let Him, will turn it all into spiritual gold. He is the Master Weaver who can take every damage, every hurt, every crippling infirmity and weave them all into His design—yes, even though their threads were spun by evil, ignorant, and foolish hands!

When you cooperate with the Holy Spirit in this process of deep prayer and inner healing, then God will not only remake and recondition you, He will not only reweave the design, but will also recycle it into a means of serving others. Then you will be able to look at it and say, "It is the Lord's doing and marvelous in our eyes."

Betty

Betty and her husband came to counsel with me. I knew that they were a deeply committed Christian couple preparing for Christian service, and that they had a solid marriage. However, recently there had been some relational difficulties between them and an increasing sense of depression on Betty's part. Her tears flowed freely that first time we met together—tears which surprised her. She thought she had turned them off many years ago, but now they seemed to turn themselves on, uncontrollably and embarrassingly.

When Betty came back the next time, she began to share her story with me. Her parents had been forced to get married because her mother was pregnant with her. It was an undesired marriage and Betty had been unwanted. (May I just say parenthetically that if this is true of your life, then sometime you need to come to peaceful terms with it.)

When Betty was three and a half, her mother became pregnant again. However, her father had impregnated another woman at about the same time. This led to serious conflict and finally to divorce. Betty's memory of all this was incredibly clear. She vividly remembered that final day when her father walked out the door and left home. She remembered being in her own little crib-bed in the room when it happened; hearing the vicious quarrel and the terrifying moment when he left. It had left an aching, malignant core of pain deep within her. It was while we were in the midst of reexperiencing that incident during a time of prayer for the healing of her memories, that the Lord took us right back into that crib.

Jesus can do that, you know, because all time is present with Him. He is the One who said, "Before Abraham was, I am" (John 8:58). Our memories are all there before Him who is the Lord of time. During that healing time, Betty uttered a wracking, wrenching cry of pain which had been buried for many years. I said to her, "Betty, if you could have said something to your father from your crib, at that moment—what would you have said?" And suddenly the Holy Spirit brought back up into her memory exactly what she had felt in that moment of total desolation. And she cried out, not in the voice of a young adult, but with the sobs of a three-and-a-half-year-old, "Oh Daddy, please don't leave me!" And all the terror and the pain of that moment came out "with sounds too deep to be uttered."

Later, as we prayed together, it dawned on me that if we were to translate Christ's cry of dereliction from the cross ("My God, My God, why hast Thou forsaken Me?") into a paraphrase for a child, we couldn't improve on Betty's words: "Daddy, please don't leave me!" And suddenly, I realized that because of what Jesus experienced on that cross, He understands the cries heard so often in our day, the cries of millions of little children, "Daddy," or "Mommy, please don't leave me!" But they *do* leave. And the Wounded Healer understands those cries and is touched with the feelings of those children.

This was the beginning of a profound healing in Betty's life. However, I wanted her to experience the ultimate wholeness promised in Romans 8:28. So we talked about trying to understand the meaning of her life. Where was God when she began life itself? Had she made peace with the circumstances of her birth through an unwanted pregnancy? She said she hadn't.

I felt led to give her a strange assignment, one I've given out only a few times in all my counseling years. I said, "Betty, I am going to give you some homework and I want you to spend time meditating and praying about it. I want you to imagine the very moment of your conception. Imagine that particular time when one cell of life from your father broke into the living cell of your mother, and *you* came into existence. That's when *you* broke into human history. As you think about that, ask yourself one question: *where was God at that moment?*"

Betty took her assignment seriously. When we met one week later, she told me what had happened: "You know, the first two or three days, I really thought this whole thing was crazy. The only thing I could think of was a verse of Scripture which kept coming to my mind, 'In sin did my mother conceive me.' But about the third day when I was reluctantly meditating on it, I began to cry. But it was a different cry than usual. A prayer was welling up from way down inside me, and I wrote it down."

She handed it to me, and with her permission I share it with you:

O God, my heart leaps with the thought that You, my loving Father, have never forsaken me. You were there when I was conceived in earthly lust. You looked upon me with a Father's love even then. You were thinking of me in my mother's womb, planning in Your divine knowledge the person I was to become, molding me in Your image.

Knowing the pain in store, You gave me a mind that would pull me above the hurt, until in Your own timing You could heal me.

You were there when my mother gave birth to me, looking on in tenderness, standing in the vacant place of my father. You were there when I cried the bitter tears of a child whose father has abandoned her. You were holding me in Your arms all the while, rocking me gently in your soothing love.

Oh, why did I not know of Your presence? Even as a child I was blind to Your love, unable to know it in its depth and breadth.

God, my dear, dear Father, my heart had turned to frost, but the light of Your love is beginning to warm it. I can feel again. You have begun to work in me a healing miracle. I trust You and I praise You. Your goodness and mercy have been with me always. Your love has never left me. And now the eyes of my soul have been opened. I see You for who You really are, my true Father. I know Your love and now I am ready to forgive. Please make the healing complete.

Betty had found the final stage of healing, when God took all the hurts she gave Him and healed them by His recycling and healing love. But then God put the frosting on the cake—He used Betty as a healed helper.

One Sunday morning I did something in my sermon that I rarely do. With Betty's express permission I used the above story. I disguised details that would identify her, since I knew she would be in the con-

gregation. At the end of the service I invited people to come forward
to the front altar if they desired prayer for emotional healing. A large
number responded. Betty was seated next to a friend who began to
weep profusely during the time of invitation, but who did not go forward. Betty moved closer, and putting her arm around her friend,
asked if she would like her to go with her and pray for her. The lady
was very hesitant, and protested that her problems were too deep and
that Betty wouldn't really understand.

Now there took place within Betty a real struggle: she knew what
she *thought* God was asking her to do, and she thought He was asking a little too much! But within minutes she knew what she had to
do. So she leaned over and whispered in her friend's ear, "Don't be
shocked: I gave Dr. Seamands permission to tell that story this morning: you see, *I'm Betty!*" Her friend looked at her incredulously.

"Yes," she said again, "I'm Betty, and I think I can understand and
maybe help." They came forward together and spent a long time sharing and praying. This was the beginning of a healing in the life of
Betty's friend. When Betty related it to me, she had the glow of a healed
helper. God had truly recycled her hurts into healing and helpfulness!

The Other Alongside

Too many of us think that we can only minister out of strength—that
only when we are victorious and can impress people with our strong
points will we bring God the most glory. But Paul claimed that there
are only two things we can glory in. The first is the cross of Christ
(Gal. 6:14), perhaps the ultimate place of weakness in all human history, the last word in injustice, which God turned into the salvation of
the whole world. The other thing in which we can glory is our infirmities, or weaknesses (2 Cor. 12:9-10). Why? Because God's strength
is made perfect in our weakness. As Christians we are called to be
healed helpers, moving not out of strength, but out of weakness.

Often in the counseling room someone will share very deep problems or perplexities. There is always the temptation to impress him,
to be the wise counselor, to move from strength and give good
advice.

But then the Holy Spirit whispers, "David, share yourself with this
person. This is not a 'client.' not a 'case' (I hate that term!); this is a
hurting human being. Let him in on your infirmities, your damaged

emotions, and your struggles. Share with him how the Spirit has helped you in your weaknesses."

Often I inwardly resist and argue with the Spirit: "But Lord, I can't do that, because he has come to me as the pastor. He respects me; he sees me as strong and wise and having all the answers."

In time, I usually yield to His gentle pressure and follow His instructions. And every time I do, this promise of 2 Corinthians 12:9–10 comes alive, as God has a chance to exercise His power, and as His strength is made perfect in and through my weakness.

Again and again I have been a part of this deep healing as God recycles the damages, the pains, and the infirmities and then uses them for someone's good and His glory.

What I have experienced in my own life, I have seen take place in the lives of many others. I dare to believe it can also happen in your life!

PUTTING
AWAY
CHILDISH
THINGS

Contents

To Helen
who for forty years
by her unconditional love,
understanding humor,
and unyielding confrontation
has helped me put away
many of my childish things.

Preface

I USED TO think that as a person entered adulthood his childish behavior patterns gradually fell away and new adult patterns took their place. But I have discovered that this is not true. Many people who are chronological adults are still emotional and spiritual children. Their quantity of birthdays may reveal their age in life, but their quality of behavior reveals their stage in life—childhood.

The New Testament tells us we are to *katargeo* childish behavior patterns and attitudes that are keeping us from maturity. This Greek word means "to put away, to render inoperative, inactive, or powerless; to remove the meaning and significance from; to cause a person to be free from something that has been binding him."

The Apostle Paul described his own growth transition this way: "When I was a little child I talked and felt and thought like a little child. Now that I am a man, my childish speech and feeling and thought have no further significance for me" (1 Corinthians 13:11, PH). "I've given up the ways of a child" (BERK).

Katargeo is a strong verb. And putting it into practice requires great effort and struggle if we are to emerge from the fight victorious and grown-up. Childish things don't simply fall away by themselves as dead leaves fall from a tree. We have to put them away, *katargeo* them, and be "finished with childish things" (NEB).

These chapters have been written to help identify some of our outdated childish patterns, and to suggest ways of breaking their grip upon us, so we can "grow up in every way into Christ" (Ephesians 4:15, PH).

David A. Seamands
Wilmore, Kentucky
1982

1

The Hidden Child in Us All

For we know in part, and we prophesy in part; but when the perfect comes, the partial will be done away. When I was a child, I used to speak as a child, think as a child, reason as a child; when I became a man, I did away with childish things.

1 Corinthians 13:9–11

SOMEWHERE, SOMETIME, YOU were a child. Although you don't remember all the details of your childhood, the child and teenager you once were is still important to you today because it continues to exist within you. The hidden child of your past is very much alive and affects everything that you do, for good or for ill.

William Wordsworth was right—"The child is father of the man." You cannot cut yourself off from your own history. You are a complex tapestry, woven with a million strands, some of which reach back to Adam and beyond him to God who created you in His image. But many of the most important threads in the complex design of who you are were introduced in your childhood, especially in the parent-child relationships.

The hidden child within can be a determining factor in life. He can lead and he can also mislead. In some people, the inner child not only survives but thrives as a bawling, brawling, sprawling character. He noisily rushes into activities he likes. He interferes with present adult life. He hurts and destroys the most meaningful relationships.

Or perhaps that inner child of your past is so timid, fearful, defeated, and self-despising that no matter how much you want to, you just can't force yourself to make friends, or speak up when you have an opinion to express, or handle heavy responsibility. He may keep you from becoming the person you have the potential of being.

Because of the power wielded by your inner child, it is essential that you know this part of yourself. However, it is necessary to insert a word of caution. We live in a psyched-up world. Everyone who has had Psychology 101 is an amateur analyst. And the greatest wrong in misguided probing is that a lot of folks like to dig around in their past to find excuses for their present behavior. They want to be able to say, "My mother and dad, my brother, my circumstances, my teacher, or that accident made me what I am today. If only this . . . if only that . . . then I would be OK."

In contrast to this self-defeating irresponsibility, I ask that you look back to find out where you are still allowing the inner child of your past to dominate your life, in order that you may become more responsible. Look back to discover where you need to change, where you need to forgive and be forgiven, where you need to be healed, and where you need to daily discipline yourself. Look back so that you may be yourself as you really were intended to be—a child of God set free by the healing power of the Holy Spirit.

As you discover where this inner hidden child is defeating you, you can *katargeo* him. You can break his power and render him inoperative. You can abrogate his sway so that you will be free to grow up in Christ in every way, especially into the perfect love which will make you a victorious and fruit-bearing disciple.

The Changeable Child

About twenty years ago, Hugh Missildine, a psychologist, wrote a best-selling book called *Your Inner Child of the Past* (Simon and Schuster). It is still a classic in its field and has been of great value in showing how the various attitudes of our parents affect the way we develop our own personality traits. I am deeply indebted to Missildine for some of the concepts used in this chapter.

This little child of the past makes himself most clearly known in the place where a child is most comfortable—the home, and in those personal contacts and relationships which feel most like home. The hardest place to live maturely is with close friends, a roommate, a sweet-heart, colleagues at work, and with family. For the little child tends to take over in close relationships.

When we are living in a casual way, we put on public selves that are polite and well-controlled. In our shallow contacts with people we usually are very grown-up, reasonable, and nice to be with. But let us move into a close personal relationship such as a deep friendship, love, marriage, or a close working partnership, and how quickly that little inner child of the past can take over. He may become unreasonable, stubborn, and demanding, or shy, fearful, and weak. We can become such completely different persons that we are surprised and shocked by what we think and feel and say.

If we stop to honestly look at our behavior, we may discover that we really haven't reacted to the present situation as it is. Rather, that hidden child of the past has surfaced to respond to some childhood event or relationship. We have not acted with maturity; rather, we have responded to circumstances entirely different from those immediately apparent.

I remember the first year I was pastor of the Wilmore Church. The county ministers took turns giving live devotions on a nearby radio station each morning. The fifteen-minute program started at 9:15. About every ten or twelve weeks it fell my turn. One day I was delayed in the office and rushed over to the radio station, arriving at 9:12 all out of breath. Three minutes later I gave the devotions.

After the program was over I walked out of the booth into the main office. The young secretary looked up at me and said, "Rev. Seamands, we like to have the speaker here at least ten minutes ahead of time, if you please." I remember my face getting flushed and my blurting out with a lot more emotion than I ever intended, "Well, I made it on time, didn't I?"

She looked a bit startled, but didn't answer because I was on my way out the door. I got in the car and drove to Wilmore by the back road. I was so upset I could hardly make it home. The whole way back I talked to myself: "Who in the world does that saucy little blonde think she is, anyhow? Doesn't she realize the busy schedule of a minister, how much time the program takes, how it ruins the morning? It takes a whole hour or more to come over here and do the broadcast."

I was practically ill before I got back to Wilmore. And then all of a sudden something dawned on me and I said to myself, "Seamands, what in the world has upset you like this?"

Now there is a good rule of thumb for measuring your reactions. When your response to a situation is way out of proportion to the event, you'd better suspect the little child within you is acting up.

With a surprising amount of feeling and emotion, a childhood experience was replayed in my mind, and I realized that I hadn't been talking to that impertinent little blonde in the radio station but reliving an incident from my childhood. All the feelings of a hurt little boy came out in that conversation.

When I saw it so clearly, I was able to ask the Holy Spirit to *katargeo* that particular incident, to move in and take the sting out of the memories, to render the experience null and void so that it would be no longer operative and active in my life. The next day I apologized to the young lady, to clear both my conscience and the atmosphere in the radio station.

The Confused Child

I suppose the area of our lives where we most see the inner child is at home, especially in the intimacies of marriage. We make a mistake when we think that only two people marry. We say, "The two shall become one." That's fine, but the trouble is that four people marry, and sometimes things get crowded around the house. There are the two adults, and there are the two children of the past. It is perfectly all right as long as the adults are running things. But home is where we relax, where we let ourselves go and become again those little children of the past. Pretty soon that hidden inner child of the husband or of the wife wants to run the home, and that's when things get interesting. When all four start acting according to their differing family backgrounds, the fun really begins!

The chief areas where these four clash are money, affection, sex, and discipline of children. If this sounds farfetched to you, then you ought to hear a husband talking to me. With tears in his eyes he says, "I don't understand myself. I love my wife so much it hurts. And when I am at work all day, I say to myself, 'This evening is going to be different.' But when I get home, what happens? All the sweet, tender, loving things I've been practicing all day get stuck in my throat. When I walk in the door, all of a sudden I am just a frightened little boy again with Mom fussing at me. Instead of telling my wife I've missed her all day,

I scold her about some fool thing. I start out to love her and I end up hurting her." Does that sound familiar?

Or maybe it's the wife who says, "You know, I'm all right until my husband begins to discipline the kids, and then I just can't stand it. I know that he isn't too hard on them. I know that I'm spoiling them and ruining them. I know they need to be spanked at times. But the minute he starts, I can see my dad all over again, and I end up fighting with my husband. I feel like a frightened little girl."

The Controllable Child

The great tragedy in all of this is that it keeps us from being free. It binds us to the past, chaining us to our childhood reactions. We are not free to love or to bring newness into our homes and into our relationships with people. We never really act, we just react. We merely respond, but seldom show creative love.

The Apostle Paul set his words about putting away childish things at the very heart and center of the great love chapter, 1 Corinthians 13. This perfect love which leads to maturity casts out fear and brings creativity and newness. But you can't find this kind of love and maturity until there is *katargeo*, until that hidden inner child of your past is dealt with.

The Holy Spirit will work in this area of your life if you give Him a chance, if you break down your pride and face yourself honestly. If this is what you want, plan to spend some time alone asking Him to show you the truth about yourself and how you relate to other people. If you see recurring patterns of behavior which continually defeat you in your Christian life, then you'd better take an honest look at them.

That will not be easy. It is difficult to look in the mirror and admit, "I wasn't in control when I acted that way. A little child inside of me was in control." It may be so painful that you will need to go to a friend who can help you see yourself. Don't imagine problems if there are none. But don't be afraid to face them if they are real.

Every week I talk to people who profess wonderful Christian experiences but who are defeated in everyday areas of their lives which hurt their influence as Christians. God doesn't mean for any of us to go on living like this. He doesn't want us to continue in defeat. Rather, He wants to give us healing and wholeness, cleansing and victory. By the power of His Spirit, He wants to enable us to put away the inner child of our past and to grow up into Him in every way.

I'll never forget what one person said to me at the end of a counseling hour: "If what you say is true, then I have never really started living. I have to go back and be reborn and start all over again." You may need that kind of rebirth and release from the captivity of the inner child of your past. Thank God, this is His intention! Make it your intention too—whatever it may cost you.

Blessed Holy Spirit, we open ourselves to You. We will not hide behind the furniture of our hearts, but come out into the open that You may show us ourselves.

O Lord, shine Your light and reveal to us our inner selves. Free us from chains which bind us to immaturity and childishness. Prepare our hearts for wholeness and fullness in Your Spirit. Amen.

2

The Healing of the Memories

Simon Peter was following Jesus, and so was another disciple. Now that disciple was known to the high priest, and entered with Jesus into the court of the high priest, but Peter was standing at the door outside. . . . The slave girl therefore who kept the door said to Peter, "You are not also one of this man's disciples, are you?" He said, "I am not. "

Now the slaves and the officers were standing there, having made a charcoal fire, for it was cold and they were warming themselves; and Peter also was with them, standing and warming himself. . . .

They said therefore to him, "You are not also one of His disciples, are you?" He denied it, and said, "I am not. " One of the slaves of the high priest, being a relative of the one whose ear Peter cut off, said, "Did I not see you in the garden with Him?" Peter therefore denied it again; and immediately a cock crowed.

But the other disciples came in the little boat, for they were not far from the land, but about one hundred yards away, dragging the net full of fish. And so when they got out upon the land, they saw a charcoal fire already laid, and fish placed on it, and bread. . . .

Jesus said to them, "Come and have breakfast. "

So when they had finished breakfast, Jesus said to Simon Peter, "Simon, son of John, do you love Me more than these?". . . He said to him again a second time, "Simon, son of John, do you love Me?" . . . He said to him the third time, "Simon, son of John, do you love Me?"

Peter was grieved because He said to him the third time, "Do you love Me?" And he said to Him, "Lord, You know all things; You know that I love You."

John 18:15–18, 25–27; 21:8–9, 12, 15–17

I REMEMBER THAT Sunday evening service in 1966 when with great fear and hesitation I preached on the theme, "The Holy Spirit and the Healing of Our Damaged Emotions." I doubt if I have preached another sermon which God has seen fit to use as much as that one. The tapes have gone all over the world and have been the means of bringing release to people held captive by their emotions.

In 1967 I received a letter from a lady who somehow got the idea that I had written a book by that title. In her letter she said, "Dear Dr. Seamands: Please send me your Damaged Emotions." I would like to have done that, but I figured she had enough of her own without taking on mine! In 1981 my book, *Healing for Damaged Emotions,* was published and I hope the lady has a copy.

As far as I can discover, the phrase "the healing of the memories" began with Agnes Sanford, an amazing Episcopalian lady whom God has used so miraculously in a healing ministry all around the world. The term is hers, but the basic idea is an old one which has long been used by Christian counselors and psychologists. If I use some terms and ideas that you have read in other books, I do not apologize. God seems to have impressed this theme on many of us at about the same time. Besides, there is an old saying that if you use one person's ideas, that's plagiarism; but if you use two, that's research!

I am neither a professional theologian nor a psychiatrist. I call myself a pastor-evangelist and counselor. I can't give you all the technical answers about the relationship between original sin and damaged emotions. Nor can I give you the exact distinction between the carnal mind and disturbed emotions. One time after hearing me preach on the inner child of the past, a parishioner kidded me: "David, all this time I've heard it was the 'old man,' and now you're saying it is a 'little child' within me causing the problem."

I don't have all the exact theological answers at this point. But I do know that as I read the theologians and the biographies of the saints, and as I honestly reflect on my own spiritual autobiography, I see plenty of imperfections in the perfect. Conversely, there can be purity of intention within imperfect expression. King David prayed: "Who can understand his errors? Cleanse Thou me from secret faults. Keep back Thy servant also from presumptuous sins; let them not have dominion over me; then shall I be upright, and I shall be innocent from the great transgression" (Psalm 19:12–13, KJV).

The Subconscious Mind

The obvious place to begin with this troublesome inner child of the past is where he really makes himself felt—in our memories. It might be tempting to go off on a high-sounding tangent to discuss the unconscious mind, but personally, I think we have overdone this a bit. At most, I like to talk about the subconscious mind or perhaps a preconscious mind.

I think the reason for overemphasis on the unconscious is to find an excuse, an escape from responsibility for our own wrong behavior. If you still prefer the term, remember that the unconscious is not an entity, not a thing. Unconscious is a descriptive word attempting to portray the depths of your personality. Whatever you call the subconscious level of your mind, the fact is that you never forget anything you experience. Although you may not be able to recall it at will, anything that ever crossed your path lives in your memory. It is filed in the storeroom of your mind. This is both wonderful and terrible. It is both the misery and the grandeur of being a human.

Greatest of all, it means that if you let the Holy Spirit reach down deep, cleanse your subconscious mind, and get into the depths of your heart to fill the storehouse of memory, God will give you power to actually make this one of the most creative parts of your personality.

Long ago I discovered the amazing power of the subconscious part of my mind in helping me prepare sermons. I have found that if weeks and months in advance, I feed certain basic ideas deep into my mind— a title, a brief outline, some thought of what I want to say—then the preacher doesn't simply work on the sermon. The sermon also works on the preacher! My subconscious mind is always occupied with that sermon, even when I'm busy with other duties.

You probably have a busy life where time is scarce. If you feed ideas into your mind, it will work on them for you. Then when you are ready, so is what you need, as a product of the great power of this deep level of mind and memory.

One night in October 1920, in Toronto, Canada, Dr. Frederick G. Banting was working on his lecture for the following day. He was a young surgeon with such a small professional practice that he had to teach in order to make a living. For several hours Banting studied the literature on diabetes. It was scant for at that time medical science offered no means of control for the dreaded disease. Banting's mind was a maze of conflicting theories and accounts of experiments with dogs.

At a late hour he went wearily to bed, only to be suddenly awakened at two in the morning. His subconscious mind had some ideas to offer. He got up and wrote down three short sentences in his notebook, and then went back to sleep. Those three sentences led to the discovery of insulin. Banting's subconscious mind had come up with the solution when his conscious mind had found none. It was his subconscious mind which brought hope and life to millions of suffering people.

But the subconscious mind can also be a tormenter, for it contains tremendous power for producing evil and misery. This especially relates to painful childhood memories. In trying to push them out of our minds, we actually bury them deeper and deeper, until they no longer can find a way out. As a result, the intense emotions we experienced but did not express, at the time the hurt occurred, have no way of being expressed now. Buried alive within our hearts, they retain amazing persistence and explosive power.

While we may think we are free of those apparently forgotten torments, this is not the case, for submerged memories cannot be stored away in peace in the same way that the mind files pleasant memories. Instead, we have to keep closing the door again and again, refusing to let these painful memories into our conscious minds. Since they can't enter through the door of our minds, they disguise themselves and try to smuggle into our personalities through another door.

The great effort required to keep these memories below the surface of the conscious mind is a constant drag on our energy. Some of us are as tired when we get up in the morning as when we went to bed at night, even though we have had eight hours of sleep. Why? All night long the battle has been raging in the depths of our personalities, causing a constant drain on our energies.

Many people live with the unresolved tensions of painful memories for years, during which the load increases. If such a person comes to the end of his endurance and finds his energies depleted, he becomes a prime candidate for an emotional crisis. If he is further weakened by physical exhaustion, illness, or traumatic shock, and then if some experience takes place which associates itself with a painful event of the past, those hidden memories he has so long tried to bury are awakened and reactivated.

When the dormant inner child of the past is thus aroused, he can take over the person's attitudes, reactions, outlook, and behavior. The submerged emotions rise up and express themselves in feelings of deep depression, rage, uncontrollable lust, inferiority, fear, loneliness, and rejection.

These painful memories are not automatically evicted or transformed by an experience of conversion or even by the filling of the Holy Spirit. They are not necessarily changed by growth in grace. In fact, these memories are often great hindrances to spiritual growth. And until a person receives deliverance from them, he does not really mature. It is as if one part of his person is in a deep freeze, or in a time machine. His body matures and his mind develops but that one particular area is still frozen. He remains a little boy, she is still a little girl, locked into that childhood stage of life.

Unfortunately these memories do not seem to be reached by our ordinary levels of prayer. Sometimes prayer seems to make the pain even worse. You feel you are in quicksand: the more you fight and struggle, the deeper you sink. I believe this situation calls for a special kind of shared praying and healing. The confusing thing is that often there is nothing wrong with the person in his present life. Not understanding this, Christian friends have been known to berate such people by saying, "There is sin in your life." Or, "You are guilty of some transgression."

Such people are made to feel guilty about disobedience to God, when just the opposite may be true. Sometimes they are the finest, most sincere Christians who are trying the hardest. They read and pray and struggle with their hangups. Their friends give them Scripture verses, books, and lots of advice. All this only adds to their agony, so they become disillusioned and sometimes despair of life.

Please don't berate a person like this! There is nothing wrong with his present adult mind. His commitment to Christ is clear, his surrender as complete as he knows how to make it. The trouble is in the child he used to be, who still lives within him, repressed and crushed down into the mind, and unexpressed until something causes it to rise up and take over.

Healing Prayer

What is to be done in this kind of situation? Often what is required is prayer for the healing of memories—the healing of that little child or teenager who underwent certain experiences which made him stop growing, experiences which imprisoned him, froze him at one stage in his growth. All those memories need to be offered to God in a prayer for healing, so that the person can be freed from his pain and compulsion.

You may ask, "What happens then? Will he no longer remember? Will the memories be erased?" Certainly not! But the power of the emotions which surround those memories—the sting, the pain, the fear, the hate, the hurt, the lust—will be broken. As we *katargeo* them, they will lose their propulsive significance. They will be devitalized, no longer effective and operative in the adult life.

Someone asks, "How is this possible? After all, those childhood experiences are gone. They took place many, many years ago. How can our prayers today possibly affect that inner child of the long-ago past? It doesn't make sense." To which I reply, in the words of Jesus, "You are mistaken, not understanding the Scriptures, or the power of God" (Matthew 22:29).

For you see, Scripture over and over again emphasizes that Jesus Christ transcends time. "Jesus Christ is the same yesterday and today, yes and forever" (Hebrews 13:8). John the Baptist, talking about Jesus, said, "Here is the One I was speaking about when I said that although He would come after me He would always be in front of me; for He existed before I was born!" (John 1:15, PH). The Jews mockingly said to Jesus one day, "'You are not yet fifty years old, and have you seen Abraham?' Jesus said to them, 'Truly, truly, I say to you, before Abraham was, I am'" (John 8:57–58, RSV).

Jesus of Nazareth is the everlasting Christ who broke through the time barrier and entered history. He lived within our time for thirty-three earthly years. But time is a finite concept. It is the way you and I experience reality—in pieces, in parts. We divide time into past, present, and future. But Christ transcends all of time. "Even from everlasting to everlasting, Thou art God . . . for a thousand years in Thy sight are like yesterday when it passes by" (Psalm 90:2, 4).

Thus our Lord is not restricted by time. He is our eternal contemporary who can walk back through time to minister to that hurting little child. Jesus can gather him into His loving arms, comforting and loving that child who so desperately wanted to be loved but never was. He can understand that little child who so intensely sought to be understood, but never was. He can reassure that child with the unconditional, accepting love he so acutely needed but never experienced. He can forgive that guilty, shame-filled little child the way he so deeply wanted to be forgiven back then, encouraging him and replacing the feelings of condemnation and dirtiness with virtue and cleanness. Yes, Jesus, the tender and everlasting Shepherd, can gather the lambs into His arms and heal their tormented, thorn-filled memories.

My experience is that the inner child of the past which most needs healing is usually one of four kinds: he is the hurting child, the hating child, the humiliated child, or the horrified child. The memories that seem to grip and grind us, that have an almost hypnotic sway and power over us, are memories of deep emotional pain, resentment, hate, fear, or embarrassment. Sometimes it is a terrible mixture of all these.

With increasing frequency, some form of sexual abuse is mingled with the memories—violation, homosexuality, betrayal, or incest. And so some people, who in their present lives are very sincere Christians, experience a near hypnotic, propulsive, and compulsive lust in their lives. Their imaginations paint terrible pictures on the walls of their minds, driving them into guilt and depression, and almost to self-destructive actions. Or, they have a deep-seated distrust and revulsion toward sex which prevents them from having meaningful relationships with their spouses.

Mike

I want to share some experiences I have had with people, in prayer for the healing of the memories. Mike was a committed Christian, a leader among youth, a dedicated Sunday School teacher who was much loved by all his students. Yet he had a deep inner struggle in his spiritual life, for he could never quite believe that God loved him. Every once in a while, strong feelings of rage, bitterness, and lust would get hold of Mike. These would be followed by guilt, depression, and a feeling that God had forsaken him and was far away.

We counseled together several times and tried all the ordinary ways of praying, but there was no real deliverance. So one day I explained to Mike the concept of the healing of memories. I loaned him some books and tapes and asked him to write down the most troublesome and hurtful memories which came to mind as he read and listened.

Finally, when I thought he was ready for this special time of prayer, we met for an undisturbed and unhurried time of openness to the Holy Spirit. We entered into an open, conversational kind of prayer in which we just talked to each other and to God, remembering that He was right there in the room.

As we did this, several pictures arose in Mike's mind, one of which was a very binding, grinding, and searing scene. This memory was central to his childhood, so dominant that he still had repeated nightmares about the event. Mike's father was well-meaning and sincere, but a very harsh disciplinarian. To punish Mike whenever he did any childish wrong, his father would shut him up inside a little room in the barn. There he would strap him severely until Mike was screaming for mercy, crying for his mother and his brothers and sisters to come and let him out. He'd run for the door of the barn, but his father would get there first and stand at the door barring the way. He would then order Mike, "Say you're sorry." He would repeat this over and over again, until the hysterical little boy would finally say he was sorry. Then his father would force Mike to embrace and kiss him.

As we prayed together and as Mike began to bring this memory to the Lord in prayer, he started to relive the emotion of it! All the resentment, hurt, and terrifying fear came into his voice. I didn't know what to say or how to pray, so I just waited on the Spirit for guidance, asking Him to pray in me and through me.

All of a sudden it came to me. As I was praying, I saw little Mike. We were confined together in that horrible barn. And I realized that emotionally Mike was still in the barn, that he had never gotten outside the door. He had lived in that barn for fifteen years without getting around his father and out of the door. Inside himself he was still screaming, still hysterical with fear, still burning with rage.

When I began to pray, I believe it was in the spirit of Romans 8:26–27, where we are told the Holy Spirit Himself intercedes for us.

"Lord Jesus, we are in the barn together. Take this little boy in Your arms, dry his tears, quiet his fears, cleanse away his hate. But, O Lord, above all, open the door and let him out."

When I said that, he began to sob uncontrollably. I continued. "Lord, Mike has never seen the blue sky. He has never lived in Your love and freedom. He is still locked in the barn. Open the door now, and let him out—set him free!"

While we were praying, it happened. It seemed as though Jesus rolled back the carpet of time and walked right into that barn. He took frightened little Mike in His arms and comforted him, loved him, and healed him. All the scars and the wounds were washed with the Balm of Gilead. Then we saw the door opening and Jesus taking that frightened, hurt, hate-filled lad out of the barn and into the clear sky and clean air of God's love.

Anne

I used to wonder along with Nicodemus who asked, "Can a man really be born all over again when he gets old?" New birth for young people we can understand—it seems much simpler for them. But let me tell you about Anne, a married woman in her middle forties, who came to see me after one of my meetings. She had several teenage children. Her marriage was about to break up because of her terrible inner conflicts and the way she was taking them out on her family. As we counseled together, I saw that she was a deeply sincere woman who had spent many hours praying about her problem. We talked several times and I loaned her some books to read. These helped her to open up and share with me many things she had never before talked about.

When I thought Anne was ready, we had our time of healing prayer together. She lifted up to God her awful childhood and teenage memories. She had an abusive alcoholic father who made sexual advances toward her, broke up the home, and then committed suicide.

We prayed for the deepest possible healing of those childhood memories and the cleansing of all her twisted emotions. Nothing seemed to happen when we prayed together. I didn't see her for about two weeks. Then she told me this most amazing story, and we knew God had answered our prayers.

It happened this way: about a week after we had prayed, she awoke very early one morning. She couldn't get back to sleep, so she lay in bed and began to pray. She said it was as if Christ Himself came into the bedroom, called her and said, "Come, Anne, take My hand. I want us to walk back through your life."

"Lord, I couldn't stand it again. It was so hard when I told the pastor."

"Anne, this time is going to be different. I am going to be with you each step of the way."

Anne then described that walk with Jesus in a most unusual fashion. The two of them were in a great art gallery where each painful incident was a picture on the wall. As Jesus led her they would stand before each vivid memory, like looking at a painting. And as she looked at them one by one, all the original emotions she had experienced swept over her. Once more she relived the fear, the pain, the shame, and the rage connected with those ghastly memories Each time she would weep bitter tears and each time an inner voice would say, "My child, just turn it over to Me; forgive everyone involved and receive forgiveness for your own hate and rage." As she surrendered each memory to the Lord, it was as if Jesus reached up and took down that particular picture.

This went on for several hours until finally, when she looked around, all the pictures had been taken down and the walls of her mind were clean and whole. The scalding bitterness and the poisonous fangs had been removed from those destructive memories.

That dramatic experience was many years ago and, although there was a lot of reprogramming which had to be done as a follow-up, it was clearly the beginning of her healing. A subsequent medical and psychiatric report confirmed this. Her deliverance and transformation has been a source of joy to her husband and family and to those who work with her.

Peter

Both Mike and Anne needed healing for childhood and teenage memories. However, many times the painful memory is more recent, a part of an adult life. This is especially true of some of the traumas surrounding our modern tragedies involving sex, violence, and the sense of betrayal in a divorce. The same principles apply and bring about release and healing when often the more ordinary means of prayer do not. The best biblical example of this is the way Jesus handled Peter's denial and restoration.

These are the only two places in the New Testament where the word for "a charcoal fire" is used. Surely this is more than coincidence. It is obvious that Jesus deliberately set the stage for His conversation with Peter on the beach that post-Resurrection morning. Peter had denied Him three times while standing near a charcoal fire in the high priest's courtyard. Now he would be asked to affirm his love and loyalty three times. Everyone knows this part, but the fact that Jesus staged the conversation by asking Peter to relive the very setting of his denial seems to be overlooked. Surely the memory of those courtyard coals had been burning like fire in the conscience and memory of Peter. Here the Master Psychiatrist led Peter to face his most traumatic memory, and used a charcoal fire to cauterize and heal Peter's pain and shame. With the sting removed, Peter would be able to use that burning memory not as a curse which crippled, but as a spark to ignite him to an even deeper devotion, even unto death!

The Prayer of Faith

I know this may all sound much too simple—like a shortcut. It is not meant to be a cure-all, for this type of healing prayer doesn't apply to everybody. However, it does apply to some. The difference is perhaps largely a difference of degree in our lives. I am trusting the Holy Spirit will apply it to those who need this deeper kind of healing experience.

While this experience can take place when you are by yourself, it doesn't usually happen that way. I believe it is the kind of healing spoken about by James in his epistle. "Confess your sins to one another, and pray for one another, so that you may be healed. The effective prayer of a righteous man can accomplish much" (5:16). Healing of the memories usually requires a very deep openness and sharing with another person, and then the prayer of faith by that other person for you on your behalf. You see, you are so intricately involved in the whole matter that you may be unable to reach the inner layers of the child of your past.

You should spend time preparing yourself and in reaching an openness to the Holy Spirit for new insights and the courage to surrender your defenses. This kind of praying should take place with someone you trust and respect, and whom you believe can pray the prayer of faith on your behalf.

It is often helpful to write out a list of the areas in your life that need to be cleansed and healed—anything that rises to bother you, memories that have powerful emotional overtones. Omit nothing, however insignificant, petty, or even foolish it may seem, as you open your heart to the probing scalpel of the Holy Spirit. Don't be surprised at what comes to your mind.

Paul Tournier says this inward examination is like entering a dark room. At first your eyes see only the most evident and the prominent objects, and you say, "Oh, there's only a table and a chair." But as your eyes become more accustomed to the dark, you begin to realize the whole room is filled with an amazing clutter of objects. Don't be afraid. Relax in the Spirit. Thank Him for every new insight, however painful.

Pray with someone in whom you have confidence, one who knows how to really pray the prayer of faith. Conversational prayer together with that person and with the Lord is easiest and best. Confess to God every feeling, every emotion you experience as you relate these memories. If you remember anything new, interrupt and share it at once, for it is the Spirit taking you to a deeper level of your mind that may need healing.

Remember that Christ is alive. He is here now. And because He transcends time, He is also back at that painful experience. Confess to Him, turn over to Him each experience, each emotion, each attitude. Let Him love and comfort and forgive you. Let Him cleanse your hates and comfort your hurts and disinfect your lusts and remove your fears. Then specifically forgive others their trespasses as He also forgives you. Let Christ's love take the place of hate. Let Christ's strength take the place of hurt feelings and self-pity. Don't be in a hurry. Allow plenty of time for undisturbed, unhurried prayer.

If you are the one who is praying the prayer of faith for others, let the Holy Spirit melt your spirit with theirs. This is not easy work. Baron von Hugel talked about the "neural cost of intercessory prayer." Such prayer is demanding and exhausting. Let the Lord fill you with understanding and empathy so you can feel the same sorrow, anger, hurt, and fear. In this way the Spirit can pray through you, putting the very words in your mouth. If the Spirit leads you in the spirit of James 5, lay hands on them, even anoint them with oil. Prayerfully and carefully obey the Spirit without embarrassment or fear. Your feelings at the time are not as important as your trusting faith.

Your friend may not have much faith, so you may need to have enough faith for both of you! It was when the four disciples let the paralyzed man down through the roof before Jesus that He saw their faith and healed the man (Luke 5:19–20). Jesus said to Jairus about his sick daughter, "Don't be afraid; just believe, and she will be healed" (Luke 8:50, NIV). In these and other instances, faith on behalf of another brought healing.

Finally, don't dictate to the Holy Spirit as to how He is to accomplish His work. It may take several such prayers, as the Spirit peels away a layer at a time. It may happen on the spot in a great rush of victory and release. It may come about several days or even weeks later. It may happen by leading that person to another healing experience—never mind, God will answer the prayer of faith for that person.

3

A Childhood Motto Which Destroys Adults

There is therefore now no condemnation for those who are in Christ Jesus. For the law of the Spirit of life in Christ Jesus has set you free from the law of sin and of death.

What then shall we say to these things? If God is for us, who is against us? He who did not spare His own Son, but delivered Him up for us all, how will He not also with Him freely give us all things? Who will bring a charge against God's elect? God is the One who justifies; who is the one who condemns? Christ Jesus is He who died, yes, rather who was raised, who is at the right hand of God, who also intercedes for us.

Romans 8:1–2, 31–34

A FEW YEARS ago I attended a Holy Spirit Conference in Michigan. One day a pastor named Brad shared with us that for many years he had been a struggling, up-and-down Christian. Outwardly he was a very successful pastor with a record of considerable accomplishment. But inwardly he was like a yo-yo, bouncing between spiritual highs and lows. Or like a billiard ball batting from one side to another, hitting pride on one side and condemnation, guilt, and depression on the other.

Brad told us, "A couple of years ago, there came to me a flash of insight from the Holy Spirit. I suddenly realized that my life was not really being ruled by love for God and for other people. Instead, for the past forty-nine years a little childhood motto instilled in me by my parents had really been running my life. All those years I thought Christ controlled my life, until I became aware that it was a motto I had adopted in my early years."

What was the powerful childhood motto? "Measure up!" Brad continued, "I'm sure my parents didn't mean to give me this impression, but what I heard them saying was, 'Sure, we love you, but we would love you more if only you would measure up!'"

The Holy Spirit began to help Brad look at himself and see the real motivation of his life. He realized that those two simple words, carried over from his childhood, were affecting him in all his present relationships, including his relationship with God. For forty-nine years he had never felt he could measure up. "But now at last I am gaining freedom from that childhood motto and am learning true freedom in the Holy Spirit."

An amazingly accurate diagnosis of some people! Instead of living by the wonderful good news of the Gospel, they are living by the directives of some childhood motto. Some of them are experts at declaring the biblical truth, but their lives are actually directed by a motto which dictates the opposite of the truth they are declaring. They confess Christ, but are controlled by an immature motto or vow.

Does a childhood motto rule your life? The Apostle Paul said that true sons and daughters of God are led and controlled by the Holy Spirit (Romans 8:9, 14). Does the Holy Spirit control and direct your life? Or is it an immature, childish spirit from your past? Or maybe it is a combination. The two can get so tangled up that you don't discern the difference. What you may think is the voice of God, may really be the voice of an immature conscience lashing you into a sense of guilt, driving you under the tyranny of self-condemnation. Sometimes this doesn't change in conversion, nor even in being filled with the Spirit.

Let's look at Brad's motto. Brad was being controlled by a God who seemed to be constantly saying, "Measure up." But this is not the God who has been shown to us in Jesus Christ. This is not God at all. Rather, it is a childhood motto which became his god and ruled him as a ruthless dictator.

You see, this is the God of the immature, childish, and neurotic perfectionist. It is not the God of the mature Christian, who by faith is receiving the perfections of Jesus Christ, so that perfection is no longer the attainment of perfect performance, but rather the gift of a right relationship with God.

Relationship? But that is exactly where this childhood motto perverts God's plan of salvation. On this deadly perfectionist path to salvation, God is an increasingly demanding tyrant. He is like Pharaoh who first says, "Make more bricks," and then demands, "Now make them without straw." He always wants a little more. He's never quite pleased with me as I am today, but always says, "You could have done better than that." The God of this motto is not the Father-God revealed to us by Jesus Christ. He is more like the godfather of the Mafia. Measure up! Perform—or else.

Conditional Relationships

The tragedy is that so much of this occurs in our homes, even in the best of them. We are all sinners, and at no place are we in more need of God's unconditional grace than in our roles as parents. Our love is so imperfect, so conditional, so varying, so full of flaws. And there are times when the conditionality is even made worse because we are so zealous to bring up our children as good Christians.

I have a young friend named Bob. When he was a child, the "Measure Up" motto was built into him by his parents. He thought it was the basis for his being loved and accepted. And since he needed to feel accepted and loved, he tried to please his parents. But they were like we all are at times. So subtly we withhold our full affection and love until we see that our children are striving at their highest level. Instead of affirming them at the level where they are, we think we are helping them to "do a little bit better." So whatever they do—eating their food or using good manners or making grades or living the Christian life on their own age level— we give our children the promise of our approval and love if only they will do a little bit better. Love becomes something just around the corner, just a hope away. The present level of achievement is subtly downgraded and belittled. We think we are saying, "We love you and want you to do better." Too often it comes across to our children as, "We will love you when you measure up," or "We will love you and be pleased with you, if only you'll do a little bit better."

This whole system of conditional relationships and attitudes was built right into Bob. And this was why, even after he grew up and realized great success in his work, he never felt he had accomplished anything. He was never satisfied, but was always belittling his own efforts. He couldn't accept a compliment graciously. When a friend complimented him, he'd explain it away. After all, he really could have done better. He felt he never achieved sufficiently to merit approval and love.

Tragically, this all became a part of Bob's Christianity. And oh, how hard he worked to satisfy his built-in Pharaoh with a lash, who kept him running faster and faster on a terrible treadmill. Striving, trying, reaching, but never quite making it. Reading more and more books on the deeper life, attending one more revival or retreat, one more trip to the altar to be fully sanctified (the very same reason he went to the altar the last time). His was an "if-only-I-could" Christian life. But nothing quite worked, and when he fell off spiritual cloud nine with a thud, a little inner voice always scolded him with, "Measure up— that's not quite good enough."

Jesus told of a loving Father who delights to give good gifts to His children, especially His gift of the Holy Spirit (Matthew 7:11 and Luke 11:13). Bob had reversed that so while he kept seeking, he never found. He asked but he never received. He knocked so loudly his knuckles were bloody, but all he got back was the echo of knocking himself, in his self-belittling and self-berating. And the door never seemed to open for him, for the inevitable consequences of "Measure up" are an unpleasable God and a Gospel which is a grinding demand instead of a gracious offer.

There is no doubt that this motto, "Measure up," camouflages and sabotages true Christian holiness more than any other. For the essence of holiness is love—deep, pure, mature love for God, for others, and for myself. The whole "Measure up" system short-circuits love at every one of those three key points: God, others, and self. It offers you a kind of God you can't possibly love. So you end up resenting and resisting Him, like the elder brother who served his father all those many years, but with deep resentment (Luke 15:25–32). Without proper self-esteem and love you can't love your neighbor. Instead you will end up resenting your neighbor just as much as you resent yourself.

Complexes

Again and again I am asked, "But how is all this possible in the life of a truly born again and Spirit-filled Christian? Surely such things are cleansed and cleared away when Christ enters a person's heart." Let us try to understand this whole process of "putting away childish things" and "growing up" from the standpoint of what we commonly call a personality complex.

We used to hear a lot about people who had a certain complex, like an inferiority complex, or a self-punishing complex. We don't use the word as much nowadays, but I believe if we properly understand its meaning it can be helpful.

One definition of *complex* is "a group of repressed desires and memories that exerts a dominating influence upon the personality." In relationship to a harmful childhood motto, we could describe a complex as an unhealthy emotional push from our past. You see, from the time we are born, we are faced with the problem of filling certain basic God-given needs: needs like food, warmth, security, sex, the need to feel worthwhile, the need to belong, the need to be loved and to give love, and the need to feel there is some purpose to our lives.

As we grow up we gradually learn certain means of meeting these great needs. We might call them emotional mechanisms, or ways of coping and fulfilling our needs. These include every form of activity, both conscious and subconscious, of the body and the mind and the spirit. By the time we have reached a certain age (and no one knows exactly when this is) we have adopted a basic pattern for handling life and finding the fulfillment of our needs. These emotional mechanisms and patterns may be right or wrong, good or bad, healthy or unhealthy, or a mixture of these.

I use the term *complex* to mean an unhealthy set of mechanisms—a wrong pattern or means of meeting life and its needs. A complex is thus a whole set of desires, responses, feelings, and ideas—a whole set of unhealthy mechanisms which have a strong emotional push. This is where some of those childhood mottos and vows come into the picture. They are in capsule form an unhealthy push from the past. Can you understand now why Christian experience does not of itself automatically cure these complexes or reprogram unhealthy childhood mottos?

Paul Tournier in his great book, *The Person Reborn* (Harper & Row, pp. 6–7), explains it so clearly in a parable. He says that a Christian experience is like a revolution. A new prince has taken over a country by means of a coup d'etat. Among the crowd that acclaims him are the followers of the fallen monarch who is now powerless. For the moment they seem to be the most zealous partisans of the new ruler. But their change of heart is not sincere, for they are the enemy who will secretly scheme the gradual undermining of the new regime. If the reigning prince wins some triumph they bow down and pretend to submit, only to raise their heads once again at the first opportunity to undermine his power.

Tournier says that this is what happens in the case of some of the deeply submerged elements in our mental make-up. They hide themselves and share in the victory we feel. But they have not capitulated and they may later succeed in sabotaging those victories if we do not unmask them. The process of unmasking them, he says, is a slow one and may require the help of medicine, psychiatry, and spiritual power.

This is an effective illustration of how a person can be a very genuine Christian and still have certain emotional conflicts and complexes which need the gradual healing and Christianizing work of the Holy Spirit. Imagine my great surprise to find that years ago one of our great theologians, Daniel Steele, used almost this same illustration in saying that a Christian can even experience the deeper aspects of sanctification and yet be plagued by what he calls "infirmities." In his *Milestone Papers* (Phillips and Hunt, p. 208), Steele talks about living in a country called "Perfect Love." He soon discovers:

> There are old residents of this country who are by no means favorites of mine, and I cut their acquaintance as much as possible—such as Ignorance, Forgetfulness, Misjudgment, Error, Inadvertence, Failure, and a large family by the name of Infirmity. In fact, I have repeatedly cast my vote for their exclusion but they insist they have a right to remain. They say they are grossly wronged when confounded with an odious foreigner called Sin, who slightly resembles them, but is wholly different in moral character. Hence, I live in peace with these old citizens, but do not delight in their society!

I realize that these illustrations are not perfect and Steele's statement oversimplified. However, for most of us they will help. Let us consider our crisis Christian experience as the coup d'etat, the moment of revolution when the New Prince takes over; and then let us look at the growth in Christlikeness and in emotional maturity as the mopping-up process whereby every part of our personality is brought under the total lordship of our Prince and Lord—Jesus Christ!

Essentially there are two complexes which result from the unhealthy inner push of the "Measure up" motto:

The inferiority complex which makes us feel inadequate and unable, and fills us with self-depreciation

The impeccability complex which makes us feel as if we should and could do better than we did and fills us with self-belittling. The impeccability complex is commonly called *perfectionism* because those who have it somehow feel that they need to do everything perfectly. They must be impeccable in their performance.

It's easy to see why these two are always interconnected, like Siamese twins. Since these people can never quite measure up, they are never satisfied with what they do, and therefore always berate themselves and feel inferior. Since they have been programmed to think that their sense of value and worth depends entirely on measuring up, they do not feel good about themselves. It's a built-in guarantee of low self-esteem and poor self-worth.

Moving Toward Maturity

In my book, *Healing for Damaged Emotions* (Victor), I have dealt rather extensively with this in several chapters on healing low self-esteem, perfectionism, and depression. However, let me make a few practical suggestions which can help you break the compulsive power of this unhealthy push from your childhood.

Try to see this for what it really is—not the voice of God, not the voice of conscience (though it may seem to be both), but a lie from your childhood and teenage past. This is where you will have to deal very definitely and decisively with it and *katargeo* it! It will help if you can make a distinction between the healthy pursuit of excellence and the unhealthy striving after standards which are beyond reach, reason, and the Word of God. This will not be easy but it is essential. And it will require time and effort: "Anyone who lives on milk, being still an infant, is not acquainted with the teaching about righteousness. But solid food is for the mature, who by constant use have trained themselves to distinguish good from evil. Therefore, let us leave the elementary teachings about Christ and go on to maturity, not laying again the foundation of repentance" (Hebrews 5:12–6:1, NIV). Another version renders it, "For those who have their faculties trained by practice to distinguish good from evil" (5:14, RSV). It is plain that God's Word considers this training and practice an essential part of leaving spiritual babyhood and growing up into spiritual adulthood.

You may not be able to do this on your own. You may need to share with a trusted friend or a pastor or Christian counselor who can help you sort out what is really coming from God and His Word, and what is simply your "never able to please" inner child pushing you toward impossible goals. Sometimes these feelings are so severe as to require a long period of time with a well-trained Christian counselor. But whatever it takes, make up your mind to "render inoperative" this insistent voice of the relentless, clamoring kid inside of you.

Cooperate with the Holy Spirit in trying to level off the roller coaster mood swings that usually go along with the "Measure up" complex. I have counseled well over a thousand people who have been troubled with this problem and find that most of them have an "all-or-nothing-at-all" outlook. Their world only has two colors—pure white or jet black. If they don't achieve perfection, then they are total failures. This keeps them on emotional and spiritual highs and lows. They often describe themselves as "spiritual yo-yos"!

I've often wondered whether or not Simon Peter didn't have a touch of this. Did you ever notice his "all-or-nothing-at-allness"? On the Mount of Transfiguration he was afraid, but found it exciting. He wanted to build booths and stay up there forever. At the Last Supper he said to Jesus, "Lord, You're not going to wash my feet. I can't let You do a thing like that!" And then when Jesus rebuked him, "OK, Lord, wash not only my feet, but my head and my hands." He swung from "Not even my feet!" to "Give me a bath!"

In those last hours Jesus said that someone was going to betray Him. Peter declared, "Lord, I don't know about anyone else. They might do it, but though everybody else in the whole world would deny You, I'll die for You!" Within a few hours when a maid kidded him a little, he scoffed, "Who? Jesus? Why, I've never even heard of the man. Who's he?"

Aren't you glad that Jesus Himself said to someone like Peter, "Simon, Simon, behold Satan has desired to have you that he may sift you as wheat. But I have prayed for you that your faith may not fail, and when you have turned again, strengthen your brethren" (Luke 22:31–32, RSV). And in the same patient way, Jesus Himself has prayed for you too (John 17:20) and is even now interceding for you (Hebrews 7:25). Through His Spirit He is here to help you, even as He helped Peter through his many mood swings and spiritual ups and downs. And, just as He finally was able to get Peter leveled off so that the unpredictable and unstable Simon became Cephas a rocklike apostle, so He will do the same for you. Peter learned how to become stabilized and steady and has told us how to do it: "Grow in grace and knowledge of our Lord and Saviour Jesus Christ" (2 Peter 3:18).

Roger and Barb

That's how it came about with Roger and Barb—a couple who came for help in their stormy marriage. In spite of regular "family devotions" and a deep commitment to Christ and their church, they found their marriage coming apart at the seams. They were all the more dejected and defeated because they were genuine believers and had tried so hard to put the Lord into their relationship—from courtship right on through several years of married life. A private time with each of them revealed they were both victims of the "Measure up" treatment. He was from a solid Christian home and she from a totally secular one, but the basic atmospheres had been almost identical. Whenever they had done any kind of outstanding performance they had been rewarded with approval. But when either one failed to do "their best" or made even the smallest mistake, their parents had reacted with disappointment and much anxiety about themselves. "I wonder what they thought your mother and father were like; they must think we're terrible parents." This kind of scene was a common occurrence. And because their parents' security and self-esteem was made to hinge on Roger and Barb's successful performances, "a heavy" was laid on them. So "Measure up," meaning, "Look what you do to our reputation when you fail," was built right into their personalities. Can you imagine what this kind of an outlook would do to the many difficult adjustments of the first years of marriage? Well, you're right; it did!

However, once they understood what was really happening between them, they were able to share their hurts and needs with one another on a deep level. Praying together in specific terms enabled Roger and

Barb to put away their childish attitudes and not to expect the kind of perfection from each other that is found only in God. It was amazing how much growth they were able to telescope into a few months. Now they rejoice that God brought them together so they could break the vicious cycle that had been operating in both families for several generations. When their first child was born they talked with me about "the joy of starting a whole new tribe" which would come to understand the unconditional love of God through their relationship!

A. W. Tozer's prayer, which precedes a chapter on the love of God (*The Knowledge of the Holy*, Harper, p. 104), is a fitting way to close this chapter.

Our Father which art in heaven, we Thy children are often troubled in mind, hearing within us at once the affirmations of faith and the accusations of conscience. We are sure that there is in us nothing that could attract the love of One as holy and as just as Thou art. Yet Thou hast declared Thine unchanging love for us in Christ Jesus. If nothing in us can win Thy love, nothing in the universe can prevent Thee from loving us. Thy love is uncaused and undeserved. Thou art Thyself the reason for the love wherewith we are loved. Help us to believe the intensity, the eternity of the love that has found us. Then love will cast out fear; and our troubled hearts will be at peace, trusting not in what we are but in what Thou hast declared Thyself to be. Amen.

4

Another Childhood Motto

And He entered again into a synagogue; and a man was there with a withered hand. And they were watching Him to see if He would heal him on the Sabbath, in order that they might accuse Him. And He said to the man with the withered hand, "Rise and come forward!" And He said to them, "Is it lawful on the Sabbath to do good or to do harm, to save life, or to kill?" But they kept silent.

And after looking around at them with anger, grieved at their hardness of heart, He said to the man, "Stretch out your hand." And he stretched it out, and his hand was restored.

Mark 3:1–5

Jesus wept.

John 11:35

And He took with Him Peter and James and John, and began to be very distressed and troubled. And He said to them, "My soul is deeply grieved to the point of death; remain here and keep watch." And He went a little beyond them and fell to the ground, and began praying that if it were possible, the hour might pass Him by.

Mark 14: 33–35

ANOTHER HARMFUL CHILDHOOD motto comes out of our misdirected culture: "Brave boys don't cry." This one has impaired many a man and wrecked millions of marriages. It can also be the subtle controlling force in a woman's life. This motto takes several forms—

unhelpful sayings such as, "Children are to be seen and not heard," or, "If you don't stop crying, I'll give you something to cry about!" And our cultural overemphasis on certain sports, the adulation of the "strong, silent person," and the inference that if one expresses his emotions he is weak—all these add strength to this destructive motto. Among Christians there are many who give the impression that it is wrong to express any other emotion than "Praise the Lord!"

Some of us had this deadly childhood motto so woven into our lives that as adults we are simply not able to express our real feelings. If feelings do surface, we don't know how to handle them. We feel ashamed or afraid or dirty or weak. We think we are very poor Christians for even having the emotions, whether we express them or not. So the translation of this childhood script in an adult Christian is, "Good Christians don't express their true feelings," or, "Good Christians must never express any negative feelings."

Rather than go into any deep discussion of emotions from the standpoint of health and psychology, I believe it will be best to counter this destructive motto by looking at the One who is not only the pioneer and perfecter of our faith, but our example in all things—our Lord Jesus Himself. So let us consider the emotional life of Jesus and see what part feelings played in His life and just exactly how He handled them.

I am so glad that Jesus was literally one of us. In fact, He was far more human in regard to His emotions than many evangelical Christians. For many of us have been badly misled by the combination of a Puritan and more recent macho tradition which has been very destructive, particularly to men. We feel it may be all right for a woman to express her emotions, but not a man—a real Christian he-man. He must not reveal his feelings. Many boys and some girls are trained this way.

And the attitude carries over into the Christian life. To be a really victorious Christian means we should always be quiet and calm and unruffled. We should never be grieved or upset, sorrowful or angry, or moved much by anything. We have falsely made a kind of a "great-stone-face," expressionless, highly controlled, unemotional stoicism the prime evidence of being an overcoming Christian.

If Jesus is our pattern, then this is a grotesque misrepresentation. It is a distorted image to put before people as an ideal. Because these unscriptural and unrealistic standards are false, they are therefore unreachable. And yet many sincere Christians try to reach them and experience a great deal of unnecessary guilt in the process. That's why "Brave boys don't cry" often follows closely on the heels of "Measure up," producing the vicious circle of striving, failing, despairing, repenting—restriving, refailing, and redespairing in which so many Christians live. Jesus was never afraid to express His emotions, never ashamed to let people see and know how He really felt. So let's look at some of life's deepest and most important emotions and see just how Jesus handled them.

Sorrow and Grief

A few years ago some English archeologists, digging in the sands of Egypt, found a tomb inside a cave which had been sealed for almost 4,000 years. They broke through the outer coverings and came on a beautiful carved stone coffin; on the outside was the name of a little girl. Centuries ago, two heartbroken parents had laid to rest their only daughter. As the archeologists were about to open the sarcophagus, they discovered another inscription. It said, "O my life, my love, my little one, would God I had died for thee!" The two men looked at each other and shook their heads, and once again sealed the cave. They were so moved by what they saw they just couldn't bear to intrude into the privacy of those sorrowing parents. They left love and death to their eternal vigil.

We can understand their reaction as they were confronted by something more important than archeological research. They were moved by a sorrow 4,000 years old. Grief over the death of someone you love is one of life's strongest emotions. What should be our reaction to this universal human experience? How did Jesus handle grief and sorrow?

There are two great incidents which give us a clue. The first is Jesus' reaction when they brought Him the news that John the Baptist, His own cousin whom He admired so deeply, had been beheaded. "Now when Jesus heard it, He withdrew from there in a boat to a lonely place by Himself" (Matthew 14:13). Isn't that what we all feel like doing when the bad news first comes? We want to get away from people and be by ourselves.

It's not necessarily self-pity or escapism. It is the natural way we first respond to sorrow. Sometime later, Jesus called His disciples and took them apart from the crowds to be by themselves. After that He left them and went by Himself to pray (vv. 22–23).

Here is a beautiful pattern we can all follow: withdrawal for a while, but not for too long. For if you grieve too long by yourself you may lose your sense of balance and perspective. You may turn in on yourself and then find you are grieving not over someone you have lost, but for yourself. So the next thing to do is to get with your closest friends. And certainly to pray, to spend time with your closest friend, the great Comforter.

Although Jesus took time to spend with His friends, and then to withdraw for hours of prayer, He never for a moment forgot the needs of others. He helped them, healed them, fed them. For Jesus there was the great healing therapy which comes from work and from doing something for someone else, even in the midst of sorrow.

The second incident portrays Jesus at the tomb of Lazarus. From this we see two more insights into how Jesus handled sorrow. "Jesus wept" (John 11:35). Thank God for that great little verse. It's not there just to help Sunday School kids who need a quick verse to recite. It has profound meaning. Jesus cried and He wasn't the least bit ashamed to admit His sorrow and to express it openly. He must have wept very freely because the following verse says that the bystanders commented, "Behold how He loved him!" But the next thing He did was to pray. And He kept reminding the mourners about the resurrection.

These are proper ways to handle grief. They are natural and normal, human and helpful. You never need be ashamed of weeping or withdrawing for a time, or getting help from your closest friends, or praying, or talking about heaven and the resurrection. This is the right way, the Christian way, to handle sorrow. And one that is good to keep in mind, for you never know when you may be struck by grief, perhaps the commonest of all human emotions. When that voice from your past scolds you with "Brave boys don't cry," talk back to it and say, "That's a lie. Jesus, the bravest of them all, cried!"

Anger

A more difficult emotion to deal with is anger—the most taboo among Christians. Did Jesus ever show anger? As He was about to heal the man with the withered hand on the Sabbath, "He looked around at them with anger, grieved at their hardness of heart" (Mark 3:5, RSV). This is the only place in the New Testament which actually uses the word *angry* to describe Jesus. Even when He drove out the money changers, it doesn't say so, though we can assume that He was angry. But this case must have been so evident—without any attempt on the part of Jesus to keep the anger out of His face or to cover the angry tone in His voice—that it is specifically recorded. There must not have been any other word than anger to express His emotion.

Bertrand Russell in his famous pamphlet, "Why I Am Not a Christian," uses this incident as proof that Jesus was not perfect as His followers claimed Him to be. Russell claims that Jesus got angry and lost His temper thus showing His imperfectness. There are a lot of us who, though we may not have said it so blatantly, may wonder about this story or the one about driving the money changers out of the temple.

I believe that Christ's anger was part of His very perfection which was never more accurately expressed than in these moments of white-hot anger. For to say that Christ never got angry would not be to say that He was perfect. It would not be the greatest compliment. Rather, it would be the height of imperfection, for it would demonstrate a great flaw in His divine character. For the Bible speaks often of the anger of God—365 times, in fact. This anger is not an outburst of childish rage. In His anger, Jesus did not slip out of character.

It's high time some of us get over our childish ideas on this subject. Anger is not a sinful emotion. In fact, there are no sinful emotions. There are only sinful uses of emotions. And there are many of us who misuse our emotion of anger, just as a blundering musician can misuse both instrument and music, taking notes intended for beautiful harmony and battering them into senseless discord. Anger is a divinely implanted emotion. Closely allied to our instinct for right, it is designed—as are all our emotions—to be used for constructive spiritual purposes.

The person who cannot feel anger at evil is a person who lacks enthusiasm for good. If you cannot hate the wrong, it's very questionable whether you really love righteousness.

Anger is not weakness; rather, it is great strength. The Bible nowhere condemns anger as a feeling. It does condemn the wrong quality of anger and warns us against inviting, nurturing, or holding on to that kind. And it plainly condemns many wrong actions which are likely to follow such angry feelings.

However, anger which fulfills the same conditions that Jesus' anger did, is the right kind. Such anger must be directed at something that is obviously wrong and evil. It must be controlled, well in hand, and under the direction of the will—not simply a heated passion out of control. And perhaps most important of all, there must not be in it any malice, bitterness, resentment, or hate.

In Mark 3 we see Jesus on the Sabbath being confronted by a man with a withered hand—a man in great need. Scores of people are watching Him. Do they hope to see Him heal this poor man and enable him to be a useful worker once more? No. They have no eye for a miracle. They're watching to see if He'll break one of their laws. They would rather see a man with a useless hand stay that way—helpless and unable to work for a living—than to see one of their religious rules broken. They were not only blind but cruel.

No wonder Jesus got angry. But look a little more closely at the verse. "He looked around at them with anger, grieved at their hardness of heart" (Mark 3:5, RSV). Note how carefully Jesus' anger fulfilled the right conditions. It was for an unselfish and a completely righteous cause: a man's livelihood and health were at stake. His anger was controlled. There was no outburst, no paroxysm. No one could say, "Jesus got so mad that He couldn't see straight!" He was the only One who was seeing straight. The people were so hardened that they had become blind and deaf—oblivious to the great need of this man.

The late Charles Jefferson once said, "So prone is anger to mix itself with base and unlovely elements, so frequently does it stir up the mud at the bottom of the soul that it is not easy to free our minds from the feeling that anger has something sinful in it; or . . . that it is an unlovely flaw in conduct, a deformity of character from which we pray to be delivered" (*The Character of Jesus,* Crowell, p. 116).

But here we see it, not stirred up by any muddy depths of passion, but flowing white-hot out of true holiness and loving concern for people.

Anger and Compassion

Above all mark the words *anger* and *grieved,* for there's the real picture. Here are two great emotions which we often think are opposites, not to be mixed any more than fire and water. But in His heart they were. There was no malice, no resentment, just great grief and compassion and love. Anger, which fell on the evil they did, and sorrow for those who did it. Anger and compassion are opposite sides of the same coin.

Did you ever stop to consider that maybe the reason your love for Christ is so lukewarm, or even cold, is because you do not get angry enough, do not hate evil enough?

Did you ever stop to consider how much good has been accomplished in the world when good people finally got angry enough at wrong to do something about it?

Martin Luther said, "When I am angry, I preach well and pray better." Dr. William Channing said, "Ordinarily, I weigh 120 pounds, but when I'm mad I weigh a ton!" The history of reform is replete with illustrations.

English prisoners used to be kept in vile, disease-ridden prisons that were described as a veritable hell-on-earth. But John Howard and his followers got angry and did something about it.

Slavery was a deeply entrenched evil in this New World until men like William Lloyd Garrison "saw in the sorrowful face of the slave the shadowed face of God." Nerved by a righteous anger that would not be silenced, Garrison shouted, "I will not retreat a single inch. And I will be heard!"

Young Abe Lincoln, watching a slave market for the first time, got sick to his stomach and a passionate white-hot anger rose in him. His fingernails bit into his hands and he whispered so fiercely that everyone heard him, "That's wrong, and if I ever get a chance to hit it, I'll hit it hard!"

Military hospitals were horrible until Florence Nightingale came along. One of her biographers presents her not as a gentle angel of mercy, but as a stubborn, angry woman with a clear call from God to unrelentingly pursue government officials until they provided humane treatment for the wounded and the dying. Those officials shuddered at the mention of her name.

Anger is not necessarily the opposite of love. Sometimes it is the result of love and its clearest expression. Never pray for your anger to be removed or taken away from you. That's as mistaken and immature as asking God to remove all sexual desires from your life. Pray rather that your temper be cleansed and brought under the Spirit's control. Pray not that anger be *eradicated*, but that it be *redirected* to that which makes God angry.

A Troubled Spirit

Finally, what shall we call this emotion of our Lord's struggle in the Garden? A troubled spirit, in the sense of trying to find and do God's clear will for His life. His struggle is difficult to describe because it was a complex combination of several emotions.

There was loneliness in it. Jesus asked His inner circle, Peter, James, and John, to stand by Him, pray for Him. "My soul is deeply grieved even to the point of death; remain here and keep watch" (Mark 14:34). Later on, "Could you not keep watch for one hour?" (v. 37) When He so desperately needed the prayers and support of His inner circle of friends, they failed Him. He was alone and hurting from loneliness.

There was the struggle of temptation in it. Before He asked the three to go with Him, He told them they were the ones who had stood by Him in His temptations (Luke 22:28). Jesus' temptations didn't end with the wilderness tempting, early in His ministry. The devil left Him for a season, hut he came back, and often. He was back now trying to use Jesus' anguish of spirit, His despair and depression, to cause Him to turn from the Father's will and seek His own. We cannot say exactly what emotions Christ was experiencing. They were so powerful as to cause physical effects: profuse sweating—as it were, drops of blood; and trembling—even falling on the ground.

Why am I going into detail here? Because of an idea many of us have. We think if we have a great spiritual struggle, if we are racked and shaken by severe conflict and temptation, if we don't easily and automatically find and affirm God's will, there is something wrong with us. We are not truly Spirit-filled.

This is a caricature of the truth. Victory is not automatic, and will usually involve a struggle within our emotions. And we should not be ashamed or try to hide it, for our Lord didn't.

We all go through Gethsemanes—our times of struggle when like Jesus we have to pray, "Father, You know my deepest feelings, what my emotions want. But Your will, not mine!"

Wholeness and Holiness

We have looked in considerable detail at the way Jesus experienced and expressed His emotions. As the perfect human, Jesus understood a principle which psychologists have only recently discovered! Any experience for which you do not make the required payment of emotion, you will later pay for with compounded interest. Jesus responded to each experience with the appropriate emotional expression. Therefore, we never find Him suffering from what we now call a "delayed reaction." Jesus did not believe that "Brave boys don't cry." Let us nail that fantasy for what it is—a lie from our childhood or teenage days. Let us be done with it, freeing ourselves from its emotional imprisonment. And then, let us grow up in Christlikeness—free to experience our emotions and to let others know what we feel.

In this way we shall become truly mature. For maturity is both wholeness and holiness. Mature holiness means recovering our true humanness. At the heart of holiness and wholeness is knowing and loving God and other people, including ourselves. The sanctifying process is essentially a humanizing process. The holier you become the more human you become, because you become more like Jesus, the only perfect human being who has ever lived. He possessed perfect sanctity, perfect sanity, perfect deity, and perfect humanity.

Unfortunately, a lot of our training from childhood mottoes has programmed us to look at holiness in a dehumanizing way. As a result Christian piety and holiness often take the form of withdrawal from the enjoyment of God's creation. Our lives become rigid, starved of genuine, free flowing love and devoid of human warmth. But we don't have to live that way. If our emotional systems have been wrongly programmed by unchristian data, they can be reprogrammed by the Holy Spirit. Instead of being God's frozen people, we can become His holy and wholesome children.

5

Childish Ideas of Love and Marriage

DON'T YOU WISH everybody would put away their childish ideas about love and marriage? You know the statistics on American marriages—one out of two is destined for dissolution. Do you realize the United States is responsible for one-half of the reported divorces in the entire world? And there are many fractured and broken marriages in this country that are not yet statistics. Though no legal action has been taken, many spouses are just living apart—nearly two million people who are emotionally and spiritually divorced.

If you add to this number the spouses who are unhappy but still together, you come to the frightening conclusion that the average still-married couple in the United States has much less than a fifty-fifty chance of being reasonably happy in their life together. Evangelical Christians aren't exempt, and are being added to the divorce statistics at an alarming rate.

Paul reminds us that growing into real maturity means getting rid of our childish understanding. In marriage nothing is more important than that. Too many people come to courtship and marriage thinking, understanding, and communicating like children. No wonder. The fantasy begins on Mother's or Dad's lap during those evening sessions before bedtime, in the story from the fairy tale book where the handsome young prince marries the beautiful young princess. For teenagers the fantasy continues in front of the television set. The mass media is the sickest and the most demonic factor in all of this, filling us with childish and unrealistic concepts. By the time young people begin to date and move into adulthood, they are still thinking and understanding like children.

In the area of love and marriage, psychologists have a fancy name for what St. Paul calls "childish things"—"romantic infantilism." What a contrast there is between this romantic infantilism—a fantasy-filled, feeling-centered love—and the love spoken of in the Bible. This love between husband and wife is so deep, so strong, so committed and enduring in quality, that it is used to illustrate the love Christ has for His church. It's the difference between reel love and real love.

Eros

"How do you know you are in love with him?" I ask some sweet young college coed.

"Oh," she says, "Every time I am around him, I really get shook up!"

I say, "Oh, you mean like a bowl of Jello?"

"Yes! That's it exactly!" she responds.

Now I like Jello. It makes a good salad or dessert. But you need a lot of other things on the menu if you are going to have a balanced, well-nourished marriage.

Don't for a moment think I am underestimating the part of marriage that shakes you up and turns you on. The feeling element is a very important ingredient in mature Christian love and marriage. Sexual love, eros, physical attraction—this is God's gift, His idea, His plan.

He intended it to be an essential part of a mature marriage. And if eros love is not a part of your concept of marriage, you are not fit for marriage. I can't think of anything worse than being married for a lifetime to someone who didn't ring my chimes!

Why is it nowadays that so many people are talking more about eros and sex, but enjoying it less? Why the growing rise in impotence related problems? Because as the song says, we have substituted fantasy for reality, "a paper doll" rather than a "real live girl."

That centerfold in *Playboy* magazine may some day prevent you from being a good lover, when you are faced with actually enfolding a real flesh-and-blood marriage partner. Fantasy may become the substitute for reality. You did notice it's called Play-*boy*, not Play*man!*

Eros, sacramental in the mind of the Christian, is vital and important. But love based only on eros, on desire, cannot be stable. No two people in the world will always seem desirable to one another. And sometimes they may even seem undesirable. Because time changes external characteristics, eros must increasingly be based on inner beauty, for there to be enduring love in the relationship.

"Falling in love" is a childish basis for a Christian marriage. You would think love was a mysterious force from outer space that unexpectedly seized two people and overpowered them, a force beyond rational control. However, if love comes that way, it can also leave that way, as mysteriously as it arrived. Several years ago a television heroine and her TV bridegroom spoke their marriage vows, claiming that they would cherish and care for each other "so long as we both shall love." They changed just one letter, and espoused a totally different philosophy of marriage than that which promises to love "as long as we both shall live."

It is childish to think that my love can be measured by the intensity of my own subjective sensations. This is merely being in love with my feelings of love. It is loving myself through another person, which is the most selfish thing in the world. Who characteristically is in love with his own sensations? With himself? A baby, of course. The modern idea of love is merely romantic infantilism. And infantilism with a gross imbalance on eros turns out to be nothing more than a young child's self-love dressed in grown-up clothes, parading on a Hollywood technicolor stage, trying to make a child's fairy-tale fantasy pass for responsible adult drama.

Philia

In the Scripture there is a second great word for love: philia. Philia is love as friendship, the kind of love that develops a common bond between people who see things in the same way, who share the same points of view, who strive together for the same goals.

The Bible forbids a believer to marry anyone who is not also a truly committed Christian. This warning not to be "bound together with unbelievers" (2 Corinthians 6:14) exists because of the nature of philia or friendship love, and the basic unity of outlook and interest it presumes. "Can two walk together unless they be agreed?" (Amos 3:3) They can't! They can't even walk together for very long, let alone love and live together in the most serious, intimate, demanding relationship between two human beings. Thus the minimum requirement of philia love is that you be one in Christ with the person you are dating or courting or preparing to marry. Without this oneness in Christ, there is no possibility of a successful marriage.

However, this does not mean that simply because two people are good Christians they will necessarily make a good marriage. We all know wonderful Christians who should have never married each other. For philia includes much more than spiritual unity. It also takes in many important factors of personality blending which make up the rivets in the bonds of matrimony.

It is foolish to overlook this vital element in our thinking about love and marriage. One childish notion, and part of the demonic delusion that comes from the mass media, goes something like this: "I couldn't think of marrying him—he's too good a friend of mine." "Why I could never fall in love with her—she is too good a friend." Did you ever hear worse rubbish? Can you think of a better basis for marriage than the fact that you are good friends? Or let's reverse that: would you really want to spend your life with someone who was not a real friend? When you are courting, a good question to ask is this: "Are we two the kind of persons who could have a lifelong friendship if there were never any sexual expression between us?" It is a pretty rough question, but an important one.

Agape

By the time we are adults, we have built a whole set of fantasy preferences for our marriage partner. However, the person best suited for you, the person to whom God may guide you, may be very different, even quite the opposite of your dream guy or your dream gal. And this is where you need to understand that third biblical kind of love which is absolutely necessary for a mature marriage, agape.

Agape is the love that comes only from God, the love that is godlike in all its characteristics. It is an other-regarding love, a self-sacrificing love. Agape is grounded not in the emotions but in the will. It is not even based on the commonalities of philia or friendship, but is settled in the commitment of the will. It is the commitment to love, in spite of and regardless of.

What is this kind of love like? If you want to know, read and reread 1 Corinthians 13. It is a manner of behavior, a commitment to care for and protect, to love and to cherish, to assume responsibility for the welfare of that person. It is covenanted devotion, and it can survive all sorts of changes of mood and circumstances.

Marriage Is for Adults

Mature Christian marriage combines:
  Eros, desire, sexual attraction
  Philia, genuine friendship, unity of interests and purpose
  Agape, deeply covenanted, committed devotion.
Married love is a very precious and precarious balance of all three. Romantic or eros love is a wonderful help in getting a marriage started. It is like the rocket that puts the space capsule into orbit and then drops away. It takes other forms of power to continue that space capsule in its successful flight toward its goal. It takes a putting away of child-ishly imbalanced concepts of love to have a successful marriage.

"I understood as a child," says Paul, "when I was a child." Yes, but marriage is an adult business. Rather than "falling in love," it might be more accurate from a Christian standpoint to speak of "climbing up into love."

Communication

The greatest problem in marriage is communication. Paul said, "When I was a child, I spoke like a child, I communicated on a childish level, but now that I have grown up, I am communicating on a mature level." Fortunately for us, Paul defined what he meant by mature communication: "So that we may no longer be children, tossed to and fro . . . rather, speaking the truth in love, we are to grow up in every way" (Ephesians 4:14–15, RSV). How beautiful and how accurate! Paul was two thousand years ahead of the times in his basic communication principles. "Speaking the truth in love" is mature Christian communication.

The greatest cause of unhappiness in marriage is the inability of spouses to communicate openly and lovingly with one another. All too often marital communication is still on a childish level.

How do children communicate? Some children speak the truth all right, but they are cruel, sharp, and hurtful. "Sticks and stones can hurt my bones, but names will never hurt me." Not true. The names can hurt even the bones, and badly. Children are very cruel at times: they speak the truth, but not in love.

Then there are children who cannot speak the truth. I don't mean that they lie. Rather, they are too afraid of their feelings to express them. Maybe every time they did express their feelings, they were not allowed to continue. Or perhaps they have never seen or heard a true expression of feelings from the people they live with. They may be loving children, but they can't speak the truth.

"Speaking the truth in love" is the secret. That is what makes a strong and mature Christian marriage. But speaking this way is a learned art. Maybe I ought to say it is an unlearned art, because often we first have to unlearn things that our homes and life experiences and our sick culture have taught us. We have to *katargeo* them. Sometimes in agony and sweat and tears and maybe a little blood, we have to put them off and change our whole way of communicating.

Isn't it incredible that a married couple can love each other, live together, make love to one another, bring up children together, yet never really communicate to one another what they are actually feeling? And we pastors have contributed to this difficulty. For we have given our parishioners the impression that expressed conflict in marriage is a sin. What this notion fails to take into account is that a husband and a wife are always communicating with each other, in one way or another. And so by failing to say what is really wrong, they express in other unsanctified ways their displeasure, their disagreement, and their anger.

Some people need to unlearn the childish unrealities they may have been taught in the name of Jesus. They need to learn that in the Christian life there is such a thing as constructive conflict, which is the grown-up way to deal with disagreements. For such people keep conflict on a childish, hurtful level. They clam up in silence, thinking they are being patient, good Christians. They walk away from any disagreement because they have been taught that this is spiritual. I often tell the couples I counsel that their basic problem is they never learned to fight like Christians! Much of what passes for "submission" is really a lack of caring enough to confront one another.

Gibson Winter reminds us that conflict is always the price of deepening intimacy between persons and can only be resolved by proper communication. Bad communication comes either from not speaking the truth or from not speaking in love. Either you do a slow burn until you are so filled with anger and resentment that all of a sudden it comes out in hurtful torrents. Or you fake your true feelings and the hurt comes out in other ways.

"When I grew up," said Paul, "I put away childish ways of communicating; I learned to speak the truth in love." That will mean confrontation, and conflict which is ultimately creative and helpful. It will result in resolving the conflict and thus deepening your love.

Helen and I are deeply involved in marriage enrichment seminars. Our favorite communication story is about a couple who attended one such weekend. Debbie wanted to serve supper by candlelight two or three times a week. And Bob would say, "I like to see what I'm eating!" or "Are you trying to poison me?" This little conflict grew until it became a big one.

Every time Debbie used candles, Bob let her know that he just didn't like it. "Candlelight again? . . . Well, I just don't like that. . . . But go on, have your candles!" Of course, that ruined the meal and left Debbie hurting. They never talked about it. It was candlelight versus non-candlelight.

Then during one of the communication exercises at the weekend, Debbie opened up. You see, she had been a foster child, and the people who finally raised her were very poor. They ate in the kitchen on a bare table. The only light in the room was one light bulb without a shade. It just hung there and swung back and forth every time the kitchen door opened. As a teenager, Debbie had vowed to herself, "When I get married I'm going to have a beautiful house with a separate dining room, and we are going to eat by soft light."

When Debbie had finished telling Bob all of this, he was really broken up. "Oh, Honey," he said, "you can have all the candles you want! I understand now." Well, when he understood about the candles, it turned out that she didn't need to have them so often anymore. That is usually the case! All we really want is for someone dear to understand where we are coming from.

Express Your Feelings

Don't worry if it seems at first that you are learning to express only your more negative feelings. For as those feelings begin to flow, you will learn to express your deep, positive ones too. It took me years and a lot of agonizing hard work to discover this. In spite of all my gift of gab and public communicating, and even my honest, open sharing as a counselor, way down deep I am really a loner. When I was eleven years old, my missionary parents brought my brother and me home on furlough. The next year Mother and Dad went back to India, leaving us with our grandmother. We thought we would see Mother and Dad in a few years, but along came World War II and they got stuck in India. The next time I saw my parents was on my twentieth birthday!

I know what it is like to be the only student in the dorm during a special vacation. It can be lonely. At that time I didn't realize that layers of unexpressed feelings were being buried. Not until I married did I discover what I was really like: a lonely, frightened little boy, who could not express his deepest feelings. Oh, yes, I could in sermons— maybe that is God's way of using our infirmities to compensate—and I could listen sensitively when I counseled others. But I couldn't express my feelings to the one I wanted to more than any other, my wife.

In those early days of our marriage, I remember saying to myself so often that tonight was going to be different. This evening when I got home I was going to be able to tell Helen that I loved her. So I would rehearse all day.

When we went to India as missionaries, I would go out in my jeep to the villages and be gone for weeks at a time. Then I would really rehearse! It's going to be different. When I get home I'll take her in my arms and say, "Honey, I love you." But the minute I got to the door, I froze. That old childhood wall came between us. I tried to batter my way through it until my hands were literally bleeding and torn. It hurt our marriage and both of us despaired.

What had to happen is that I needed to share my deepest self with Helen. What self? That frightened, lonely little boy with all of his weaknesses. I'd been scared to do that all of my life. Oh, I had such a brave front. Helen could express her feelings; she told me her fears and how people got her down. But not I. I was always brave. When Helen expressed inadequacy, I interpreted it as feminine weakness. And I was afraid that if I ever told her how I really felt, we would both dissolve and go down the drain together! So I was bold—"Oh, don't let that get you down." All the time, inside was this scared, lonely little boy.

But God is faithful. One day the dam broke and I shared my real self, the terrified, lonely kid inside of me. I told her everything, at times sobbing uncontrollably. And you know, the most wonderful thing happened! I found out that she wasn't weak, but was amazingly strong. She opened like a flower to the sun. She sustained me and gave me strength. And best of all, when my false front cracked and she saw what I was really like, then I could express my love freely. The log jam was broken and the stream could flow freely. I could express my deepest feelings, both positive and negative.

Christians with conflicts? Yes, God's people who are to be creative and mature. No longer are they to be children tossed about by feelings and circumstances, but adults who speak the truth in love, as they grow up in every way.

Mature Christian love in a good marriage is the result of commitment and work. Helen and I work harder at our marriage than at anything else in the world. For you see, the most childish, the most immature misunderstanding of all about marriage is simply this: that love is self-sustaining and that a good marriage comes about automatically because two fine, committed young Christians marry one another. If you will get rid of that unbiblical notion, then you will make progress. Marriage is hard work, but you can enjoy it. And you will find that the work is worth it, because the one thing you are going to be doing a million years from now is loving. So you'd better get in practice now. And marriage is the best preparation for heaven that I know about.

6

Childish Ideas of God and His Will

I urge you therefore, brethren, by the mercies of God, to present your bodies a living and holy sacrifice, acceptable to God, which is your spiritual service of worship. And do not be conformed to this world, but be transformed by the renewing of your mind, that you may prove what the will of God is, that which is good and acceptable and perfect.

For through the grace given to me I say to every man among you not to think more highly of himself than he ought to think; but to think so as to have sound judgment, as God has allotted to each a measure of faith.

Romans 12:1–3

AN ASTRONOMER WAS in conversation with a preacher who wanted the brilliant scientist to think about God. The astronomer just shrugged him off saying, "Preacher, I have a very simple theology: just do good and love your neighbor as yourself." To which the preacher answered, "Yes, and I have a very simple astronomy: 'Twinkle, twinkle, little star.'"

Some of us have this kind of theology, especially when it comes to our concepts of God and His will. The question we are really addressing is this, "How does God work to achieve His will in this world?"

If you are like some people I know, you may be thinking, "That's such a theoretical, highfalutin sort of question. It may be good for a philosophy class, but what has it got to do with me and my everyday life?"

I would like to share three true stories with you that illustrate how important it is to be rid of inadequate, immature concepts of God and how He works His will in this world.

A young couple had taken their baby to the hospital after midnight. Their neighbors called me at three o'clock in the morning, and I was there waiting for the couple when they returned from the hospital to their home. The young mother was wringing her hands, weeping in anguish because her baby was dead. She sobbed out, "Oh, my baby! My baby!" Then she said, "I'm sure it must be God's will. . . . But if the specialist could only have gotten there in time he could have saved him." Do you hear her agonizing confusion? Did this mean that if the doctor had come in time he would have been able to outmaneuver and bypass God's will?

• In 1973 a tragic story appeared on the front pages of every newspaper in the country. A sincere couple in California heard some fly-by-night healer-evangelist preach against using medicine, so they went home and took the insulin away from their four-teen-year-old diabetic son. You know what happened—in a matter of hours he was in a coma, and within a few days he was dead. Then they waited for three days, claiming that God was going to resurrect the boy. Finally the authorities forced them to bury him.

Does this mean that God does or does not want us to take insulin if we have diabetes? Does it mean that God works for healing in this world only by direct action? Without the use of any secondary causes?

If God balances the imbalanced chemistry in your body through some drug and thereby saves your life, or if He gives me good vision through a pair of glasses, or if He gives you new life through heart surgery or the implantation of a pacemaker or through some operation, are these too God's will?

• About ten years ago an outstanding medical student had finished his residency. He married a fine Christian lady who was also a doctor, and they were planning to be missionaries. Only six weeks after the wedding, they went to visit her parents. Her mother who was a former mental patient became deranged, suddenly pulled out a revolver and shot and killed the young husband. I actually heard people saying that it was God's will. In what sense could such a monstrous thing be described as God's will?

What Is God's Will?

How does God achieve His will in this world? This is not some far-out question, believe me. Rather, it is gut-level Christian living, so important that you may need to put away a lot of childish and immature ideas about it. Paul said, "Be babes in evil, but in thinking be mature" (1 Corinthians 14:20, RSV). And you ought to become mature before the disaster happens, because then you will have an anchor in the storms of life, an anchor which holds you steady when "sorrows like sea billows roll," and you feel as though you do not have strength to hold onto anything. Leslie Weatherhead's little book *The Will of God* (Abingdon) has been a source of comfort to many a struggling Christian. In this chapter, I am using some of his basic ideas which have been most helpful to me.

There are millions of people outside the kingdom of God who resent and hate God because of their misunderstanding about His way of working in our world. And there are millions more in the kingdom who are confused about the subject. I believe our confusion arises because we use the phrase "the will of God" to include several layers of meaning. There are at least three:

The intentional, perfect will of God
The circumstantial, permissive will of God
The ultimate will and purpose of God.

The Intentional Will

The intentional will of God is God's perfect will for you and for the world. It is His ideal purpose for your life. Jesus stated it negatively: "It is not the will of your Father who is in heaven that one of these little ones perish" (Matthew 18:14). In God's intention for you, He pours Himself out in fatherly goodness.

It is high time we get rid of all our childish and unbiblical notions which lead us to believe that everything which happens in this world today is the will of God, in the sense that it is what God intends and plans to happen. So much of what occurs is evil and harmful and destructive, and falls within the second meaning—the circumstantial, permissive will of God. But this should not be considered the intentional will of God.

We must realize that the intentional, perfect will of God can be defeated by the will of man for the time being. If this were not true, humans would have no real freedom whatsoever. All evil that is temporarily successful, temporarily defeats the perfect will of God. There are a thousand and one tragedies which are the furthest from God's intention for those situations . . . the starving children of Cambodia, the millions of street people in India, the horrors of concentration camps, the 50,000 people who are slaughtered annually on American highways, and the countless victims of child abuse and violence. Or it may be as simple as you being a single person without any real prospects of marriage—a widow or widower or divorcee. All the way down to the fact that last week you may have flunked a midterm exam. The list is endless. You may call these things evil, or the fruit of human sin, ignorance, folly, and selfishness. You may call these things accidents. You may call them the inevitable consequences of personal and social sin. But do not call them the intended, planned will of God!

There are people who seem to get a lot of comfort from thinking their tragedies are the intentional will of God, but ultimately there is never any real comfort or support in something that is not true. If you base your support on an idea of God which is untrue, then in your hour of real need you will be left without meaning. You may end up resenting God, and do yourself great emotional and spiritual damage.

The Permissive Will

The circumstantial or permissive will of God is operative in our fallen cosmos. Paul said, "We know that the whole creation has been groaning in travail" (Romans 8:22, RSV). Not only do we humans have imperfections and infirmities, but the radical defect of imperfection goes through all of nature with its disasters. Sin is so serious that it has caused a radical imbalance and imperfection in the created cosmos. Because of that imbalance, because of human folly and sin, because man's free will creates circumstances of evil that cut across God's plans, there is a circumstantial or permissive will of God.

When an infant accidentally fell out of a fifth-story window, someone asked whether the death of that child was God's will. Do you see how important it is that we get our thinking straight before we answer that question? After another tragic accident, I said at the funeral that God never intended it to happen. And I was deluged with calls all week from people who asked, "You didn't mean what you said, did you?" To which I responded, "I certainly did! I cannot say that God intended that accident to happen." I couldn't worship a God like that.

In circumstances surrounding such accidents God wills that the law of gravity will operate. God's laws and His causes are continuously working. It is God's will that a baby is made out of flesh and blood, not out of plastic or rubber. According to the law of gravity, when flesh and blood tangle with concrete the result is going to be a smashed body. The very law that enables the child to stay on the face of the earth is the force which can kill. The law is not suspended if we sin or are careless; nor is it suspended if we are the innocent party in an accident.

It is within the circumstantial will of God that the principle in Romans 8:28 is so vital for our Christian lives. Many things which are permitted to happen to us in this world are the price of: (1) a world of reliable laws, where we can count on things, and (2) a world of free moral choices. Certain events happen within God's circumstantial will, but not directly because God intends or wills them. The wonderful assurance of the Scripture is that God will not allow anything to happen to us which by itself can defeat His ultimate purposes or defeat His children.

As Weatherhead so beautifully puts it, "Nothing can happen to you that God cannot use for good." And that puts us on entirely different ground, because it is never the event in itself, but rather the fact that God is at work that makes a circumstance turn out for good. God Himself does not change or undo the nature of a tragedy—the evil of it, the awfulness or pain of it. However, God can work with us, changing the meaning of that event to our total life, working out His will in the circumstance.

Because God can use all things, anything becomes grist for His will and His mill. Therefore, no Christian can ever say, "Well, you see, I wanted to do this, and I wanted to do that, but I was a victim of a terrible home situation, a tragic accident, disease, injustice, loss—so what could I do?" There are no circumstances which are so deadly of themselves that they can down the Christian or defeat God—not even death itself. God is never beaten by any possible combination of circumstances.

The Ultimate Will

The ultimate will of God can never be finally defeated. Weatherhead uses this very beautiful illustration. Picture some children playing in a tiny mountainside stream. They divert the stream by making little dams of mud and stones, and they float their toy boats in the puddles and ponds. But the stream continues to surge down to the river and the valley. Now picture men building great dams, changing the course of rivers with lakes and locks, diverting their flow. Yet even they cannot prevent the streams from flowing into the sea.

In our lives, so many things—our sins and mistakes, the accidents of history, the sins of others against us—may divert and temporarily defeat God's plans and purposes. But even in new circumstances created by evils, ills, and accidents, God will provide other channels to carry out His ultimate will.

What is meant by the omnipotence of God? It does not mean that by sheer exhibition of power God gets His own way. This would make our freedom an illusion, and moral growth an impossibility. That God has power means He has the ability to achieve His purposes. To say that God is all-powerful means that nothing can happen which will ultimately defeat Him.

With evil intention the establishment of Jesus' day took the innocent Son of God and crucified Him on a cross. Purely from a human standpoint, it was the most heinous crime in history. But six weeks later Christ's disciples were preaching about that very same death on the cross. God had made man's crime His instrument to save the whole world.

Accidents, disasters, and moral evil create terrible pain. But to those of us who love God, who are called and who cooperate with His purpose, our suffering cannot separate us from His love, or defeat the working out of His purpose in our lives.

Bible scholar William Barclay of Glasgow University was a prolific writer. Barclay's famous commentaries on the New Testament are known around the world and have been translated into many languages. While we would not agree with some of their theological conclusions, they are unexcelled for background material on the New Testament. "How did William Barclay do it?" is a question that has been asked over and over again. Writing newspaper columns, authoring books, appearing on TV programs, working as dean of a college, taking time to be with students and to listen to them—how did he do it? In a manner different than most of us will ever employ.

You see, some years ago when William Barclay discovered that he was going deaf, he was faced with a decision: should he turn in on himself in self-pity and end his career? What a blow! Would anyone say that deafness was God's intended, perfect will for William Barclay or for anyone else? I doubt it. But knowing himself to be within the circle of God's permissive, circumstantial will, and grasping all the power in the promise of Romans 8:28, William Barclay decided that he would make use of his new world of almost total silence. Shut off from all the other sounds of life, he gave himself in total concentration to the inner sounds of God's Word. Even when a hearing aid did help, he would often shut it off in order to be in a world of silence. Instead of self-pity, he wrapped Romans 8:28 around his deafness and used it to work out God's purpose through his life.

May God help us to reach a truly biblical understanding of this whole matter. As Paul would say, I too want to say in conclusion: "Brothers, sisters, think on these things. Be mature in your thinking, because some day the emotional balance and spiritual life of yourself, or of someone else, may depend on your mature understanding of this matter."

O Lord, we struggle with deep and difficult things in our lives. We know from personal experience the agonies of trying to discover Your ways and Your will for our lives. Save us from childish half-truths which can destroy our faith. We pray that You will help us put life together in a mature way, to understand and to work with You in the accomplishing of Your will in our lives and in the world. In Jesus' name, Amen.

7

Childish Ideas of Prayer

And it came about that while He was praying in a certain place, after He had finished, one of His disciples said to Him, "Lord, teach us to pray just as John also taught his disciples."

Luke 11:1

"Pray, then, in this way:
   'Our Father who art in heaven,
   Hallowed be Thy name.
   Thy kingdom come.
   Thy will be done,
   On earth as it is in heaven.
   Give us this day our daily bread.
   And forgive us our debts, as we also
      have forgiven our debtors.
   And do not lead us into temptation,
      but deliver us from evil. For
      Thine is the kingdom, and the
      power, and the glory, forever.
   Amen."

Matthew 6:9–13

WE ARE CONTINUING to look at God's will, but we are bringing it down now to the place where it affects us the most, in our praying. False and immature concepts of prayer are terribly destructive factors in the lives of Christians who are trying to grow up. And they keep millions of people from even entering the kingdom.

In one of Somerset Maugham's best-known novels, *Of Human Bondage*, there is the story of a little boy named Phillip. Born with a clubfoot, Phillip is crippled and very self-conscious about his deformity. One day he hears that God can do anything if we will only pray and ask Him for it. So before going to sleep one night he looks down at his twisted foot and asks God to straighten it out for him by the next morning. He then falls asleep fully expecting that by the next day his foot will be normal. But when he awakens and pulls back the covers, Phillip discovers that his foot is still misshapen and ugly. He is hurt and disillusioned. The experience is the beginning of his loss of faith.

This kind of story is repeated countless times in the lives of grownups. I have spent innumerable hours with people whose faith has been similarly shaken because God didn't answer particular prayers for them. Many times things are made worse for them because well-meaning but ill-informed Christians have encouraged them to pray. They have quoted Scripture verses about God's power and sometimes have gone so far as to practically guarantee that God would answer their prayers.

It was this way with Connie, a young adult who had just come through a traumatic divorce. She told me through bitter tears that she had been a gung-ho Christian for many years. She listed many involvements in the life of her church, her faithfulness in daily devotions, her generosity in giving. At her place of work everyone knew her as an outspoken witness for her faith and she had won several of her co-workers to Christ.

As she talked to me, she still couldn't believe what had happened. Her husband had run around on her and finally left home. She did not believe in divorce, and had done everything in her power to hold the marriage together. But here she was—divorced, alone, lonely. Worst of all she was angry at God and utterly confused. God had let her down. Practically everyone in her church had been praying for her marriage. Scores, including her pastor, had said repeatedly that she had nothing to worry about, for this was agreed prayer by a large number of God's people who were sure God would bring her husband back to her and put the marriage together again. So she was angry not only at God but also at the church and her Christian friends.

Connie had been badly hurt and she felt shattered. She sobbed as she told me the whole story.

I could repeat a hundred incidents like that. The scenes would be different, the names and details would vary, but the basic plot would be exactly the same. Hurting people—confused, disillusioned, sometimes rebellious and angry—but always with a shattered faith. Why? In a complex world, they had tried to build part of their adult life on the sandy foundation of a childish, simplistic concept of prayer, and their house had collapsed. They were like the builder in Jesus' parable who had not dug deeply enough.

There is a German proverb which says, "Lies have short legs." Untruths and half-truths just don't go very far. They can carry you for a while, but not for long. Let's dig deeply into this whole question and find some of our immature and inadequate ideas on prayer. And then let's *katargeo* them quickly before they do us irreparable damage.

The Impossibilities of God

One of the favorite questions I use in my church membership training class with youngsters is this, "Can God do anything?" Almost always every hand goes up and they all answer, "Of course. He's God, isn't He?" I keep quizzing them, "Are you sure? Absolutely sure? Can you think of anything that God can't do?" After a few minutes of this, there is usually at least one kid who begins to catch on to my question. Very hesitantly he will answer, "Well, maybe He can't do anything that's bad or sinful." Then we always have an interesting discussion together as I point out to the children how important it is to have a God who can't do some things.

It is important that we all come to understand the flip side to the verse we hear so often, "With God all things are possible," namely, that with God some things are impossible. This is one of the fundamental differences between the Christian faith and the Moslem religion. Islam says God can do anything and everything. It will accept no limits to His power which is absolute and arbitrary. We Christians, on the other hand, say that God's power is unlimited except by His own moral nature and by certain self-imposed limitations He has built into His world, including the moral beings He has created. So the best place to begin getting this whole matter straight is to think about some of the things God cannot and will not do.

God Cannot Violate His Nature

Let us commence with the most obvious of all and one which is a foundation stone in the Christian doctrine of God. God cannot sin. He cannot do anything evil, for that would go against His own perfect moral nature. Both Hebrews 6:18 and Titus 1:2 speak of a God who cannot lie. So when we repeat our creeds to the effect that we "believe in God the Father Almighty," we do not infer that His might or power include the ability to do wrong. God's power is unlimited, but it is morally conditioned—it is limited by His perfect nature of holy love. God can do anything which is consistent with His own holy self, but He cannot violate His own nature. God can do anything except not be God!

I remember one of my missionary colleagues telling me about his experience with a converted cannibal over in Africa. One day the new convert came by to ask if it might be possible for him to take a brief vacation from being a Christian—just for a few hours—while he went and killed a certain rival chief who was an ancient enemy. He assured the missionary he would be right back afterward to continue his Christian life. Before we laugh at him, let's remember the many times we have all half-consciously wished we could take a similar vacation. The poor ex-cannibal was disappointed when my friend explained to him why that could never be. It was because of who and what God is.

God cannot cease from being God for a while. He cannot act out of character. Thus God cannot lie or sin or commit any moral evil. James taught this in a different connection, "Let no one say when he is tempted, 'I am being tempted by God,' for God cannot be tempted by evil, and He Himself does not tempt anyone. Every good thing bestowed and every perfect gift is from above, coming down from the Father of lights, with whom there is no variation, or shifting shadow" (James 1:13,17). John applied this same principle, "God is light, and in Him there is no darkness at all. If we say that we have fellowship with Him and yet walk in the darkness, we lie and do not practice the truth" (1 John 1:5–6). This means God is pure light and there are no dark spots in Him. Therefore, nothing dark or evil can come out of Him. It further means God cannot make a deal with sin: He cannot tolerate it. To do so would be to violate His own moral nature of holy love.

Of course, this also means that from a moral standpoint God cannot change. If anyone is going to do the changing, we will have to.

We need to always remember this for it seems to be one of our life-time battles—trying to change God, trying in some subtle way to pull Him down to our level. Because we love Him and want to have fellowship with Him, we often try to do it on our terms. But God cannot come to terms with us, for that would be contrary to His own nature and that is impossible for God just because He is God—I should say, especially because He is God! God cannot lie, He cannot sin, He cannot act out of character, He cannot do anything which goes against His own pure and perfect moral nature.

God Cannot Violate His Own Laws

There is a second category of things which God cannot do which bears directly upon this matter of proper perspective in prayer. These acts do not concern His own nature, but the nature of the world He has created. Some would say it is too strong to assert God cannot do these things: they would prefer to say He does not do them only because of the kind of world He has created. But this is the only world that we as humans have to live in and we are the only moral creatures of our kind. So for all practical purposes, since God created us and our world and its laws the way He did, then as far as we are concerned it's the only one we operate in.

To say He could have created it all differently is a lot of theory. The world is as it is, and we are who we are. We and God work within the fallen framework of this world. By creating this kind of a world, God has imposed certain limitations on Himself which, as far as we are concerned, make up some of the things which are impossible with God. Using the same principle we did in the first category, we could say that God cannot do anything which is contradictory to itself.

That may sound complicated, but it really isn't. Do you remember your big discussions when you were a kid: "Can God make a rock so big that He couldn't move it?" Or that old favorite which is actually another version of the same question, "What happens when an irre-sistible force meets an immovable object?" The problem here is that you are trying to put contradictory things together when it can't be done. In this world you can't have something that is square and round at the same time, a design shaped like both a rectangle and a triangle, or an object that is black and white at the same time. This is just another way of saying that God made this world to operate according to certain laws. We don't know all those laws; we've been a long time discovering some of them and we've got many more to go. These laws really come out of the character of God Himself and express His inner stability and reliability. That's why we can call our universe a cosmos instead of a chaos.

When we fail to realize this and to reckon with it in our prayers, we are on a collision course and someday could get hurt so badly that our faith itself would be badly dented or even destroyed. Much disillusionment with prayer is caused by childish misunderstanding of how God works in relationship to this world.

Let me use an extreme illustration. Let us say there is a married couple who, though they desire a child very much, have so far not been able to have one. They could pray in several different ways which would in every case involve either that they would be able to have a baby or that God would enable them to adopt a child. We can't imagine any couple who would pray for God to somehow drop a baby into their laps from heaven. But why not? Can't God do anything? It's not hard to see the foolishness and the falseness in this kind of reasoning.

Let's go a step further. Let us say that through some tragic accident you have to have your leg amputated above the knee. Would you pray that God would grow a new leg for you? Why not? Doesn't the Bible say, "All things are possible with God?" You would correctly reply that God just doesn't do things that way. Certainly in the final resurrection that leg will be fully restored, but not in this life.

Perhaps this is the right place to thank God for all the wonderful discoveries of science and modern knowledge. They have cleared away tons of false information and foolish ideas and have given us true insights into the mysteries of our vast universe. That's why we need never be afraid of any new discovery of science. All the facts are God's facts. Today we can be much better, saner, more knowledgeable Christians than ever before because many wrong ideas once held have been cleared up and we can know more truth. It is truth that sets us free and this is just as true in regard to prayer as to everything else.

All this in no way means that God is a prisoner of His own universe. God can intervene with higher laws than we know anything about. An airplane does not break the law of gravity when it flies; it supersedes it with a higher law—the law of aerodynamics. God often operates by higher laws which transcend the ones we know about. The miracles of the Bible represent God's freedom to work in this way. But even then there is a certain beautiful congruity, a certain lawfulness about those miracles.

C. S. Lewis in his book, *God in the Dock* (Eerdmans), has a most illuminating chapter on this. He points out that when the devil asked Jesus to turn stones into bread, it was more than a mere temptation to take a shortcut to popularity. It was a typically devilish suggestion, for the devil is essentially a magician.

God works miracles, not magic, for no one makes bread out of stones—not even God. He turns seeds into wheat or corn or rye and out of that we make bread. When Jesus fed the Five Thousand, He didn't take stones from the brook and turn them into bread and fish. He took loaves and made more loaves, fish and multiplied them into more fish. And this is what farmers do every year and the fish do in season—produce more bread and more fish. It takes them a long time to do it through the laws of nature. But Jesus Christ, being the Lord of both time and nature, can speed up the process into a few moments. Lewis points out that this kind of fittingness and lawfulness is true of all the miracles. God does not contradict Himself or violate the sacred order which He has built into this world.

God Cannot Violate Human Freedom

All this leads to a third limitation on the power of God. It comes out of the second and is also self-imposed by the way He has made this world of things and persons. God cannot violate human freedom. He has created a race of persons with freedom to make choices. He did not create fleshly robots, mechanical beings over which He has complete control. He created human personalities made in many ways like Himself—in His own image—with a spirit akin to His own, beings with self-consciousness and self-determination. Limited, yes, by the kind of world we live in, but with enough freedom to choose so as to be responsible to Him.

Let's think of how God works, regarding our salvation. God desires to save us from our sins, bring us into His very own family as His redeemed children, and change us so we will love and serve Him— and do all this without at any point overriding or overruling our freedom. Yet how can He save us without at the same time destroying the very thing He wants to save? God cannot redeem us by mere omnipotence, by the sheer exercise of His power. That would violate our personhood and destroy what He most desires—our freely chosen love.

How often I have heard from children and teenagers in the counseling room: "Why doesn't God just make me be good?" But that wouldn't be goodness. It would be slavery and God is not interested in slaves but in sons and daughters! God will not overpower us into goodness; He can and does work through every possible means to get our attention, to call us, to woo us and win us. But He will never ravish us or violate us as persons.

God cannot save us against the consent of our will. Sometimes we point out such things as the conversion of Saul on the road to Damascus, as if God had simply forced him into submission. Certainly it was a powerful revelation of the living Christ. But I remind you that Paul, writing about it years later said, "I did not prove disobedient to the heavenly vision" (Acts 26:19), plainly implying that in spite of all that display of supernatural power, he still had to give the consent of his will. He could have been disobedient if he had chosen to.

Actually all this leads right to the cross. There is only one way God can save us and preserve our freedom—the way of suffering love. That was the basis of Christ's appeal to the murderous and rebellious Saul, "Saul, Saul, why are you persecuting Me . . . I am Jesus whom you are persecuting" (Acts 9:4–5). That's what captured Saul's heart and made him a love slave of Jesus for life. Yes, God can suffer for us, appeal to us, unrelentingly love us. But He cannot force us against our wills. He cannot violate our moral freedom.

Mature Prayer

We have gone into considerable detail about all this because it is the basic groundwork for a mature and biblical concept of prayer. Without this understanding prayer can remain a very childish matter, built on a mixture of fantasy and fairy-tale magic. Someday it can even become a dangerous boomerang, returning to badly damage your faith.

It is reported that the saintly George Mueller, that remarkable man of faith whose prayers literally fed and clothed thousands of British orphans, once said, "Prayer, apart from Scripture, is ninety percent illusion." It is all right for children to fantasize and live with some imaginary illusions while they are little, but when they grow up they must put away those things. To fail to do so can result in getting hurt.

After seeing the movie *Mary Poppins,* one little girl jumped off her rooftop with an open umbrella.

Let's think again about Connie whom we mentioned at the beginning of this chapter. What was the real problem back of her shattered faith? It was the fact that another person's will was involved—her husband's. In such instances we can never guarantee the outcome of our prayers, because God cannot violate that person's power of choice. God actually did answer the prayers of Connie and her church friends. God convicted her husband deeply; he was really miserable and unhappy in his sins. But he would not give them up. He used his very Godgiven power of choice to say no to Gocl. And a tragic divorce was the result. This incident is like so many involving prayer—it was a mixture of truth and error which we commonly call a half-truth. The trouble with a half-truth is that you can always get hold of the wrong half. This was what happened to Connie and her friends. They prayed in great faith because they knew some great truths:

• God certainly wanted the husband to repent and change his behavior.

• God certainly wanted the marriage to be saved, and therefore,

• God would do everything in His power to bring this about. But they went a step too far when they guaranteed to Connie (and themselves) that it had to happen. This was false because they forgot to add one more truth to the above three:

• God cannot force anyone against his will; He will not violate our moral freedom. Therefore, the husband could still refuse to do the right thing and could insist on a divorce. Because they ignored this important basic fact they ended up with a half-truth which turned out to be very destructive.

In his classic book on doubt, *In Two Minds,* Os Guinness deals extensively with the devastating effects of doubts which arise from faulty ideas about God. He says, "The devil's stock in trade is the world of half-truths and half-lies where the half-lie masquerades as the whole truth" (InterVarsity, p. 47). He also points out, "Poor teaching is the largest single cause of those doubts for which the doubter is not initially responsible. When what is taught is such a distortion of God's Word that doubt is inevitable, the basic responsibility is not the doubter's but the teacher's" (p. 207).

Half-Truths Can Kill

How well I remember a sad instance from our days in India. A brilliant young Methodist missionary, Spirit-filled and fruitful in his service, was stricken with appendicitis. He was about to go to the hospital for an operation when some superspiritual friends persuaded him that it would be a great act of faith and a powerful witness to the non-Christians of the community if he did not submit to the operation, but instead had a healing service and trusted God to heal him. Unfortunately, he agreed to their misguided suggestion. Within a matter of hours his appendix burst and a few days later he was dead. All India mourned the loss of this marvelous young missionary with such a promising future. Here again we see what pain such immature half-truths about prayer can bring.

As in this example and the one in the previous chapter about the parents taking insulin away from their son, many of the worst tragedies occur in the realm of half-truths about healing. I have known people who trusted God to heal their poor vision. They threw away their glasses. Then after weeks of suffering, they had to once again have their eyes tested and put on glasses. The basic issue is not whether God heals in answer to prayer, but how God brings about this healing.

It is evident that God's usual way of healing is to use the best of human knowledge and medical skill. Ever since He gave the command to mankind to have dominion over the earth and subdue it (Genesis 1:28), it has seemed as if God would rather wait for humans to do just that, and bring about most of the healing through the use of natural means. This is not to say that God cannot occasionally cut through natural means and heal in supernatural ways. But this is definitely the exception, not the rule. We get into trouble when we try to make the exception the rule. Though people prayed for centuries about some of the great plagues and scourges of mankind, God seemed content to wait until humans achieved enough dominion over His world to find the cures. And so came vaccinations which wiped out smallpox, and insulin for diabetes, and Salk vaccine for polio, and antibiotics which have saved millions of lives. Why didn't God directly intervene before this? Because that is not the way He works in this world of natural law and secondary causes.

Faith, Prayer, and Presumption

Unless we really grow up in our thinking about prayer, we can easily fall into what the Bible calls presumption. A synonym for presumption is audacity. In this act, we overstep our limits and ask God to overstep His. There are at least eleven references in the Bible to the matter of presumption. They are all in the Old Testament except for 2 Peter 2:10. In every case presumption is considered a sin, an affront toward God, an overstepping of our bounds with Him. In several instances in the Old Testament its punishment was death. The psalmist wisely prayed, "Keep back Thy servant from presumptuous sins; let them not rule over me; Then I shall be blameless, and I shall be acquitted of great transgressions" (Psalm 19:13).

When Jesus resisted Satan's temptation to jump from the top of the temple, He was refusing to tempt or test the Father by an act of presumption. Many of our childish and immature prayers, based on half-truths and misquotations of Scripture, come dangerously near to being presumption instead of true faith. We need to grow up into Christ in our ideas of prayer lest we fall into errors which bring dishonor to the name of God.

In Catherine Marshall's book, *Meeting God at Every Turn,* she tells of her two-year bout with tuberculosis. She describes her pilgrimage and how God had to bring her step by step from the "oversimplified presumption of the new pupil" to the place where she saw the difference between "presumption that masquerades as faith and real faith." It was not until she was finally able to pray this prayer that a slow but steady healing came about: "Lord, I understand no part of this, but if You want me an invalid for the rest of my life—well, it's up to You. I place myself in Your hands, for better or for worse. I only ask to serve You."

The Problem of Unanswered Prayer

We would be unfair if we did not take at least a brief look at the question of unanswered prayer. For while the biblical principles we have described can help us understand most of our situations, there are still many times when we feel as if we have prayed from our highest and best understanding and are still left puzzled and confused. Let's face it—at those times the Bible itself may not seem helpful, for it too is full of unanswered prayers.

- Moses prayed to enter the Promised Land but died with his request refused.
- Habakkuk cried from his tower, "O Lord, how long shall I cry and Thou wilt not hear?"
- The psalmist pled in his depression, "Why art Thou so far from helping me, and from the words of my complaint?"
- Paul prayed three times that his troublesome physical handicap, his "thorn in the flesh" which was hindering his service for Christ, would be removed. But instead he was promised "sufficient grace" to make the best of it and let it make the best of him.

Leonard Griffith suggests that if some twentieth-century moderns were writing the rest of Paul's biography, it might run like this:

> After these things, Paul began to lose interest and fell away from the church. . . . His thorn was there to stay; obviously prayer could not budge it. He read some books on prayer; still it did not seem to work. Perhaps he could get along just as well without praying. Why not? He went back to his trade and made tents. He amassed quite a fortune for those days—before he died. The years grew very tranquil and undisturbed in their slow and equal pace from day to day. It was a great relief to be rid of all the wearing obligations of religion, except, of course, that he was never quite happy (*Barriers to Christian Belief*, Harpers, p. 112).

No, the problem is certainly not new. But when it is our personal problem with pain, then we need to find our own personal answers. May I borrow from many of the ancient classics on the subject of prayer and suggest some possible reasons for our unanswered prayers:

- We do not ask for the right things. How often we don't realize what we are asking for. Paul's words in Romans 8:26 apply here, "For we do not know how to pray as we should." James puts it, "You ask and do not receive, because you ask with wrong motives" (4:3). So often we pray for things which, if God did provide, would turn out for our worst instead of our best. God is well aware of what we really need. But we often ask for our wants instead of our true needs. Sometimes God does not answer the want we express in prayer in order that He might answer what He knows to be the real need behind it.

The most classic illustration of this in Christian history is the story of Monica, the mother of St. Augustine. In his *Confessions* he described his mother praying all night that God would block her son from setting sail to Italy. She saw her son going from bad to worse and couldn't imagine what would be in store for him if he went far away from her influence, and especially to Italy with all its licentiousness and alluring splendors. But while she was praying, her son set sail to Italy. It was there he met the mighty preacher Ambrose and fell under the right influences. It was there he became a Christian—in the very place from which his mother's earnest prayers would have kept him. Augustine, understanding this aspect of the mystery of unanswered prayer, later wrote a prayer of thanksgiving: "Thou, in the depth of Thy counsels, hearing the main point of her desire, regarded not what she then asked, that Thou mightest make me what she ever desired."

• We ask for things we should be taking care of ourselves. I saw a TV evangelist actually using a vending machine to illustrate prayer. If we put our prayers of faith in the coin slot, the answers appear where the merchandise falls out. This is to make prayer like room service and God an eternal bellhop, a celestial errand boy. We must never make our prayers a substitute for what God intends us to achieve by ourselves. There were times when God interrupted the prayers of Moses and of Gideon, and in effect said to them, "Don't speak to Me about these matters; go and speak to the Children of Israel." It was not a time for prayer but for action.

God sometimes has to remind us to keep the division of labor straight—to remember what is His work and what is ours. The writer of the Book of Hebrews often mentioned things that Jesus "learned" by suffering and obedience and discipline. What kind of Christians would we be if everything was accomplished simply by praying for it? We would remain spiritual children living in a fantasy land of magic wands.

Griffith offers this incisive illustration:

When a boy asks his father to do his homework because he wishes to play, will the father—assuming he is equal to his son's homework—do it? Not if he loves the lad and cares for his growth of character. The father . . . may encourage him, assist him, stand by him, and see him through but he must not do for the son anything that the boy can possibly do for himself (p. 116).

We often say, "Not our ability, but our availability," which is intended to call attention to the fact that it is all accomplished by His power, not ours. But let us remember that our availability includes putting at God's disposal the best that we have and allowing Him to use it as a channel of His power. And our best is usually hard won and slowly achieved.

• We are not ready for God's answer. The longer I counsel people, the more I respect the matter of timing. *Chronos* is the ordinary word for time used in the New Testament. It's just plain human time, and we get words like chronology and chronometer from it.

The word used for God's time is *kairos*. It means the right time and the ripe time, like the phrase for the advent of Jesus, "the fullness of the time" (Galatians 4:4). I may spend many hours counseling someone only to discover that it is just not their *kairos* time. The books and tapes I loan them, the sessions together don't seem to be going anywhere. We often talk about it together and break off our sessions for a while. It can often be years later they come back with, "Now I understand what you were saying; now it's all making sense to me. I reread those books and they really came alive. Could we talk together again?" This time it's different; progress is amazingly swift, growth rapid. Our prayers had not been answered because the person wasn't ready.

John 5:6 is an amazing verse: "When Jesus saw him lying there and knew that he had already been a long time in that condition, He said to him, 'Do you wish to get well?'" Did it take thirty-eight years of illness to make the man so desperate that he would finally drop his excuses, quit blaming others, and be ready to believe and obey Jesus?

When I was a youngster I had asthma. It got worse in my teens and by my freshman year in college was so bad I was unable to take the spring semester exams. I prayed constantly for healing, others prayed for me, and once I underwent the anointing and laying on of hands for healing. The prayers were never answered.

Years later, in my early morning quiet time, God showed me through one sentence in a devotional book that I needed to have a healing of my memories. This involved forgiving someone on a deeper level than I had ever done before. It took several days of heart searching and prayer. I never even prayed about my asthma problem. I just allowed the Spirit to take care of those resentments and hurting memories. It's hard to believe, but I haven't had any asthma from that day to this!

Yes, a lot of prayer had gone up for my asthma, but I was not ready to receive God's answer until my deeper problem was taken care of. This is true for many areas of unanswered prayer in our lives. There are many things God cannot give us until we are ready for them. The saints have always reminded us that Yes and No are not the only answers to prayer. Many times God gives us the other one—Wait.

One characteristic of a child is the inability to wait, a need for instant gratification. People who still have a childish outlook on prayer find it difficult to wait upon the Lord. We are to be "imitators of those who through faith and patience inherit the promises" (Hebrews 6:12). Guinness describes this kind of waiting on God as a kind of suspended judgment. He reminds us that sometimes we may not know why, but we can know why we trust in God who knows why. Thus patience and waiting are signs of a mature relationship with God; they reveal our belief that He is truly trustworthy.

Relationship. That's a good place to bring this to a close. The great devotional writers of the past believed that there is really no such thing as unanswered prayer if we keep our lives in harmony with God. That God always answers prayer in one of two ways: either He changes the circumstances or He supplies sufficient power to overcome them. He answers either the petition or the person.

When you understand this, you have put away an immature view of prayer. Your first interest is no longer the gift, but the Giver.

8

Childhood Confusions Versus Adult Distinctions

"He who is without sin among you, let him be the first to throw a stone at her."

Jesus said to her, "Woman, where are they? Did no one condemn you?" And she said, "No one, Lord."

And Jesus said, "Neither do I condemn you; go your way. From now on sin no more."

John 8:7, 10–11

He had to be made like His brethren in all things . . . For since He Himself was tempted in that which He has suffered, He is able to come to the aid of those who are tempted.

For we do not have a high priest who cannot sympathize with our weaknesses, but one who has been tempted in all things as we are, yet without sin.

Hebrews 2:17–18; 4:15

You have forgotten the exhortation which is addressed to you as sons,

"My son, do not regard lightly the discipline of the Lord,
Nor faint when you are reproved by Him;
For those whom the Lord loves He disciplines,
And He scourges every son whom He receives."

All discipline for the moment seems not to he joyful, but sorrowful; yet to those who have been trained by it, afterwards it yields the peaceful fruit of righteousness.

Hebrews 12:5–6, 11

WE HAVE NOW dealt with several different areas where wrong concepts left over from childhood give rise to wrong feelings and actions. In some instances these came out of hurtful experiences and relationships which left scars on our memories. They needed a special kind of healing experience before their emotional bondage could be broken. There were others which came from immature notions in regard to basic Christian truths. These needed the corrective of mature, balanced biblical principles.

Now let us consider some childish confusions and the necessary distinctions we need to make if we are to conduct ourselves as grown-up Christians.

It has been said of children that they are "the world's greatest recorders but the world's worst interpreters." It's difficult to know just where some of these childish confusions came from, and maybe we don't need to know. But the task still remains of sorting them out so we can put away their childish results.

The Distinction Between Acceptance and Approval

Among evangelical Christians we find a lot of confusion between acceptance and approval. This can have its roots in families where parents did not make it plain to their children that disapproval of what they were doing did not mean rejection of them as persons. When a child is being punished for something not approved by his parents, it is easy for him to get the idea that they don't like him or accept him as a person. Thus a kind of mathematical formula is implanted in the youngster:

Approval means acceptance.

Disapproval means nonacceptance or rejection.

So punishment and discipline equal disapproval and rejection.

Therefore approval means, "I am loved and accepted."

Disapproval means, "I am not loved but rejected."

This may or may not be the parents' fault. However, if you are a parent it would be well to look closely at just how you discipline your children. Be sure to make it crystal clear that while you do not approve of what they are doing, you do accept and love them as your children. You need to be especially careful with highly sensitive youngsters, going out of your way to make sure they understand this distinction. Because you love them you must correct their wrong behavior. You do not approve of their conduct, but you will always love them and accept them regardless of what they do. Make clear to them that your acceptance of them does not depend on your approval of everything they do.

However, sometimes children pick up this confusion from their teachers or other authority figures and even their friends. Wherever it comes from, it can create emotional and marital havoc in immature adults. They tend to then record and register any disapproval—even a suggestion, let alone a criticism—with the old formula of nonacceptance and personal rejection. This is a built-in guarantee of personal hangups, interpersonal blowups, and spiritual breakups.

It is also the surest way to become a pharisaical Christian. When we carry within us this confusion, it means that we cannot accept and love ourselves unless we can approve everything we do. It follows then—since we treat our neighbors as we treat ourselves—that we shall surely apply this same childish formula to them. Thus we will not be able to approve of everything they do. When this gets mixed in with a spirit of legalism and a religion which consists mainly of prohibitions and regulations, the result can be especially deadly.

Jack came to see me regarding what he called "a personal family matter." It turned out that he was upset because his brother Joe had walked out on his wife and children after almost twenty years of marriage. The brothers had been very close and Jack felt hurt over Joe's behavior. But what was really bothering him was his confusion over what his attitude should be toward Joe. He had not invited him to his house or even spoken to him for more than a year. Now Joe had recently written and asked if he might come for a visit. Jack was afraid that if he was friendly to Joe, he might give the idea that he approved of what Joe had done. Or the people in his church might think that he approved of divorce. So he hadn't even replied to Joe's letter. He kept telling me that he knew his feelings were wrong but he just couldn't help it. "That's the way I was raised," he said, "and I simply cannot lower my moral standards for anyone—not even my brother."

This same dilemma could be duplicated under many different circumstances. Some Christians are afraid to be friendly or even to show ordinary kindness to a sinner for fear the person might get the idea they approve of his sins. There are entire churches who suffer from this confusion. Their attitude is, "We must make sure people know where we stand on this issue." The same personal problem that Jack had is worked out on a group scale. In both instances, it reveals a deep childish insecurity. It is possible to hold the highest moral standards and at the same time be accepting and loving toward those who have violated those standards. The person who feels shock and shows rejection toward those whose behavior he disapproves is not revealing his own high moral standards. Instead he is revealing a fearful and insecure area of his own emotions which he has never dealt with. He desperately needs to put away childish confusion and grow up into Christ.

This maturing begins by looking at Christ's clear-cut distinction between acceptance and approval. He was so filled with confidence and inner security that He could walk with deep compassion among the publicans and sinners, gluttons and winebibbers, thieves and harlots. Yet not once did He ever lower a standard so that anyone might think He was approving of their behavior. This is what the Pharisees accused Him of, but that was only the projection of their own problem onto Him.

The way He dealt with the promiscuous Samaritan woman at the well (John 4:5-42), or the cheating IRS official, Zaccheus (Luke 19:1–10), or the woman caught in the very act of adultery (John 8:3–11) gives us a pattern to follow. His words to the second woman are the perfect combination, "Neither do I condemn you; go your way; from now on sin no more." Here is loving acceptance and redemptive disapproval, personal compassion and moral challenge, beautifully put together by Christ so that distinctions are not blurred.

Many of us will never feel any real peace with God about our own personal salvation until we break the stranglehold of this childish confusion. God does not wait to accept us and love us until He can approve everything about us. If He did, we would all be hopelessly and eternally lost. And if He doesn't wait—with His high and holy standards—why should we wait to accept ourselves and others?

The Distinction Between Temptation and Sin

It is James who tells us to consider it a joy when we fall into various temptations. He even goes so far as to say that the man who endures temptation is blessed. However, that is not our usual view of the matter, and with some people it is made much worse by a fundamental confusion of temptation and sin. Let us look carefully at the Scriptures and some practical aspects of temptation so that we will not fall prey to Satan's slimy suggestions which keep us feeling guilty and under condemnation.

First, let us forever fix in our minds that everybody experiences temptation. Dante had an allegorical picture of the Christian life as a journey in which a man climbed up a winding mountain road. When he began the journey, he was a young man. After he had climbed a short while, a snarling wolf leaped out of the bushes and tried to tear him to pieces. To Dante this was the wolf of lust, of bodily passion, and represented the major temptation of a young person.

As he climbed higher and came into middle life, a giant tiger sprang on him. This was the tiger of pride, and represented the great temptation of middle age—pride of position, of name, and of status. Finally, near the top, at the time of old age, a great, hairy-maned lion came bounding after him. This was the great temptation of the later life—money and financial security.

In his classification of the three great temptations of life the point Dante was trying to make is this: There is no level of Christian life where you will be free from temptation. There is no person, however Spirit-filled, however saintly and mature, who will not face temptation of some kind.

Many people who seek counsel on the deeper life mistakenly think that if they can just reach a high level of spiritual experience, they will not have to face temptations anymore. The New Testament takes the history and geography of the Children of Israel and uses them as a symbolic picture of our spiritual experiences. For example, the Israelites in Egypt stand for the slavery and bondage of sin; the miracle of the Red Sea represents our salvation and deliverance; the journeys are the normal growth of the soul; the forty years in the desert picture the self-filled, carnal Christian, defeated and discouraged; the Jordan represents the place of full surrender; and the promised land of Canaan represents the higher level of Spirit-filled living.

What was the primary activity that characterized the life of God's people under Joshua in Canaan? Warfare. They had entered the land but now they were to possess all of it! The whole Book of Joshua is the story of great warfare in possessing the land. At every level in your Christian life you will face temptation. Because you are a free moral agent, your power of choice is never taken from you. God never changes you from human to vegetable or animal, or into a moral and spiritual robot. As Oswald Chambers so often said, God can give us pure hearts in an instant, but He cannot quickly give us Christian character. That takes time and can come only through a series of right moral choices.

Temptation is the proving ground of those choices and no one is exempt, not even our Lord Himself.

Still this false and childish fantasy persists and some respond, "Yes, I know all that. But surely if I am truly filled with the Spirit, I would not undergo such strong temptations." Where did this idea come from? Surely not from the Word of God and certainly not from the biographies of the saints. They freely admitted their struggles with all kinds of temptations.

Let us look at the passage in James 1:13–14—"Let no one say when he is tempted, 'I am being tempted by God.'" No, the temptation hasn't come from God. Then from where? Read on: "But each one is tempted when he is carried away and enticed by his own lust."

Now the word lust is not a good translation for today. In the 1600s, lust meant the whole range of human desires. Nowadays, we have come to use it only in a sexual sense. For example, this same Greek word is used in Luke 22:15 where Jesus Himself said, "I have earnestly desired to eat this Passover with you." It is also used in Matthew 13:17, where Jesus said, "Many prophets and righteous men desired to see what you see." Obviously the word can mean a desire or longing which is good as well as bad. In James the word simply refers to what we would call today our inborn natural urges—natural desires such as hunger for food, the desire for sex, or for recognition or companionship. So we should reread it, "Each one is tempted when he is carried away and enticed by his own desires." (In Greek "carried away" is a term used for fishing, the lure of bait, and "enticed" refers to a hunting trap.)

Now follow it carefully: "Then when lust—or desire—has conceived, it gives birth to sin. And when sin is accomplished, it brings forth death." It takes two to conceive in order to give birth to sin. What are the two? The person's natural desire plus the satanic suggestion, the temptation. So on the one hand we have a natural basic desire, of itself God-given; and on the other hand, we have the evil temptation, the bait, the trap, the satanic suggestion to misuse that drive, to pervert it and fulfill it in an unlawful and improper manner. But remember the two have not as yet come together. They have not as yet conceived, that is, been joined. The two have not become one; they are still separate.

What is it that can either keep them apart or allow them to come together, conceive, and give birth to sin? Your will! As long as your will says, "No, I will not allow these two to come together; I will that they stay apart," it doesn't matter how strong the desire or how alluring the bait and the temptation, you have not sinned.

A very crude illustration: I have been working out in the yard. It's nearing noontime; I don't need to look at my watch. My stomach has been telling me the time in no uncertain terms. I am hungry; I look up and see an apple tree. Some luscious apples stare me in the face. I'm hungry; I would like to eat an apple; my mouth even waters. So I go over and am about to take one. But on closer inspection I see that the tree is not in my yard; it's in my neighbor's yard and so belongs to him. Now I'm hungry and my desires want me to eat. I am tempted, but I say No; my will comes between the hunger and the apple. I have been tempted. I have not sinned. My will has prevented a joining, a conjunction of the two. If my will would assent, then the two would come together and sin would result.

This is a simple illustration, and for some matters too simple. But it illustrates the main point. Now transfer this same idea over to other areas of temptation, say a sexual desire or the desire for recognition or belonging. All these are basic, good in themselves, God-given desires. To have the desire is no more sinful than when your mouth waters at that apple. But the secret is in what you do with the evil suggestion. If you will refuse to toy with it, you are in the clear. "You can't keep the birds from flying over your head, but you can keep them from nesting in your hair!" Temptation is *not* sin. A thought of evil is not sin, but allowing it to settle down until it becomes evil thinking is sin. Having the desire is not sin; accepting the evil suggestion to fulfill that desire in the wrong way is sin.

Brent, a college youth, came to counsel with me. After listening to his camouflage of so-called intellectual difficulties he was having with the Christian faith, I asked, "Why don't you tell me what's really bothering you?" He did. He was angry with God. "Why?" I asked. "What did He do to you?" He replied, "That's the problem; it's what He *didn't* do for me. Last year during the Spiritual Emphasis Week I asked Him to take away my sexual desires. The struggle was too much, so I asked Him to remove them."

Brent's real problem was he had never gotten clear in his mind the distinction between temptation and sin. We spent a long time together until he saw it clearly. When he was able to see the foolishness of his anger against God, he could be restored in his Christian walk. Years later I had the privilege of performing his marriage ceremony to an attractive Christian young lady. At the reception he whispered to me, "I'm sure glad God didn't answer that prayer." I laughingly replied, "Amen!"

Don't ask God to take away your sexual desires, or your ambitions, or to remove your temper from you. He cannot answer these prayers. He can and will give you self-control over your sexual desires. He can enable you to have one all-consuming ambition—His glory. And He can cleanse and redirect your temper so that, like Jesus, you will get angry at the things you ought to get angry at. Know the difference between temptation and sin.

The Distinction Between Hurt and Harm

The confusion between being hurt and being harmed is another hang-over from our childhood and teenage years. It is almost impossible for a small child to understand this difference. Whatever the circumstances or the motive behind it, anything which causes pain to a child is seen as a hurt. A parent or friend might do something only by accident, and he might feel terrible about it afterward. It makes no difference to the child—it hurts and therefore he cries.

As we grow up, we slowly begin to see the difference. When I used to wrestle with my dad, sometimes he would accidentally hurt me. I remember looking at his eyes. If I saw pain there I knew he hadn't meant to do it, and even though sometimes my pain was severe and I wanted to cry, I didn't. I didn't realize then that I was learning an important lesson.

Of course, I was fortunate because my dad is a wonderful Christian man. He recently celebrated his ninetieth birthday by returning for a brief visit to India where he had spent forty years as a missionary.

But what about a family where there is really no difference between hurt and harm—where discipline and punishment, alcohol and anger, put-downs and throw-downs all get mixed together so that when someone is hurt he is also harmed? It can be difficult for a person out of that background to make this distinction. He may have memories that need healing and a whole response system which needs reprogramming before he can really become mature in Christ.

For the maturing process requires discipline. It is a sign of God's love and concern for us. "Those whom the Lord loves He disciplines. . . . God deals with you as with sons; for what son is there whom his father does not discipline? . . . He disciplines us for our good, that we may share His holiness" (Hebrews 12:6, 7,10). This means that God does not hesitate to hurt us if this is necessary to help us become mature sons and daughters of His.

He will hurt us but He will never harm us. He will hurt us if that is necessary to wean us away from dependence on feelings to total dependence upon Him. He will hurt us if that is necessary to wean us from self-sufficiency to total dependence on Him. This means He will sometimes hurt us by allowing us to undergo falls and failures until we realize that apart from Him we can do nothing or be nothing. God is not afraid to hurt us, but the hurt is always to heal and help us, never to harm us.

Perhaps I can best illustrate this by an intimate and painful page from our family life. Our son Steve was born while we were missionaries in India. Helen and I saw immediately that he had a twisted clubfoot. The crucial time for treating this deformity is the first forty-eight hours after birth, but we were 500 miles from a hospital having an orthopedic physician—a difficult two-day journey. It was almost a month before we could travel with Steve to the Presbyterian hospital where his little foot could be placed in a plaster cast.

Because that clubfoot got a month's head start, to straighten it took several years and required three painful operations.

I'll never forget the day when our wonderful orthopedic surgeon in Lexington, Kentucky called Helen and me in. He placed a bottle in my hands. It was all wrapped in cotton, so it would be soft but firm. He said, "Daddy, I'm going to give you a tough job. If we're going to help this foot heal after the operation and keep it from reverting to the old twist, you're going to have to turn it back the opposite way."

Every evening there were some traumatic minutes in our family. Helen had to hold Steve—he was just a toddler—and I had to take his foot and put it over that bottle and twist it as far back in the opposite direction as it was turning in the wrong direction.

You can imagine Steve's response—his cries of pain. Sometimes when he'd plead with me to stop and I didn't, he would scream,

"Daddy, I hate you!" My stomach would churn. I'd get sick of the whole business.

But years later, when I saw him playing Little League baseball, when I sat on the sidelines of the college tennis courts and watched Steve and his cousin win the tennis doubles tournament three years in a row, I said, "It was worth it."

When I see him walk with no noticeable limp, I say again, "It was worth it."

In the coming days your heavenly Father may say to you, "We are now going to get down to the business of straightening you out, until you grow up in every way into Christ." When He does this, it will hurt. But do not let any childish experiences throw you into confusion. Always keep in mind this important distinction: God may hurt you, but He will never harm you.

9

Childish Dependency on Feelings

And I, brethren, could not speak to you as to spiritual men, but as to men of flesh, as to babes in Christ. I gave you milk to drink, not solid food; for you were not yet able to receive it. Indeed, even now you are not yet able, for you are still fleshly. For since there is jealousy and strife among you, are you not fleshly, and are you not walking like mere men?

For when one says, "I am of Paul, " and another, "I am of Apollos," are you not mere men? What then is Apollos? And what is Paul? Servants through whom you believed, even as the Lord gave opportunity to each one. I planted, Apollos watered, but God was causing the growth. So then neither the one who plants nor the one who waters is anything, but God who causes the growth.

1 Corinthians 3:1–7

THE WORD THAT the Apostle Paul used for "childish," *nepios*, is seldom used in Scripture. In each case it suggests an adult who displays the irresponsible characteristics of a child, an adult whose development has been arrested. This same word is used in Hebrews 5:11–14, condemning those who are still needing to be spoon-fed or nursed on milk because they are babies (babyish). Paul used it in writing to the Corinthians: "And I, brethren, could not speak unto you as to spiritual men, but . . . as to babes" (1 Corinthians 3:1). He followed this with a catalog of their babyish actions.

This reference to infantile behavior is clearly not a matter of chronology, since all the passages were written to adults. Such babyishness does not go away by itself with the mere passing of time. Age will not necessarily fill you with maturity—just wrinkles! Therefore, babyish behavior has to be dealt with very decisively, says Paul. Why? Because it results from a defective form of love. If we are to find mature love as described in 1 Corinthians 13, we must put this babyishness out of our lives.

The chief characteristics of toddlers are their total self-centeredness and their inability to wait for anything. Little children want the time lag between desire and fulfillment to be very short. They demand immediate gratification. They are also almost totally dependent on feelings.

Many adults are babyish in these very same ways—self-centered, demanding immediate gratification of desires, and overly dependent on feelings.

Feelings are important, and there is a central place in the Christian religion for the emotional life. The fruit of the Spirit is love, joy, peace, and all three of these include feelings. Christianity is not a form of stoicism. It in no way relegates the emotions to a second-class status, but recognizes that wholeness must include the emotional life. One of the characteristics of life in the Holy Spirit is the free flow of all that is deepest in the human personality. The Spirit frees us to experience and express our emotions.

Feelings and Personality

The way you express your feelings in other areas of life will show up in your Christian life. If you have difficulty with feelings in your general living, you are not going to be a totally changed person emotionally after you are converted or filled with the Spirit. You will have similar difficulties with feelings in your Christian life. Some people have more trouble along these lines than others do. I think Paul's young disciple, Timothy, was sensitive, prone to depression and discouragement. When he felt low, Paul would have to "stir him up to remembrance" and get him going again.

Some people suffer disillusionment because they believe their Christian experiences should alter their basic personality patterns and temperaments. God is not out to change your fundamental personality structure. He can use you to His glory; He wants you just exactly the way you are. In the play, *Green Pastures*, Noah in his great moment of acceptance and surrender says, "Lord, I ain't much, but I's all I's got!" That is a very profound statement. The sooner you rejoice in who you really are, the better. For God wants to use you—the unique and irreplaceable you.

We all have problems in certain areas of our lives. As we vary in talents and in gifts, so we vary in our difficulties. However, most people have some problems with their temperament or disposition. Therefore, one of the healthiest things a new Christian can do is to take a good look at himself, accept the basic facts about his personality and not berate himself because he isn't like someone else.

Our feelings are the most variable and the most unreliable part of our makeup. They are mysterious. They are inexplicable. You cannot directly create a feeling and then command it at will. Feelings are dependent on many factors, some known, some unaccounted for. The saints of old recognized this. The sixteenth-century French saint, Fenelon, wrote about "dry spells," those rather feelingless periods in the Christian life. He offered a list of things that can produce these dry moments. Some of the items sound very spiritual, but right in the center of the list is this one: "They also may be caused by well-meaning guests who stay too long in your home." (And you wondered if you were sinful for feeling the same way!) He had the sense to see that feelings are created by a great variety of causes. For example, do you sometimes awaken in the morning in a mood that is completely different from the way you felt the night before? And you can't figure out any good reason for it?

This is why it is so utterly childish to let our feelings control us and, above all, to let them become the thermometer of our spiritual health. It is only a small step from this control to guilt and resentment and thinking something is wrong with us because we have not had a particular kind of experience or feeling. For then we begin to compare and we "if only," wanting to be someone we're not.

Now let us think about some areas of our Christian lives where we need to *katargeo* very decisively our babyish dependency upon feelings, and to find a mature and balanced wholeness of Christian living.

Feelings and Assurance

Some people are dependent on feelings as the basis for their assurance of salvation. I doubt if any other subject brings as many people to the pastor as the matter of feelings in relationship to salvation. Because feelings are so variable and unreliable, it is dangerous to rely on them in this way. This does not mean that the Spirit's witness with my spirit that I am His child will not deeply involve my feelings and emotions, because it certainly will. But feelings must never be made central. They are not meant to take first place in assurance, and if you put them there, you are doomed to be an unhappy and unstable Christian who does not follow the divine order of things.

This divine order was stated so simply by David, "O taste and see that the Lord is good" (Psalm 34:8). You cannot reverse that and say, "O see and taste." Experiencing before tasting is impossible. The truth of God's promises in Scripture comes first, those promises attested by the life and death and resurrection of Jesus. The truth as seen in the person of Jesus Christ has to be accepted, acted on, submitted to, and believed in before it produces the right feelings. The emphasis in the Bible is on grasping the truth, on establishing the relationship which produces the feelings. That is the divine order. Fact, faith, and feeling. Taste and see—faith, belief, acceptance, grasping, and then the seeing and the feeling that the Lord is good.

The surest way to become a defeated, morbid, unstable Christian is to always ask yourself, "Well, how do I feel?" To base your relationship to God on the condition of your feelings is a certain sign of spiritual babyhood. The sure road to maturity is to learn to live above moods and feelings. This is going to require discipline. And it will require particular effort for feeling-centered individuals who have never learned in other areas of life to seek truth before feeling.

I like the suggestion which comes to us from our dear missionary friend from India, Sister Anna Mow. She gives her formula for those blue days when you feel depressed and condemned, and are prone to doubt your salvation because you just feel so bad. On those blue days, Anna Mow talks to herself. And that's a good idea. I do that occasionally too, simply because I enjoy intelligent conversation! This is what Anna says to herself when she is not feeling good:

- Did I get enough sleep last night?
- Have I hurt someone, intentionally or inadvertently?
- Do I feel resentment or self-pity?

If all is well in these three areas and Anna can find no reason for her spiritual indigestion, she just throws back her head and laughs at herself. And what a wonderfully contagious laugh she has, as she says to herself, "All right, Anna Mow, you stay here in the blues if you want to. I'm going on with the Lord."

There is a profound truth in Anna Mow's simple formula. You are not just your feelings. At any given moment you are greater than the sum total of your thoughts and feelings. Your selfhood is above and beyond any feelings you may be having, and you can transcend your feelings. One of the most important steps of growth in the Christian life is to reach the place where you affirm this truth about yourself.

I remember when our son did it. After his senior year in high school, he sold books door to door in a distant state. Our phone bill that summer was absolutely phenomenal, because when things weren't right Steve would get on the phone—collect, of course. And we could tell from the first word if he was down. I remember saying to him on the phone again and again, "Steve, you are at the age where you have to face one of the greatest decisions in your life: Are you going to take control of your life and run your feelings? Or are your feelings going to take control of you and run your life?" He went away as a boy. He came back a young man because he made a fundamental decision about himself that summer.

It is a great turning point when you decide that you are going to run your life. Some of you are still on the cradle roll because you have never made that decision.

The disciples said, "Lord, teach us to pray." Jesus did not answer, "Well, now, when you feel like praying. . . ." No. He said, "When you pray, say, 'Our Father.'" You may say, "But, Lord, I don't feel like saying, 'Our Father.'" "The kingdom of heaven," said Jesus, "suffers violence, and violent men take it by force" (Matthew 11:12). It is not Christian merely to say what you feel; it is Christian also to say and to pray what you know you ought to feel.

E. Stanley Jones said that sometimes you have to feel yourself into a new way of acting, but at other times you have to act yourself into a new way of feeling. Faith is basically action. It is belief acted upon and lived out that in time produces a certain kind of feeling. That is God's order. Don't try to reverse it or you will be a childish Christian, unstable in all your ways.

Feelings and Guidance

Many people depend on feelings as the basis for Christian guidance. One of the great promises of the Christian life is: "For all who are being led by the Spirit of God, these are the sons of God" (Romans 8:14). Nothing is more vital in life than the fact of God's guidance. But many of us misunderstand this to mean that God always leads us by direct feelings and inner impressions. A common phrase now for guidance is "the hot line to heaven" which means a strong, inner emotional push which may be quite independent of outer influences. Some Christians go to ridiculous lengths on these things, even to the point of praying about what stamp to buy at the post office. I hear of college students who pray about whether they should go to a certain campus activity and then about whether they ought to take a date to the event. I don't know whose prayers are getting answered because a lot of the girls sitting alone in the dorm are praying that the boys will have enough sense to date them. There is obviously a clash of prayers here.

This perpetual praying for a feeling or an inner voice on what to do runs all the way from the smallest daily decisions to the most serious matters of life. Now the error occurs not about the fact that God does indeed speak through the subjective inner voice, through feelings and impressions. I have had experiences when God did speak that way. The error lies in making feelings and impressions the main source of God's guidance, unchecked and unbalanced with the other, more regular ways in which God guides us.

Feelings and impressions come from three sources: from God, from the devil, and from the inner workings of our minds—our personality patterns, temperament and disposition, emotional hangups and scars, from the damaged emotions of our lives. These are a third source that can be used by either the Holy Spirit or Satan. This is why John warns us, "Beloved, do not believe every spirit, but test the spirits to see whether they are of God" (1 John 4:1, RSV).

A young lady was driving along a country road when she was seized with a strong impression, an overwhelming impulse, that she was to go back and find someone she had passed on the road and witness to him. She was so troubled about it that she came to me for advice. I strongly advised against it; it was obvious to me that there were deep emotional factors in her that Satan was using, not to guide but to misguide. She didn't take the advice but went anyhow. It is a long story and is filled with incidents both ridiculous and dangerous. All that she accomplished was to bring a bad name on the Lord and on the Christian school where she was a student.

The Apostle John's warning means that every subjective Christian experience must be examined and evaluated. It is your moral and spiritual responsibility to test the spirits before you dare to say, "The Lord told me to do this," or, "The Lord led me to do that."

Let me say a couple of things about the matter of guidance. In the everyday decisions of life, you do not need to seek special guidance from God. Many people quote Isaiah 30:21 as the basis for this kind of specific guidance for the daily details of life. "And your ears will hear a word behind you, 'This is the way, walk in it.'" But by failing to quote the rest of the verse they really misquote it and distort its true meaning. The complete verse goes on to say, "Whenever you turn to the right or to the left." In other words, it is only when you start to turn either to the right or to the left and thus start to get off the track that you will hear the voice saying, "This is the way, walk ye in it." As long as you are walking in the right path, obeying the directions of the Lord, you may not hear any special voice of guidance, because you do not need it.

If you are a child of God, the Holy Spirit lives in you, you have surrendered your life to Him, you have given Him the controls—then live! Live self-forgetfully, joyously, freely. Live on the assumption that what you are doing is right, because you have power steering: you are led by the Spirit. To stop and expect some feeling or impression on every simple detail of daily life is a vote of no confidence in the Holy Spirit who indwells you and leads you. It is also unnecessary, and one of the surest ways to drive yourself and everybody around you crazy.

In special times of decision when you need a more specific word from God, remember that guidance is cumulative. Guidance comes through

- God's Word
- outer circumstances (open and closed doors)
- your own best reasonable thinking
- the counsel of other Christians
- the inner voice of your feelings.

These are like five great lights God gives us for guidance. No good ship's captain would just go by one light in the channel. He would crash his ship on the rocks or wreck it on a sandbar. Not even two lights or three lights. The trained navigator lines up all of the lights, and then knows he is in the clear, deep channel, and that he can sail safely to his destination.

I remember talking with a missionary pilot just after he had completed a long and difficult course to get his license for instrument flying. After he told me about it, one idea stuck in my mind. He said, "You know, instrument flying is so different from ordinary flying by sight, because you have to learn that you just can't fly by your perception. Sometimes you have to go against your feelings. You just keep your eyes on those instruments. Sometimes you feel as if you are going opposite of what the instruments tell you. You sure can't fly by your feelings."

And you can't fly the Christian flight by your feelings either. Keep your eyes on the instruments: God's Word, the pattern of Christ, the counsel of mature Christian friends, your own best thinking, the outworking of circumstances, and your inner feelings. As much as possible, balance them all together. Put off that childish overdependency on feelings and impressions as the basis for guidance.

Feelings and Good Works

Some people depend on feelings as their motivation for doing good works. John Wesley preached a devastating sermon in which he warned against "the sin of waiting to feel good before you do good." How often we say, "Well, I just didn't feel like doing it." James wrote, "Whoever knows what is right to do and fails to do it, for him it is sin" (James 4:17, RSV). He did not say, "Whoever knows and feels like doing it." Like little kids we so often wait on feelings as the basis of our motivation—"Well, I did it because I felt like it." Or, "I didn't do it because I just didn't feel like it." In a world like we live in today—where on every hand we hear and see Jesus Christ in dire need, when we can see Christ poor and naked and hungry and imprisoned—we don't need to feel some special kind of urge to Christian service and good works.

Paul told the Ephesian Christians that they were not saved by their good works. We love to quote that part, but we need to go just a little further where he said they were saved unto good works (2:8–10). There are so many unhappy, self-centered Christians who could go a long way toward solving their problems and growing up, if they would quit sitting around taking their spiritual temperature, feeling their emotional pulse, and waiting for some good inner feeling to push them out into the stream of God's service.

To wait to feel good before you do good works is a sin. You can begin now to do some of the good works and services that you know need to be done.

10

Childish Concepts of Self and Self-Surrender

I have been crucified with Christ; and it is no longer I who live, but Christ lives in me; and the life which I now live in the flesh I live by faith in the Son of God, who loved me and delivered Himself up for me.

Galatians 2:20

Do you not know that your body is a temple of the Holy Spirit who is in you, whom you have from God, and that you are not your own? For you have been bought with a price; therefore glorify God in your body.

1 Corinthians 6:19–20

WHAT DOES THE Bible mean by the word *self*? What do we mean by self-surrender, or complete consecration, crucifixion of the self, death to self, putting self on the cross and Christ on the throne? These are terms we toss about. Yet understanding of these concepts is central to the Christian life. If there is cloudiness and confusion, if our minds are filled with immature or sub-Christian ideas; a lot of wrong thinking, wrong feeling, and wrong living are sure to follow.

Dag Hammarskjold was perhaps the most famous Secretary General in the history of the United Nations. When his plane went down in Africa it was such a mystery and for awhile was thought to be sabotage. He was killed in an open field on a clear night. No one could figure out why it happened until the map the pilot was going by was found in the wreckage of the plane. The pilot had the map open to the city of Ndolo which is a town in Zaire. But Hammarskjold intended to go to the city of Ndola which is in Zambia. The pilot crashed thinking he had 1,000 feet more to go on the runway. One letter made the difference between life and death. If you have the wrong mental map of self and of self-surrender, your Christian life will surely end in despair and disillusionment. No concept is more important to a mature understanding of what Christ is asking from you.

Let's think together about some false and harmful ideas of self and self-surrender, to see if we need to put these away.

Self-Extinction

As a very zealous, youthful Christian I loved the passage in Galatians that says, "I am crucified with Christ." Oh, I liked that! "It is no longer I who live, but Christ who lives in me." I loved that too. But I did not like the little phrase in-between: "Nevertheless I live" (Galatians 2:20). I didn't consider the phrase quite spiritual enough, until I got to India as a missionary. Then I realized that those three words are most inspired. You see, the Far East tries to solve the problem of the self by getting rid of it. Buddhism says, "Snuff out the candle of self: Nirvana." Hinduism goes at it a little more gently: not self-extinction, but self-absorption into God. The personal, individual selfhood is to be so united with God that it is like a raindrop falling back into the ocean from whence it came, losing its own identity.

"I am crucified with Christ," said Paul, "but I'm still alive. I haven't been destroyed or absorbed or dissolved. I haven't been wiped out." The highest point in the scheme of salvation is when we reach heaven to enjoy fellowship with God throughout eternity. The Christian faith does not have the slightest hint in it that your selfhood or mine will be extinguished when we get there. Forever fix in your mind that your ego comes from God Himself and that selfhood is eternal, imperishable, and indestructible. God does not desire to destroy it. He can fellowship with it and reward it in a heaven; He can isolate it and separate Himself from it in a hell. But it persists. St. Bernard was right when he wrote concerning this essential personhood, "It cannot be burned out, even in hell."

Be careful of falling into error or confusion about self-surrender. "God, take self out of me. God, I want to get to the place where I never think of myself." Such praying is not Christian at all and will mess up your life. This is especially important for young people who are going through the agonies and confusions characteristic of teen years. Adolescence is the age when you are all legs and arms, and falling over yourself. You are like the centipede who in trying to figure out which leg to put in front of the other one, went down in a heap. You are self-conscious, and in your desperation you cry out for consecration and spirituality which will somehow remove from you the intense consciousness of your existence.

Listen, teenager—if God answers that prayer, you are going to be in bad shape! They will call the ambulance because you'll be in a coma. Even at the height of spirituality you never lose the human gift of self-consciousness.

Self-Disparagement

There are Christians who equate self-denial with self-disparagement. They do this because they do not understand the proper place of self-love in the Christian life. They reject self-love because they see it as the very essence of sin. It is dangerous to think of self as something detached and essentially evil.

Jesus said that we should love God with our whole hearts and love our neighbor as we love ourselves. Love for self is as necessary for maturity and wholeness and holiness as is love for God and for other people. Indeed, loving God and loving my neighbor require a measure of self-acceptance and self-love in which I hold my own selfhood in esteem, integrity, identity, and respect.

In the great marriage passage of Ephesians, we read that the measure of a man's love for his wife is his love for himself (5:28–29). Commenting on this chapter, John Wesley wrote: "Self-love is not a sin; it is an indisputable duty." Selfishness is a sin, as is self-centeredness, for these are distortions and perversions of love. Never fall into the trap of thinking that crucifixion of the self, self-denial, or self-surrender mean self-contempt or self-despising. Even the word selflessness is very misleading. The opposite of pride and self-centeredness is not selflessness or self-contempt, but God-centeredness. "I live, yet not I." Yes, my ego is still alive, but it is not a self-centered, self-filled ego. It is a Christ-filled, Christ-centered ego. Don't make self-belittling or selflessness the goal of your Christian life.

St. Augustine said many wonderful things, but he also made some horrendous blunders. It has taken us centuries to get over some of his extremities regarding the body and sex and self. One of those blunders is in *The City of God:* "The difference between the city of the world and the city of God is that the one is characterized by love of self to the contempt of God, and the other (the city of God) is characterized by love of God to the contempt of self." This is very wrong, very unbiblical, and the way many of us live. We think we are pleasing God. We think we are producing the sanctified and holy life through this kind of counterfeit holiness. In reality, we produce a guilt-ridden piety, a joyless self-negation, an unattractive goodness. Instead of delivering us from self-centeredness and pride, self-contempt leads us into a religious self-centeredness and pride.

In his famous letters to Wormwood, that abominable genius Screwtape gives some subtle advice on the matter. Wormwood is on his first assignment. He always refers to the young Christian he is tempting as the patient. Screwtape writes to Wormwood, "You must therefore conceal from the patient the true end of humility. Let him think of it not as self-forgetfulness but as a certain kind of opinion (namely, a low opinion) of his own talents and character" (*The Screwtape Letters,* C. S. Lewis, Macmillan, p. 72).

Another time when Wormwood has tried all forms of temptation and the young Christian is not falling for any of them, Screwtape writes him, "Your patient has become humble; have you drawn his attention to the fact?" (p. 71)

Self-despising is not pleasing to God, and it is not the answer to the problem of pride. It actually increases the problem. Psychologist Karen Horney has said, "Self-hate is pride's inseparable companion, and you can't have one without the other." How often self-incrimination becomes an inverted form of good works, of inner penance which we must do, thinking we are pleasing to God. It is a badge of membership in an elite holy club which prides itself for self-belittling and guilt. So an amazing thing happens: condemnation of self becomes the basis of "a good conscience."

Some of us wouldn't know how to live if we didn't feel guilty; we'd go to pieces from spiritual anxiety. That guilty self becomes the basis of a "good conscience," while a good conscience somehow creates a feeling of guilt. It reminds me of a cartoon I saw. Two convicts in a prison courtyard are whispering about a third. The first convict says to the second, "You know, the thing I can't stand about that guy is his guiltier-than-thou attitude."

"Love your neighbor as you love yourself," said Jesus. Self-love, not selflessness, is the basis of interpersonal relationships. Selflessness between people can turn out to be mere compliance and appeasement. It is often used to rationalize copping-out on the tough, real-life questions of right and wrong. And, of course, selflessness in the hands of a Christian bully can become an exquisite instrument of torture, of spiritual and emotional blackmail. If he can make you feel guilty by saying to you, "You're thinking about yourself," then he can control and manipulate you into doing whatever he wants.

The heart of the Christian life is love, loving God with the whole self and loving others as you love yourself. Don't translate that—"Love your neighbor instead of yourself." "Love your neighbor as you love yourself," Jesus said. This requires not less of a self, but more of a self filled with power and love.

Self-Actualization

Another inadequate answer to self which has come about in recent years through a veritable explosion of OKness psychology is self-actualization. It says, "Accept yourself, express yourself." In this school of psychology, the self does not need to be surrendered, only developed. Perhaps one of the reasons for this solution is that we Christians went to an extreme with our self-despising. While it contains much that is true and helpful, it is not a biblical answer to the problem of the self. Alan Reuter, a Lutheran counselor, has written an interesting book, *Who Says I'm OK?* (Concordia) While Reuter expresses appreciation of the OKness psychology, he reveals its inadequacies and shows how it can become another false god on the market, another means for escaping the true selfhood that God wants. This approach leaves self at the center of your life. It feeds the very disease it is trying to cure, that is, a self which is independent of God and sufficient without Him. It promotes personhood centered not on God, but on self. Such worship of a false god—whether done in a pagan way or in a relatively religious way—does not answer the problem of the self. It may only pamper our childish selfcenteredness and keep us from true maturity in Christ.

Self-Surrender

Any false and immature understanding of the self and self-surrender leaves the person self-sufficient, self-righteous, self-willed, seeking his own glory. In a word, basically unsurrendered. Many a Christian accepts God's sovereignty in every other realm of life except over his inner self. This is often so subtle that only the Holy Spirit can reveal the error. Such a person may be willing to work for God, to pray and to witness. Yes, and even to preach with the tongues of men and angels, to move mountains by faith, to give everything to feed the poor, and even to give his body to be burned and to die as a Christian martyr. The unsurrendered self will go to great lengths to prevent its dethronement. It will rise to heights of sacrificial service. I have seen missionaries travel thousands of miles, crossing many oceans, but fail to take the last step required for self-surrender. That last step is to the cross of Jesus Christ. It was there, says Paul, that when Christ died we were united with Him in the likeness of His death . . . for our old self was crucified with Him (Romans 6:5–6). We will be looking at this more specifically in the next chapter.

It is only when I surrender myself to God, when I allow Him to take center stage of my life, when I put myself under His authority, when I am filled with His love, that I can love Him with my whole self. Only then do I possess the true self-esteem and self-love that enables me to love other people. You cannot reverse these two and come out right. Then the true self can be cultivated, accepted, realized, actualized, and developed to its fullest potential. When God is truly God, then I can truly be who I am. "I've gotta be me," says the song. Sure! But I can't be me until He is truly He. When God is the center, then I can like the me I am, because my self is on-center.

I have to laugh at the philosophers and the psychologists who say that the Christian concept of self-surrender destroys the self, inhibits our manhood or womanhood, prevents self-development, and keeps people from being at their best. The lower I kneel at the feet of Jesus Christ, the taller I stand in my own unique selfhood. Chained to Christ as His bondservant, I become free and for the first time can like who

I am. The self is released from trying to be someone it isn't and was never intended to be. As a result you and I can become what we were meant to be.

"Nevertheless I live," says Paul, "yet it is not I." I'm not destroyed, I'm not extinguished. I'm alive, yes, but better still, Christ now lives in me and the life I live is really His life being lived in me and through me. And now I can say, "Sure, I'm OK, and you're OK."

Many Christians feel that self-surrender will destroy them. Why do they think this? Because of false, immature, and even unchristian ideas of what self-surrender is, ideas which bring fear and hesitation, which keep them from that which gives the greatest joy and fulfillment of life—total surrender to Christ.

One night I preached a sermon entitled, "Unconditional Surrender," and the Holy Spirit gripped the heart of a young man named Ed. He came to the counseling room that week and said, "Doc, that is what I need to do, but I'm afraid." Now Ed was quite an athlete and especially talented in gymnastics. I will never forget his illustration. He said, "I need to surrender; I want to, but I'm afraid. I'll tell you how it feels. It's like I am over in the gym and grab hold of the bar. I'm ready to work out on it when all of a sudden they pull the bar up until it is almost to the ceiling. Way up high, and I'm just hanging on for dear life. The Holy Spirit is saying to me, 'Ed, let go. . . . Surrender. . . . Let go, Ed.' But I'm so far up that when I look down there are clouds below me. And Doc, I can't see where I am going to land." He looked me straight in the eye and continued, "All I ask is that God show me where I am going to land."

I replied, "Ed, that's the catch. Real self-surrender is when you give up your right to yourself. That means you give up the right to ask where you will land. But Ed, you have nothing to worry about because you will land in the arms of love."

But Ed was afraid and hesitant. Though we met and prayed several times, he never really let go. He graduated and I didn't see him for several years. Then one fall during the Homecoming weekend Ed came back to Wilmore. On Sunday morning the church was filled with guests. After the service I went to the back of the church where a long line of alumni wanted to greet their former pastor. They were quickly passing by me when suddenly I recognized Ed. His face was glowing, radiant. He came and shook my hand so warmly and said, "Doc, I just want to tell you one thing: I let go, I let go." He had found out that he didn't need to be afraid. He could let go because he would land in the arms of Perfect Love. And so will you.

O God, we rebuke Screwtape and all of his emissaries for filling our minds with fearful ideas. They tell us that if we really let You take over, You will destroy us, hurt us. O God, rebuke the powers of evil that so many of us struggle with, and help Your children to find the joy and fulfillment of the Christ-centered self. Answer our deepest prayers. In Jesus' name we pray, Amen.

11

The Ultimate Crisis of Life

For if we have become united with Him in the likeness of His death, certainly we shall be also in the likeness of His resurrection, knowing this, that our old self was crucified with Him, that our body of sin might be done away with, that we should no longer be slaves to sin; for he who has died is freed from sin.

Now if we have died with Christ, we believe that we shall also live with Him, knowing that Christ, having been raised from the dead, is never to die again; death no longer is master over Him. For the death that He died, He died to sin, once for all; but the life that He lives, He lives to God.

Even so consider yourselves to be dead to sin, but alive to God in Christ Jesus.

Romans 6:5–11

THE WORD ULTIMATE means something beyond which there is nothing more important or decisive. Self-surrender is the ultimate crisis of human life.

The Ultimate Spiritual Battle

Self-surrender is the ultimate crisis because it represents the ultimate spiritual battle. Everything else in Christian experience is a preamble to this. Everything else is the work of the Holy Spirit in prevenient and wooing grace, paving the way for this great divine/human encounter.

Self-surrender begins in our inheritance, in the home with all of its influences, in the conviction of our sins, the agony of struggling with guilt, the painful attempt to win God's approval by trying to do better and be better by lopping off this sin and that sin, and even in the putting on of religious disciplines. Then comes the realization that we are dependent completely upon grace. Next is the joyous discovery that we don't have to do our moral housecleaning before we come to God, but can come as we are, receive His full and free and absolute forgiveness, and know the joyous experience of conversion, of becoming a new creation.

This is followed by growth in grace, the ups and downs of Christians who, having begun in the Spirit, fall back into the way of the law. Then the desperate attempt to please God, to be all that we think He wants us to be, often with the mistaken notion that following and obeying a holy law can make us holy. And all along, at every step of the way, the Holy Spirit is working with us on the emotional hangups we have been talking about, helping us to put away childish things and grow more and more mature.

All of these important steps are the growing pains through which God "leads His dear children along," until we finally see what the real challenge is. Everything up to this point has been a minor skirmish in comparison to the ultimate battle to which we are being led lovingly, ruthlessly, relentlessly, wooingly but oh, so firmly. We are being taken by the Holy Spirit to the place where we see that the real issue is the surrender of self to the lordship of Jesus Christ. As the Holy Spirit leads us, sometimes gently, sometimes rather roughly, but always lovingly, suddenly the surroundings look familiar. For we see that He has brought us to a spot we recognize, a skull-shaped hill we call Calvary. It is at the cross that the crucifixion of the self-centeredness of my ego is going to take place. And this is the greatest battle of every life.

Jesus made it clear that anyone who does not renounce all that he has cannot be His disciple: "Whoever does not bear his own cross and come after Me, cannot be My disciple" (Luke 14:27, RSV). The words I want you to notice especially are: "Come after Me." I believe this is a far deeper call to commitment and surrender than Jesus' first call, "Come unto Me."

"Come unto Me" is the first step. But it is after disciples come to Jesus that He begins to make things harder for them. Some leaders say to their followers, "I'm going to ask very little of you." Jesus never says that. He tells us to count the cost. He makes His demands more stringent; He ups the price; He winnows and sifts out those who follow Him. He seems afraid of having too many, so He thins out the ranks. He separates the dabblers from the disciples.

The Holy Spirit takes us through this process of self-exposure so that we will see what the real issue is. For our basic sin lies much deeper than the daily sins which are its outward form, deeper than the infirmities and hangups which, though not sinful in themselves, do predispose us to certain sins. The real sin is the unsurrenderedness of the ego. This sin is the root; the sins are the fruit.

It is so subtle, so undiscernible to the naked eye that only the Holy Spirit—through this process and through the Word of God, which is the sharp, two-edged sword, piercing to the innermost depths—can bring us to the place where we see the ultimate battle, namely the need for the crucifixion, the death of self-centeredness.

"I am crucified with Christ: nevertheless I live; yet not I, but Christ liveth in me." Galatians 2:20 is the most self-surrendered verse in the New Testament. But strangely enough, it is also the most self-filled verse in the New Testament. Did you know that there are eight personal pronouns in that one little testimony? "I"—five times. "Me"—three times. It is self-filled and self-surrendered at the same time. Confusing? A contradiction? No, it's the great paradox at the very heart of the Christian life and must be understood if we are to go on to real maturity.

We need to identify the three facets of the ego. The difficulty is that we use the personal pronoun "I" to cover all three of the facets.

"I have been crucified with Christ"—that is one facet of the ego. It needs the death-dealing effects of crucifixion.

"Nevertheless I live"—that is obviously another facet of the ego. It is the selfhood which survives self-crucifixion, a selfhood which is indestructible and eternal. Christ is not at all interested in crucifying or destroying it; He is only interested in liberating it and in developing it to its fullest and highest. This indestructible, imperishable ego will be alive, either in heaven or hell, a billion years from now, and God Himself cannot destroy it. He wanted it for His eternal fellowship!

"Yet," says Paul, "not I, but Christ lives in me." That's the answer: the Christ-filled, the Christ-possessed, Christ-centered ego.

The first facet of the ego is the one which is fallen, diseased, perverted, and twisted. It always turns in on itself and raises its will. It prevents my true self from reaching its highest potential and being what God planned for it to be. This facet of the ego with its malignant self-centeredness and self-sufficiency needs to die. We talk about Custer's last stand, which was a bloody battle. The crucifixion of self is everyone's last stand because it is the ultimate battle.

It may take a long time to travel from conversion to self-surrender. One of the mistakes in our philosophy of holiness and sanctification is to ask people to do something that is psychologically and emotionally impossible: namely, to move too quickly from conversion to self-surrender. It seems that God has to bring most of us through a series of steps until we arrive at total desperation. And only God can do that for us. No preacher, no amount of emotional manipulation can do this. There is a temptation to subject new Christians to spiritual pressure until they say, "Yes, it's done." But by so doing, we turn them into spiritual phonies. Some people have been so badly damaged they need healing before there is a real self to surrender. Not everyone is ready for the message of self-surrender at the same time. We need to leave people in the hands of the Spirit who prepares them for the ultimate crisis.

It took me four years to get from "here to there." In the battlefield of my spiritual life where the Holy Spirit led me deeper and deeper, I surrendered many attachments, many relationships, many ambitions. I was healed of many hangups and damaged emotions. I answered the call to preach and to go to the mission field. But I hung on to myself until the Spirit in His gracious work, largely through the reading of Oswald Chambers' book, *My Utmost for His Highest*, took the veil from my eyes. One lonely summer, as a student at Asbury College I saw it, but I didn't realize what had happened until three weeks later. So don't give me that stuff about "if it happens to you, you'll always know it at the time." That isn't so. There are a lot of things on the market that just ain't so! I got in through the back window and didn't know it. But one miserable July night on the third floor of Morrison dormitory, I saw my self as I never had before: I saw all of its loathsomeness, its deceptiveness, its rebelliousness.

You see, before my conversion I felt convicted as a guilty criminal who had broken God's laws. But now I felt a different conviction. It was not that I was breaking God's laws. Rather, it was as if I were guilty of treason against the state, that I had within me an unyielded being that questioned the very right and rulership of God Himself. One statement of Chambers kept hammering at my heart: "Total surrender is when you give up your right to yourself." Isn't it amazing! Oswald Chambers said that a quarter of a century before J. B. Phillips translated the New Testament and rendered Jesus' command in Mark 8:34 like this: "If anyone wants to follow in My footsteps, he must give up all right to himself, take up his cross and follow Me."

Surrender is the ultimate crisis because it is the ultimate battle. There are many different figures of speech that may help you at this point. You may picture your heart as a house with many rooms. This is an act whereby you turn over to Christ, room by room, every portion of your personality, particularly the control room, the throne room, the ruling room. Or you may picture the various areas of your life where you need to surrender to God's will—your plans, ambitions, sex life, romance, marriage, leisure, and choice of a life's vocation.

Or picture your own image of who you are, and what you think other people think about you, your name, your work, and your spiritual reputation. I believe that was the crux of my battle. You see, I wanted people to think I was "spiritual." I wasn't particularly interested in worldly things, so they weren't hard to give up. But I did want people to think I was spiritual, and that was a hard battle. I had to take my spiritual reputation and hand it over to Christ.

What was the first step in the *kenosis*, the self-emptying and the self-surrender of Jesus? He, "who, being in the form of God, thought it not robbery to be equal with God made Himself of no reputation" (Philippians 2:6–7). He emptied Himself. That was the first step. Have you ever given your spiritual reputation over to Christ? We live in such bondage to other people because we want them to think we are spiritual. This leads to neurosis in the Christian life and to introspection and slavery.

Some people mistakenly illustrate self-surrender this way—You take a blank sheet of paper and on it write a long list of things you want. "Lord, give me this, give me that, give me the other." It is like a grocery shopping list. Then you sign your name and hand it over to God saying, "Lord, I surrender. Take my life and let it be."

But that is not what surrender is all about, so let's start over. Take the blank sheet of paper and sign your name at the bottom. Now hand it to God and say, "Lord, You fill it in. And whatever You fill in, my name remains signed at the bottom forever."

The All-Inclusive Crisis

Self-surrender is the ultimate crisis because it is the all-inclusive crisis, encompassing all other crises of life. Dr. Henry Clay Morrison used to say in his down-to-earth way, "When you come to the altar for consecration, you are bringing two bundles with you: one bundle is the 'known' of your life, and the other is the 'unknown.' In full consecration you put them both on the altar."

This causes a lot of confusion and anxiety, particularly among young people. Self-surrender is both a definite crisis and a never-ending process. When we talk about self-surrender we are talking about a commitment of your will to the lordship of Christ. Now you can do that at any given time, provided you are ready. If the Holy Spirit has "ripened" you, it is your *kairos* time. If it is your *kairos* time, it is God's time.

When you surrender, what are you giving? Your will. You are surrendering your willingness to Christ, but the content of that will is something that you will fill in from now on throughout your life. Long ago I realized that if I didn't make it very clear, in asking Christians to surrender, I was really asking them to do something that was psychologically impossible, because you cannot surrender to God something of which you are not aware. Let's put it positively: you can only surrender to God that which you first acknowledge to yourself. You can surrender your willingness to God, you can make a total surrender of your right to yourself, you can make a full commitment to surrender. But you won't actually be surrendering anything specific until you face some particular issue of the will in a real life situation. And that is the confusing part. You may make a total surrender to the lordship of Christ, and then come to something two weeks later where there will be a struggle between your emotions and your will. Right away Screwtape gets on your shoulder and says, "Ah, huh! You really didn't surrender a couple of weeks ago in church, did you!" And unless we have a mature mind, we will be prone to fall for that deception.

God said to the children of Israel, "All of Canaan is yours, but you must possess it. It is yours provided you put the soles of your feet upon it" (Joshua 1:3). You may fully surrender your willingness to

God's will, but all that you are doing is renouncing your right to your will. You are saying, "God, I will to choose Your will in every situation in my life." You surrender your right to make your choices on the basis of what you would like, and you commit yourself to find and follow, discover and do God's will. Yes, that is a crisis, but it also has to become a daily process, because we actually surrender concrete things and situations only as they come up into our awareness.

When you make this full surrender you are promising, "God, my will is Yours," which is really saying, "Now, God, when anything comes up, I will choose what You choose." But, you see, you have not yet surrendered anything, you have not yet actually chosen anything. And when you do come down to actualizing it, you may encounter a struggle between your emotions and the commitment you once made. Complete surrender doesn't computerize you into automatic, robot-like choices.

I don't know of a better illustration of this than Jesus' great struggle in the Garden of Gethsemane. Most people do not take a profound look at that experience. It was a terrific struggle during which Jesus fell on the ground three times in agony. What was the struggle all about? Had not Jesus long ago made a total surrender of His life? Was not Jesus' will in absolute agreement with His Father's will? Of course. Had He not said all of His life, "My food is God's will; My will is God's will; My joy is to do the will of My Father"? Yes, there is no question about the depth of Jesus' total surrender to and alignment with the Father's will. But there was still a profound struggle in the Garden between Jesus' emotions and His will. Every surrendered Christian knows what that means. The most sanctified saint has been through this and may go through it again tomorrow. I find it interesting that Jesus accepted His emotional struggle without any shame! And the New Testament writers make no effort to cover or soften it.

So let's not give young Christians the false idea that surrender is something you do once for all. You may make the commitment of intention once for all. You may say, "Not my will, but Yours be done," and mean it for the rest of your life. But to actualize this, to make it real in concrete situations is a lifetime process. It is something you get better at as you mature in the Spirit-filled life. All of us would live saner, safer, sweeter, more effective lives if we could honestly admit to ourselves and to God that we, like Jesus, experience a struggle at times between our emotions and our will.

A young lady who came to me for counseling was deeply in love. But she was beginning to realize that, as much as she loved the young man, he was not the right one for her because of some genuine spiritual differences that she saw as insurmountable. So she wrote him a letter, they talked about it, and then she broke it off. Some days later she came to me in tears, depressed, all torn up. What was wrong? Well, she had some well-meaning friends who assured her that there must be something wrong with her spiritually or she wouldn't be having such a struggle. She was crying a lot, couldn't do her work, and wasn't concentrating on her studies. She knew she had done the right thing and didn't have the slightest intention of going back on her decision, but her feelings were giving her a rough time. Instead of helping her bear the burden, her well-intentioned but misinformed friends had added a burden of spiritual guilt to her already overburdened heart. I said to her, "Honey, of course, you can cry. Of course, you are feeling blue. Of course, you are struggling. But tell me, what is the direction of your will?" She replied at once, "That hasn't changed, because I know what I must do." We opened the New Testament and read together the story of Christ's struggle in the Garden of Gethsemane. She saw the point. Her commitment to God's will was firm and steady. But her emotions were battered and putting up a struggle. Someone has rightly said, "Your will can go ahead by express, but your emotions sometimes travel by slow freight."

When I am in conflict, the best thing I can do is to take my feelings to God in ruthless honesty and tell Him what they really are. Then I reaffirm the full surrender I made many years ago and apply it to this specific situation.

You can surrender your will. You can make the all-out surrender now if He has readied you for it. This is the great battle, and the great crisis. But it is not the end. Rather, it is an open end, in which you begin a lifetime process of specific surrenders to the Lord.

The Essential Secret of Life

Self-surrender is the ultimate crisis because it is the essential secret of life itself. It is the means of finding my true self, of becoming what God planned for me, of discovering my personal uniqueness. Self-surrender is the death which is followed by resurrection. It is a paradox, for if you lose your life, you will save it; but if you try to save it, you will lose it. The *New English Bible* translates Mark 8:34–37 this way: "Anyone who wishes to be a follower of Mine must leave self behind; he must take up his cross, and come with Me. . . . What does a man gain by winning the whole world at the cost of his true self? What can he give to buy that self back?"

We give up our self-centered and twisted selves to find our true selves. The aim of God in self-surrender is not the destruction of self; it is the birth and the growth of the true self He intended you to be.

In his book, *How You Can Find Happiness,* Sam Shoemaker gives this testimony:

> I can well remember a time in my life, long after my first decisive spiritual experience, when I was facing the need to take another big step forward. I could almost see my "self" shrinking out of sight under the withering effects of an honest facing of my faults, and, like Alice in Wonderland when she was shrinking, I wondered whether I wouldn't go out like a light if this process went on! But this was not the real case: when I let go deeply inside, my true "self" was never more fulfilled and expressed, and I realized that all this fanfare of resistance and self-will is the protective device of the ego to keep the true "self" from emerging and being victorious. This fear of giving up, of giving in, is a contrivance of the ego. As Fenelon said, "If we looked carefully into ourselves, we should find some secret place where we hide what we think we are not obliged to sacrifice to God." But until that false ego dies, the true self cannot live. And the death of an ego is the greatest of all human crises (Dutton, pp. 91–92).

Self-surrender is the ultimate crisis because it is the answer to life. This self dies in order to truly live. This captive self surrenders not to be destroyed, annihilated, or absorbed, but to be liberated, to be its true and best self. George Matheson's great hymn captures these truths most beautifully.

Make Me a Captive, Lord

Make me a captive, Lord, and then I shall be free;
Force me to render up my sword, and I shall conqueror be.
I sink in life's alarms when by myself I stand;
Imprison me within Thine arms, and strong shall be my hand.

My heart is weak and poor until it master find;
It has no spring of action sure, it varies with the wind.
It cannot freely move till Thou has wrought its chain;
Enslave it with Thy matchless love, and deathless it shall reign.
My will is not my own till Thou hast made it Thine;
If it would reach a monarch's throne, it must its crown resign;
It only stands unbent, amid the clashing strife,
When on Thy bosom it has leant and found in Thee its life. Amen.

12

Reprogramming Grace

IN THE PRECEDING chapters we have dealt with the many different ways the inner child of the past manifests itself and interferes with our adult lives. We have seen that this growing up procedure requires us to *katargeo* that child in several areas of our lives. There are powerful childhood and teenage memories which need to be healed. There are subtle childish acts of concealment and defense which need to be unmasked. There are unhealthy childish complexes and compulsions that need to be broken. There are unrealistic mottoes whose dictatorial power over us needs to be challenged. There are unruly feelings which need to be saddled, and shackled feelings which need to be freed. There are infantile lies which need to be rebuked, babyish confusions which need to be cleared, and naive concepts which need to be straightened out.

This process requires both negative and positive efforts. As we *katargeo* the negative behaviors, we must be sure that mature, positive feelings, understandings, concepts, and actions take their place. That's why this process requires the whole person in every aspect of personality—thought, emotion, will, and behavior. It requires growing up in our personal relationships—with ourselves, others, and God.

Most of us would agree that the greatest problem in our lives is ourselves. As Samuel Hoffenstein put it, "The trouble with me is that everywhere I go, *I* go too, and that spoils everything!"

A little boy came in from school one day and asked his mother, "Mama, how do wars get started?"

She replied, "Well, if you're talking about the last war, it got started when Germany attacked Belgium."

Dad, who had been buried in the evening newspaper, came up for air and said, "No, Son, it wasn't Belgium; it was when Germany attacked Poland."

But the mother insisted, "No, I'm sure I remember correctly; it was Belgium."

"Now what do you know about it?" corrected the father. "You didn't go to college. I did, and I minored in world history. I tell you the war began when the Germans attacked Poland."

It wasn't very long until the parents were arguing heatedly; soon they were shouting at each other. The little boy tugged at his mother and she snapped at him, "Well, what do you want?" He said, "That's OK, Mama. Now I think I know how wars get started."

From within that hidden child in all of us some incredibly immature behavior can emerge. So much of what we are is rooted in the early developmental years of our lives. This is not to deny the biblical fact of original sin and the fallenness of our natures. Nor is it to belittle our own sins, in which "we have each turned to our own willful ways" (Isaiah 53:6). But it is to remind us that it is all further complicated by a vast range of childish things which could be classed more as infirmities and cripplings—weaknesses which predispose us toward certain kinds of sins, limitations which make us more liable to certain kinds of temptations.

Responsibility

Some years ago I saw an ad which claimed that a certain lawn food was supposed to help the grass grow thicker and healthier. It said, "The shoots grow down before they grow up, and what they find to root in will determine how they grow up." Our adult lives are deeply rooted in our childhood/teenage years and deeply affected by them. I was fascinated by a magazine article written about a well-known college football player which stressed this:

You could say that we become what we are, not so much in the
sanctuary of the womb or the groves of academe, but in that
Elysian drive-in joint known as High School. . . . It is there that
we are nurtured, our personalities shaped, our bodies structured,
our habits and moods and values all having jockeyed for position in the chaotic halls of puberty. High School is enduring. . . .
No one is completely delivered from the days of High School"
(*Sports Illustrated,* August 31, 1981, p. 38).

Thank God his conclusion is not true. We can be delivered from the
scars and damages and lies of our early years. Thank God His redeeming grace can break the chains of our sinful past, and His reprogramming grace can dissolve the compulsions of our wrongly computer-
ized past.

I heard a beautiful testimony from one of the converts in a Bill Glass
Prison Crusade in the South. He was a huge man with his arm in a
sling. They told us he was known as one of the tough guys of the
prison. He accepted Christ as his Saviour on the first night of the crusade. A few days later he said, "You know, something's happening to
me. I don't really understand it and I sure can't explain it. I got up
this morning and I didn't scream and holler like I usually do. Even
my cellmates commented about it. The only way I can describe it is
it's like someone took the old tape which had been playing in my mind
since I was a kid and put a new tape in and it's playing new talk and
new music."

This was an amazing insight for a comparatively uneducated person. He was already beginning to experience the renewing and reprogramming process. Sometime later he discovered another important
factor and added, "But you know, I've got to keep working on it and
see to it that the right tapes are playing."

He had discovered his responsibility. Just in case anyone has gotten the wrong idea from anything we've said—the reason we try to
discover damages from the past is not to blame someone else. Rather,
it is to clarify our insights and outline the real issues, so that we can
direct our prayers and efforts to the right places

It is amazing to what lengths some people will go to avoid their own
responsibility. In March 1978 a Colorado man brought a "malparenting
suit" against his mother and father. He sued them for $300,000 for
"lousing up his life," claiming they had intentionally done a terrible

job of parenting and had made him what he was. The judge dismissed the suit saying there must be a "statute of limitations" on parenting and a time when an adult takes responsibility for his own life. If not, then next will come suits against brothers, sisters, teachers, and even friends.

Jesus had an amazing way of cutting through all excuses and attempts to scapegoat others. He always made people face up to their responsibility. If we were all honest we would agree that the problem is really in ourselves. Just as the fingers and the thumb are rooted in the palm of the hand, so our problems are rooted in the self. And this self needs three spiritual experiences to come into wholeness: forgiveness, healing, and surrender.

The Forgiven Self

When an airplane crashes, a lot of attention is focused on the "little black box." This is the crashproof, fireproof, waterproof steel box which contains the recording of everything the pilots said and did just prior to the accident. When the investigators get that then they are able to make an accurate determination of who or what was at fault.

In a sense God has built into every one of us a device similar to the flight recorder. Our memories contain the unerring and unerasable record of our every word and action. Conscience is a part of this—so many of us constantly struggle with a sense of unresolved guilt. Sometimes it is a mixture of real guilt and childish pseudoguilt. In any case we are like the psalmist who said, "My sin is ever before me." Note, he did not say "was." He put it in the present tense. We say the trouble is our past, but the real trouble is that the past is not in the past. It is in the present and we wear it around our necks like a chain.

If it is true that forgiveness is the most therapeutic fact in all of life, then guilt must be the most destructive. We are simply not built for it, so we automatically try to atone for it, to get rid of it somehow. Often we carry it around in our bodies and minds and it affects our entire personality. Or we put it into a bag and dump it onto someone else.

There is only one place we can put our guilt to find a true sense of forgiveness—on the back of the crucified Christ. Isaiah 53:6 says, "All of us like sheep have gone astray. Each of us has turned to his own way. But the Lord has caused the iniquity of us all to fall on Him."

And 1 Peter 2:24 declares that "He Himself bore our sins in His body on the cross." We do not have to bear guilt and condemnation any longer. But there will be no moving away from childish burdens of guilt and moving into mature freedom and peace until we can *katargeo* our guilty and unforgiven selves.

I have written much about the healing of the memories. Not long ago I was suddenly struck with the thought that God too has had a healing of His memories. In one sense, the Cross involves the mystery of God's memory. There are several places in Scripture which imply that God no longer remembers our sins against us: "Do not remember the sins of my youth or my transgressions" (Psalm 25:7), and "Do not remember the iniquities of our forefathers against us" (79:8).

In commenting on this remarkable fact, Corrie ten Boom puts it in her own inimitable way, "When God forgives He forgets. He buries our sins in the sea and puts a sign on the bank saying, 'No Fishing Allowed.'" The most helpful word I ever heard on this was from a young man who said every time he started to pray, he would remind God of a certain failure in his past. One day when he started to do this it was as though God whispered to him, "My son, enough of that. Stop reminding Me of that sin. I distinctly remember forgetting it a long time ago!"

The first step toward Christian adulthood is to be done with any subtle form of inner penance and self-condemnation for already forgiven and forgotten sins. The guilty self needs to become the forgiven self.

The Healed Self

There is a figure of speech we often use to express the idea of a wrong response to something: "That's like waving a red flag in a bull's face." Whenever a bull sees the color red he gets furiously angry. This is why the Spanish matadors use red cloaks in their bullfights. Whenever the bull sees the red, he automatically lowers his head, paws at the ground with his feet, and charges.

Our personalities are something like that, and one way to look at our childish responses is to consider them as various colored flags of life. Jesus must have realized this basic principle when He warned His disciples, "Keep watching and praying, that you may not enter into temptation; the spirit is willing, but the flesh is weak" (Matthew 26:41). He recognized that every person has his own set of predispositions. Note that word: *pre*—prior, beforehand—and *disposition*. Predispositions are those things within a person which are prior to his disposition, and which push it in a certain direction. These are the person's own private set of flags which, when waved before him, trigger off certain responses. These unchristianized complexes and unhealthy pushes from the past keep dragging him back and pulling him down. In spite of repenting and reading, pleading and praying, his childish responses keep playing the same old record.

One Sunday when we were serving Communion, the crowd was unusually large and it seemed to be taking far more time than normal. The longer it took, the more upset I got. I became overanxious and began to perspire. All of a sudden I saw myself as I really was and said, "This is utterly ridiculous. Here I am, standing here in my holy robe at the altar of the church, getting flustered because we are going to be a few minutes late." And then I saw something else. I saw myself as a young boy with my schedule-maniac grandmother. She was the kind who had to be at the train station forty-five minutes ahead of schedule just to be on time. I could almost hear her prodding me, "Hurry up, David. What's taking you so long? Hurry up, or we'll be late." Then I prayed silently, "Lord, set me free from this. I do this every time something makes the service run over a few minutes, and I'm tired of letting that flustered little boy run my life." I was able to relax and can say that it has not troubled me since. Up to then a tight schedule was like waving a red flag in my face—it produced in me a response of hurried overanxiety. But what about you?

• Red Flags of Resentment. When your husband or wife, child or friend says or does a certain thing, is there an immediate negative response of resentment? If so, deep down within you a red flag has been waved. The place you experience this most strongly is in the closeness of marriage and the home. Someone has described these predispositions as the "furniture of marriage"— the basic personality equipment and responses people bring into marriage. It can be as simple as a wife saying, "Honey, would you please take out the garbage?" The red flag has been waved and the bull—I mean, the husband—roars and charges. Or the husband cautions his wife about the grocery bill and she bristles, remembering her penny-pinching childhood.

• Yellow Flags of Fear. We sometimes say of a person, "He's yellow," meaning he is afraid or cowardly. Fear can cause some powerful and paralyzing reactions. The Bible points out the three greatest fears.

First is the fear represented by Adam after his sin, recorded in Genesis 3:8–10. When God asked Adam where he was, he answered from his hiding place behind a tree, "I was afraid and I went and hid myself." Adam was afraid that when God found out what he had done and who he really was, he would not be accepted. In Adam's case he had experienced the purest kind of unconditional love. His fear came from guilt and self-accusation.

Today we often see this fear in people who have experienced a highly conditional love. Whatever the source, guilt or inadequate love, this is a very deep-seated fear—"If I am known, known for who I really am, I will not be loved or accepted." The answer to this fear is found in God's great promise, "For God hath not given us a spirit of fear, but of . . . love" (2 Timothy 1:7, kjv).

God's unconditional love and grace, which always accept us where we are today, are the answer to this fear of rejection.

Kathy was struggling with both resentment and fear when she came for help. She found it hard to understand acceptance and affirmation. There was always the fear she would be rejected, especially by men. She remembered many times when her father had turned her away: he never had time for her, never listened to her. Once she had seen a wall plaque in a store with some loving sentiments on it. She saved up her money and gave it to her dad. He looked at it and said rather gruffly, "We've got enough junk lying around the house now." She said she remembered something being turned off inside her that day. Later, when her father mellowed and wanted to be more understanding and affectionate she was still angry and afraid. It had affected her relationships with people and with God. Gradually she learned to forgive and to accept affirmation and love. Through our counseling and the friendship of a loving Christian family, she came to understand the "Daddyness" of God. As she shared and let herself be known, she realized she was accepted and loved.

Another fear is the one expressed by the one-talented man in Jesus' parable (Matthew 25:14–30). His was the common fear of not being useful in life. He buried his one talent because he was afraid the Master would be harsh and overdemanding. This kind of fear troubles many who were brought up on the Measure Up philosophy of life. They see God and people as asking them to do too much and to be too much—more than they are capable of. "But God has not given us a spirit of fear, but of . . . power." God never asks of us what He will not supply. "The One who calls you is faithful and He will do it" (1 Thessalonians 5:24, NIV). As we have heard so often, "It is not our ability but our availability."

There is a fear which Job expressed: "For what I fear comes upon me and what I dread befalls me. I am not at ease, nor am I quiet, and I am not at rest, but turmoil comes" (3:25–26). This is the fear that I will not be adequate, I will not be able to cope with life. So many talk to me about the fear that they will have a nervous breakdown as their mother or father did. Or they are afraid to marry because their marriage may end up in divorce. So many people today fear that they will reproduce the tragedies and traumas of their homes. Again the Word comes to the rescue. "For God has not given us a spirit of timidity but of power and love and discipline." God is in the business of breaking vicious cycles. He is the God who specializes in the new start. Not just the second chance, but the first chance—the chance to start a whole new positive cycle of love and goodness. He is in the business of tearing down ancient yellow flags of fear.

• Black Flags of Abuse. So many people have the black or at least gray incidents of life which leave them feeling soiled, dirty, and ashamed. These may have happened during the sensitive childhood years, the stormy years of pubescence and adolescence, or the impressionable years of young adulthood. They involve the area of sexual experiences. It is difficult to say whether this kind of tragic and traumatic experience is on the increase, or if it is just being talked about more openly. My personal opinion is that sexual abuses are definitely increasing, because of the sexual wilderness in which we live, where there are so few moral fences.

My files are filled with letters from people who have come for help and liberation from sexual experiences which have left deep scars so that they have not been able to respond naturally and normally during courtship and then in the intimacies of marriage. But these are also some of the most joyous and exciting letters of deliverance, cleansing, and healing. A woman freed from the binding chains of a lesbian relationship wrote:

At this point I am just waiting on God and His direction. I feel as though a malignant tumor has been removed from the center of my being and I am very restful and quiet. At the same time I feel a sense of excitement and anticipation. It is as though Jesus is reaching down inside of me and gently pulling out pieces of myself to show me what is there. . . . Some things I know have been turned over to Him. Others have been healed and where I used to feel sick I now feel whole. He is teaching me who I can be in Him.

Many subsequent years of happy married life confirm the depth of her healing.

My favorite letter is from Irene. I had spent many hours with her when she was a student in college, which led to a long session of prayer for the healing of those scalding and sordid memories of sexual abuse by her own father. I didn't hear from her for many years and then came a long letter. Her father had been taken seriously ill and had asked to see her before he died. She made the trip in fear and trepidation.

I wasn't sure how I would feel about Daddy—whether my emotions had really been healed as I trusted they were, or whether when coming into close physical proximity I would still feel that wave of nausea and all the words of love and concern, even though they came from my heart, would have to be forced through my lips. . . .

The two weeks I was there with Mom and Dad were fantastic. I could almost feel the Lord hugging me close to Him, with His arms around me, guiding everything I said and did! It was a beautiful, unforgettable experience that I praise the Lord for. I wouldn't have missed it for anything! I was filled with His special joy and peace. Outside of Christ I would have been a nervous wreck and no help to anyone.

When I saw Daddy there seemed to be an instant rapport and understanding between us, and with honest and joyful love I threw my arms around his frail, thin body, kissed him and told him I loved him. He had tears streaming down his face. He knew and I knew that everything in the past was forgiven and washed in the blood of the Lamb. There was healing and wholeness and unspoken understanding. My heart soared! The healing and love for which I had trusted the Lord so long ago was mine, not just when I was far enough away from the problem to be able to accept it in theory, but right there in Daddy's arms. I wanted to call you right away to share it all with you, but I wouldn't have been able to explain the call to Mama, so I just promised to write you.

She then went on to describe the privilege of helping lead her father to a personal experience of Christ in his final weeks of life and their fellowship together.

The White Flag of Surrender

Paul reminds us that God has given us weapons of warfare which are strong enough for "the destruction of fortresses." For we are "destroying speculation and every lofty thing raised up against the knowledge of God, and we are taking every thought captive to the obedience of Christ" (2 Corinthians 10:4–5). The Final sign of the capture of a fortress is when the enemy flag is torn down.

One of the most exciting and interesting experiences of our missionary career was to witness the transfer of power from Britain to India. We gathered with thousands on August 15, 1947 to watch as the British flag (the Union Jack) was slowly lowered and the tricolor flag of the newly independent India was hoisted in its place. The local police band added a touch of humor by playing "London Bridge Is Falling Down!" In spite of the musical selection, it was an awesome and exciting hour.

But I have had an even greater privilege—of being with hundreds of people when, through the wisdom and the power of God, ancient strongholds of childishness, infirmity, and immaturity were pulled down and the Christian flag raised up.

But before this could happen there was always a series of struggles. These took many forms which involved all parts of the total personality—mind, emotion, and will. There were all kinds of major and minor skirmishes, in which childish things were done away with. Ultimately there came the decisive battle when the full surrender was made, when the defeated and oft-times battered self ran up the white flag of unconditional surrender. Then the Christian flag was hoisted and Christ could claim full lordship over His own.

Have you ever noticed what the Christian flag really is? It is simply a clean white flag with the cross imprinted on a small section of blue. It is the emblem of the conquering Christ implanted on the sign of our surrender.

A man was once asked, "Sir, are you a Christian?" He was thoughtful for a few moments and then replied, "Yes—in spots." My prayer is that you will allow the Holy Spirit to make you a spotless and mature child of God.

HEALING
OF
MEMORIES

Contents

To my many counselees
who honored me with their trust,
enriched me by their sharing,
and taught me most of what I know

Preface

about the miracle of inner healing.

MEMORIES ARE NOT simply mental pictures of the past. Rather, they are present experiences of the total person . . . feelings, concepts, attitudes, and behavior patterns. Thus they tend to make us repeat those actions which accompany the pictures on the screen of our minds.

This is the way the Bible speaks of memory when it urges God's people to call something to remembrance. Scripture never compartmentalizes us into physical, mental, and spiritual beings, but emphasizes the life of the whole person.

The real tragedy of hurtful memories is not simply the emotional pain they bring or the powerful push from the past we feel within us. Rather, it is because of the pain and the push, we learn wrong ways of relating to people and coping with life. In time, these become our very personality patterns—our way of life.

Time alone cannot heal the memories of experiences so painful they have been pushed out of our conscious minds. They require a special kind of spiritual therapy. This includes a period of counseling and preparation, a session of deep healing prayer, and a time of follow-up for relearning.

Healing of Memories is for lay people who want to be free of painful memories which affect present behavior and Christian growth. It is also for professionals who want to help others be free of the tyranny of the past.

David A. Seamands
Wilmore, Kentucky

1

The Mystery of Memory

MITZI WAS EXCITED. "It's all beginning to make sense—the pieces are fitting together. At least now I understand *where* I need help and *what* I need to be praying about. And there's hope—no, better than that—Harry and I *know* there's healing ahead and that's making such a big difference in everything."

I couldn't keep from liking this fine young couple—both so attractive and intelligent, obviously deeply in love with one another, and strongly committed to the highest ideals of a Christian marriage. But like so many others, they had discovered from the very start that they couldn't seem to keep from hurting and being hurt by each other. As we counseled together, it became clear that the heart of the problem was Mitzi's hypersensitivity and her unrealistic expectations. Some people have been described as "accidents waiting to happen." It seemed that Mitzi was one deep reservoir of pain waiting to be tapped into. All her life, pastors and teachers had told her to just forget the past, claim victory in Christ, and develop new skills for coping with the present and future.

So Mitzi was surprised when I encouraged her not only to become aware of the painful memories but even to write them down so she could share them with me and her husband. She did this conscientiously and prayerfully.

Now we both felt the time was ripe and so had scheduled the in-depth healing prayer session. One by one, Mitzi visualized before the Lord some of her most hurtful and humiliating childhood and teenage experiences. As we prayed, our imaginations were literally "back there" in time. She was not simply remembering the past. She was reliving and refeeling incidents, often in remarkable detail, *as if she were actually there now*. Although it was a struggle, Mitzi was forgiving the many people who had hurt her; and in turn, she was receiving God's forgiveness for her long-held resentments against them.

When, during the prayer time there was a long unexpected pause, I gently suggested that if the Spirit was showing her something new, she should go ahead and share it with the Lord. The tone of her voice became that of a little child as she began her prayer, "Dear Jesus," and told Him something she had not remembered for many years. She was about four years old and, together with her family, was visiting her grandmother. Grandma had woven a tiny blanket for her doll. Mitzi was a painfully shy child. It was almost impossible for her to even say "hello" "hi" or "thank you" to anyone. When Grandma gave her the blanket, her parents said, "Isn't that nice of Grandma to work so hard and make such a pretty blanket for your dolly? Now Mitzi, tell her thank you." Mitzi whimpered out her childish prayer, "O Jesus, You know how badly I wanted to say thanks to Grandma, but there was a big lump in my throat and I just couldn't say it. Dear Jesus, I tried so hard, but it wouldn't come out."

Now Mitzi shook with sobs. I tried to comfort her, asked her to imagine herself sitting on Jesus' lap, like the children in the Bible. This gave her the necessary encouragement to go on. The deepest hurt was yet to come. "My little sister was there and said she wanted the blanket. So Mother and Dad told me if I didn't say thank you, they'd give it to her. And when I couldn't say it, they did. They gave it to Patti! *O Jesus, You know how much I wanted to say it. But no one understood, no one cared. It's not fair, it's not fair!*"

As we continued praying, Mitzi saw how much this and other similar experiences had influenced her life. She had allowed deep bitterness to enter her heart. She had carried it against her parents and her sister. Now it had become the pattern of her life. Whenever she sensed injustice or misunderstanding, she became tongue-tied, filled with bitterness, and unable to communicate. Thus she could never resolve problems. In subsequent sessions, we worked together to help her learn new ways of openness with Harry and with other people. To this day, Mitzi insists that that time of healing prayer was the turning point of her life.

What happened to Mitzi and the many others we shall be describing? They had a deep experience of Christ which brought about the healing of festering memories which had been poisoning their inner lives and their outer relationships with others. This experience is what many of us call the healing of memories and what this book is all about. But before we go further, I want us to take a general look at the subject of memory itself, as seen by modern science and in the Scriptures.

Memory in Scripture

The Bible deals with the awesome power of memory in the same way it does many other concepts—with very little description or theoretical discussion. In a complete concordance of the Scriptures, you will find the noun *memory* listed less than half a dozen times. When a memory becomes something more concrete, like a *memorial,* it jumps up to twenty-five references. But when it becomes a verb as *to remember,* or *call to mind a remembrance,* then there are over 250 such references. About seventy-five of them refer to God and His memory. Many of them are requests for God to remember something—His covenants, His promises, or His people. Or they are requests for Him *not* to remember something—sins, failures, and the like. The remaining 175 describe the memory or the forgetfulness of people. Among these are many commands to remember or not to remember certain important matters.

In Scripture, memory is considered one of the most important aspects of both God's mind and ours. It is central to God's nature as well as to forgiveness, salvation, and righteous living. God's ability to remember or not remember is a part of the divine mind or knowledge which filled the biblical writers with awe. Since we have been created in the divine image, we too have this ability. Though ours is limited, the biblical writers considered this human facility a reason for wonder and praise.

Take, for example, Psalm 139. While the awestruck psalmist begins by contemplating the vastness of God's mind and His ability to know and remember everything, he soon switches over to himself. He is amazed at how the Creator has made him. "Such knowledge is too wonderful for me, too lofty for me to attain. . . . I praise You because I am fearfully and wonderfully made; Your works are wonderful, I know that full well" (Psalm 139:6, 14, NIV).

How amazingly accurate God's Word is. For to this very day, the most brilliant scientists, doctors, and psychologists are hard-pressed even to formulate theories on memory. This, in spite of the fact that it is the basis of almost everything we do in life.

The Incredible Giant

What is this mysterious process we call memory? How are we able to recall mental pictures of places and people we experienced years ago? Our immediate answer is that the past is all stored somewhere in the brain. But what we've done is to answer one mystery with another! For in spite of great advances in research during the last fifty years, the brain remains the most unexplainable part of our human equipment. When the *Reader's Digest* published its famous series on the various parts and functions of the body, it began with the brain. It classified it, along with the heart and lungs, as *one* of the giants of the body. We now know it is *the* giant; for while you can be kept alive by an artificial heart and lungs, there is no substitute for the brain. The legal definition of death is when brain activity ceases. There are times when the brain's activities slow down and relax, but they never stop as long as we're alive.

The brain itself is about three pounds of "messy substance shut in a dark warm place—a pinkish-gray mass, moist and rubbery to the touch, about the size of a soft ball" (*Our Human Body*, the Reader's Digest Association, p. 99). Perched like a flower on top of a slender stalk—the spinal cord—it is connected by the finest fibers to every nook and cranny of our bodies, from the roots of our hair and teeth to the tips of our fingers and toes. It is the center of the most elaborate communication network in all of creation. Statistics from medical scientists boggle the mind. There are an estimated 13 billion nerve cells inside the brain itself. Most of those cells make contact with, that is, have junctions with 5,000 other nearby nerve cells. Some have as many as 50,000 such junctions or *synapses*. The word *astronomical* isn't big enough to describe this, for the number of connections inside one brain far exceeds the number of stars in all the galaxies! But that's only the beginning.

The informers of the brain are our sense organs, posted like sentinels at strategic points throughout the body. Take the skin, for example. In it are 4 million structures sensitive to pain, 500,000 which detect

touch or pressure and another 200,000 which keep track of the temperature. Add the *big ones* to this—the ears, eyes, nose, and tongue—and
you are beginning to get the picture. The best way to picture the brain's
network is to imagine thousands of telephone switchboards, each one
big enough for a city like New York or London. Every circuit is operating at full capacity, receiving requests and plugging them into the
proper circuit in a fraction of a second. This is only a faint idea of what
takes place in your brain when you do the simplest daily tasks, like
remembering a friend's address.

A Little Lower Than God

You can see why memory is called a mystery. For though memory is
rooted in this incredible brain system, it is also a part of the mind which
is above and beyond the network. The human mind is greater than
and distinct from the system through which it operates.

Scientists who enter brain research soon find themselves involved
in philosophical theory which goes far beyond the purely material.
Deep questions surface: How does the brain, a physical substance,
interrelate and interact with the mind, a nonmaterial reality? How do
our emotional attitudes and our spirits affect our bodies and minds
the way they do?

The Bible is not a scientific textbook and does not give us formal
answers to such questions. Instead, it gives us a picture of the whole
person as created by God. Although we are made in God's image, we
can no more fully understand all about our own minds than we can
possibly understand God's mind. When the Scripture talks about body,
soul, and spirit, it takes for granted the full *unity* of a human being.
Nowhere does it isolate a person's brain from the rest of the personality, anymore than it isolates the body or the soul. It always emphasizes the whole life of a person.

Have we gotten away from the subject of memories? No, for memories are the experiences of whole persons as they remember something,
and not simply brain-stored pictures of the past. Memories include
feelings, concepts, patterns, attitudes, and tendencies toward actions
which accompany the pictures on the screen of the mind. This is the
way the Bible uses the concept of remembrance, or stirring us up to
remember something. When Scripture commands us to "remember the
Lord," it does not mean to simply have a mental picture of God. It is

a command to whole persons to orient all our thoughts and actions around God. The same is true when it tells us to "remember our Creator in the days of our youth." Or "remember the Sabbath Day to keep it holy." This is far from simply asking us to engage in mental or spiritual exercises in thinking and reflecting. It's an appeal to whole persons to set certain priorities and to live according to spiritual principles of worship and action.

This wholistic idea of memory is in complete accordance with all the latest findings in brain and behavior research. The tendency now is to look on the entire body as an extension of the brain, almost as if each cell of the body were a miniature brain/mind in itself. Everything is connected and interrelated. As with the circulation of the blood, so information and instructions, giving and receiving of responses, flow back and forth from the brain to all parts of the body. Related to all of this and *yet transcending it*, is the unique selfhood of individual persons.

In the *King James Version of* Psalm 8:5, we read that God has made man "a little lower than the angels." But the newer translations render it more accurately with, "Thou hast made him a little lower than God." Truly it is this remarkable gift of memory which enables us to gather all the knowledge of the past and use it in our imaginations to create new and wonderful pictures for the future. No wonder the psalmist goes on to exult in his status:

> Thou . . . dost crown him with glory and majesty. . . .
> Thou hast put all things under his feet. . . .
>   O Lord, our Lord,
> How majestic is Thy name in all the earth!
>   (Psalm 8:5, 6, 9)

Where Do Memories Begin?

Verse 2 of Psalm 8 contains those famous words, "From the mouth of infants and nursing babes Thou has established strength." Only in the last few years have we come to realize the truth of those words in reference to memory. Again and again I have been amazed at the power which painful memories from infancy seem to have in adult experience. Years ago when I first began the ministry of inner healing, I was very skeptical of these early memories. Slowly but surely, I have been forced to abandon my skepticism and in several instances have had to pray for the healing of some memories which could only have begun before birth. One young man was not healed of his almost compulsive recurrences of suicidal depression until his mother finally told him she had witnessed the suicide of a family member, when she was almost eight months pregnant with him. He had kept talking about strange and terrifying scenes of death which we could never trace. Now we prayed for the Holy Spirit to heal whatever evil influences that experience had on him. We asked God to heal all the roots of the family tree, changing it from a tree of death to a tree of life. It was the beginning of his release from fear and depression.

People who have been adopted need to make peace with that fact. It doesn't matter if they've had the finest set of parents in the world. I said almost these very words one day to Mavis as she sat in my office. God had been doing miracles of healing in her life, but there were still some areas which disturbed her. Mavis loved her stepfather deeply and had a good relationship with him. She had never known her real father, who had died before she was born. Mavis was a brilliant student with a keen and logical mind, and what I was saying sounded quite "off the wall" to her. But she agreed to read chapter 12 from my book, *Healing for Damaged Emotions*, which tells the story of Betty. This is how Mavis described the painful yet healing experience which took place.

Suddenly and without warning, tears began to flow down my cheeks as I sat reading the story of Betty. Her dad had left her when she was three and a half years old. During a healing session with Dr. Seamands, she had uttered this painful cry to her daddy (as if she were a child again), "O Daddy, please don't leave me!"

I identified with these words so personally as I read them. They came alive and touched something deep within me, something I had not realized was there. It was as if I were the one who had uttered them over twenty-two years ago, while still in my mother's womb. You see, my father died of cancer three months before I was born.

Not understanding all that was happening to me, I decided to go and take a walk. These strange tears and emotions were too strong, too real to be ignored or repressed. For the next hour I slowly wandered about town during the early evening hours. I resolved to let myself feel whatever might arise from within me.

And feelings concerning my father's death came in abundance. To say the least, they surprised me.

It was as if I were actually back within my mother's womb at the hospital bedside of my father. Inside the womb I fought to be heard, to somehow be acknowledged. I kicked and struggled with all my might so my father could see me, touch me, hold me, kiss me, love me before he died. Over and over again I kept saying, "Daddy, please don't die, please don't die. *Please* don't die. You haven't even seen me yet. You don't even know if I'm a boy or a girl. O Daddy, please don't die!"

As I continued to walk, the tears never seemed to subside. For the first time in my life, I was mourning the death of my father. A few tears had fallen at the thought of his death, as I had grown up, but never had I experienced such emotion and meaning in my tears and pain. Now, as an adult, I was experiencing the same anguish and struggle as I did many years ago, while I was in my mother's womb.

Even still, I am skeptical as I think of a prebirth infant mourning the death of her father. Yet I cannot deny the thoughts, emotions, and healing I experienced so unexpectedly. They were simply too deep, too real, too spontaneous to be denied.

Time magazine of August 15, 1983 carried a cover story on "Babies, What Do They Know? When Do They Know It?" Reporting on hundreds of medical and behavioral experiments being conducted in the United States, France, Austria, as well as in other parts of the world, the article described

> an enormous campaign aimed at solving one of the most fascinating riddles of human life: What do newborn children know when they emerge into this world? And how do they begin organizing and using that knowledge during the first years of life? . . . The basic answer, which is repeatedly being demonstrated in myriad new ways: *Babies know a lot more than most people used to think. They see more, hear more, understand more, and are genetically prewired to make friends with any adult who cares for them* (pp. 52–53, italics mine).

One of the most important results of these studies is the conclusive proof that long before an infant can speak, he is thinking and learning and remembering. As this article states, "Intellect is at work long before any language is available as a tool.... Babies develop an important ability to recognize categories. This was once thought to require language—how can the unnameable be identified? But babies apparently can organize perceptions without a word." The article goes on to show how children very early learn their own unspoken language of shapes, sounds, colors, smells, as well as a language of responses and relationships with people. They *remember an amazing variety of specific things long before they can speak or have words to identify objects or people.*

How far back can we push the frontiers of memory? The *Time* article states, "The search for data is being steadily pushed back from childhood to earliest infancy *and even before birth!*" (p. 53, italics mine)

Dr. Thomas Verny, a Canadian neurologist and psychiatrist, makes a strong case for prebirth memory in his best-selling book, *The Secret Life of the Unborn Child.* Dr. Verny traces the prenatal development of the child and comes to this conclusion:

> The first thin slivers of memory track begin streaking across the fetal brain sometime in the third trimester, though exactly when is hard to pinpoint. Some investigators claim a child can remember from the sixth month on; others argue the brain does not acquire powers of recall until the eighth month. There is, however, no question that the unborn child remembers or that he retains his memories.... We can safely deduce that certainly from the sixth month after conception his central nervous system is capable of receiving, processing, and encoding messages. Neurological memory is most assuredly present at the beginning of the last trimester, when most babies, if born, can survive with the help of incubators (Summit Books, pp. 142, 191).

Dr. Verny documents his claims with scores of interesting illustrations of both prenatal and very early infant memories.

To many of us this sounds farfetched, but it didn't to our grandparents who accepted prenatal influence as a matter of fact, though they carried it to ridiculous extremes. I can still hear my grandmother suggesting to a neighbor that perhaps the reason why a certain little boy down the street had such a long, ugly nose was that his mother had visited the zoo too often and spent too much time watching the elephants! But we are discovering that a lot of those old wives' tales contained a kernel of truth. Most primitive peoples are careful to keep expectant mothers away from frightening experiences.

In a carefully controlled study of 2,000 women during pregnancy and birth, Dr. Monika Lukesch, of Constantine University in Frankfurt, West Germany, came to the conclusion that *the mother's attitude toward her baby has the greatest single effect on how an infant turns out.* And just as important, Dr. Lukesch found that the quality of a woman's relationship with her husband rates second and has a decisive effect on the unborn child.

Dr. Gerhard Rottmann, of the University of Salzburg in Austria, came to much the same conclusion; he even showed that the unborn child is capable of very fine emotional distinctions. This is illustrated by the biblical story in which the Virgin Mary visits her cousin Elizabeth to tell her of the visit of the angel and the promised Messiah. This causes Elizabeth to joyously exclaim, "Behold, when the sound of your greeting reached my ears, the baby leaped in my womb for joy" (Luke 1:44).

We should be careful not to overemphasize the area of prenatal awareness, for our knowledge of it is still very sketchy. My desire is simply to point to the wonder of it all, and to suggest that for the healing of memories, in some instances, we may have to deal with factors that precede birth. God informed the youthful Jeremiah about his prenatal call, "Before I formed you in the womb I knew you, and before you were born I consecrated you" (Jeremiah 1:5). By this reminder, God reinforced Jeremiah's call and commissioning as a prophet. Surely the same God who used this remarkable power for good is able to heal the scars and hurts of painful memories, however far back they may go.

As overwhelming as is the mystery of human memory, there is one aspect of the divine memory which is still more incredible. It is Jeremiah who most clearly tells us about it. "I will forgive their iniquity, and their sin I will remember no more" (31:34). How can an omniscient God not remember something? This verse is found in a passage about the New Covenant, which we now know includes the Cross and all that God in Christ has done to wipe out our sins. Perhaps God Himself has had some kind of healing of memories so that, wonder of wonders, when He forgives, He really does forget as well. Certainly, we are in the presence of great mystery. Mystery leads to wonder, and wonder leads to praise!

2

What is Healing of Memories?

UNFORTUNATELY, THE PHRASE *healing of memories* has come to have various meanings. In the minds of many Christians today, it is a kind of quickie cure-all, a shortcut to emotional and spiritual maturity. Because emotional healing has, at times, been carried to extremes, some people have abandoned it altogether, calling it unscriptural and even unhealthy. I can certainly understand their fears. My own experience in this realm has taught me that there is no area where the wheat and the tares are more closely sown together than in psychology. Being the infant science that it is, it is filled with all sorts of newly emerging theories and approaches. It is only quite recently that the insights and proven truths of psychology are being integrated with a truly Christian approach to counseling. It is important to recognize that all truth is God's truth, whether it be at the Lord's table or in the laboratory test tube. We keep our balance by continually running all truths through the sieve of God's Word.

Healing of memories is a form of Christian counseling and prayer which focuses the healing power of the Spirit on certain types of emotional/spiritual problems. It is *one* and *only one* of such ministries; and should never be made the *one and only* form, for such overemphasis leads to exaggeration and misuse. It is very important that Christian workers possess both sufficient knowledge and Spirit-sensitized discernment to know when it is the right tool of the Spirit for healing.

One of the main purposes of this book is to help counselors and other Christian workers know when to use it and when not to use it.

In the usual course of memory healing, there are three phases. They are not always distinct and sometimes blend together. However, to help us clarify, we will look at them separately.

A Time of Counseling

God may use another person or a group to bring about the insights we have been unable to discover on our own. Counseling is often necessary to uncover the hidden hurts, the unmet needs, and the repressed emotions which are preventing us from getting to the truth which will set us free. In many instances, there can be no true healing and spiritual growth until we are released from painful memories and unhealthy patterns which now interfere with our present attitudes and behavior.

When I answered my office phone one afternoon, a man's anxious voice plunged me right into the situation—"We've got marriage problems," he said a bit curtly. "Can I send my wife to see you?" I usually find appointments by proxy do not work out too well. Soon a feminine voice on another line assured me she had asked her husband to take the initiative. Within a few days, I was listening to Patty tell me about a faltering marriage, a new lack of affection for her minister husband, and a whole spectrum of physical and emotional difficulties which had obviously driven her to the brink of breakdown. I also sensed a deep commitment to God and to her marriage. Patty's childhood story sounded like a textbook case for healing of memories—a broken home, several instances of sexual abuse by family members, family illness and poverty which overloaded her with work and responsibility at an early age. It was as if a Pandora's box full of painful memories had suddenly flown open to cause her present defeat.

However, when we went over the details of her scarred and sordid childhood, I was deeply impressed with the mature way she had handled it all. Sexual traumas and painful experiences had not kept her from being feminine in her outlook and completely normal in her responses to her husband. Her early experiences, painful as they had been, had actually helped make her a better mother to her children. In the end, it became clear she did not need a healing of those hurts from her past. An early teenage conversion and a loving church had enabled her to make peace with them rather remarkably.

We discovered that the real problem was a deep-seated bitterness she had allowed to take root in her heart a couple of years before. You see, her husband had felt the call to preach late in life. This meant leaving a lucrative position, thus forcing certain economic sacrifices upon Patty. Certainly this had reactivated her early fears of being poor and had added intensity to her resentments; but the crux of her difficulty was her more up-to-date feeling toward her husband. Gradually she had allowed this to affect her actions, so that she had been walling him out of her life and blaming him for other unrelated matters. This had blocked the flow of their hitherto healthy love life so that the whole relationship was breaking down. She had to face the ugliness of her sinful resentment and the subtle ways in which she had been getting even with him. In confession and prayer, she found grace to forgive him and to accept forgiveness for her wrong attitude and her hurtful actions. When they communicated all this to one another, God's love was able to wash away the barriers and restore deep love on both sides.

I have deliberately chosen an illustration where counseling revealed that a healing of memories was *not* necessary, to point out the need for personal counseling. It is often difficult to determine whether healing of memories is called for, and it is at this point that I have many reservations about using this form of emotional/spiritual healing with large groups of people or in mass meetings. Some clergy attempt this, and I surely would not limit God's power. I know that He uses sermons on inner healing to reveal to us our needs, and this is, in a sense, mass counseling. I have also seen some wonderful miracles of healing that had their beginnings in this kind of a public service. But I have strong reservations about trying to lead a whole audience through this process. Like much that takes place in the field of healing today, it is more magic than miracle. It's very rare to see long-term and lasting results, with permanent changes in attitudes and relationships, apart from a process that includes all three of the phases about which we are writing. The first is opening up to a counselor, pastor, or trusted friend. "Confess your faults to one another and pray for one another, so that you may be healed" (James 5:16).

A Time of Special Healing Prayer

This is one of the distinctives about the healing of memories. So that
the Holy Spirit may actually touch the barriers to health, a full use is
made of conversational prayer with emphasis on visualization, imagination, the pinpointing in time of the specific situation which produced
the painful memory, and a deeply empathetic faith on the part of the
praying partner.

In this special prayer, we allow the Spirit to take us back in time to
the actual experience and to walk through those painful memories with
us. It is then, through the use of our sanctified imaginations, that we
pray as if we were actually there at the time it took place, allowing
God to minister to us in the manner we needed at that time.

*This prayer time is the very heart of the healing of memories. It is in prayer
that the healing miracle begins; without it, the whole process may simply be
a form of autosuggestion, catharsis, or feeling therapy. This special time of
prayer cannot be bypassed, if there are to be lasting results.*

At times we do not receive what we pray for, because we ask for
the wrong things and from the wrong motives (James 4:2–3). It is important that our praying be on target. One of the miracles which often
takes place during this special prayer time is that *the Holy Spirit becomes our Counselor who clarifies the content and purifies the motives of
the prayer itself.* Often we begin by praying about the memory of a
particular incident, or about a particular relationship, because we have
thought one of those was the heart of the problem. Then, during the
time of prayer, the Spirit peels away that layer and opens us up to
deeper levels of our own minds and helps us *to discover what the real
issue is.* This is extremely important and later we shall spend a lot of
time on it. Because of our fallenness and the sinful responses we make
to people who hurt us, we often develop very selective memories. That
is, our recall of some things can become distorted because of the intensity of the emotions connected with them. Do you remember our
description in chapter 1 of the junctions or *synapses* which pass along
the electrochemical impulses and thus send information to the brain?
There are hundreds of these in which *information can be altered before,
during, or after it has been received* (See *Our Fragile Brains*, D. Gareth
Jones, InterVarsity Press, pp. 43–44.)

Our attitudes of mind, emotion, and spirit play a big part in memory
processing and can often throw us clear off the track when it comes

to finding out insights necessary for healing. This is why Jesus' words about truth are so essential, "You shall know the truth, and the truth shall make you free" (John 8:32). His favorite name for the Holy Spirit was "The Spirit of Truth" (John 14–16). Sometimes, after we have gone as far as we can through counseling, it is during this time of prayer when the Spirit of Truth focuses like a great laser beam on the real need and brings His healing light to bear upon it.

Jack was a young man in his thirties, single, attractive, and with a good job. Recently he had been having bouts with depression. Although he had been a Christian for many years, he was filled with a generalized guilt which made it difficult for him to believe that God really loved him. He described his feelings this way: "There are invisible chains around me; I keep asking God to break them, but feel He won't do it—not for *me*. I have a sense of hopelessness, unworthiness." He shared with me his obvious abilities in art and music: "People tell me I have a lot of talents. I'd like to use them for the Lord, but I get all tied up in knots and can't express them. So I get angry at myself and feel that God is disappointed in me too."

At work he had difficulty standing up for his proper rights; as a result, his boss and coworkers took unfair advantage of him. They even told him they did. Why did he allow this? "I'm afraid I will be rejected even more than I *was*." I noticed the past tense and asked what that meant. In the next few sessions, he shared with me the picture of a home filled with constant rejection, putdown, and even physical abuse. Some of his worst memories were awakening from a night's sleep because his father was yelling at him and hitting him. This often occurred a few hours after a bedtime routine, when he would have to make up a story about his own wrongdoings, to satisfy his father's insistent accusations! His mother had "spells" when she would scream and throw things, breaking valuable belongings. The home was an atmosphere of utter unpredictability.

During our conversations, most of his feelings seemed to be directed against his parents. He casually mentioned an older sister, but only in passing. However, during the healing prayer time everything changed, and a great river of rage erupted against the sister. She somehow had a very unique and privileged position in this irrational family, and on scores of occasions could have protected and saved Jack from a great deal of suffering. Instead, she had increased it. Whenever she introduced him to her friends she would say sarcastically, "Don't pay attention to anything Jack does—he's mentally retarded." She actually added her suspicions to those of his parents and made his position worse. After they had both left home, Jack talked to her once about the fact that they were never shown any physical affection. He was deeply hurt when, instead of giving any understanding or comfort, she said angrily, "What'd you want me to do about it, hug you?"

When the Holy Spirit began to translate some of the deep sighs and groanings which came out of the pit of his painful memories (Romans 8:26–27), it became obvious that this was the place Jack needed the deepest healing. He had by far the greatest struggle in forgiving his sister, not his parents. It was only after a long time of wrestling with his resentments, and allowing the Spirit to "tear them from his heart like a bunch of leeches," that he forgave her and in turn received God's forgiveness for his years of hidden bitterness. And it was all the result of the prayer time. After all, the Holy Spirit is the true Counselor who leads us into all truth.

Whether or not the prayer time is an occasion of new perceptions, it is always a time of new power. And this power is what saves the healing of memories from being just another form of therapy in which people "psych themselves out" and "feel good." The prayer time is when the probing power of God Himself penetrates into the deepest levels of our personalities. Hundreds of times I have had people say to me afterward, "I really wondered . . . I felt changed and different but I was skeptical. Would it last? Would my attitude be different when I actually had to face the offending person or be back in the situation? Well, I found out that I really had been healed. God did it, and as I look back, I realize it all happened while we were praying together." And this usually leads to a prayer of thanksgiving and praise.

A Time of Follow-up

The painful memories need to be integrated into life and invested with new meaning. During this time the counselee, the counselor, and the Holy Spirit work together to reprogram wrong attitudes and behavior patterns so as to insure permanent changes. The ultimate goal here is not simply relief from the pain of the past or some level of mental and emotional health, but a growth in Christlikeness and a maturing work of sanctification and true holiness. Then the "healed helper" will be able to actually use his or her painful memories as an instrument of blessing in the lives of others.

Sometimes this follow-up requires a great deal of hard work, for *the healing of memories does not automatically computerize us into perfect performance and guarantee different behavior.* The real tragedy of hurtful memories is not simply the intense pain we feel from them and the powerful push from the past they stir up inside us. *It is that because of the pain and the push we have learned wrong ways of coping with life situations and wrong ways of relating to people, until these have become the basis of our personality patterns—our way of life.* These patterns must be changed by the sanctifying power of the Spirit working through our daily disciplines. The difference now is that we can be freed from the pains and the pushes and the compulsions.

3

Why Do Some Memories Need Healing?

~~~~~~

AN UNKNOWN AUTHOR has said, "Memory is the power to gather roses in winter." Obviously, this refers to the joyous aspect of good memories. Proverbs 10:7 comments on this, "The memory of the righteous is blessed." Paul wrote to the Philippians, "I thank my God every time I remember you" (1:3, NIV). Truly happy memories like these were Paul's roses in winter. They brought color and warmth to the damp and desolate atmosphere of the Roman jail where Paul was a prisoner when he wrote the letter.

I once conducted a service for some emotionally disturbed people in a Kentucky hospital. Many of them had come from the mountains in the eastern section of the state. The chaplain had shared with me some of their backgrounds—poverty, unemployment, a high incidence of child abuse, alcoholism, and family tragedy. In my message I talked about God's grace which could comfort them and heal the emotional wounds which had been a factor in producing their breakdowns. To close the service, the chaplain gave them the opportunity of choosing a favorite hymn. I was surprised when several selected the well-known Appalachian Gospel song, "Precious Memories, How They Linger." In the midst of their overwhelming mental pain, they were making every effort to remember only the roses of their past. But their physical and emotional conditions were living proof that they had refused to face up to or make peace with their many thorns.

Time Heals All Wounds—Or Does It?

It's time that we take a closer look at one of the great myths about healing—that time heals all wounds. The falseness is in the word *all*. True, there are many wounds which time by itself can heal. If the mind can consciously endure the pain when it is being experienced, then, as time passes, the intensity of the painful memory will lessen. With sufficient time, only the memory of having suffered will remain. There will still be pain in the memory, but it will be bearable. It will be somewhat like a successful operation which does not develop infection. It can certainly be very painful, but it will gradually heal without complication. Someday only a sensitive scar will remind us of the suffering we went through. *Yes, time can heal all unrepressed and uninfected painful memories.*

But time by itself does not and cannot heal those memories which are so painful that the person's mind cannot tolerate them. The evidence shows that such experiences are as alive and as painful ten or twenty years later as they were ten or twenty minutes after they were pushed out of consciousness. What cannot be faced and borne is denied. Let us use an extreme illustration, to show how wonderfully God has provided us with a built-in protection system for one of His most precious gifts to us—our minds.

People in serious automobile accidents almost never remember the actual moment of impact. That final experience of binding and searing pain is rarely, if ever, within recall. They often remember many things just prior to that moment. They will say, "I could see that we were going to hit that bridge," or "I remember the truck bearing down on us," or "I can see in my mind when we started over the cliff." But they do not remember the experience of going through the windshield, or when they were thrown out of the car, or actually hitting the abutment. Thank God they don't! Can you imagine what it would be like to go through life with that kind of a mental picture permanently stored in the memory? Such a person would not be able to maintain sanity. He could not bear the overwhelming emotional pain which would accompany such a memory. So God in His mercy has provided a kind of mental and emotional fuse which simply blows itself when the circuits get overloaded.

This illustration contains both the physical and emotional factors which make it easy for us to understand *how* and *why* the fuse blows.

Mental pain can produce similar results. I shall never forget the sad and bewildered face of a Korean War veteran who was shown on TV many years ago. His painful battle and prisoner-of-war experiences had left him without any identification tags and with almost complete amnesia. He couldn't even remember his own name and personal identity. We all ached for him as he looked out through our TV screens and asked, "Can anyone tell me who I am?" Fortunately, for him and many others, the memories were restored.

Repressed Memories

Sometimes serious crimes are solved when long-forgotten events are recalled that provide important clues. The Associated Press carried the following story in our local newspaper on December 21, 1979 (*The Lexington Herald*, Lexington, Kentucky):

WOMAN'S MIND UNLOCKS CLUE TO
DAD'S MURDER 35 YEARS AGO

RAEFORD, N.C.- Edward Leon Cameron disappeared 35 years ago. Sheriff Dave Barrington went looking for him last week and turned up a bizarre murder locked since childhood in a woman's mind.

For years Mrs. Perry had not been aware that something grotesque, too horrible to think about, was suppressed in her memory. But, according to Barrington, it resurfaced during (treatment). . . .

It was April 8, 1944, and Annie Blue Cameron was just short of her 10th birthday. That night, she now remembers, she overheard her parents quarreling in the family's farmhouse.

The next day, she "opened the door to the front bedroom and saw her father's body on the floor. . . . He appeared to be dead," reads a search warrant drawn up last week. "The next week after school, (she) went to the outhouse. She looked down the hole and saw her father's face barely submerged under the excrement."

But those events were frozen in the minds of a little girl and her mother, Winnie Cameron, who gave up her terrible knowledge only in death.

Barrington said the story began to unfold after Mrs. Perry sought psychiatric help. . . . Mrs. Perry had been unwilling to discuss the case with anyone but the authorities, and the nature of her psychological problems has not been discussed.

Mrs. Perry, now a reading teacher at Valencia Community College in Orlando, Florida, eventually got in touch with the FBI. And last Christmas she confronted her mother in a telephone call, taped by the authorities with her permission.

"Ma, I feel like you had something to do with my father's death," said Mrs. Perry, according to the sheriff. Mrs. Cameron refused to discuss it, he said.

On December 1 of this year, Mrs. Perry called her mother again. "I want to talk to you again about what I discussed last Christmas," she said. "Is my father's body still in that toilet?"

Her mother replied, "I will tell you after Christmas."

The digging started December 12. Mrs. Perry and her sister, June Ivey, helped law officers locate the place where the outhouse had stood.

"At 1:20 P.M., we hit the remains. . . . It was a rib," Barrington said. "After that it was just bone after bone all afternoon." Only Cameron's skull and a few other bones remain unearthed.

"Mrs. Cameron was in the house most of the day (Dec. 12)," Barrington said. "She only left the next morning at 8 A.M. That was the last time she was seen by my department alive."

Late Friday afternoon, the Cameron son . . . found Mrs. Cameron, 69, lying beside her car on a back boundary of the family's farmland, a .32-caliber pistol clutched in her hand. On the car seat lay an envelope. . . . Barrington (said) it contained a confession.

Some time ago I was giving a seminar at the Duke University School of Medicine Department of Psychiatry and mentioned this incident. A young resident told me he was from the very town where all this had happened and vouched for the truthfulness of the facts in the newspaper article.

This incident illustrates one of the mysteries of memory—the ability to block out of our minds things which we are not able to face. The saddest part of this is that though we may block out the pain quite *unintentionally*, we still suffer the consequences. Often, as in the case of Mrs. Perry, it's not until those memories literally explode and begin to affect our daily lives that we are forced to do something about them.

Many of us have hurtful memories which we try to push out of our minds. Such memories cannot be healed by the mere passage of time any more than an infected wound could be. The infection turns inward and actually worsens because it spreads to other areas, affecting and infecting them. So it is with certain painful experiences, especially those that happen during the important years of early childhood and teenage development. In severe situations, a dissociation or splitting off and storing away of the experience can take place. It then seems to be deposited into a part of the memory which is not immediately available to conscious recall. No one completely understands the mental, emotional, and neurological process. But we do know that it requires a great deal of continuous emotional and spiritual energy to keep the memory in its hidden place.

It could be compared to a person trying to hold a bunch of balloons under water. He succeeds for a while but finally runs out of energy; then they pop up here and there, in spite of his desperate efforts. Such repressed and fixated memories can never really be forgotten. Nor can they simply be filed away in the same way our minds store pleasant memories, with their accompanying good feelings. For the harder we try to keep bad memories out of conscious recall, the more powerful they become. Since they are not allowed to enter through the door of our minds directly, they come into our personalities (body, mind, and spirit) in disguised and destructive ways. These denied problems go underwater and later reappear as certain kinds of physical illnesses, unhappy marital situations, and recurring cycles of spiritual defeat.

As I was writing this chapter, I was interrupted by a long-distance call from another state. A man had read *Healing for Damaged Emotions* a few weeks before and wanted to talk with me. He had been a Christian for over seven years, faithful in his Bible reading, prayer life, and fellowship with other believers. But there were areas of life where, as he said, "The needle seemed stuck in repetitive emotional patterns." He went on to say that although he had tried every Christian discipline he knew, he simply could not figure out what the problem was. While reading the book, he felt as if the Holy Spirit had stripped off a layer of his memory so that he could remember some things which were related to his "broken record" problems. There was no particular trauma; rather, it was a whole atmosphere, an environment with a pervading tone he had absorbed while growing up. And though he hated it, he discovered he was *unintentionally* trying to reproduce that very same climate in his present relationships. He kept stressing the fact he had not realized what he was doing *until he remembered*. Now that he understood, he was able to share the memories with a counselor and receive even deeper insights. And through praying with his wife, he was seeing changes in himself and in his home atmosphere. I hung up the phone thanking God for an up-to-date confirmation of the effects of buried memories.

The man's story is also a needed balance to some of the more extreme illustrations I have used. For often, we are not able to pinpoint particular experiences or happenings. Instead, as with this man, it can be an aggregate of surrounding influences, an all-pervasive atmosphere which encompasses us with *a whole set of generalized memories which require healing*. I'm sure this is a part of what Jesus had in mind when He spoke of the destructive effects of some actions upon children, and then uttered one of His most severe judgments upon those who "offend these little ones" or "cause them to stumble" (Matthew 18:6–7 and Luke 17:1–3). Truly, "it would be better for him if a millstone were hung around his neck and he were thrown into the sea."

Creating Trust Conditions for Conscious Recall

People who carry hurtful memories will allow them to come into conscious recall (remembrance) only under certain *trust conditions*. This is why an understanding and empathetic counselor is often needed, someone whom the hurting person can trust and who can lead him or her into the presence of a caring and trustworthy God. In fact, it is precisely at this point that the Gospel is truly good news—the incredible news of the understanding and saving companionship of God Himself. Christ's sufferings on the Cross *for* us and *as* us provide the *trust conditions* which enable the sufferer to bring those painful memories into the light of consciousness so they can not only be faced but healed.

The creation of these trust conditions needs to begin with the way we present the Gospel and in the very atmosphere of our churches.

4

Creating the Atmosphere for Healing

AT THE END of World War II, the Japanese government was faced with a massive problem. Even though the peace documents had been signed, there were thousands of Japanese soldiers in the mountains and jungles of South Pacific islands who would not come out of hiding, surrender their arms, and return to a life of peace. They had been so thoroughly brainwashed by their officers with stories of what the Americans would do to them if they gave themselves up that they fully believed surrender would mean either torture or instant death. Finally, the Japanese Emperor made a speech explaining the situation and pleading with his men to come home. The speech was broadcast by radio and also recorded and repeatedly boomed toward the mountain caves and the jungles by loudspeaker. In essence he said to them, "Come out, the war is over. Peace has been established. You will not be harmed, but welcomed and protected."

Since it was the voice of their Emperor himself, almost all of the troops accepted his assurance and came out. There were stragglers, of course, but within months all but a few had surrendered. After some years, it was assumed that all the living had been accounted for. However, it was not until March of 1974 that the last soldier finally came out of hiding, twenty-nine years after the war was over! By now the two countries were on friendly terms. When they asked the man, now in his sixties, why he had waited, he said it had taken him that long to get over his fears.

In chapter 3, we said we allow certain kinds of painful memories to come into conscious recollection or remembrance only under the right kind of trust conditions. Without those conditions we are like the old Japanese soldier. Our fears will not, cannot, allow us to lower our defenses so that our buried memories can come out of hiding. In a very real sense, God, the loving Heavenly Father, the Emperor of the Universe, has sent us all His special message of peace. Perhaps it is best expressed by Paul, in 2 Corinthians 5:19, "God was in Christ reconciling the world to Himself, not counting their trespasses against them." Here is the very heart of the Good News—"Come out, you don't need to be afraid any longer. There is peace between us. You will not be harmed or punished, but welcomed and accepted."

Why is it, then, that so many people do *not* feel free to open themselves up to the healing grace of God? Why are they still hiding behind all manner of defenses? *The reason is that all too often the atmosphere in our churches, the attitudes of other Christians, and the very way we proclaim the Gospel do not create the trust conditions which are necessary for healing.*

The Pastor as Prophet and Priest

There are different functions of preaching, different kinds of sermons, and different goals at which they are aimed. Many sermons represent the *prophetic role* of the messenger. He stands as God's representative and proclaims God's Word, "Thus saith the Lord." As prophet he should, like Jesus, speak with authority. In this role the minister's aim is to proclaim truth, expound the great doctrines of the faith, and uphold biblical standards for ethical living. As prophet he speaks of sin, righteousness, and judgment, and calls people to repentance, salvation, sanctification, and holiness of heart and life.

When he preaches in his *priestly or pastoral role*, the content and the aim are different. As God's representative he offers the nourishment of the Word, building up and encouraging the people. He brings comfort to the sorrowing and hope to those in despair. In the words of Charles Wesley's beautiful hymn, "Jesus, Lover of My Soul," the pastor's aim in this kind of preaching is to "raise the fallen, cheer the faint, heal the sick, and lead the blind."

Most of our preaching falls somewhere between the prophetic and the pastoral approach. Indeed, to be what God intended preaching to be, there should be a balance between the two aspects of the Gospel—moral demand and gracious gift. Of course, our Lord Himself combined the two most perfectly, as in His words to the woman taken in adultery, "Neither do I condemn thee; go, and sin no more" (John 8:11, KJV). Most ministers try their best to be faithful to both emphases and generally are able to meet the needs of most of their listeners. What they often fail to recognize is the increasingly large number of people in their congregations who need to be reached by an even deeper level of preaching. Edgar N. Jackson, in his book, *A Psychology for Preaching*, reports on a questionnaire given to 4,000 people. Its purpose was to find out what people want from their pastors through sermons. Half of them expressed a concern about intensely personal matters—the futility of life, insecurity in personal relationships, loneliness, marital problems, the control of their sexual desires, the effects of alcohol, false ideas of religion and morals, feelings of inferiority, the problems of illness and suffering, and feelings of guilt and frustration. Another fourth were chiefly concerned with family problems, parenthood, childrearing, and relational conflict. The remaining fourth were concerned with the more traditional religious problems (Harper and Row, pp. 75–77).

Here is a cry for help which needs to be heard and answered through our evangelical preaching. A lot of spiritual needs arise out of immaturity, inner conflict, emotional and relational hangups. People want to know how to live this abundant life we are always preaching about, in the nitty-gritty of daily living.

To these normal human problems we in North America must add a whole list of abnormal ones. Truly, we have sown to the wind and are reaping the whirlwind, as an increasing number of people, including many born-again and Spirit-filled Christians, are coming into young adulthood with serious emotional problems which deeply affect their spiritual lives. In our increasingly sick society, the situation seems to grow worse by geometric proportion, like a population explosion.

Our tragic overemphasis on sex has become almost a national obsession:

- the explosive rise of divorce in the last four decades,

- the alarming increase in child and spouse abuse, incest and sexual violation,
    - the growing addiction to liquor and drugs,
    - the breakdown of moral standards, discipline, and the sense of responsibility.

All of these have helped make our society an assembly line for turning out disturbed people with damaged emotions. And many of these damaged emotions are deeply buried in layers of memory which will not respond to the kind of preaching we ordinarily hear. In fact, we can say some of our traditional preaching actually causes such people greater fear and hardens their defenses so that those memories are driven still further underground. Even in sermons of comfort or encouragement, it is possible to present the Good News in such a way as to deepen people's despair. Many times when I ask people why they don't share their problems with their pastor they tell me it is because they already know what he will say. He will simply make them feel guiltier than they already do. When I pursue this further by asking them how they know this, they usually reply, "I can tell by the way he preaches." It would be easy for evangelists and pastors to dismiss this judgment as unfair. The fact is that it hurts because it is so often true. *Too often our preaching discourages people even more and deters them from seeking the help and healing they so desperately need.*

Preaching for Emotional and Spiritual Healing

Years of experience in this area have taught me that a special kind of preaching is needed to encourage a healing of memories. It is distinctive in its content, style, and aim. The task of this type of preaching is:

- to give the sufferer the courage to lower the defenses which have prevented his healing,
- to enable him to bring out into the open his buried inner fears, anxieties, conflicts, and shame,
- to help him exteriorize his hidden and deeply internalized memories in the presence of the Cross,
- to create what is, perhaps, to him a completely new image of God, an empathetic Father who is not shocked but understanding of whatever is uncovered in His presence, because He has known about it all along and has never stopped loving.

The Content of the Preaching

The heart of this special kind of sermon is found in certain fundamental aspects of the Good News we have in Christ.

• Incarnation—Emmanuel, God is with us. The Apostle John wrote, "The Word was made flesh, and dwelt among us" (John 1:14, KJV). Matthew quoted Isaiah's prophecy, "Behold, a virgin shall be with child, and shall bring forth a Son, and they shall call His name Emmanuel, which being interpreted is, God with us" (Matthew 1:23, KJV).

Among us . . . With us. What does this mean that God is with us? When we think of how we use the word *with*, we get a clue. Sometimes we go to a friend who is suffering from disease, or pain, or great loss. We want to convey our deepest feelings of sympathy. So we say, "I want you to know that I am with you in this, with you all the way." This is a meaning of the Incarnation we need to convey. Isaiah prophesied about the coming of Emmanuel, and Matthew explained the meaning, "which being interpreted is, God with us." In our preaching to people suffering from mental and emotional pain, we need to speak of the real humanity of Christ. It is not that "the Word became words." Words are needed, but they are not enough, not even for God Himself. The Word became *flesh*. God has come down into the arena of human living and suffering. *He has become one with us by becoming one of us.*

• Identification—God is in our pain with us. Perhaps I can best illustrate this point by telling two true stories which were reported in the Canadian newspaper, *The Calgary Herald.*

On June 5, 1978, seven-year-old Martin Turgeon slipped off the wharf and fell into the Prairie River. The dozen or more adults standing on the same pier did nothing—except watch him struggle a few moments in the water and then drown.

Why didn't anyone help? Well, just a short distance upstream, untreated sewage is dumped into the river. The water is highly polluted and very smelly. One witness quoted an onlooker as later saying, "We weren't going to jump in there—the water was much too dirty." A policeman who came on the scene shortly thereafter remarked bitterly, "It makes you wonder about how human people really are. The boy probably could have been saved."

Contrast that incident with this one. In August of 1977, John Evering-ham, an Australian journalist working in Laos, was expelled by the Communists. Engaged to marry a national of that land, Keo Sirisom-hone, he was forced to leave her behind. For ten months John care-fully planned how to rescue Keo. Finally, on May 27, 1978 he set out on his mission of rescue. Outfitted with face masks, fins, and a scuba diving tank equipped with two breathing devices, he plunged into the rain-swollen Mekong River which separates Laos from Thailand.

Because of the murky water, there was zero visibility below the surface, and John had to use a compass which was on his face mask. He battled swirling currents, crawling along the muddy bottom where he was occasionally tossed about by whirlpools. When he surfaced he discovered that he had underestimated the current. He was still sev-eral hundred feet off shore and being carried past the spot where Keo was waiting, disguised as a fisherwoman to avoid any suspicion. Exhausted, Everingham swam back to the Thai side.

This time he entered the river further upstream. Let me quote him at this point. "I made it, and crawled out on the bank. Keo seemed to have given up and was dejectedly walking away in the distance. I yelled at the top of my lungs. She turned and saw me and, running forward, fell into my arms." Keo had never learned to swim so John put a slightly inflated life vest around her neck and one of the breath-ing regulators in her mouth. With their faces just at the surface of the water and a quick-release strap binding them together, John pushed hard into the river. After a desperate struggle they made it together, falling exhausted on the bank on the other side—in Thailand!

John's story illustrates Emmanuel's identification with us in our terrible human predicament. He is not a God who stands by, unwill-ing to get involved, but a God who loves us so much that He is will-ing to plunge into the turbulent and murky waters of human life and be identified with us all the way:

• in His very conception, submerged in the amniotic fluids, the waters of the Virgin Mary's womb,

• in His birth and infancy, fleeing the swirling waters of King Herod's insane death decree,

• in His boyhood, learning through the waters of growth and development, maturing from the discipline of earthly parents and religious authorities,

- in His thirty years, immersed in the waters of obscurity, soaking in Scripture, being saturated in patience and divine wisdom,
- all through His life and ministry, plunging into the polluted waters of sin-corrupted lives, baptized with sinners, eating with them, and risking their contamination,
- and finally, engulfed in the whirlpools of deceit, denial, and betrayal, entering the murky depths of death itself . . . even the death of the Cross.
- Crucifixion—God is in our pain with us and for us, all the way, even at great cost to Himself. Now we have reached the very core of the Good News—the Cross. Jesus identified with the worst of us right to the end, as He was crucified with two criminals. Here in the deepest waters of all, "He suffered death, so that by the grace of God He might taste death for everyone" (Hebrews 2:9, NIV).

This identification in death was crucially important, as the author of the Book of Hebrews tells us . . . "He too shared in their humanity so that by His death He might destroy him who holds the power of death—that is, the devil—and free those who all their lives were held in slavery by their fear of death. . . . For this reason He had to be made like His brothers in every way. . . . Because He Himself suffered when He was tempted, He is able to help those who are being tempted" (Hebrews 2:14–18, NIV). Here is complete identification with us, the ultimate proof that God understands our pain and our suffering. The point of this passage and others from the Epistle to the Hebrews is that because God now fully understands, we never need hesitate to bring anything to Him. Indeed, we are urged to "approach the throne of grace with confidence, so that we may receive mercy and find grace to help us in our time of need" (Hebrews 4:16, NIV).

We do not really convey the meaning of this invitation if we limit the death of Christ to atonement for sins. Certainly the Cross means that Christ died for our sins; but if we confine it to that, we are missing one element in our preaching and teaching which millions of hurting people need to hear. For by His Cross, Christ reconciles to God both sinners and sufferers. When Christ descended into hell, He not only brought cleansing from the guilty memories of our sins which condemn our consciences; He also brought healing for those painful memories which arise within us to torment and enslave our personalities. Many of these memories come from injuries and infirmities which we did not choose. Rather, we were victims of the sinful choices of others. And that is exactly what Christ allowed Himself to be on the Cross—a victim of the choices of others. As He voluntarily subjected Himself to the ultimate penalty for our sins, He went through the most painful experience of human life—undeserved and unjust suffering. He deliberately submitted Himself to the twin mysteries of sin and suffering. Our preaching is much too simplistic if we limit the Atonement to the forgiveness of sins.

There are those who would immediately ask, "Whose sins?" In the passage from Matthew regarding sins against children, which we quoted in chapter 3, Jesus went on to say, "Woe to the world because of the things that cause people to sin! Such things must come, but woe to the man through whom they come!" (Matthew 18:7, NIV) Yes, we have all sinned and need the forgiveness which the Cross provides. But because we are also sinned against, we need assurance from the Cross that God understands the complicated and contradictory emotions we experience, the inner hell of tangled feelings which erupt from unhealed memories.

One of the angriest moments in my counseling ministry was while I was listening to a sobbing young lady unfold her story. Judy had heard a well-known evangelist preach and had gone to him for prayer and guidance. In great agony she shared with him how her minister father had repeatedly molested her sexually, beginning at the age of six. She confessed her confused feelings which constantly kept her depressed and spiritually defeated—a jumbled mixture of guilt, shame, sexual ambivalence, anger, and sadness. His immediate reply was that if she would "repent" for her part in all this, God would "straighten out" her feelings. He faithfully expounded the "plan of salvation." He was so full of answers that he did not even take time to listen to her questions or to hear the full story, which included the fact that her mother, in a fit of rage, had broken Judy's leg when she was only three years old.

The miracle of God's grace is such that, in spite of the sickness of her home, this young lady was a genuine Christian. She had indeed experienced forgiveness and the new birth in Christ. What she desperately needed was to be healed from the sordid scars of the past and to learn a whole new way of relating to God, others, and herself.

This is why the preaching of the Cross in its fullest sense is so central to create the trust conditions necessary for the healing of memories. How beautifully the ancient Communion liturgy puts it: "Through faith in His blood" we receive "the remission of our sins," and "all other benefits of His passion." Let us be sure that our version of the Good News includes this benefit which so many wounded spirits need. In His first sermon in the synagogue, as recorded by Luke, Jesus' proclamation of the Good News included the description of the Messiah from Isaiah 61:1–2. "He has sent Me to bind up the brokenhearted, to proclaim freedom for the captives." Surely the brokenhearted of our churches need to know that He has borne their griefs and infirmities, as well as their sins.

• Living Reality—of an empathetic and understanding God. What does all this mean? How does it affect our daily lives? And how does it create the atmosphere for the healing we have been talking about? It changes our concepts and feelings about God and thus produces a climate of trust in which deeply submerged memories can emerge.

Why is this true? Because God now knows how we humans feel. Yes, God has always known this, because God is God and knows all things. So how can we say God *now* knows? That seems to mean that He has learned something new, and this would make Him less than perfect, thus less than God. In the sense that God is omniscient, He has always known; but now, *He actually knows* from experience. Those wonderful passages in Hebrews imply there is a deeper sense in which God now *knows and understands* because of the sufferings of Christ. I hesitate to use a very personal illustration, but it's the only one I know that can explain what I mean.

Prior to our going to India, Helen and I spent a year of study in a missionary training school, where we had a valuable course in Tropical Medicine. One of the facts we learned was that fifty percent of all babies in India die before the age of five. We knew the fact of infant mortality. But two years later when our ten-month-old son, David, died within a few hours after an attack of fulminant bacillary dysentary, and we buried him that March morning in the red soil of Bidar, India, Helen and I came to know about infant mortality in a new way.

Of course, God understood what it meant to be a human being. But because of the Incarnation, His ultimate identification with us in the sufferings and death of Christ, God now fully knows and understands, not simply from factual omniscience but from actual experience.

Now we are sure that He knows and cares. Because He has been one of us, because He has lived out our life at every point, from a human womb to a human tomb, we know He is "touched with the feeling of our infirmities" (Hebrews 4:15, KJV). And because we are sure that He *knows*, life need never be the same for us.

• Participation by His Spirit in our Healing. An empathetic, understanding God who knows and cares is the most therapeutic factor in our inner healing. But in a sense, all we have said is past tense—it is the Jesus of history. Thank God He has not left us there. The Jesus of history becomes the Christ of present and personal experience through the work of His Holy Spirit. It is the Spirit who takes all that He made *possible* by His sufferings, death, and resurrection and makes it *actual* in our lives now. The Holy Spirit is the *paraklete. Para*—alongside, and *kaleo*—to call. The One Called Alongside. And Romans 8:26–27 assures us that the Holy Spirit helps us with our infirmities, our cripplings, and our weaknesses. The Greek word for *help is* a compound of three words meaning "to take hold of on the other side." It is a beautiful and sensitive picture of the knowing, understanding, caring God who is now participating with us in our healing.

This assurance is set in the context of Romans 8:18–28, where Paul is talking about the pain and suffering of living in this fallen and imperfect world. Even the created world of nature "has been groaning as in the pains of childbirth right up to the present time." Yes, it is truly a hurting world. Then Paul goes on, "Not only so, but we ourselves, who have the firstfruits of the Spirit, groan inwardly as we wait eagerly for our adoption as sons, the redemption of our bodies." Yes, the world of nature groans and, although we are Christians, we too groan. But we are not left alone. *God Himself, in the presence of His Holy Spirit, also groans with us.* "In the same way, the Spirit helps us in our weakness. We do not know what we ought to pray, but the Spirit Himself intercedes for us with groans that words cannot express" (vv. 22–23, 26, NIV).

This must be at the heart of our preparatory preaching, this incredibly Good News which for many of our suffering hearers seems too good to be true. We must preach it with all the love and empathy and understanding we can receive from the Spirit, always sharing openly from our own lives where we have experienced this kind of inner healing and understanding love.

Redemptive Acceptance in the Congregation

In addition to the content of the preaching, there is another supremely important aspect for creating trust conditions. The pastor may preach the kind of sermons we have been describing. However, unless the attitudes of Christians in his church radiate the same kind of redemptive acceptance, there will not be the necessary climate for healing. Most of the fears and anxieties which keep people from opening up are caused by *pain from unhealthy interpersonal relationships*. As we have already seen, the memories of those relationships go far back in their lives, perhaps even before birth. These people learned a whole language of harmful relationships even before they learned to speak. It is essential that they now learn a new language of helpful relationships. But to learn it, they must first hear it spoken. That is why the people who make up the church play such an important part in the healing process. Supportive Christians need to surround struggling and suffering persons with an atmosphere of understanding and love. Sometimes in the name of love they may have to confront, but this will always be done in a spirit of restoration rather than judgment. If it has to be *tough* love, it will still be tough *love*.

Can we honestly say this is the kind of atmosphere we find in most of our churches? Christian businessman, speaker, and writer, Fred Smith, of Dallas, Texas has written an incisive modern parable on this theme. With his permission I am quoting much of it:

"DON'T TAKE ME TO THE HOSPITAL—PLEASE"

This scene didn't make sense. There he lay in the street bleeding; the hit-and-run driver gone. He needed medical help immediately. Yet, he kept pleading, "Don't take me to the hospital, please."

Surprised, everyone asked, "Why?"

Pleadingly he answered, "Because I am on the staff at the hospital. It would be embarrassing for them to see me like this. They have never seen me bleeding and dirty. They always see me clean and healthy. Now I am a mess."

"But the hospital is for people like you. Can't we call an ambulance?"

"No, please don't. I took a pedestrian safety course, and the instructor would criticize me for getting hit."

"But who cares what the instructor thinks? You need attention."

"But there are other reasons too—the admissions clerk would be upset."

"Why?"

"Because she always gets upset if anyone for admittance doesn't have all the details she needs to fill out her records. I didn't see who hit me, and I don't even know the make of car or license number. She wouldn't understand. She is a real stickler for records. Worse than that, I haven't got my medical insurance card."

"What real difference would that make?"

"Well, if they didn't recognize me in this mess, they wouldn't let me in. They won't admit anyone in my shape without an insurance card. They must be sure it isn't going to cost the institution. They protect the institution. Just pull me over to the curb. I'll make it some way. It's my fault I got hit. Why should the nurses get their clean uniforms dirty with me? They would criticize me."

With this he tried to crawl to the gutter while everyone left him alone. Maybe he made it—maybe he didn't. Maybe he is still trying to stop his own bleeding.

Does that strike you as a strange, ridiculous story? It could happen any Sunday . . . in a typical church. I know it could happen because last night I asked some active Christians what they would do if Saturday night they got hit and run over by some unacceptable sin. Without exception they said, "I sure wouldn't want to go to church the next morning where everybody would see me."

In the good-natured spirit of the conversation, we decided if caught—hit and run over by sin—we would be better off to go to the pool hall instead of the church. . . . There we would find sympathy and understanding.

We kept exploring: Is the church for imitation saints, dressed up and smelling good, or is it for the bleeding who know they have been hit and run over and who want to get well? Somehow the question stops being one for the entire church as it becomes singularly mine—one individual—one sinner saved by grace—one human being striving to insulate myself in a superior group or becoming involved in the total need.

"Behold how they love one another." The winners and the losers, the healthy and the sick, the hurt and the well. I need to be a giver and receiver in a church where the hurt will say expectantly, "Take me to the church, please."

The healing of memories requires a corporate fellowship of believers as caring as the paralytic's four friends, who risked tearing up the roof in order to bring him into the presence of Jesus for healing. People will allow their most painful memories to come into conscious recollection (remembrance) and thus risk the possibility of healing only within *trust conditions*. You may be wondering just how we can achieve those conditions. I remind you that the Good News is Christ crucified and resurrected. Listen to John's account of what happened on that first Easter evening. "On the evening of that first day of the week, when the disciples were together, with the doors locked for fear of the Jews, Jesus came and stood among them and said, 'Peace be with you!' After He said that, He showed them His hands and side" (John 20:19, NIV). *The risen Christ came right through the doors which had been locked out of fear.*

Praise God, our risen Lord can still walk right through the defenses and doors which have long been locked out of fear. He can still bring peace to pained and troubled hearts. He does it by *speaking words of peace* and by *showing His scars*, the price He paid to bring us that peace. It's up to us, His disciples, to gather together in His name, in His Spirit, and create the atmosphere for His healing appearance.

5

Biblical Foundations for Memory Healing

〜〜〜〜〜〜〜〜〜〜〜〜〜〜〜〜〜〜〜〜〜〜〜〜〜〜

IT IS OF utmost importance to understand that the healing of memories has a solid foundation in the Scripture, which is our final authority in all matters of faith and practice. Some people have totally rejected all forms of inner healing because the precise definitions do not appear in the Bible. If we applied that reasoning to everything, we could be led to fanatical and even dangerous extremes—not wearing clothes with buttons; not driving cars; not using pianos, organs, or PA systems in church; refusing penicillin for a sick child and thus being the cause of his death. We would actually be denying that all truth comes from God and that we have a spiritual obligation to use every new insight and discovery in any area of life for God's glory and human good. The real question is not whether a practice appears in the Bible in the specific form or language we use today. Rather, the question is whether it is contradictory to or consistent with principles stated in Scripture. In accordance with this basic tenet, we Christians are grateful for all the new truths, insights, and discoveries which continually come to us from many fields such as medicine, sociology, mathematics, physics, and psychology. As we look at the biblical teachings, we find the principles upon which we base the healing of memories.

Put Away Childish Things

It is necessary to put away childish things in order to grow up spiritually. There are two different Greek words in the New Testament which refer to childhood. It is important that we keep them distinct.

Paidion is a word which refers to the time of childhood, in a healthy and normal sense. We get our words *pediatrics* and *pediatrician* from this root. *Paidion* is the word Jesus used when He brought a little child before the disciples and told them they needed to have the same qualities of humility and teachability as the child. He went so far as to tell them, "Unless you are converted and become like children, you shall not enter the kingdom of heaven" (Matthew 18:3). While we tend to tell children to grow up and become more like adults, Jesus was always telling adults to become more like children! Today, we would use the word *childlike* to express this idea. The Bible urges us to be more *childlike* in our faith, humility, acceptance, and openness to others. We are never to grow away from these *childlike* qualities.

The other word is *nepios*, which refers to childhood in an unhealthy and abnormal way, in the sense of remaining in a stage of protracted infancy and childhood when one should have grown beyond it. Nothing is more delightful than a child who acts like a child; and nothing is more dreadful than an adult who keeps on acting like a child. This kind of behavior can be downright disruptive and is sometimes destructive. Today we describe such a person as *childish*. If his behavior is extremely childish, we go further back to an even earlier stage of life and say *babyish*. *Nepios* is the word Paul used in Romans 2:20, Galatians 4:1, and 1 Corinthians 3:1 when he described people who were spiritually immature. In his great love chapter, 1 Corinthians 13, he wrote, "When I was a child, I spake as a child, I understood as a child, I thought as a child; but when I became a man, I put away childish things" (v. 11, KJV). Here he was referring to a combination of emotional and spiritual immaturity. Does this verse seem to be out of place in the middle of the great love chapter? It isn't at all, for the characteristics and behavior of *agape* love require a certain level of emotional and spiritual maturity. And that level can never be reached until we first put away childish things.

Paul's word for *put away* is the strong Greek word *katergeo*, which means "to render inoperative, inactive, or powerless; to remove the

meaning and significance from; to free from that which has been keeping one bound or tied up." Maturity doesn't come simply because we
grow older. We can be chronological grown-ups and psychological
children at the same time. To be finished with childish things requires
action by the person.

This biblical principle forms a fitting foundation for the fact that
some people must undergo a healing of memories. Certain problems
which prevent maturity we call *hangups*. We say people's hangups keep
them *in a bind*. The words are amazingly accurate. When people have
never faced their painful memories or been loosened (unbound) from
them, they are still *hung up at a certain age and stage of their development*. Yes, their bodies are of adult size and their minds fully developed. But their emotions never grew past a certain level. At that particular point they got stuck, hung up; hence the term, personality or
emotional hangups. Many of those hangups come as a result of memories which bind and hold us in a vicelike grip. Such painful memories
are like weights tied to a swimmer's body. They keep pulling him
down, so that he is just barely able to keep afloat, or they consume so
much emotional and spiritual energy that he is not able to make any
progress.

Phil and his wife, Janet, came to me for help after seeing a marriage
counselor for several months. They loved each other very much and
were both strongly committed to holding their marriage together. They
expressed their willingness to work hard at it, and that's exactly what
Phil had been doing. The main problem between them was that Phil
could not express the deep love he felt for Janet, either in words or in
physical affection. Of course, this affected their relationship in many
areas. She was simply not receiving a normal share of emotional fulfillment and this made her irritable and impatient. He tried to compensate for his problem by being helpful around the house—in fact,
he was too helpful and often got onto her turf. She interpreted this as
interference and a put-down of her housekeeping. She said, "I appreciate his wanting to help, but it makes me feel as if he's not satisfied
with the way I do things." And so there was set up a vicious circle of
negative emotions which kept escalating.

The marriage counselor seemed to have only one approach: analyze
the situation and see what the problems are. Then by prayer and effort,
change the behaviors which are creating bad feelings. It is certainly a

very sound approach and I have seen it work wonders in many situations. However, it is not the only one, for there are many people who are unable to change attitudes and actions until they first deal with the hangups which are preventing change. Often the intrapsychic (inner) causes of the breakdown in interpersonal relations must be dealt with first.

After Phil's mother died, when he was a boy of ten, he lived alone with his father for many years. After a while, the father began drinking heavily and at times would abuse him, occasionally even in sexual ways. The house was unkempt and dirty and Phil could never bring friends home. For several years, there was a steady stream of women who spent the night with his father. At an early age, Phil was overloaded with responsibility and became a loner. In one of our sessions, as he was sharing his story, he allowed himself to plug into his emotions. With moist eyes and a trembling voice he said, *"I guess I learned to cope with all this by just never allowing myself to feel anything. I didn't dare let myself feel good in the occasional happy times because I knew they couldn't last. And I didn't dare allow myself to cry or feel down because I just had to keep going. I guess the truth of the matter is that I've been afraid to let myself feel. And now I don't know how."*

Phil had an unusual request—he wanted Janet to be with him when we went through the prayer time for the healing of those painful memories. She was very understanding and held him, yes, like his much-needed mother, while we all wept and prayed together. Phil needed to courageously face many unpleasant and painful memories. As they came to mind he had to do a lot of forgiving of his father and receive a lot of forgiveness from God for his resentments.

When he became free from these chains of the past, he and Janet were both able to begin making the proper behavioral changes which had been recommended to them. This was by no means easy; it was hard work and required much encouragement and counseling, *but at least it was now possible, whereas before it was not*. Why? Because the kind of love required for those changes was not possible until first some "childish things" were put away—*katargeod*—rendered inoperative and powerless to interfere with his present adult efforts. The healing of his memories freed him so that he could now allow himself to feel. This was an absolutely necessary first step in learning how to express his feelings for Janet. And this kind of inner healing was perfectly consistent with the biblical principle we have stated.

Accept Christ as a Present Helper

Jesus Christ is our eternal contemporary, the Lord of time and our healer; and His Holy Spirit is our present and available helper. The most distinctive part of the healing of memories is the time of prayer. Through the use of imagination, we try to recreate the painful memory and then actually visualize it as it once took place. We pray as if we were actually talking to God on the spot and ask Him to do for us what we would have asked, had we prayed then and there. We ask Him to heal the little child or teenager who underwent those experiences—things which really did fixate the child at that place, which made him get stuck at that stage of growth. How can this be possible when the events may have happened many years ago in time? How can our prayers today possibly affect that inner child or youngster of the long-ago past?

The Scriptures tell us that Christ is the Lord of time—past, present, and future. In a very real sense He is our eternal contemporary, "the same yesterday, today, and forever" (Hebrews 13:8). When John the Baptist introduced Jesus to the people, he said, "Here is the One I was speaking about when I said that although He would come after me He would always be in front of me; for He existed before I was born!" (John 1:15, PH) In another passage there is a wonderful mix-up of tenses. When the Jews taunted our Lord, "You are not yet fifty years old, and have You seen Abraham?" He answered them with, "Truly, truly, I say to you, before Abraham was, I am" (John 8:57–58, RSV).

If Christ could make these statements during His incarnate earthly existence, how much more can we now make them of the risen, ascended, and glorified Christ! He transcends all time and space, which are, after all, finite concepts of the limitations on our human lives. As Jesus demonstrated on numerous occasions following His resurrection, He was not limited by either time or space, but could appear anywhere and anytime. In a sense, it all is present tense with Him. Because we are bound by time and space, we say Christ "walks back into time" in order to minister to some hurting person. Because of our finite limitations, we do not understand *how* He does this, but we can certainly *visualize Him doing it*. Indeed, on the basis of Scripture, we have every right to picture Him as *here and now*.

But is all this mere autosuggestion? A sort of self-hypnosis where we "psych" ourselves out by the use of mental pictures and strong imagination? No. The promises regarding the work of the Holy Spirit's participating presence and power assure us He really is here. It is the Holy Spirit who makes the trancendent Christ intimately immanent. The Spirit assures us He is truly alongside us, "taking hold along with us over on the other side." Later we shall look at some of the pictures of Jesus which are helpful in healing of the memories. While they are pictures based on biblical symbols, the *form* of the mental images by which we visualize His presence is the product of our imaginations. But the *fact* of His presence pictured by these images is guaranteed by the promises of Scripture.

There is a lovely hymn by Henry Twells which we often sang prior to the monthly evening healing services in our church. It beautifully expresses the healing power of Christ who is always with us in the present tense (*The Book of Hymns*, United Methodist Publishing House, p. 501).

> At even, ere the sun was set,
> The sick, O Lord, around Thee lay;
> O in what divers pains they met!
> O with what joy they went away!
>
> Once more 'tis eventide, and we,
> Oppressed with various ills, draw near;
> What if Thy form we cannot see?
> We know and feel that Thou art here.
>
> O Saviour Christ, our woes dispel,
> For some are sick, and some are sad,
> And some have never loved Thee well,
> And some have lost the love they had.
>
> And none, O Lord, have perfect rest,
> For none are wholly free from sin;
> And they who fain would serve Thee best
> Are conscious most of wrong within.
>
> O Saviour Christ, Thou too art man,
> Thou hast been troubled, tempted, tried;
> Thy kind but searching glance can scan
> The very wounds that shame would hide.

Thy touch has still its ancient power,
No word from Thee can fruitless fall;
Hear, in this solemn evening hour,
And in Thy mercy heal us all.

Pray Specifically

We need to be specific in our confessions and prayers. One of the great emphases of Scripture is the need for ruthless moral honesty in facing our sins, failures, and needs. In the very first story of human disobedience in the Garden, we see the human tendency to cover up when any kind of emotional pain is involved. When the Lord God came down for His usual time of fellowship with Adam and Eve, they hid from His presence among the trees of the Garden. When God called out to Adam asking where he was, he answered, "I was afraid because I was naked; so I hid myself" (Genesis 3:8–10). Ever since then, we humans have been afraid to be open and uncovered, not only with God but also with others *and ourselves*. It is this fear gone to extremes in our fallen, distorted personalities that we see in repressed memories which cause us pain. We cover and hide them rather than face them. This covertness permeates our personalities in every realm. It is the leading cause of our fear and guilt and, more than anything else, disrupts our relationships.

The biblical prescription for this endemic human disease is honesty, openness, repentance, and confession. Jesus called the Holy Spirit "The Spirit of Truth" (John 14–16). The Apostle John used the word *truth* twenty-two times in his Gospel and nine times in his First Epistle. In 1 John, we see a direct correlation between truth, confession, and our relationship to God, others, and ourselves. Let me explain.

Centuries before the branch of learning we call psychology ever began, John described what we now know as our defense mechanisms. These are simply the various ways we humans keep from seeing the truth, and protect ourselves from fear and anxiety. They don't change the reality or truth of the situation; they only change the way we look at it. We actually protect ourselves by deceiving ourselves, so that we won't have to change. Let's look at the Apostle John's words:

And this is the message we have heard from Him and announce to you, that God is light, and in Him there is no darkness at all. If we say that we have fellowship with Him and yet walk in darkness, we lie and do not practice the truth; but if we walk in the light as He Himself is in the light, we have fellowship with one another, and the blood of Jesus His Son cleanses us from all sin.

If we say that we have no sin, we are deceiving ourselves, and the truth is not in us. If we confess our sins, He is faithful and righteous to forgive us our sins and to cleanse us from all unrighteousness. If we say that we have not sinned, we make Him a liar, and His word is not in us (1 John 1:5–10).

Now let us see how both John and the psychologists describe the three main defense mechanisms. These are given in the order of their seriousness.

• Denial. This is the simplest and most direct of them all. We just plain deny something; we lie about it. We refuse to acknowledge it; we don't want to look at it or discuss it. John comments on this: "If we say that we have fellowship with Him and yet walk in darkness, we lie and do not practice the truth" (v. 6).

• Rationalization. This means of defense is more complicated and, therefore, more serious. It is not as outright as lying, but is more sophisticated. Here we try to give reasons which justify our behavior. Someone has said there are two reasons for everything we do: a *good* reason and the *real* reason! We not only deceive someone else, but now we deceive ourselves; it is a deeper deception than denial or lying because we are often unaware of it. John deals with this: "If we refuse to admit that we are sinners, then we live in a world of illusion and truth becomes a stranger to us" (v. 8, PH).

• Projection. This is the worst of them all because here we take deception one step further and blame others for our problems. In fact, we project our failures onto someone or something else and say *they have the problem.* John describes this so accurately: "We make Him (God) a liar and His Word is not in us" (v. 10). Whereas we began by telling the lie ourselves, we end up by saying God is telling the lie. "I'm not the liar; *He is!*"

Now I realize this passage of Scripture is set in the context of moral and spiritual matters. But it has a definite bearing on our subject, for its principles also extend to the emotional/spiritual areas of life. One of the reasons that unhealed memories can cause such disruption in our lives is that they usually contain many negative emotions, such as fear, hurt, anger, guilt, shame, and anxiety. Again and again these feelings arise and we wonder where they are coming from. We feel confused because we are unable to pinpoint the cause of the feelings. This makes us feel guilty, because "Christians are not supposed to have such feelings." So we not only have the problem, but we double back on ourselves with added guilt for ever having the problem. The difficulty lies in the fact that *we are unable to pray specifically about it.* It's like trying to fight a fog. What we desperately need is to be able to discover the place of specific need—to find out what the real problem is so we can then deal with it. The principle involved here is a very important one: *We cannot confess to God what we do not acknowledge to ourselves.* And so we make our generalized confessions, give and receive generalized forgiveness, and end up with a hazy, foggy, generalized relationship with God.

We do not intend it to be this way; but because *a lot of specifics are protected by our defense mechanisms and hidden in our buried memories, we cannot find emotional and spiritual relief from their onslaughts.* We need to uncover the situations, experiences, and attitudes which are causing the negative emotions and allow the Holy Spirit to deal with them specifically. And this is exactly what happens so often during the healing of memories prayer time. Instead of the general prayers, "O Lord, please help me to have better feelings toward my parents, or help me to forgive my brother, or sister," now the specific hurt is mentioned in detail. "O Lord, I was so hurt that day Daddy threw my toy across the room and broke it because I had accidentally spilled water on his book, and then he made fun of me when I cried. I was so angry, I really hated him for that. I was really glad when he had the accident that afternoon." Or, "Father, I have never really forgiven my teacher, Mrs. Slade, for humiliating me that day in front of the whole class, and accusing me of something another kid had done. And I've wanted to get even with Johnny for lying about it. I forgive them for what they did to me; and I need You to forgive me, Lord, for these years of resentment toward them." And on and on it goes. *Specific memories* which have finally been allowed to surface, resulting in *specific confessions of specific feelings; specific forgiveness* given and received, resulting in deep inner healing and cleansing. This principle of specificity is central to the healing of memories and is in perfect accord with the biblical truths regarding repentance, confession, and healing.

Time and again I have seen the turning point in a person's healing come when his memories plugged in to some important details he had pushed out of his mind. Joyce was a competent social worker in her late twenties. Engaged to be married, she had moved to our part of the country to be near her fiancé. Within six months he broke the engagement. She was crushed and sought help, for the shock of the rejection forced her to realize that this was a pattern in all of her relationships with men. Although Joyce had been a Christian for several years, she had a lot of trouble with mood swings, depression, and a general sense of hostility toward men. She commuted to work in a car pool and the other women didn't like when it was her turn to drive. They told her she scared them because she drove "angrily." Two of her companions were married. Joyce noticed that the happier their marriages were, the angrier she got; she was jealous of their good relationships. On the job her coworkers watched her short fuse and volatile temper. Besides her broken engagement, it was what one of them had said to her that jolted her into realizing she needed counseling. "Joyce, you certainly are an even-tempered person—you're always mad."

In counseling, Joyce told of a home in which there was an unbelievable amount of drinking, conflict, and fighting. Caring Christians had helped her find a church family and a new life in Christ. But the lack of fatherly affection and love left its toll, and she constantly sought to fill the empty hole in her heart through a series of boyfriends. It was always the same pattern—desperately reaching out for affection, she would become too physically involved with her steadies. Although her Christian moral standards prevented her from going "all the way," she would become very intimate with them. This would result in a loss of self-respect and usually end up in a breakup. Joyce was very discouraged and angry at her own compulsions. She was sure this was God's way of punishing her and that He would never allow her to have a lasting relationship and a husband.

We went through a long list of hurts and hates, humiliations and guilts during a lengthy prayer time. A whole river of emotion was released, and after considerable struggle she found grace to forgive and be washed of her bitterness. Then, when I thought we were about finished, the Spirit pulled back the veil of remembrance and sharpened her memory. Specific details of a sordid night spent with a man became crystal clear. She cried out in agonizing prayer as she relived the terrible feelings she experienced. "O Jesus, I feel so terrible. I have let myself down, and failed You in my witness. I have lost all respect for myself; I have no faith in myself to carry out my convictions. I give up on myself—and I feel that You have given up on me too."

She then realized that that night had been a turning point of self-hate and despair. Ever since then she had felt God was punishing her; she had been punishing herself by her self-destructive sexual behavior. In prayer, she now allowed a merciful and loving God to minister to her as she relived that awful night. He forgave her and gave her back her sense of virtue and self-worth as a woman. It was a blessed time of cleansing and restoration. What a joy it was two years later to be the officiating minister at her marriage to a deeply dedicated young man. The most beautiful part of the ceremony was when they both shared how God had taken the broken pieces of their lives and reconstructed them, now giving them the gift of a new beginning. We've talked about transformation several times since. She always reminds me that the healing change began when she could confess to God a lot of specifics which, prior to then, she had prayed about only in generalities.

Minister to One Another

The Body-Life principle means that Christians minister to one another for healing. James enunciated this truth in his epistle: "And the prayer offered in faith will restore the one who is sick, and the Lord will raise him up, and if he has committed sins, they will be forgiven him. Therefore, confess your sins to one another and pray for one another, so that you may be healed" (James 5:15–16).

Our Lord Himself, in His great teachings on prayer, gave us the promise of corporate prayer. "I say to you, that if two of you agree on earth about anything that they may ask, it shall be done for them by My Father who is in heaven. For where two or three have gathered together in My name, there I am in their midst" (Matthew 18:19–20).

The kind of prayer which takes place during the healing of memories fits perfectly with the commands to "confess to one another," and to "agree" about the subject before they ask for an answer. The Scriptures recognize that some petitions require a corporate, open, and sharing kind of prayer before they will be answered. Once again both the "confession" and the "agreeing" assume the specificity which God honors. I think it is significant that the verse prior to the "agreeing" promise tells us, "Whatever you shall bind on earth shall have been bound in heaven; and whatever you loose on earth shall have been loosed in heaven." And the verses which follow contain some of the most important teachings on the subject of forgiving and being forgiven that we find anywhere in the New Testament. Surely all this fits most perfectly in the context of praying for the healing of memories. It seems in God's plan there are certain kinds of healings—physical, emotional, and spiritual—which can come about only through the ministry of other members of the Body of Christ.

Confession and Restoration

I would be remiss if I did not close this chapter by pointing out that this particular biblical principle is now being fully confirmed by the latest findings in medicine and psychology. In the *Lexington Herald-Leader*, Lexington, Kentucky, September 23, 1984, an article appeared from the *New York Times* News Service. It was entitled, "Confession May Be Good for Body," and it went on to say, "Confession, whatever it may do for the soul, appears to be good for the body. New studies show persuasively that people who are able to confide in others about their troubled feelings or some traumatic event, rather than bear the turmoil in silence, are less vulnerable to disease." It then reported on several different experiments which confirm the "long-term health benefits" of sharing our most painful secrets with others.

Dr. James Pennebaker's research shows that "the act of confiding in someone else protects the body against damaging internal stresses that are the penalty for carrying around an onerous emotional burden such as unspoken remorse." Similar research conducted at Harvard University shows that those who do not share have "less effective immune systems." Dr. Pennebaker, of Johns Hopkins School of Medicine, publishing his findings in *The Journal of Abnormal Psychology*, confirms these discoveries.

How interesting that modern science is just now catching up with the plain teachings of Scripture. David declared these truths thousands of years ago.

How blessed is he whose transgression is forgiven,
Whose sin is covered!

How blessed is the man to whom
the Lord does not impute iniquity,
And in whose spirit there is no deceit!
When I kept silent about my sin, my body
wasted away through my groaning all day long.
For day and night Thy hand was heavy upon me;
My vitality was drained away
as with the fever-heat of summer.
I acknowledged my sin to Thee,
And my iniquity I did not hide;
I said, "I will confess my transgressions to the Lord."
And Thou didst forgive the guilt of my sin.
Therefore, let everyone who is godly pray to Thee
in a time when Thou mayest be found. . . .
Thou art my hiding place:
Thou dost preserve me from trouble:
Thou dost surround me with songs of deliverance.

(Psalm 32:1–7)

Is there an example in the Bible where the principles we have described were actually used to heal someone's painful memories? Yes, in the way Jesus handled Peter's denial and restoration. There are only two places in the New Testament where the word for a "charcoal fire" is used. In John 18:18 we are told that Peter stood with the servants and officers in the courtyard warming himself before a "charcoal fire." It was there he denied Jesus three times. Later, on the beach that post-Resurrection morning, when Jesus prepared breakfast for the disciples, He deliberately set the stage for Peter (John 21:9). Once again there was the "charcoal fire." Jesus, master Physician and Psychiatrist, forced Peter to stand near a charcoal fire. Oh, how his memories and his shame must have burned within him. Three times he had denied his Lord and three times he was asked to affirm his love for Him—standing before those hot red coals. Jesus used a fire of coals, somewhat like a "coal off the altar of fire" used by the Lord in Isaiah 6, to cauterize and heal Peter's pain and shame. As he faced pain in all of its specifics, his memories were healed, and he was restored and recommissioned for service.

6

*Indications
for the Healing
of Memories*

Wʜᴀᴛ ᴀʀᴇ ꜱᴏᴍᴇ of the symptoms which point to the possible
need for the healing of memories? I say *possible*, because all along I
have been stressing that the healing of memories is one, and only one,
form of inner healing. I would reemphasize that here. The kinds
of emotional/spiritual dysfunctions which will be described do not
automatically mean memory healing is the only spiritual therapy that
should be considered.

When painful memories have not been faced, healed, and integrated
into life, they often break through defenses and interfere with normal
living.

*One of the evidences of this is recurring mental pictures, scenes, or dreams
which bring disturbance and disruption to the emotional and spiritual life.*
During the counseling process, I always ask a question something
like this: "Do you have certain pictures in your mind which keep coming back? Which won't seem to let you alone, but keep repeating themselves over and over again? Or perhaps which keep recurring in your
dreams? Mental images (memories) which are so strong they actually
interfere with your present life?" If the answer is affirmative, I request
that the person tell me about them.

While the particulars may be drastically different, the facts are the
same. There are certain mental pictures which keep coming back like
TV video replays. Sometimes they are like the replays in slow motion,

which means that *the emotions which go along with the memories are very intense.* It is like the super-slow motion of the game, when you actually *see and feel* the determination or the pain on the player's face! Often these recurring play backs are strongest just before dropping off to sleep, or while waking during the night, or just before awakening in the morning. Sometimes they are in dreams (nightmares) in which the victims discover themselves screaming, struggling, or in a cold sweat. These can be so intense as to affect their ability to cope with life the following day.

The characters and the plots of the recurring scenes are as varied as the lives of those involved. However, I have noticed the contents and the pain seem to have certain of the following common denominators.

Hurts

In one sense, anything which causes physical pain or mental and emotional anguish could be called a hurt. I will confine this discussion to some of the more common experiences of life which cause emotional suffering by striking a blow to a person's selfhood. Our present word *hurt* comes from the older Middle English words *hurten, hirten,* "to strike or harm," which in turn come from the Old French *hurter (American Heritage Dictionary of the English Language).* Whatever strikes or harms our ego causes us hurt. This can happen to us at any level of life, from the prenatal stage, infancy, childhood, the teens, through young adulthood, and on to old age. At the very heart of many of our hurts is *a sense of rejection.* The more important or significant the rejecting person is to us, the greater is our feeling of being rejected by him.

The most painful kinds of rejection occur during the earliest years of life—preschool and the early grades—because there is no way of explaining the reason for an action which infants or children interpret as rejection. Children cannot understand why they are being treated that way, and they don't know how to cope with it. There may be very logical reasons for what is taking place, but there is no way of communicating them or of their being properly understood. For example, many of the most deeply felt rejections result from accidents, illnesses, unavoidable delays, or even deaths. Parents, family members, relatives, teachers, pastors, or friends are forced by the circumstances to give something or someone else prime time and priority attention. This is experienced as a rejection and can leave a painful scar on the memories.

Jeff, a very earnest Christian young man, came seeking help for his low self-esteem, depression, and spiritual defeats. He had an almost constant fear of being abandoned by family, friends, and even by God. Strange feelings of lonely uneasiness which stirred up hazy memories would come back to him again and again. In various ways this uneasiness was the theme of many situations which haunted his dreams. But it was all so foggy that he was hard put to describe it very clearly. Of one thing he was sure—*rejection was in the center of it all*. We had no difficulty in observing Jeff's reactions. In such situations, the core of hurt is so painful that the person develops the additional problem of becoming terribly afraid of being hurt (in Jeff's case, rejected) in the same way again. This becomes a vicious circle—like a dog chasing its own tail and occasionally biting it! So the fear of additional rejection and further hurt grows and grows until it affects the person's perception of life. The fear becomes an expectation and this finally becomes the *hurtful filter* through which he screens the most ordinary experiences of life. All this causes him to *feel* a great deal more pain than he is actually experiencing in his present circumstances.

With Jeff, it was easy to trace this painful progression; he was now living in a kind of carefully insulated space capsule which protected him from more of the anticipated wounds. So we began where he was and slowly moved backward in time, using various methods we will describe in a later chapter. We, of course, also surrounded our sessions with much prayer, constantly asking for the understanding and discernment which only the Holy Spirit can give. One of my earliest mentors described this process by an unforgettable picture which has been of great help in my counseling. He advised me, "Sometimes you just have to keep on rowing and praying, praying and rowing, until the Spirit shows you the right place to land!"

One day the Spirit showed Jeff and me the proper memory dock, and after landing, He guided us to explore a labyrinth of hidden caves filled with feelings of abandonment and rejection. It had all begun at the birth of a baby sister, when Jeff was four years old. His mother had undergone a difficult pregnancy and an extremely painful delivery. To make matters worse, his sister had been born with a correctable birth defect which required a lot of attention and considerable expense. Up to this point, Jeff had been the center of the family care and affection. Now there was a drastic shift. Under the most normal circumstances, this "redistribution of love" is difficult enough. In Jeff's case, it was traumatic. In many families, the older child makes the adjustment by becoming "Mama's Little Helper" and is thus made an important part of the enlarged system. But the nature of the newborn's problems excluded Jeff from even this role. Quite unintentionally, Jeff was left out and felt extremely hurt by what he perceived as deliberate rejection. There were extended periods when the sister required treatment by specialists in a distant town, and Jeff was left with an unmarried aunt who did not comprehend the change in Jeff's behavior. Instead of giving him much-needed extra understanding and love, she only added extra discipline and punishment. Jeff's hurt and rejection were compounded by confused feelings of fear, anger, and guilt. He was sure that it was something he had done which had caused the whole situation—his mother's morning sickness, the difficult delivery, and the birth defect. Like every child, he had ambivalent feelings of love and anger toward his mother and baby sister—*was God punishing him for those wrong thoughts and feelings?* He pushed those unacceptable feelings out of his mind, but life seemed to become increasingly unfair and painful. To a grown-up this may sound ridiculous, but on a four-year-old level, it has a consistent sense of logic and reason.

As we shared and prayed together, Jeff began to recall in graphic detail the vicious circle of hurt, fear of more hurt, and the distorted perceptions which presumed additional rejection and hurt. As a series of memories emerged, he was astounded at the deep feelings of rage and bitterness toward his sister and aunt which erupted along with them. During the prayer time I was reminded of the story in John 5. . . . you remember, the people claimed God sent an angel to trouble the waters of the pool which then became healing waters. In a similar way, God stirred up Jeff's mind for emotional and spiritual hydrotherapy. The only way healing became possible was for him to step right down into this pool of troubled memories, painful as this was. It took several trips (dips) into the pool to receive adequate wholeness. Each time, we asked Jesus to give Jeff the understanding, love, affection, and forgiveness he needed at a particular stage of his childhood. Finally, the propulsive and compulsive intensity of his recurring memories and dreams was dissolved, and Jeff was able to learn mature and Christian ways of relating to others. Of course, he had to work hard at reprogramming his outlook and learning new relationships. However, *because of the healing of his memories he was now free to do so.* Prior to this, in spite of much effort and spiritual discipline, he had not been able to do so.

Humiliations

Another common theme of these recurring painful flashbacks is embarrassment, shame, and humiliation. A party game or TV program based on "My Most Embarrassing Moment" may be very entertaining. Those are the incidents we have worked through and can even laugh at. But memories involving times when we were deeply humiliated produce the most painful emotions we experience, and are some of the chief causes of low self-esteem and depression. Stanley, a minister in his forties, shared this story with a small group at a Yokefellow retreat one weekend. It was his first day at school and he was very proud of the fact that he could write his name. So when the teacher asked who could write his name, he was the first pupil to volunteer. He took out a piece of paper and spelled it out in big block letters—STANLEY.

"She said, "You've spelled it wrong. It's spelled STANDLEY."

He replied timidly, "No, Ma'am, there's no D in my name."

"Write it again," she said sternly, "and spell it right this time."

Stanley wrote it again, without the D. She scooped up the paper, held it before the whole class, turning so all could see, "Look, boys and girls. Here's a boy who's so stupid he doesn't even know how to spell his own name. Now Stanley, write your name again and put the D in it this time, do you hear?"

So he did as he was ordered. His spirit was crushed and he felt shattered inside when some of the children around him tittered with laughter at his deep crimson blush.

Stanley commented on the incident to his share group, "That scene seems stamped on my mind forever. I cringe and hurt inside every time I think of how the class laughed when she told them how stupid I was. And worst of all, for some weird reason, I accepted her evaluation. The crazy thing is that I still feel stupid. I know it doesn't make any sense—my wife, my accomplishments, my people—all tell me I'm not stupid. But there's an inner voice that says I am." He added, "Not long ago I was talking to one of my members who has a Ph.D. He told me he had been helped greatly by our conversation and paid me a genuine, high compliment. And you know what? Something inside me said immediately, "Well, he may have a Ph.D., but he must be pretty dumb not to see how stupid and inadequate I really am!"

It's amazing how insensitive parents, teachers, and other authority figures can be to the devastating effects of public put-downs on children. With the best of intentions, these adults often use the put-down as a form of discipline or a way of changing behavior. Because it brings rapid results, they think it is legitimate. They fail to realize the deep damage to the fragile self-esteem of tenderhearted youngsters, because of agonizing memories which are literally branded on their minds.

Scripture has much to teach us at this point. God's Spirit usually came to people and dealt with their shameful failures privately. How careful Jesus was to do this—He confronted people with their sins and mistakes when they were alone with Him. Indeed, He went out of His way to defend and build them up before others, waiting for the opportune private moment to take up the negatives. In His advice, in Matthew 18:15–17, Jesus was careful to lay down principles for dealing with all such situations. First we speak to people privately and try to correct situations. Only when that doesn't succeed do we gradually add others (witnesses) until finally there is the public admonition. When Paul gave the updated version of the fifth commandment (parent-child relationships) in Ephesians 6:1–4, he exhorted fathers not to do anything which would deliberately goad their children to resentment.

However, not all the recurring memories of humiliation are necessarily public. Some of them involve private situations when cruel and thoughtless remarks are etched deeply on the walls of the imagination.

One beautiful woman, who battled low self-esteem for many years, shared with great pain the mental picture which arose almost every time she put on her makeup. She had been brought up in a very strict home where her father considered any form of makeup sinful. One morning, in her preteens, she used some face powder to cover the skin blemishes which often occur at that age. Here are her very own words as she recalled this hurtful humiliation, "My Dad laughed at me and sarcastically commented that I looked like a white-faced heifer." And then she added with significant emotion, "*And not once while I was growing up did he ever tell me that I looked nice.*"

Thinking back, we were able to understand why her dad had done this. He was afraid that her attractiveness would "get her into trouble with the boys." Downgrading her appearance was his mistaken way of protecting her virtue. Sad to say, this is a mistake many parents make, when they have handsome sons or beautiful daughters. That they mean no harm does not lessen the emotional wreckage. All too often their attempts to control by guilt, shame, and humiliation become the seedbed of painful memories which someday will need healing.

Sometimes memories of humiliation are not connected with specific incidents, but are part of the overall atmosphere of the growing years. We find this especially in connection with an alcoholic parent. The family becomes a part of the system which has to cover for mother's or dad's drinking problem. So the child or teenager becomes adept at making excuses for not being able to invite friends in. A way of life which includes half-truths and plausible reasons fills the youngster with shame and deceit. Feelings of being different from others and always cheated out of fun times poisons their memories with the pain of humiliation.

Horrors

I am using this strong word to cover the gamut of fears and terrors which can lie embedded in the lower layers of the mind and one day rise to fill us with all kinds of anxieties. It would require an encyclopedia to cover all the different ways the roots of fear become embedded in our memories. It is said there are 365 "Fear nots" in the Bible— one for each day of the year. This is because God knows what it's like to live in this fear-filled world; He understands that these deep-seated fears are some of our greatest obstacles to faith.

Some of the most common and disabling fears shared with me for memory healing include the following:

fear of the dark,
fear of being abandoned or left alone,
fear of failure, not accomplishing anything worthwhile,
fear of losing one's mind or control of one's emotions,
fear of sex, sexual thoughts, and desires,
fear of people and trusting others,
fear of cancer and other serious illnesses,

fear of God and the final judgment,
fear of committing the "unpardonable sin,"
fear of the future,
fear of death of others close to us, or our own.

Among Christians, many of these fears are greatly intensified by a sense of guilt for having the fear in the first place. Good Christians are not supposed to be anxious or afraid—after all, Jesus is always with them and so there is nothing to be afraid of. Besides, the Bible says, "Perfect love casts out fear" (1 John 4:18). And so they become all the more afraid and are trapped in a vicious cycle of being afraid to admit they are afraid!

The fact is, many of these fears are rooted in frightening experiences, unhealthy teachings, and poor relationships somewhere in the past, especially during the early years of childhood. They have been pushed to the bottom level of the mind so often that the person may have only the haziest memories of them. Often there are not specific remembrances and the individual is plagued with general, global feelings of anxiety which attach themselves to first one thing and then another.

It was like this with Jack and Jill, brother and sister in a very emotionally disturbed family. The father was a religious tyrant and the mother a religious doormat. He ruled "by the Book," meaning his own inflexible (and usually wrong) interpretations of the Bible, backed up by an unpredictable temper which sometimes bordered on violence. The mother survived and tried to maintain peace and hold the family together by "sweet submission." The result was an atmosphere where everyone walked on emotional eggshells before the father. And before the Heavenly Father as well, because of the faulty earthly model and his dogmatic half-truths. It was the kind of religious home which Christian counselors confront so often. We are always amazed at the amount of emotional and spiritual wreckage wrought in the name of twisted Scripture—especially the Ephesians 5:21—6:4 passage which describes marriage and family relationships.

The memories which caused Jack's fears were so deeply submerged that when they came out, they were mixed into a great variety of biblical and theological questions. I could expect a regular phone call from Jack every few weeks. They always went something like this, "I was reading in the Bible recently and came across a passage where it says thus and so, and this has bothered me a lot. I'm afraid that I . . ." or

"I don't understand how. . . ." This would be the preface introducing an area of great anxiety which was troubling Jack's spiritual life. It was not until Jack could recall and face the painful and horrifying climate of his developmental years that he was able to be healed of its memories and find wholesomeness in both his emotions and his beliefs.

Jill's fears came out in a quite different way—all kinds of illnesses, some very real and some imaginary. Jill's mother had paid an awful price for her failure to confront the true situation and express her real feelings. When she could stand it no longer, she took to bed. This brought her some much-needed attention, even tenderness, from her husband. He, in turn, used it as another means of controlling the children—"Be quiet now; don't upset your mother and make her sicker than you already have."

Jill had learned well from her mother, and her life also had an unpredictable atmosphere; different, but equally fearful. Crippling pains, a forty-eight hour virus, or even some kind of heart condition could strike at any time. And so Jill, like the woman mentioned in Mark 5:26, "endured much at the hands of many physicians, and . . . spent all that she had and was not helped at all." It seemed as if Jill wore a coat of fear and kept looking for an illness to hang it on. Healing of some ancient memories, and then lots of practice at learning other ways of coping with responsibility, have enabled Jill to lead a reasonably stable life.

Hates

We come to an area which is at the very heart of our subject—resentment, bitterness, and hate. In a later chapter we shall show how to deal with our hates, through the prayers for forgiving and being forgiven. At this point, we are considering hate as one of the major ingredients in those recurring mental replays which are a sign we may need a healing of some painful memories. For everything we have described in this chapter usually brings with it strong resentments. Sometimes we are quite conscious of these and struggle against them in prayer, but seemingly to no avail. Sometimes we are simply aware that general feelings of rage are within us, but we are unable to pinpoint the causes. They seem to be submerged just below the level of our conscious recall. This is often the cause of depression among

Christians, this frozen and buried resentment. At other times, the stress from this repressed hate expresses itself through the body language of sickness. There are many illnesses which may have their roots in unhealed resentments. There is the classic story of the youngster who overheard his dad telling someone his mother had colitis. He sighed and asked his father, "Who has she been colliding with now?"

You remember when Jesus was riding into Jerusalem, in that event we call the Triumphal Entry, that the religious authorities told Him to make the people stop shouting their Hosannas and expressing their emotions. Jesus replied that if He didn't allow the people to express themselves, "the very stones would cry out" (Luke 19:40). There is a living parable in this story. When Christians fail to express their true feelings, their bodies cry out through the voices of pain and illness. This is especially true of resentments buried so deep they are not even allowed to enter into conscious memories. These occasionally burst through into the mind and then the slow motion video replays occur. Scenes and pictures arise and rage takes over. Christians are particularly confused when they then "take it out" on someone nearby—a spouse or a child they dearly love. This, in turn, fills them with remorse, guilt, and spiritual defeat. They are further bewildered because they can't figure out where it all comes from. Most likely they unwittingly drilled into some ancient and untapped river of resentment which, like a sudden oil strike, "blew" up. When this keeps happening and doesn't seem to be helped by discipline, prayer, and deeper experiences in the Spirit, we should look for the causes in the pressure and pain of unhealed memories.

Perhaps the most puzzling and shocking experience of all is when devout Christians find themselves overrun by feelings of anger against God Himself. This is terribly hard to admit. I have spent many sessions gently leading counselees to the place where they finally realized their resentment against God. The shock has been so great that some have momentarily passed out in my office, or have became nauseated to the point of vomiting. For they love God and want to serve and please Him and are devastated when they discover this submerged anger against Him. After the initial trauma passes, they are able to take their bitter feelings into His very presence and let Him wash them away in His love. Later, as we look back, we see this very act of remembering and feeling was the necessary breakthrough and the beginning of their healing.

It was this way with one man who shared with me some of the worst stories of child abuse I have ever heard. It was hard to imagine the ingenious ways his mother used to hurt him, exquisite acts of physical torture and verbal decimation. Being a good Christian, he had never really faced his true feelings about all this. Instead, he kept assuring me how much he loved his mother. Little by little, the painful details came out and he became aware of a violent rage against her. But underneath this was an even deeper layer of anger. One day, right in the middle of our prayers for healing these horrible memories, he cried out in anguish, *"And God, where in the hell were You when all this was going on?"* A flood of violent emotion gripped him. In his fear he shook like a leaf. But it wasn't long before he experienced a flood of God's love washing over him like ocean waves. Years of reprogramming and therapy have been necessary for his wholeness, but there is no doubt that this moment was the beginning of a great healing in his life.

In a truly remarkable book, *May I Hate God?* by Pierre Wolff (Paulist Press), the author shows how our anger and resentment, which we think will only separate us from God, can also become the doorway to greater intimacy with Him. It is a small book and I recommend it to those who are afraid to face this painful area of their spiritual lives. I have found it very useful in preparing people for the healing of memories prayer time.

And so we have taken an entire chapter to consider the primary symptom which indicates the need for memory healing—that is, recurring mental pictures and memories which are so intense they interfere with present behavior.

We are now going to spend the next two chapters on a second symptom—distorted and destructive concepts of God.

7

Distorted Concepts of God

◇◇◇◇◇◇◇◇◇◇◇◇◇◇◇◇◇◇◇◇◇◇◇◇◇◇◇◇◇◇◇◇◇◇◇◇

INSIDE EVERY ONE of us is a mental picture of God. We often speak of this as our concept of God and talk about it as if it were something completely in our minds. We forget that, along with what we have been taught about God, experiences, memories, and feelings play a large part in forming this picture. *The most determinative factor is our "feltness" of who God is and what He is really like.* It is surprising the number of genuine Christians who are caught in an inner conflict between what they *think* about God and what they *feel* about God (and how He feels toward them). Their head *theology* is excellent but their gut-level *knee-ology* (what they feel when they pray) is terrible. This is the source of many emotional hangups in Christians and one of the strongest indicators for a healing of memories. Years of experience have taught me that regardless of how much correct doctrine Christians may know, *until they have a picture and a felt sense that God is truly good and gracious, there can be no lasting spiritual victory m their lives.*

The Good News and the Bad News

How is it that the Gospel which we proclaim as Good News so often becomes bad news that affects our feelings?

To understand this, let's borrow a concept from foreign missions—cross-cultural evangelism. In a short time, a missionary becomes aware of the fact that what the people hear him say can be very different from what he has actually said. He proclaims (encodes) something, but the listener hears (decodes) something else. While working in India, I soon learned to be very careful about preaching on the text "You must be born again" (John 3:7). The Hindu decodes those words through his belief system of reincarnation and a cycle of rebirths. So he hears it as, "You must be born again and again and again," going through many reincarnations until one finds salvation (release) from the cycle.

Or, let's bring it closer to home literally. I say the word *home*. To some the word means "heaven," and their mental images and feelings correspond to that. To others it means "hell," and they see and feel correspondingly. Our concepts are composite mental pictures made up of many different pieces which come to us from various sources. Chief among those which contribute to our concept of God are life experiences, interpersonal relationships, and teachings we have been given. Certainly, what we have been *taught* is extremely important. But what we have *caught* is equally so. In fact, *our feelings about God can drastically affect our ideas of God.* This is because those feelings are part of the dynamics which determine the way we perceive the teachings given to us. *This crucial fact is overlooked by so many pastors and Christian workers.* They assume if the doctrines and ideas they preach and teach are biblically correct, they will automatically clear up a person's concepts of God and enable him to believe in God and trust Him. They imagine that the Holy Spirit, as it were, somehow drills a hole in the top of the hearer's head and pours the pure truth into him.

With many people, nothing could be further from the truth. For although the Holy Spirit is the One who reveals the truth, what the listener hears and pictures and feels still has to be filtered through him. The Holy Spirit Himself does not bypass the personality equipment by which a person perceives things. *And when those perceiving receptors have been severely damaged, the biblical truths get distorted.*

In this sense the facetious remark—"Man creates God in his own image" contains an element of truth. Even for the most healthy and normal Christians, clarifying their concepts of God is a lifelong task and a central part of reaching maturity in Christ. This is one of the main reasons why the Incarnation was so necessary. The Word had to become *flesh*. God had gone as far as He could in revealing Himself through *words*. For at their very best—as in the greatest prophets of the Old Testament—words are subject to the distortions of sinful and damaged hearers. Only when the Word became a human life was it possible for us to see a true picture of God, "full of grace and truth" (John 1:14). But the problem of distortion is still partially with us, for the content of the words we read in the Bible which describe Jesus and the character of God is greatly influenced by our memories and relationships.

How the Good News Becomes Bad News

Because it is so important for us to understand the connections between what we hear about God and what we feel about Him, I have illustrated the process on the chart. Beginning at the top, you will see the Good News as revealed to us in Jesus Christ. If you have seen Him, you have seen the Father (John 14). While this list of God's characteristics is not complete, it is sufficient to give a true picture of the goodness of God. You will note that the lines coming down are straight. This represents their truthfulness—the truth and grace revealed in Christ.

As you continue reading downward, you will notice that the lines become jagged and twisted. This means something is happening to the straightness and truthfulness of the Good News about God as they pass through unhealthy interpersonal relationships. In every case now, the Good News has become distorted into the Bad News and the person perceives God as the opposite of who He really is. Compare the truth on the chart with the distortion. The loving, caring God has become hateful, or at least unconcerned.

Many times I ask counselees, who have already given me their theological picture of a loving God, how they think God feels about them. All too often they say, "I don't think He really cares for me; I'm not sure He knows I exist. If He does, I'm not sure He's concerned." In contradiction to their theological view, they *feel* that God is mean and unforgiving, holds grudges against them, and constantly reminds them of past sins; that He is a very legal God who keeps accounts on them. As in the song about Santa Claus, "He's making a list and checking it twice!"

Sometimes I ask people who are having a difficult time describing their God to draw a picture of Him. As you might imagine, I have an interesting collection of drawings. Several depict a huge eye which covers a whole page—God watching everything they do, waiting to catch them at some failure or wrongdoing. Others have drawn angry

HOW THE GOOD NEWS BECOMES THE BAD NEWS

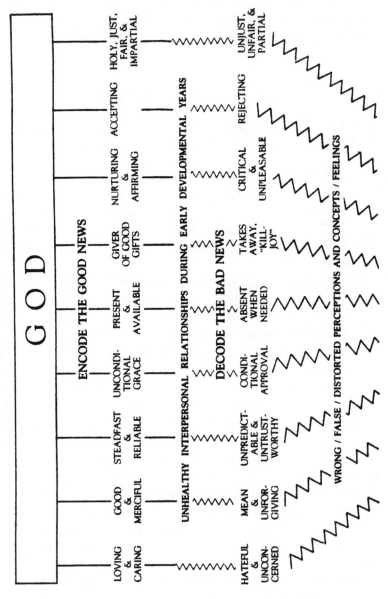

GOD

ENCODE THE GOOD NEWS

| LOVING & CARING | GOOD & MERCIFUL | STEADFAST & RELIABLE | UNCONDITIONAL GRACE | PRESENT & AVAILABLE | GIVER OF GOOD GIFTS | NURTURING & AFFIRMING | ACCEPTING | HOLY, JUST, FAIR, & IMPARTIAL |

UNHEALTHY INTERPERSONAL RELATIONSHIPS DURING EARLY DEVELOPMENTAL YEARS

DECODE THE BAD NEWS

| HATEFUL & UNCONCERNED | MEAN & UNFORGIVING | UNPREDICTABLE & UNTRUSTWORTHY | CONDITIONAL APPROVAL | ABSENT WHEN NEEDED | TAKES AWAY, "KILL-JOY" | CRITICAL & UNPLEASABLE | REJECTING | UNJUST, UNFAIR, & PARTIAL |

WRONG / FALSE / DISTORTED PERCEPTIONS AND CONCEPTS / FEELINGS

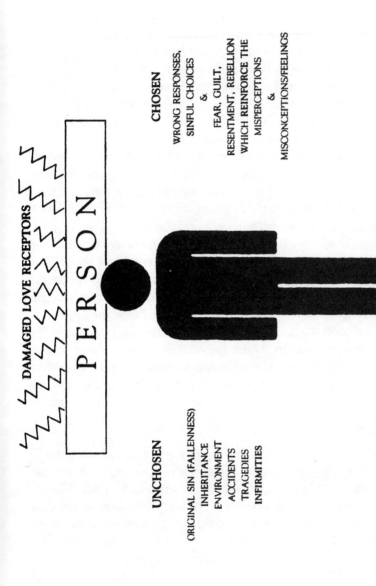

DAMAGED LOVE RECEPTORS

P E R S O N

CHOSEN

WRONG RESPONSES, SINFUL CHOICES
&
FEAR, GUILT, RESENTMENT, REBELLION
WHICH REINFORCE THE MISPERCEPTIONS
&
MISCONCEPTIONS/FEELINGS

UNCHOSEN

ORIGINAL SIN (FALLENNESS)
INHERITANCE
ENVIRONMENT
ACCIDENTS
TRAGEDIES
INFIRMITIES

WHY THE HOLY SPIRIT SOMETIMES NEEDS A TEMPORARY ASSISTANT
(LIKE A PASTORAL COUNSELOR)

human faces, or birds of prey with sharp beaks and talons. One young theological student said he couldn't draw very well but next time he'd bring a picture of his God. I was very curious about it. It happened to be the Christmas season and he brought a magazine with an artist's drawing of an extra large, angry and demanding Scrooge sitting behind a desk, quill pen in hand with his debit-credit ledger before him. Standing in front of the desk facing Scrooge was small, terror-stricken Bob Cratchett. Pointing to Scrooge he explained, "That's God," and then to Cratchett, "That's me." And just think, this young seminarian made an A in his theology class!

Follow the chart across. Instead of trusting a God who is predictable in His steadfastness and reliable in His faithfulness, many Christians are filled with fears and anxiety because at a deep gut-level they sense God to be untrustworthy. They sing about "amazing grace," talk about it in Sunday School, and even witness about it to others. But on a performance level, they live fearful of a God who accepts and loves them only when they "measure up." They quote verses about God *always* being with them, but ask me, "Why is it that God never seems there when I need Him?" Their God is not, as Scripture puts it, "the giver of every good and perfect gift" (James 1:17), or the One who desires to give good things to His children (Matthew 7:11). Rather, He is a killjoy who delights in taking from them whatever they really enjoy. "Why is it that God always seems to take from me everyone I've ever loved?" It's as if they feel God constantly keeps an eye on them, and as soon as they truly love someone or are having too much fun at something, He gets jealous and says, "Give it up, or I'll take it away from you."

They do not see God as a nurturing and affirming parent who is always encouraging His children in their development; or as a good father or mother, pleased with every step of growth. Instead His face seems critical and unpleasable. He is indeed the inner voice that always says, "That's not quite good enough." So they feel rejected by God, unaccepted by Him because they are unacceptable to Him and thus caught in the vicious circle of trying to please an unpleasable God. They become POWs—not prisoners of war but Performance Oriented Workers. The final distortion is yet to come, for as I pointed out in *Healing for Damaged Emotions*, these Christians usually have hidden anger against God. Therefore, they come to feel He is unfair and partial in His judgments. He is an unjust God to them, but treats everyone else fairly. This is why they often freely tell others about a loving God and explain the plan of salvation by grace, but are unable to apply it to themselves.

Now we come to the crux of the whole matter. Notice what it was that brought about the twisting of the lines and the distorting of God's character—*unhealthy interpersonal relationships, especially those which occurred during the early development years of childhood and adolescence.* More than any other factor, these faulty relationships cause the emotional damages which distort spiritual perceptions. You will notice on the chart that the twisted lines actually go in both directions. They proceed down from the bad experiences and relationships and also come up out of the persons. This means that what began from outside sources gradually has been internalized. It is now the way they actually perceive other people, themselves, and God.

It's a way of life. We could liken their condition to a kind of spiritual paranoia. Paranoid persons can take the most loving, affirming statements and twist them into insults, rejections, and even threats. In the same way, Christians with *damaged love receptors* can rake the Good News and turn it into Bad News. This is why so many of them have an uncanny knack of missing the wonderful promises of God's mercy, love, and grace, and consistently selecting Bible passages which emphasize wrath, punishment, judgment, and the unpardonable sin. Unless Christian workers truly understand the dynamics of this, *they will not be able* to *help these damaged persons.* They will actually *harm* them, overloading more oughts and guilts upon them by giving them the spiritual disciplines of Bible reading and prayer.

Finally, look at the columns on either side of the person in the drawing. The fact that we may have been victims of painful experiences and hurtful relationships does not excuse us from responsibility. Certainly, there are many *unchosen* factors of life, including our fallen natures which in themselves tend to produce distorted pictures of God. There are other factors over which we have neither choice nor control—our biological and psychological inheritance, our geographical and cultural environment, and the accidents, tragedies, and traumas of life. These make up our unchosens which, in many cases, have caused what Scripture would term our *infirmities.* Infirmities are the weaknesses, the cripplings, the inborn and ingrown defects of body, mind, or spirit. They are not in themselves sins but are, rather, those qualities of our personalities which predispose us and incline us to ward certain sins. They are the weakened places in our defenses which undermine our resistance to temptation and sin.

On the opposite side of the figure are the *chosen*—the places where we are responsible. We have chosen to make wrong responses to God and to other people. We have held onto our resentments and bitterness and have deliberately decided to disobey God. This has brought us fear and guilt, and has further reinforced our warped perceptions and feelings about God. So, however much we have been victims of the sins and evil of others, we have also sinned, and we must accept our share of responsibility for our problems. We have much to forgive but we also have much for which we need to be forgiven. Yes, it is a complex picture; but its purpose is not to confuse, but to clarify, to help us discover and be healed of those images and feelings which distort our concepts of God. For, in spite of all our commitment to the most rigorous Christian disciplines, we will never find lasting "righteousness, peace, and joy in the Holy Spirit" (Romans 14:17) until we find a Christlike God, the kind of God who, like Jesus, tells us He no longer considers us "slaves" but "friends" (John 15:15).

Will the Real God Please Stand Up?

This section title is the name of an exceptionally helpful article about clarifying our concepts of God (Joseph Sica, *Marriage and Family Living*, August 1983, pp. 18–21). Mr. Sica traces the different ways children experience their parents during the various stages of growing up. He then lists some of the faulty concepts/feelings of God which can develop.

• The Legal God "keeps an accounting of what we do. He waits for us to step out of line, to trip up, to falter, so He can mark us as losers."

• The Gotcha God resembles Sherlock Holmes and wears a detective's trench coat and dark glasses. Like a disguised private investigator, He is always following at a short distance. The moment we step out of line, He jumps out of the bushes and yells, "Gotcha!" He is much like the "comer policeman" God J.B. Phillips writes about in his excellent book, *Your God Is Too Small*.

• The Sitting Bull God "relaxes in a yoga position on cotton candy clouds, expecting burnt offerings and homage all day."

• The Philosopher's God, Aristotle's "unmoved mover" of the

universe, is withdrawn, cold, and distant. He is much too busy running the galaxies to get involved in our petty problems. As one man described Him, He is silently sitting in His office, studying the encyclopedia, His door closed with a "Do Not Disturb" sign on it.

• I have added another, The Pharaoh God. He is an unpleasable taskmaster who is ever increasing His demands, always upping the ante. Like Pharaoh of old, His commands move from "Make bricks," to "Make more bricks," to "Make bricks without straw." He is the very opposite of the Heavenly Father-God of Jesus. He is more like the horrible godfather of the mafia who always says, "Measure up or else."

Picturing Relationships

Why are these distorted concepts of God so damaging? Think of them in relationship to people. It is a basic principle of all interpersonal relationships that the ideas and feelings we have about people always affect the way we see them and relate to them. Our mental pictures of people determine how we assume they will act toward us, for we expect people to be like our pictures of them. Our pictures also determine how we will act toward them. For example, if I think a person is honest when he is actually a crook, he may cheat me when I trust him. But the opposite can also happen. If I assume he is a crook when he is actually honest, then I become the loser because I won't trust him. In both instances I have lost, and for the same reason—my wrong picture of the person.

If this is true in human relationships, how much more important is it in regard to our relationship with God! Most of our failure to love and trust God stems from our pictures of God as unlovable and untrustworthy. And most of our anger against Him is not really against the true God but against our unchristian or subchristian concepts of God. The only encouraging thing about all this is that God knows and understands us. He is not angry with us for our lack of trust or our anger toward Him. Rather, He is very saddened that our false picture of Him keeps us from getting to know Him as He truly is. He is far more brokenhearted about it than we are. That's why He longs to help us find healing from the hurts which have contributed to the distorted concepts/feelings about Him.

8

Difficulties from the Distortions about God

ᘏᘏᘏᘏᘏᘏᘏᘏᘏᘏᘏᘏᘏᘏᘏᘏᘏᘏᘏᘏᘏᘏᘏᘏᘏᘏ

Wrong CONCEPT/FEELINGS of God lead people to various kinds of spiritual problems. Some of these are possible indications of the need for a healing of memories. While many of them are related, it will be helpful if we look separately at some of the most common ones.

The Inability To Feel Forgiven

One of the most precious beliefs of evangelical Christians is called "the witness of the Holy Spirit." This theological term means the inner knowledge and confidence that we are the redeemed children of God. Note the word *redeemed*, for there are two ways in which the Bible speaks of God's children. *All humans are God's children in the sense of being created.* Because God created humankind, He sees no barriers based on race, culture, sex, or education. But in another and deeper sense, the Bible is very plain that *not everyone is a child of God.* Jesus Himself described some people as children of the devil (John 8:44). Being spiritual children of God means a totally new relationship with Him and requires *redemption*—forgiveness and new life. Redemption comes about by grace, through faith in what Christ has done for us in His life, death, and resurrection. And the assurance that we have received redemption is given to us by the Holy Spirit who comes to live within us. The clearest Scripture about this was written by Paul: "For you have not received a spirit of slavery, leading to fear again, but you have received a spirit of adoption as sons by which we cry out, 'Abba! Father!' The Spirit Himself bears witness with our spirit that we are the children of God" (Romans 8:15–16).

Like many Christians, I misunderstood this passage for many years. I mistakenly thought this witness was solely the work of the Holy Spirit who overwhelmed and overpowered us with assurance. His witness would be so strong that we just couldn't help knowing and feeling that we were redeemed. But my counseling experiences have made me aware that the verse doesn't say that at all. It says that *His Spirit bears witness with our spirit.* That is, this inner assurance is not simply a witnessing to us, but a witnessing together with our spirits. His Spirit (capital S) witnesses along with our spirit (small s)—the divine and the human working together. This is in perfect accord with the biblical principle that it always takes at least two to constitute a true *witness* (Deuteronomy 17:6; Matthew 18:16). So it is the Holy Spirit and our spirits agreeing together which creates inner confidence that we are forgiven and accepted as children of God.

But what if our spirit has been so badly damaged that it simply cannot maintain this witness? What if the receiving and perceiving capacity of our personality is so distorted it cannot think/feel of God as Abba, as Papa? And cannot think/feel that He could possibly call us son or daughter? Because of unresolved and unhealed past experiences with parents, family members, teachers, spouses, or even leaders in the church, many Christians have such poor concepts of God they are unable to maintain an assurance of this kind of relationship with Him. In chapter 1, we referred to the fact that children learn a language of relationships long before they can learn a language of words. And the painful memories of unhealthy relationships often cry out so loudly that they interfere with learning the new relationship with God.

It is a known truth that children learn from the concrete to the abstract, from actual experiences with things and people to thoughts and concepts about them. They only gradually think in terms of abstract ideas as they grow older. So concepts like love, acceptance, faith, justice (fairness), and dependability are based on real experiences with actual people, particularly those people of most significance to them. This combination of concepts and feelings based on relationships is the very foundation for their basic experience of God's mercy, forgiveness, and the witness of the Spirit.

The things we teach our children about God's character are certainly important. We are to bring up our children "in the discipline and instruction of the Lord" (Ephesians 6:4). But, as we have already pointed out, this teaching should be given within an atmosphere and climate where *the experienced character of the parents and other significant adults is consistent with the expounded character of God.* When there has been contradiction between the two, we usually see a lot of emotional and spiritual wreckage and persons with damaged love receptors. These are the ones who find it very difficult to maintain a consistent assurance that they are the loved, forgiven, and redeemed children of God.

Two things are often necessary to correct the damage. *First,* a healing of the primary relationship which caused the problem. With the assistance of a counselor or trusted friend, they need to go back to the hurts which caused the damages and find healing for those memories. This will allow them to break free from the painful pressures of the past. *Second,* they need to develop trusting relationships. This begins by learning to trust the counselor or pastor. But it should continue as they become a part of a new network of relationships with other Christians in the church or small support group. Here they can experience openness and unconditional love and come to believe that they are accepted, even when they are not acceptable. How many times Helen and I have seen the beginnings of this great transformation during a marriage enrichment weekend, when a small group of Christian brothers and sisters have enveloped someone with a kind of unconditional love they have never experienced before. Many of them later testify that it was then they really felt loved and forgiven; this assurance has stayed with them.

The Inability To Trust and Surrender to God

Another common spiritual problem which may indicate the need for memory healing is the inability to trust God and surrender to Him. Much of what we have written about the preceding difficulty applies to this one also. However, an important principle distinct to this inability is that God created us so that we would not trust or surrender to anything we are afraid of. This is a part of a divinely implanted protection system. In the presence of the dangerous or the fearful, our alert systems go into action. Our bodies produce chemicals which arouse our defenses, and our minds and spirits quicken their pace. This is a God-given survival mechanism, so that we don't go rushing out to embrace snarling bears or hissing cobras. Rather, we hesitate in the presence of that which we are afraid to trust.

This same principle makes it very difficult, if not impossible, for some people to surrender to God. When we ask individuals to trust God and to surrender to Him, we are presuming they have concepts/ feelings of a trustworthy God who has only their best interests at heart and in whose hands they can place their lives. But according to their deepest gut-level concept of God, they may hear us asking them to surrender to an unpredictable and fearful ogre, an all-powerful monster whose aim is to make them miserable and take from them the freedom to enjoy life. They believe that if they seek first the kingdom of God and His righteousness, then, "all these things will be *subtracted* from them." This is their inward translation of Matthew 6:33.

Within an emotionally healthy person, there is enough original sin and selfishness to insure a continued struggle in fully surrendering his or her will to God. But we are talking about a deep-seated commitment-anxiety which goes far beyond that. And behind this anxiety is always a distorted concept of God which makes it almost impossible for such a person to surrender to Him. Unless Christian workers are aware of this, they will not be able to lead these damaged persons to surrender, but will only increase their problems by presenting an overdemanding God who always asks them to do what they cannot do and never helps them get over the barriers which keep them from doing it.

You pastors and counselors who are confronted by suspicious Christians who sincerely desire to grow in Christ, but who are held back by this kind of deep-seated commitment-anxiety, need to check out their gut-level concepts/feelings about God. Is He really fit to trust and to love? I often ask my counselees that very question. One man, who was very knowledgeable in Scripture, answered me by reversing Jesus' words in Luke 11:11–12, "I guess down deep I really feel that God is the kind of Father who, when I ask for bread, gives me a stone, and when I ask for an egg, gives me a scorpion." Is it any wonder he was finding it difficult to make a full surrender to a Gnd about whom he felt that way? Or that he was angry and resentful?

When you delve into the reasons for this distorted idea about God, you will usually discover a picture of God that blends with a picture of unfair, unpredictable, undependable and, therefore, unworthy parents or other significant persons in their lives. The memory of painful experiences with them is so strong that they are now unable to trust anyone enough to surrender. If you and your counselee will work together to bring healing from the rejections and resentments surrounding those memories, you will be on the way toward discovering the God who can be respected, trusted, and loved.

Rather than pressuring struggling Christians into saying, "I'll try to trust," it is far better to help them understand and find healing for the true source of their dilemma. Then they can go on to say, "Lord, I trust You with my inability to trust You, or anyone else, for that matter." This is not just a play on words hut an important shift in their personal center of gravity. When that center moves from being ego-centered to being Christ-centered, they have made a good start toward surrendering to Christ. They are beginning to risk the kind of openness and integrity which Jesus accepted and honored when He healed the son of the man who said with tears, "Lord, I believe; help Thou my unbelief" (Mark 9:24, kjv).

Intellectual Questions and Theological Doubts

The third category of problems which can indicate the need for the healing of hurtful memories centers in intellectual questions and doubts. You may be wondering why something so obviously *mental* is included in a list of *emotional* symptoms. As I have already said, Scripture speaks of persons in terms of wholeness. This is particularly evident when it comes to our beliefs and doctrines, for there is a basic unity, an interdependence of the emotions, the mind, and the will. Within the central citadel of the self, each one affects the others. This reflects the Hebrew belief that faith involves the whole person—feeling, thinking, and acting. We deceive and flatter ourselves if we imagine our theological beliefs are purely rational, a matter only of mind and thought. Our religious beliefs are greatly affected by our feelings and our way of life. Did you ever notice how illnesses—even something as simple as the common cold—affect our faith, our prayer life, our patience, and how we think and feel about God, ourselves, and others? When we move that feeling factor over into the religious realm, it becomes more intense, especially when we are attacked by questions and doubts about the Christian faith. *It is not simply that reason attacks our faith, but that deep-rooted emotions overwhelm our reason as well as our faith.* Those emotions are so powerful they can outvote and overpower our faith. How often have I heard, "Of course, I know better with my *head*, but my feelings are so strong I just can't help doubting that God really cares." Yes, in spite of our desperate attempts to cling to the reasons for our beliefs, our emotional scars may still sabotage our theology and fill us with doubts.

The finest book written in recent times on the subject of doubts is *In Two Minds* by Os Guinness (InterVarsity Press). He covers every possible angle of doubt in both a scholarly and a practical way. In a chapter entitled, "Scars From an Old Wound," he discusses those doubts which are purely psychological in origin. He describes the problem so clearly with this beautiful illustration. Picture healthy faith as a person who has a firm grip so he can reach out and take hold of anything he wants to. Now imagine that this person has an open wound in the palm of his hand. The object he desires to hold is in front of him, and his muscular strength is sufficient. But the unbearable pain which will result makes it very difficult or even impossible to grasp the object.

This is exactly what happens to many Christians with unhealed emotional scars. The very process of trying to believe exerts great pressure on an emotional wound that is too painful to bear. In fact, the questions and doubts which seem to be coming from their *heads* are actually arising out of some deeply buried hurts in their *hearts*. Something has so deeply damaged and distorted their concepts/feelings of God that they yield to doubt so they will not have to reopen those painful wounds. William James, the father of American psychology, understood this problem clearly. He claimed that religious and theological doubts which are emotionally rooted cannot be solved by reason. Early in my ministry, I discovered he was right.

Since I have worked near educational institutions for a large part of my life, people have constantly approached me with various "intellectual problems regarding the Christian faith." Many of these people have been genuine seekers after truth, and I have never hesitated to spend hours helping them achieve a reasonable and defendable faith. But I soon learned to recognize that no amount of biblical study or theological reasoning could dispel the questions and doubts of certain people. Since the doubts were emotionally rooted, even after one aspect of their problem was cleared up, another would arise, and then another and another. I also discovered a fairly predictable list of theological problems which troubled these people, like, "Are the heathen lost?" "Predestination—does God choose only some to be saved?" "How do I know whether or not conversion is simply psyching myself up?" There were also many troublesome Scriptures, some of them the harsher passages from the Book of Hebrews (6:4–8; 10:26–31; and 12:15–17). And, of course, there was that all-time favorite, the unpardonable sin. Did you ever try to argue someone out of thinking he had committed it? If so, you've discovered it's usually a complete waste of time.

With certain damaged Christians, these are not intellectual problems at all, but emotional problems appearing in theological disguise. They are unhealed hurts which are so entangled with their concepts/feelings of God that they have become a part of *the way these people keep from feeling their pains.* As Guinness reminds us, *true intellectual doubts need answers, but emotionally rooted doubts answer needs.* Until those basic, inner needs are met and old wounds healed, the doubts still remain. For it is less painful to bear the pain of the doubts than to face the pain of the traumatic memories of events which caused them.

This is an important area with which pastors or counselors need to be well acquainted. Otherwise, they will try direct and overly simplistic remedies which will not help people but drive them into deeper despair. For these people truly *want to believe,* sometimes more than anything else in the world. This desire is exactly where some of their questionings come from—*they want so much to believe that they cannot stand to risk the terrible pain of believing and then being let down.* For this disappointment is what they have experienced somewhere back in their lives.

For example, can someone who has never experienced any genuine love, but only hate, rejection, and even cruelty as a child, really believe God loves him? Can a son who has gotten nothing from his unpleasable mother but criticism, nagging, correction, and put-downs really believe/feel that he is pleasing to God and that "there is therefore now no condemnation for those who are in Christ Jesus"? (Romans 8:1) Isn't it to be expected that he would gravitate toward some of the more judgmental Scriptures, like the ones from Hebrews I've mentioned?

What kinds of theological questions would you expect from a daughter who said of her father, "I never knew whether I'd get hugged or slugged, and I never knew what made the difference"? Or, the young lady who said, "When Dad went out the door, we never knew when he'd be back—a few hours, several days, or a couple of years"? Or the one who told me with deep sobs, "I just covered my face with the pillow and cried when Daddy would have sex with me"? Without a major healing, can these women really have a proper theology about God as the Heavenly Father who loves and cares for us and will never forsake us?

Yes, these are extreme cases, but they clearly illustrate the point. Not all theological questions and doubts are a sign of disbelief, unbelief, or rebellion. In many instances, they are symptoms of the need for a deep, inner healing. It is only *after* this takes place that such people are able to reshape their faulty doctrines and properly understand the Scriptures.

Problems with Neurotic Perfectionism

Since I have written extensively on perfectionism in *Healing for Damaged Emotions,* I will not go into great detail here. However, the thousands of letters and phone calls I have received from its readers only reinforce my earlier conviction that this is one of the commonest emotional viruses infecting Christians today. Let us not confuse the biblical doctrine of Christian perfection with its greatest hindrance and counterfeit, neurotic perfectionism. Biblical perfection is a level of maturity and sanctification in which the holiness of Christ is imparted to us by the infilling Holy Spirit, so that we are enabled to live a life of habitual victory over sin. Like our justification, this is purely a gift of the grace of God. It is received and lived by faith, and is basically a matter of relationship. It does not depend on perfect performance (works) but on faith in His perfect performance. Everywhere in Scripture we are admonished to make this level of living the aim of our sanctification. Christian perfection goes by many names, depending on one's theological background. Unfortunately, it is called by some the "Higher Life," or the "Deeper Life," or the "Spirit-Filled Life," but that is because these Christians seem content to live on a lower, shallower, and half-filled level of life. As the norm for all Christians, and because it is God's will for His redeemed children, true Christian perfection is the healthy pursuit of Christian excellence by those who, out of gratitude because they are accepted and loved as they are, want to please God and be at their best, *on His terms.*

Although neurotic perfectionism may resemble what we have just been describing, it is actually the greatest enemy of true Christian perfection. For neurotic perfectionists strain compulsively and constantly to make themselves acceptable to God and to measure their relationship to Him in terms of performance and accomplishment. They are restive achievers, not resting believers. The root cause of this is the concept/feeling of an unpleasable God. Their God is an increasingly demanding tyrant who requires perfect performance. He is a punitive judge who has no tolerance for imperfection. At the slightest failure, He expresses His displeasure and covers them with condemnation and guilt. This leads perfectionistic Christians to twist the truth, so that *they rate their behavior before God higher than their relationship to God.* They place conduct before faith, deeds before trust, achieving before receiving, work before worship, and performance higher than relationship.

It naturally follows that perfectionists have oversensitive consciences and live under "the tyranny of the oughts." They try to placate their anxiety by the false humility of belittling themselves and overemphasizing doctrines and duties, rules and regulations. But even though they constantly try harder, they are guilt-ridden, fearful, and subject to mood swings and depression. This is because the basis of their relationship with God is performance, not grace. At best, it is a Galatian mixture of the two. Many such Christians unconsciously take the very channels of grace—repentance, confession, prayer, Bible reading, and Christian service—and turn them into works. Their attempts to find inner peace and be pleasing to God by reading another chapter, praying another hour, and taking on another job at the church, never succeed. Then they feel caught in a trap from which there is no escape. They are literally "damned if they do and damned if they don't!" This is the ultimate despair of neurotic perfectionists and it drives many sincere Christians to emotional or spiritual breakdown—or both.

To make matters worse, such people often have major problems with loneliness, for their relationships are lacking. Because they are sure that others (like God) will reject them when they discover their imperfectness, they literally beat others to the punch by becoming oversensitive, defensive to criticism, and inhibited in communication. All this, in turn, worsens their relationships with others. They unintentionally set themselves up for the very rejection and disapproval they so much fear. In response to the vicious cycle, their inner voice says disapprovingly, "It's just like I told you—people won't accept you unless you're perfect." The cycle is completed when they then react with anger and resentment toward the others who "ought" to have responded with acceptance and love anyhow. Then everyone is included in their frustration and despair, especially those closest to them.

Christians suffer from varying degrees of the perfectionist virus. There is some of it in all of us because it is part of growing up in Christ. Even those who have been brought up by the best of parents, and in the most ideal of situations, still have to battle wrong concepts of God. Our own sinfulness, both unchosen and chosen, and Satan, the father of lies, will see to that! Perhaps the most amazing thing about the love of God is that *He accepts us in spite of our distorted pictures of Him,* and works with us until we gradually come to know Him as He truly is. Most of us begin our spiritual pilgrimage with a mixture of law and grace. It's only by experiencing His great faithfulness through our many failures that we finally come to the place where we can really sing that line in the hymn, "Rock of Ages,"—"Nothing in my hands I bring, simply to Thy cross I cling."

However, there are many who, in spite of their moral earnestness and faithful disciplines, do not grow out of perfectionism and into freedom and maturity in Christ. Instead, they continue to be performance-oriented and even sink into the neurotic levels of perfectionism we have been describing. They are very sincere but very unhappy Christians, carrying out their daily duties in quiet despair. If they are parents, they unknowingly create a legalistic, graceless home atmosphere of conditional love which spreads the deadly infection into one more generation. Thank God this does not have to be. They can be cured by experiencing God's unconditional grace at the deepest levels of their being. But this requires right concepts/feelings about God, and is sometimes impossible without a deep inner healing of those memories which have contributed to the distorted pictures of Him.

Mary and Rabboni

Some years ago a lady named Carrie came to counsel with me following a sermon I had preached on the need some Christians have for inner healing. She was a very intelligent, attractive, Spirit-filled Christian, and highly successful in her profession. During the sermon, the

Holy Spirit had pulled back a veil so that she became aware of a deep anger against God. Since Carrie was in her fifties and had been a diligent Christian almost all her life, this came as a great shock to her. We counseled regularly for several months, slowly working through many layers of repressed emotions until finally the Spirit led us to the place which needed healing. The memories returned slowly, going all the way back to when she was about ten. It was during World War II, and Carrie's favorite brother was in the army. One day an army officer came to the door and delivered the terrible news of the death of her brother. Carrie's parents were devastated, her mother going to her room to shut herself up for days. Carrie literally had to take over. She had to be the strong one and shoulder many of the household responsibilities. *She never had a chance to express her grief over the loss.* She loved that brother more than anyone else in the world, and though she was hurting badly, no one cared enough to listen to her sorrow. Into her crushed and overloaded heart crept an anger against God for allowing her brother to be killed, and against her family for never allowing her to express her tears. She had to become a ten-year-old superwoman whose needs were totally unmet.

Now, with these painful memories, came a chance to express her grief. But there also came the realization that because of what had happened then, she had become a closed person, rather perfectionistic and overdemanding in her outlook. The core of her anger and pain was this, "I've always been forced to do and be someone I'm really not." And this had carried over to the way she perceived her superiors *and God,* who always seemed to be pressuring her into being more than she really was. With Carrie's permission, let me share her letter which describes the turning point in her healing.

After talking with you yesterday, I came home for lunch and, as I usually do, reached for a book. I've been reading in *Rabboni* (by W. Phillip Keller) and had reached the chapter "The Forgiveness of God." Without really thinking, I started to read. Suddenly, it was not just a book, but God was using it to say, "You're forgiven." It seems incredible, but for the first time in my life the reality of being forgiven came home to me. I haven't words to express the song that began inside—the wonder of feeling forgiven and free.

The realization of forgiveness came as a result of thinking on your answer to my question, "What do I do now?" Your reply, "Do nothing," seemed too simple; yet finally the truth came home that that was the exact answer I needed, for God had already done it. There may be lots of reprogramming ahead, but today I think it will happen, for I'm finally on the road.

This was indeed the beginning of a new road of grace and freedom in her life. Like Mary in the greatest recognition story of the Bible (John 20:1–16), Carrie found her Rabboni, her Master, in a new relationship.

Perhaps it would be fitting to close this chapter with a prayer from St. Augustine, who early in his Christian life faced the problem of a wrong concept of God.

Should I call on You for help or should I praise You? Is it important to know You first before I call on You? If I don't know who You are, how can I call? In my ignorance, I might be calling on some other object of worship. Do I call on You, then, in order to know You? . . . It's settled: let me seek You, Lord, by asking for Your help in my life.
(*The Confessions of Augustine in Modern English,* Sherwood E. Wirt, Zondervan, p. 1)

9

Preparing for the Prayer Time

〜〜〜〜〜〜〜〜〜〜〜〜〜〜〜〜〜〜〜〜〜〜〜〜〜〜

Up TO THIS point we have been laying the foundation for the healing of memories. Now I will begin to describe the counseling and prayer sessions and the manner in which I conduct them. In this way, I hope the final chapters can become a kind of manual for both counselors and counselees who desire to use this special form of spiritual therapy. Since the prayer time is the very heart of it, this will be described in considerable detail in the next chapter. But first, let's look at some ways to prepare for it.

Preparation of the Counselee

It is very essential that counselees be properly prepared for the time of prayer. To rush into it without really knowing what needs to be done, and what the real issues are, is to practice magic, rather than to participate in a miracle, as it should be. God is not a respecter of persons, but He is a respecter of conditions and principles. He works through the laws of the mind and spirit. Indeed, there are certain principles which govern healing and prayer itself. That is why, in almost every situation, there must be a time of counseling which precedes and follows the prayer sessions.

At the very outset, I explain to people that I will probably be giving them homework. This makes them aware of the fact that no one (not even God) can help them without their consent and cooperation. The picture of the Holy Spirit helping us with our infirmities (Romans 8:26) is one of participation on our part with the One who "takes ahold over on the other side" of our problems. The purpose of homework for counselees is to help them get in touch with the repressed memories and feelings which are causing them emotional and behavioral problems. At the heart of all remembering is association, for associations are the links which cause our minds to recall experiences. By remembering one picture, we then recall another, because our minds have somehow associated the two. When the memories are clearly recalled, there is a strong possibility of reexperiencing the emotions which originally accompanied the experience. The reverse is also true. That is, if we can experience certain feelings, there is the possibility the memories associated with those feelings will reenter our consciousness.

It will help us at this point to recall some of the findings of Dr. Wilder Penfield, the world-renowned Canadian neurologist. Beginning in 1951, Dr. Penfield did years of extensive research on the brain and memory. He began with the fact that the whole nervous system uses a very slight amount of electrical current to transmit its sensory information to the brain, and the brain in turn uses that current to record and store the data. He experimented by stimulating the memory areas of the brain with small amounts of electricity and discovered that every experience we have ever had is recorded in minute detail by the brain. Whether or not we can consciously recall them, they are still stored in our memories.

Even more important for our study, *the feelings which went along with the experience are also recorded in the brain.* In fact, they are recorded in such a way that they cannot be separated from the memory of the experience itself. So, remembering is more than just repicturing or recalling. *It is more accurate to speak of it as reliving an experience.*

Penfield went on to show that because of this capability to relive experiences, we humans can function on two psychological levels at the same time. We can be conscious of living in our present surroundings now and, *at the same time,* so vividly be reliving a previous experience that we feel as if we are living in the past. This is why memories have such power over us and furnish us with so many of the concepts and feelings of our present experiences. We not only remember what we felt, but we tend to feel the same way now.

The purpose, then, of the preparation time, is to help the counselees bring into their consciousness both the pictures and the feelings of those painful memories which they have partially or totally pushed out of their remembrance; to help them, hear, feel, and understand what they experienced and to bring it before the Lord for healing. I don't mean to be facetious in saying that if Penfield accomplished this by electrical impulses, surely the Holy Spirit can also do it if we ask Him to. And so, through reading, listening to tapes, and opening our hearts to Him in quiet meditation and prayer, He can reawaken memories and enable us to become aware of those painful experiences which are interfering with our growth in Christ.

Reading and Listening Assignments

After several conversations with counselees, if I sense God leading me toward this form of inner healing, I suggest certain reading assignments. What I recommend depends largely on the problem areas with which they are struggling.

To help people open themselves and become aware of hidden hurts, I have found these books most helpful:

Your Inner Child of the Past, Hugh Missildine, Simon and Schuster
The Art of Understanding Yourself, Cecil Osborne, Zondervan
Healing for Damaged Emotions, David A. Seamands, Victor Books
The Key to a Loving Heart, Karen Mains, David C. Cook—especially helpful to women, because it is written about the home.

The following books apply to specic areas of need:
• Concepts of God
Your God Is Too Small, J. B. Phillips, Macmillan
May I Hate God? Pierre Wolf, Paulist
Putting Away Childish Things, David A. Seamands, Victor Books
• Guilt, Low Self-Esteem, Depression
Happiness Is a Choice, Minirth and Meier, Baker
Guilt and Grace, Paul Tournier, Harper and Row
Free for the Taking, Joseph R. Cooke's great book on grace, Revell
• Relationships with Parents
Cutting Loose, Howard Halpern, Bantam
• Struggles over Forgiving Others
Healing Life's Hurts, Dennis and Matthew Linn, Paulist
Forgive and Forget, Lewis B. Smedes, Harper and Row
Healing Where You Hurt, Jon Eargle, Bridge Building Ministries
• Incest and Sexual Abuse
A House Divided, Katherine Edwards, Zondervan

- Homosexuality

The Broken Image, Leanne Payne, Crossway Books

- Grief and Loss—General

A Grief Observed, C. S. Lewis, Seabury

- Death of a Child

But for Our Grief, June Filkin Taylor, Holman

- Miscarriage or Stillbirth

Empty Arms, Pam Vredevelt, Multnomah

Some people find it more convenient or beneficial to listen to tapes. They can do this while driving to work or in the evenings in the privacy of their homes. I have found tapes to be extremely useful in helping people become aware of their needs. A catalog of my own cassettes is available from Tape Ministers, Box 93396, Pasadena, California 91109.

Writing Assignments

As people read books or listen to tapes, they should keep notes of whatever thoughts and memories come to them. The important thing to remember is this: *nothing is too insignificant or seemingly stupid and silly to record.* For though it now looks stupid or petty from an adult standpoint, at the time it was very important and brought deep hurt. Perhaps the most painful part of the memory is at that very point— the significant others involved in the incident didn't realize how much it meant and that's what hurt the most! Whatever comes to mind, as one reads or listens, should be jotted down. Sometimes it is very productive to keep a diary or journal during this period.

For counselors who would like to learn more of this technique, I would highly recommend Morton Kelsey's book *Adventure Inward: Christian Growth Through Personal Journal Writing* (Augsburg).

Ways of Getting in Touch with Our Emotions

The real purpose of the homework assignments is to help people become aware of the true feelings connected with their repressed memories. The most subtle trap to avoid in this whole process is "the paralysis of analysis." This is where it all turns into a great big *head trip.* It is possible, through an extensive time of counseling, for counselees to very clinically describe an extremely painful past. They can analyze it all in their heads, realize the problems which need solving in their heads, and work out the solutions in their heads. But after it's all over, they will discover that nothing has really changed. It was all a kind of fascinating intellectual and spiritual game. *Everything took place in their heads, but their hearts and ways of living were untouched.*

I do not mean to downgrade the place of the mind in our healing. We have consistently stressed the biblical idea of the whole person, and this certainly includes our minds. There must come a time of reprogramming our thoughts and transforming us through the renewal of our minds. With some Christians, it is possible to go directly to this and help them realize their full potential of life in Christ. But with others, Christian workers need to realize this cannot happen until they are first freed from their emotional hangups. When we tell such damaged persons the only thing wrong with them is "wrong thinking" or that they should "stop living in the flesh and claim their rightful life in the Spirit," all we do is increase their guilt and deepen their despair. I have spent many hours picking up the pieces for disillusioned Christians who have been pushed into trying this shortcut. *It simply will not work, not because of any lack of desire on their part, or lack of power on God's part, but because God cannot violate His own principles in bringing them to wholeness and holiness.* As in the case of the lady described in chapter 8, their deeply buried negative emotions must first be brought into the light and dealt with.

Therefore, I again want to stress the importance of tapping into these submerged feelings. Many people are terribly afraid of doing this; fearing they will lose control of their emotions, they keep it all on a head level, always wanting to analyze. "But I want to know *why* . . ." is a phrase they will use over and over again. All this does is to reinforce their defenses and drive their real feelings even deeper into the concrete of their personalities. That's why, when we give counselees their homework, we must constantly emphasize the importance of allowing feelings to come to the surface.

Through the years, my counselees have taught me many important truths. They have suggested methods of reviving hidden memories and frozen feelings. On one occasion, I gave a young lady the usual reading and writing assignments. Before we met again she went home for the holidays. While she was there, the Spirit prompted her to go through all the old family pictures which were stored in the attic. She decided to arrange all her pictures in chronological order, beginning with the earliest baby photos right up to the present. It was fun to do—for a while, until she began to discover a rather pronounced change in her pictures. What began as pictures of a cheerful baby and continued as a happy little girl started to change. The difference in her posture and facial expressions was markedly different. There was a kind of furtiveness and sadness in her face.

As she laid out all the pictures side by side, wondering about the difference, she began to tremble with a strong sense of anxiety and fear. Memories she had pushed out of her mind for years forced their way back in. We had not been able to clarify them through the counseling process. Now they began to sort themselves out and she was able to pinpoint some very painful experiences of sexual abuse by a lesbian baby-sitter. Because of this visual experience through pictures, it did not take long to lead her to the place of healing, when she returned for counseling. Ever since then I have suggested to others that they look at old photos, family pictures, and high school or college year-books. This use of pictures has proved very helpful in situations where we were unable to push memories back to where the real hurts originated.

Taking journeys to places associated with painful memories can also bring back buried emotions. Former hometowns, schools, even churches connected with painful memories, can all be used by the Spirit to bring pain to the surface. One divorcee, filled with great guilt and self-despising because of her past life, told me she had gone back to the very place out in the country where, as a teenager, it all began. She said, "I drove out by myself and parked the car where we had parked that night. Then I got into the backseat where I first threw away my self-respect. And there, on the backseat of the car, I sobbed it all out and asked God to take the burning sting out of these memories."

Today, as the lovely wife of a pastor, she has a very special ministry to hurting teenagers and young divorcees who are trying to find a new life. She is truly one of God's healed helpers!

The Counseling Sessions

While there is much that can be accomplished by those who take their homework seriously, it is usually not possible to find full healing by oneself. The divine principle of healing—confession to one another and prayer on our behalf by another (James 5:16)—emphasizes the need for a counselor's help. Look once again at the figure in chapter 7. Since unhealthy, destructive relationships of the past have distorted some people's sense of perception, it stands to reason that healthy, constructive relationships in the present are necessary to restore a proper sense of perception. This is why a healthy trust relationship with a counselor is often absolutely essential.

I define a counselor as a *temporary assistant* to the Holy Spirit. Both of the italicized words are important. *Assistant,* because the goal of all Christian counseling is to assist people to become emotionally and spiritually mature enough to relate directly with the Holy Spirit, the Great Counselor. *Temporary,* because dependence on the counselor should never become permanent. If it does, then the counseling itself becomes a part of the problem and not a means of solution; a part of the disease, not the cure. It is only a *temporary* means to an end, the goal of total dependence on the Spirit. However, this in no way underestimates the crucial importance of counselors in the healing process. All through history God has used humans as assistants, not only to carry out His work, but also to "stand in the gap" as His intermediaries who show people what His character is really like. There are vast numbers of people who feel like the scared little girl whose mother was trying to comfort her with the assurance of God's presence. "I know that," she said, "But I need a God with skin on Him!" The counselor fills this need. For many counselees, this is the first time in their lives they have experienced a stable, trustworthy, and truly loving (accepting yet confrontive) relationship. Thus the very being of the counselor is the commencement of healing.

But the *doing* is also of great consequence. This is not the place to go into detailed instructions of the *listening process* involved in this procedure. Those who find themselves in the role of counselors— pastors, Sunday School teachers, various church workers, or trustworthy friends—must develop the art of listening. Fortunately, it is a learned art and can improve as we practice it. We've all had the experience of simply listening to someone open their hearts to us and then tell us, much to our surprise (since we hardly said anything), "Thanks so much; you've been a great help to me." What we need to remember is that perhaps no one ever cared enough or valued their opinions enough to listen to them before.

Your listening should be *perceptive,* listening with your eyes as well as your ears. Watch for those signs of body language—tearful eyes, sighing and swallowing which literally push rising emotions back down into their hiding places, as well as blushes and blotches on the face and neck. Listen for "motor mouths," those who use talk so that they won't be able to feel anything. There is also the nervous laughter which is so incongruent with what is being described. It can be disrupting; but remember, it's really a very hopeful sign. That kind of laughing means people are getting in touch with some deep emotions and they don't know what to do with them. Laughter is the one acceptable Ametican emotion. "Brave kids never cry," and are often not allowed to express any negative emotions. But they can always laugh, even when "they are crying on the inside." Don't be afraid to gently confront people and help them become aware of the impressions you are receiving. An important part of their self-awareness is *understanding the meaning* behind what they say and do.

Again, your listening must be *prayerful*. While carefully concentrating on what is being communicated to you, at a deeper level you must be using your spiritual radar to *tune in to the discernment of the Holy Spirit*. In addition to the sensitivity of your own spirit to the human spirit sharing with you, you must be prayerfully receptive to the inner voice of the Divine Spirit. Remember, however, that you are a fallible human being and need to handle the impressions you receive with great humility. Some people think they have an infallible "hot line to God," and use their impressions too quickly and bluntly. I often have to remind myself of the time when a layman dropped by to see the great New England preacher, Joseph Parker, and found him pacing the floor of his office. "What's the trouble, Doctor Parker?" he asked. Parker replied, "It's really very simple: *I am in a hurry, but God is not!*" You need to be in prayerful alignment with the Spirit, but also be willing to "test the spirits" (1 John 4:1) to see if the impressions are really from Him. I have discovered that *the hasty thing is usually the wrong thing.*

On the other hand, after careful and prayerful consideration, do not be afraid to obey His leadings. Many times I have felt the Spirit was helping me discern what someone's real problem was, even though they had not directly mentioned it. And when I finally shared it with them, although this was often quite painful, it proved to be the place which actually needed the most healing.

Playback, Role Play, and Coaching

Many pastors and laypersons will be called on to assume the role of counselor. What I write here is intended to help such nonprofessionals who can be very important links in the healing chain. The preparation counseling for healing of memories demands all the human wisdom and skill we can possibly acquire, plus the discernment of the Spirit. This is because we are often attempting to help people to remember things they really don't want to remember, and to face pain they have long been trying to avoid. So in addition to careful and prayerful listening, our responses can be very decisive in the process.

Counselees are often unaware of what they are really saying. Counselors shouldn't always directly tell them what they are hearing. Instead, they should help them become aware of the true meanings behind what they have shared. In this way, counselees will also become aware of what they are feeling and thus be able to pray much more fruitfully.

When counselors pick up important clues, they should learn the *playback* technique of feeding it back to the counselee so that he hears it the same way. In chapter 11, I have included the story of Larry's healing. This illustrates the use of careful listening and playback in helping people recognize hidden needs.

Role play is another way of helping people reach feelings. Such questions as, "What would you have liked to say to him/her if you'd have had the chance?" or "What did you really feel like doing, if you'd had the opportunity?" If it's a matter of what they would like to have said, it is much more effective to ask the counselee to act as if you are that person and to say it directly to you. Their tendency will be to keep it all in the third person—"I would like to have said. . . ." Try to guide them into speaking directly to you, or possibly to an empty chair in which the person involved is supposedly sitting. Thus, "Dad (Mom), I wish you would listen to me when I try to tell you what I'm feeling," or "(Person's name), I am feeling very rejected by you."

Role play cannot be forced on people but should flow naturally from the conversation. It can be a powerful tool in helping people realize what they were actually feeling during the original situation. Often they are surprised at the rush of painful emotions which comes out while they are speaking. I once lost a few buttons off my coat when a counselee got carried away by the anger generated through the role playing, but the results made it worthwhile!

We must keep constantly *coaching* for memories, meanings, and feelings. They are all important. They all need to be *owned* before they can be *disowned*. This is simply the psychological way of stating the same truth we talked about in chapter 5—we cannot confess to God what we do not first acknowledge to ourselves. It's amazing how tenaciously people will deny their feelings because "Christians are not supposed to feel that way, especially not *Spirit-filled Christians*." This is denying reality and is a form of untruthfulness. Until it is brought up and out into the light, it cannot be healed by the One who is called the Spirit of Truth.

This emphasis on becoming aware of true feelings is not just some modem psychological "feeling therapy," which brings about an emotional catharsis so that people will feel better. It is the bedrock scriptural reality of confession, repentance, and forgiveness. The word *confess* comes from the Old English words *con* and *fess*. To confess is simply to *fess* "say or speak" and *con* "along with." To confess is to know and say along with God what God already knows and says about certain things in our lives. This is what we are helping people do through our counseling times. We are helping them know the truth which makes them free through insight and awareness. Better still, we are helping them to know the Son who in redeeming and healing power will make them free indeed (John 8:32, 36)

The Final Assignment

When it is agreed that everything has gone as far as it can by sharing together and by the kinds of homework we have described, the counselee should be asked to do the final assignment. From all that has been discussed and prayed over, let the counselee make a list as the guide for the prayer time. This list should include the most painful and recurring memories which have been seen as causing the main emotional and spiritual hangups. These do not need to be written out in great detail; just a brief phrase or sentence for each item is enough, so that it will be remembered and prayed over. The list should be as specific as possible, in the sense that persons be remembered by name, and incidents or attitudes and atmospheres be listed specifically. One man called it his "hit list." When I asked him why, he explained it this way, "Because those are all the people who hurt me so much I hate them and want to hit them for it." Although he may have overstated his case, I think he had the general idea of what the final list should include. Counselees should bring their lists with them. The list should also be undergirded. by prayer for a spirit of willingness to follow the Spirit's directions during the prayer session.

The Preparation of the Counselor

When the counselee is ready, it is time for the counselor to prepare for the crucial time of prayer.

First, counselors should review all their notes—what they have jotted down during the counseling sessions plus any ideas and impressions which may have come to them while praying for the particular person.

Second, they should spend time in meditation and prayer, asking the Spirit to give them emotional and spiritual empathy with the counselee. They need to become so one with them in prayer that they will actually participate in their pain, feel their sufferings, and "bear their burdens."

After this prayer for empathy, they should then exercise faith for the healing of their counselee. Faith has been called a form of "sanctified imagination." This means we pray using our imaginations to visualize people as healed and freed from the painful chains of their past; that we picture them as changed and made new, as whole persons in Christ.

Finally, counselors should pray for the emotional and spiritual energy necessary for this time of prayer. Once, after healing a woman, Jesus spoke of virtue going out of Him. Baron von Hugel writes of "the neural cost of prayer." Every counselor knows how tiring and draining a difficult counseling session can be. But that doesn't compare to the energy required to walk people through a healing of memories prayer time. It is a very exhausting experience for both parties. Counselors should ask God for the extra physical, emotional, and spiritual strength necessary for this experience. Believe me, they will need it!

10

Conducting the Prayer Time

BECAUSE THE PRAYER session is so important, it is essential that it be planned properly. The session requires *unhurried time* and *an unpressured schedule.* This means that it should not simply be an hour worked into a regular counseling schedule. It should not be subject to clock-watching by anyone. The pastor or counselor should not be anxious about some other person impatiently waiting for an appointment, or a committee meeting that is about to begin. To allow for this kind of freedom, I always schedule at least a two-hour block for the prayer session.

I want to go through the memory healing process with you, step by step. I will describe the prayer session in detail, instructing, explaining, and illustrating as if we were actually going through it with a counselee who has been adequately prepared.

The Opening Explanation

Begin by explaining or reminding the counselee about the concepts of prayer which are basic to memory healing. Remind him or her that Jesus Christ is Lord and, therefore, the Lord of time. (See the section, "Accept Christ as a Present Helper," chapter 5.) Describe how Jesus will be walking back into time with you and dealing with the situation as He would have, had you asked Him at the time. Once more clarify the reason for this—"The real problems are not with the adult, the grown-up person you are just now. So we need to reach back into the past and let Jesus deal with your child in those places which need the actual healing. This is because you seem to be stuck or hung up at those particular places of hurt. So far as possible, I want you to talk to God as if you are now the child (or young person, or adult) you were at that hurting place in your life."

Next, explain, "We will be using a very free-flowing conversational type of prayer. We will just talk to God as openly as we have been talking together. Nothing fancy, no windups or closings, just talking to Him as if He's sitting right here with us.

"I am going to feel free to interrupt your prayers if I feel you are getting off target—like being too negative, telling God how bad you are. Or, I may point out some new insight or discernment from the Spirit.

"And you should also feel free to stop in the middle of the prayer to look at your list, to ask a question, or share something the Spirit has reminded you of, something you have not recalled until now."

If distorted concepts of God are a real part of their problem, try to assist the visualization process by helping them find their most comfortable picture of God. Since they are going to be talking very personally to God, this is an important matter. Strange as it may sound, I often ask people which will be easier for them, talking with *God* or with *Jesus?* In most instances they will say something like, "I feel better with Jesus; I guess I'm scared of God." Or "Jesus is okay, hut I can't stand God." Once in a while this is reversed, "I don't know, Jesus seems too near, *a little too real.* God seems farther away, a little safer, I guess."

If there have been unhealthy and harmful relationships with parents, avoid using the term *Father* for God, even though that is your usual way of praying. I will long remember a prayer time with a lady who had been a victim of incest. Toward the end of the hour, she suddenly began to address God as "Heavenly Father." She stopped right away, burst into fresh sobs and said, "Oh my God, You know that's the first time I've ever been able to call You that!" Sometimes it is best to use a more or less neutral term such as *Lord*; but I have discovered that most of the time, people are comfortable with imagining a picture of Jesus for this prayer time.

Make clear what the content of the praying will be. They are to tell God what they have been telling you, not hesitating to look at their list, if they feel it necessary. They should make sure they tell God what they are feeling as they relive the experience they are describing—that is, what the child, teenager, or young adult was feeling at that time.

The Counselor's Opening Prayer

I always open in prayer. Though there is no set format, that prayer will usually contain words something like this:

"Lord Jesus, we quiet our hearts before You at this time. . . . We know that You have been in on all our conversations, so You know all the things we have talked about. We're glad You understand us even better than we understand ourselves.

"We need Your help now because we don't know exactly how to pray. But You've promised us in Your Word that at times like this You will send Your Holy Spirit to actually come into our hearts and to pray in us and through us; and even when we don't know exactly what to say, You will take our sighs and groans and pains and translate them into prayers. We ask that You will do that right now—come into John's/Mary's heart and pray for him/her. Give him/her the very words to pray and awaken the very feelings he/she needs to relive.

"Now, Lord Jesus, I want to bring before You a little ___ year-old boy/girl named _____. He/She wants to talk to You about some things which have caused a lot of pain. I know You are going to listen. So I bring You_____.

"Now, _____, just talk to Jesus and tell Him whatever is most on your heart."

The Counselee's Prayer Time

Usually it won't be long before the counselee will start praying. However, if there is a long pause, be prepared to wait it out patiently and prayerfully. If the hurts are very specific, counselees will usually begin with some of the earlier incidents of childhood. If it's more a matter of atmosphere and climate, they will often begin with later general impressions and then move back to the specifics. However, this is completely up to them—whatever is uppermost in their minds is where they should start.

It is impossible to regularize or formalize this prayer time. This is one reason why many counselors are afraid to get into memory healing—its direction cannot always be controlled and its contents cannot always be predicted. Frankly, it can be somewhat frightening, and counselors must simply "hang loose in the Spirit" and be ready for almost anything.

Sometimes, it takes quite a long time for counselees to really open up in prayer. You should not hesitate to interrupt and redirect their praying, if you feel they are being too general and thus trying to avoid facing painful issues. Even during the prayer time, make every effort to help them relive the original emotions.

Coaching and encouraging are perfectly legitimate. Statements like these are appropriate and helpful: "Why don't you also tell Jesus what you were feeling when that happened?" or "Don't be afraid to let the feelings come up and the sounds come out as you talk to God about that." Or, if it seems they are struggling to maintain tight control over their emotions, "Don't be in a hurry let's just stay with that memory for a while and let our emotions plug into it. I have the feeling there is a lot of unexpressed pain in that one." If there is a rush of feelings with sobs and tears, wait patiently, praying silently in your heart. This time when the counselee shares his deepest hurts with the Lord is extremely important and *should never be rushed.*

Sometimes, if the Spirit imparts a deep sense of discerning empathy, you should feel free to enter into the very prayers of the counselee by praying *as if you were the counselee, and using the editorial we.* For example, "O Lord Jesus, You know how *we* felt, *we* really wanted _____ to die," or "*We* felt so ashamed and guilty *we* wanted to kill ourselves," or "Lord, *we* were really angry at You, the fact is *we* hated You for taking Mother away from *us*—she was all *we* had." This approach often gives the counselee the courage to face their bitterness against God or someone else they are supposed to love, and to verbalize it openly.

At other times, if there is a lull in the counselee's prayers, it is helpful to clarify issues and emotions by asking such questions as, "What are you sensing to be the real issue in this? What was it that hurt you so much and made you so angry?" Or, "I'm sensing there is more involved than _____. Is there a word or feeling that the Spirit is giving you about this?" Here are some of the words counselees have given in reply:

abandoned	shamed	worthless
totally alone	dirty	desperate

annihilated	unjust	hopeless
panic-stricken	trapped	wiped out
like garbage	rejected	betrayed

Don't be surprised if, when counselees reexperience a situation, they revert back to that time. Their voices may become like those of children, and they may say and do things appropriate to that stage of life. They may also express in words now what they weren't able to (or allowed to) then. Like, "Mama/Daddy, please don't leave me, or (hit me), or (do that)."

Questions can also come pouring out—addressed to the people involved then, or to you, or to God, such as,

"How could he/she have done that to me?"

"Why did they adopt me when they didn't really want me?"

"Where was God in all this?"

"How could they do that when they said they loved me?"

"How could I have ever done such a thing?"

"If I could only understand why!"

Questions represent many different things. They may be an attempt to figure it all out, so it can be kept controlled on a purely intellectual level, so the pain of it never has to be faced. Or questions may mean the expression of the deepest kind of feelings—*great anger* against God, others, and self, or the *sheer agony* of not being able to comprehend how such painful experiences could ever happen in the first place.

When New Memories and Insights Emerge

One of the most amazing experiences which can happen during the prayer time is the emergence of the heretofore unremembered. You may hear comments like this: "I just can't believe it, I had never remembered that before." Or, "It's amazing. Up till now, I could never remember anything before I was ____ years old, and now all those things have become clear to me." The new insight can be one of the most important results of this prayer time. This is where the Holy Spirit literally prods us with His divine electrodes, somehow interjecting His light and power into the synapses of the nervous system and bringing to conscious recall those memories which have been forcibly stored in some deep layers of the brain/mind. No wonder the Spirit is described in Romans 8:27 as "He who searches our hearts" (NIV). Here is a supernatural work of the Spirit, the Great Counselor, who is able to open our hearts (subconscious minds) to ourselves. Many times during the counseling sessions, the counselee and I have both started down a certain path of felt need. Then, while praying, some new or enlarged memory has emerged to become the means of showing us a different trail which ultimately led to the true place of healing.

George came seeking help for the usual syndrome of emotional and spiritual problems accompanying perfectionism. He was oversensitive to the approval or disapproval of others, generally angry and impatient with the faults of "professing Christians." He never felt quite acceptable to God and was often troubled by fairly severe depression. We agreed that God had graciously helped him find the right kind of wife—warm, accepting, and understanding. But, as is often true of perfectionists, that was part of his problem—he found it difficult to accept this affection and love, though he truly loved her and desired to express that love more than anything else. During counseling he shared several incidents when, as a supersensitive child, he had been deeply hurt and had begun to draw back from people. One harmful experience kept troubling his memories. As a lad in his preteens, he found a lot of his dad's hidden porno magazines. When he confronted his parents about them, his mother became very angry, but his father just laughed at him. Later his mother talked to him about it in private. She put down his dad and lectured George about sexual evils, hoping he would never become "a dirty-minded man like his father." When George made out his list, this was one of several hurting memories he had written down. In prayer, we took up the childhood hurts and he forgave his peers and others whom he felt had rejected him. When we began praying about the porno incident, he was able to forgive both his parents for their part in it and to receive forgiveness for his long-held resentments against them.

During his prayers, however, he recalled other things which turned out to be the real memories which were affecting his present life and marriage. For he had repressed the fact that he looked into those magazines, was sexually aroused, and felt very "dirty" about it. His mother's lecture drove this feeling even deeper underground. This began an attitude in which, unable to accept his own teenage sexual development, he had become very prudish about sex and had assumed an extremely critical and self-righteous attitude toward others. He suddenly remembered the cruel and unchristian way he had treated a pregnant teenager during high school. She had looked to him as a Christian friend, desperately seeking his help, but he had rejected her in very pharisaic fashion. He then remembered several other incidents like this and began to see the true nature of his judgmental and critical perfectionism. He also realized why he was unable to accept and enjoy his wife's love and intimacy—he had been clinging to a false sense of prudish moral superiority, thinking he was thereby a better Christian than she was. With these new memories and insights, we were then able to pray at the place of real damage and receive deep healing. It only took a small amount of follow-up and reprogramming on George's part to bring about a marked change in his spiritual and marital life. And it was all made possible because the Spirit searched out some repressed memories during our time of prayer.

Letting Christ Minister to the Past

As we have already stated, the uniqueness of memory healing is walking back into our past with the Lord and asking Him to heal us at a specific time and place of need. In the first two chapters of my book, *Putting Away Childish Things,* I wrote of this in general terms and gave several illustrations of Christ's ministry to the "hidden child in us all." This is where counselors can be at their best as temporary assistants to the Holy Spirit. For it is during such prayer times, after counselees have shared their most agonizing memories with God, that we as counselors can most helpfully mediate. Our prayers should be to Jesus, asking for His direct intervention and healing presence. We should ask Jesus, whom we believe is present with us in the memories which are being relived, to minister to the counselee for their particular need at that time.

For example, let us suppose a counselee has just told God about some extremely painful experiences of rejection. In the incident there is deep humiliation and the person is left feeling stupid, worthless, and unloved. The counselee is filled with emotions and stops praying to weep.

This is the perfect time for the counselor to pray, using the imagery of Jesus blessing the little children: "Lord Jesus, You who took the little children in Your arms, do that now for _____ , one of Your children who is hurting so badly. Let _____ sit on Your lap and put Your arms around <u>him/her.</u> Tell _____ how much You love <u>him/her</u>

and how sorry You are that he/she hurts so much. Let him/her feel Your approval, and know how pleased You are with him/her."

Another beautiful biblical picture of Jesus which is so helpful for such times is the Good Shepherd. You can pray, "Lord Jesus, You who are the Good Shepherd promised to take the little lambs in Your arms and give them Your protection and love. Do that just now. Let _____ feel your arms around him/her in warm and tender care. Like a good shepherd washes and binds up the cuts and bruises of his lambs, wash his/her wounds and pour in Your healing balm."

The basic idea behind this imagery is to match the particular aspect of the character of Christ to the specific needs of the counselee at that time. So, for feelings of rejection we visualize the One who knows what it's like to be "despised and rejected of men," and who went out of His way to care for people's needs. If counselees are overcome by the terrors of loneliness and abandonment, we picture the Christ who understands us, since He was forsaken by all His disciples, and who even experienced what it's like to not be able to feel God's presence, as He cried out, "My God, My God, why hast Thou forsaken Me?" Christ understands this feeling of loneliness so well that He promises never to leave us abandoned or orphaned.

When they are filled with the confused emotions which accompany memories of sexual abuse, or the guilt and shame of sexual sins, we imagine Jesus in all His purity. He is pure but not prudish, sinless but not censorious. For painful childhood experiences, we ask for Christ's tender and pure embrace; for the whisper of His assurance which restores a feeling of purity. For experiences in which they bear responsibility, we pray for His arm around their shoulder and His non-condemning words of forgiveness. We spend time kneeling beneath the Cross, receiving the washing and cleansing which restores feelings of virtue and self-respect.

For those struggling with torturous memories of unpleasable parents, teachers, and disapproving Christians, our prayers should picture Jesus lifting them from their groveling position until they are standing tall and straight before Him. Then we listen as He says to them, "_____ , you are My beloved son/daughter, in whom I am well pleased!"

We have only scratched the surface of the possible application of this principle of "imagineering"—visually matching pictures of specific hurts with pictures of His special healings, based on His actual ministry as presented in the Gospels.

Forgiveness—The Heart of Healing

We come now to the subject of forgiveness which is the very crux of the healing of memories—forgiveness in the sense of *forgiving and being forgiven.* It would be impossible for me to exaggerate its importance in the healing process. It is at this point where the greatest struggles of prayer will take place, and where counselors will expend the most spiritual energy. It is also here where counselors will be most sorely tempted to give up; for that very reason, this is usually where the battle is won or lost. Let us take a closer look.

There is no question that forgiveness is the key relational issue in the Bible. This is true for all our relationships—with God, others, and ourselves. We often speak of grace and of our salvation being unconditional. This is true in the sense that there are no *conditions of merit* we humans can meet. There is nothing we can do in order to *earn* or *achieve* God's grace. It is given to us freely as the gift of His love.

But in another sense, forgiveness is conditioned by our response. It is still unconditional, because the very ability to respond depends on His grace. Without that prevenient or preceding grace, we would not be able to say either yes or no to His offer. But God has so created us that forgiving is basic to our responding to His gift of grace. It would seem He has made us so that unless we truly forgive others, we make it impossible for Him to forgive us. Not impossible in the sense that He withholds His offer of forgiveness until we first forgive; no, for in one sense, as Paul states in 2 Corinthians 5:18–19, God has already forgiven our sins through Christ's death on the Cross and offers us His forgiveness freely. It is impossible because He has made us psychologically so that we are not able to *receive* His forgiveness unless we forgive. This is plain throughout the entire New Testament, and is the one condition our Lord stressed again and again. In His model prayer, in Matthew 6:12, He stated, "Forgive us our debts, as we also have forgiven our debtors." And in His commentary on this prayer, He explained, "For if you forgive men for their transgressions, your Heavenly Father will also forgive you. But if you do not forgive men, then your Father will not forgive your transgressions" (Matthew 6:14–15).

In Matthew 18:23–35, we have His parable of the unforgiving servant, which ends with the angry master turning the culprit over to the jailers for torture. Jesus then made this application of the story, "So shall My Heavenly Father also do to you, if each of you does not forgive his brother from your heart." In Mark 11:25, Jesus once again set a condition when He said, "And whenever you stand praying, forgive, if you have anything against anyone; so that your Father also who is in heaven may forgive you your transgressions."

It is clear that God has built this supremely important principle into the very structure of all interpersonal relationships. It is based on the nature and character of God Himself; and since we are made in His image, it has been built into us. So we are talking about a basic biblical and psychological principle. Every experience of memory healing of which I have been a part confirms this. If we want forgiveness without forgiving, we are asking God to violate His own moral nature. *This He cannot and will not do.*

The essentiality of forgiving is the reason I have put so much stress on being honest about feelings. For the first step toward forgiveness is *to acknowledge feelings of resentment and hate.* When people experience severe hurts, they usually end up hating the persons who caused these hurts. *If they then bury the hurts, they also bury the hates.*

But God has so structured our personalities that we cannot do this and get by with it forever. We cannot long ingest and integrate hidden resentments, anymore than our stomachs can digest and incorporate bits of broken glass. In both, we are going to feel a lot of inner unrest and pain! Both require serious operations. The healing of memories is a form of spiritual surgery and therapy.

My Personal Experience of Inner Healing

In order not to hurt anyone, I have had to wait until both of my parents were gone before I could share the details of my own healing. I was born in India of Methodist missionary parents who gave forty years of service there. My mother died in 1981. Dad was ninety-two when, on his twelfth postretirement "shuttle-service" visit to India, in 1984, he fell ill and died. He is buried in his beloved India. I will always remember our final week together when I flew out to be at his hospital bedside and have "closure" with him. It's impossible for me to say how much I owe to him. His saintly life as my earthly father certainly made it easy for me to believe in my Heavenly Father.

But Mother and I were a different story. We were both nervous, high-strung personalities, and from the very beginning found it difficult to get along together. I remember my childhood struggles with ambivalent feelings toward her, feelings I was never able to express or share with anyone. We came to the States when I was eleven, and a year later my parents returned to India, leaving my brother and me in the good care of a loving grandmother. Mother was far away, so getting along was no longer a problem. A conversion experience in my early teens brought many changes in my life. I felt I had dealt with my resentments, and my new life in Christ gave me a much better attitude toward her.

I had always suffered from asthma. In my teens it grew worse until, by the time of my freshman year at Asbury College, it became so serious I was unable to take my spring quarter exams. In spite of many prayers on my behalf, the asthma continued and I accepted it as a handicap I must learn to live with. By now I was a committed, growing Christian, and during my college days I entered into a deeper experience and life in the Holy Spirit. I also strongly felt the call to missions. So together with a lovely college classmate God had brought into my life, four years, two degrees, and one child later, we left for India as missionaries.

Our work went well for the first ten years. Then one day when I was thirty-four, I was reading a book by Glen Clark during my devotions. The Holy Spirit made one sentence from the book leap out at me. It said that some forms of asthma may be caused by resentment toward parents. I stopped short. Could it be possible? During the next hour, the Spirit peeled off a layer of my mind and I began to remember some deeply buried resentments against Mother. They were specifics I had not dealt with; in fact, I had not even really recalled them for years. The Spirit also showed me that I had not faced some of my true feelings toward God. You see, I had been separated from my parents when they got stuck in India during the early years of World War II. They had left me at twelve and I did not see them again until the morning of my twentieth birthday. And after all, it was God who had called them to be missionaries in the first place. Oh, I had spiritualized it all, basking in the glow when people would say, "Isn't it wonderful, your parents are missionaries!" The gut-level truth was that I felt angry about those lonely teen years. All my friends had their parents with them and places to go on holidays.

For the next few days, I shared some of these thoughts with Helen, and we talked and prayed about them. I forgave and was forgiven. And I experienced a cleansing/healing from my resentments at a deeper level than I'd ever known before. But then came the serendipity. How truly gracious God is! In the midst of the struggle, we had forgotten all about my asthma. But God hadn't, and He gave me something I never even thought to ask for. Can you believe it? I've never had a wheeze of asthma since then!

I always hesitate to tell about this, for fear some may jump to conclusions about their own physical ailments. I cannot make generalizations from my particulars. I can only share my experience with you and trust the Holy Spirit to guide you into the truth of what He has in store for you. The main reason for sharing my personal experience is to emphasize the central place of forgiving and being forgiven in the healing of memories.

Important Ingredients for Forgiveness

During those days of prayer and struggle, the Spirit dealt with several aspects of my resentment-forgiveness problem.

• First, I had to take a look at some of my very specific hurts and be willing to relinquish all feelings of resentment. Was I holding on to a secret desire to get even in any way? At first I thought to myself, "Of course not." For by then I had learned from relatives some of the tragedies of Mother's life—an alcoholic father who had spent a few years in prison, and some other painful childhood traumas. I could explain the causes of many of her neurotic problems; but *explaining is not the same as forgiving.* We may trace all sorts of fancy psychological schemes about those who hurt us and not face the fact of our resentments against them.

Finally, I realized where my real problem lay. Of course, I understood her background and therefore I would forgive her. But first, *"Let me just once tell her all the ways she has hurt me. I just want her to know what she's caused me to feel—that's all."* This is a most subtle form of resentment—a way of wanting to get even. The Spirit asked me to turn that over to Him. Some counselors believe and teach there can be no true forgiveness unless we *always* go at once, confess our bad feelings to the person(s), and attempt to bring about *immediate reconciliation.* I believe this is a dangerous teaching and I have seen much hurt come as a result of it. God has His own perfect timing for this kind of resolution, *if it is ever to come about.* With some individuals, like Joyce Landorf's *Irregular People,* it may never happen. God asks us to give

Him our complete willingness for reconciliation, but the timing is His. My first struggle was to fully and unconditionally forgive.

• Then the Spirit brought a second aspect to my mind. From then on, I would assume full responsibility for who I was and what I did. Up to that time, I had the most wonderful, built-in excuse for all of my failures. It worked automatically, like the doors which open as we go in and out of a supermarket. Whenever I failed in any way—in my ministry, marriage, or spiritual life—that automatic excuse-making gadget inside my mind went on, and a sign read, "You failed because you had that kind of a mother. If only she hadn't done that to you, you would have been okay; it's her fault, not yours!" Wow, it was the most comforting device! You see, it guaranteed that I (that is, the true me) had never really failed. With this built-in device, I was able to maintain my perfectionistic, unreal superself intact. If I gave it up, what would happen to me? The Spirit was relentless, "Remember, if you really forgave her, then that gadget's gotta go. From now on, *you alone are responsible.*" Frankly, this was more difficult than the first issue.

• Then a third matter emerged, and for me, it was the hardest of all. Way back in a closet in my heart, I had hidden a secret bargaining point, a place of leverage with God. If I really forgave, stopped my scapegoating, and let her off the hook, then surely God would see to it that somewhere in the future she would give me the affectionate love and affirmation I had never received from her. Surprise! The inner voice of the Spirit was gentle but firm, "Can you relinquish that possibility? What if you never get that from her? What if she is never able to give you that kind of love? Are you willing to accept her and love her just as she is, even if she doesn't change a great deal?" This was an agonizing surrender for me. It was almost as if the Lord was asking too much this time.

Later, when I began to observe similar struggles in my counselees, I understood what was really at stake. *I was really trying to offer my forgiveness and love in return for the guarantee of a promissory note.* But just as God offers us unconditional forgiveness, so we must give it to others. Paul's great words in Ephesians 4:32 helped me the most, "And be kind to one another, tenderhearted, forgiving each another, just as God in Christ also has forgiven you."

Finally, standing beneath the Cross, I found the grace to surrender all claim on the future—for that too was a form of unrelinquished resentment. Then I was to give my forgiveness in the same way I was seeking to be forgiven—freely and fully.

• Let me add a fourth fact which I learned later, during the reprogramming stage. Forgiveness, like most matters related to our spiritual growth, is both a crisis and a process. The few days back in India were the crisis point, when, by an act of my will, I obeyed the Spirit and forgave. But there were many, many times afterward when the old feelings returned, or when I remembered some new item on the "hit list," and ancient feelings came alive. The crisis of forgiving really means committing ourselves to be willing to continue the process, whenever it is necessary.

I discovered that resentments are like all other human feelings—they are unpredictable and sometimes they can strike us when we least expect them.

In this respect, feelings of resentment are much like feelings of grief. I have mentioned the death of our first son while we were in India. Ten years later, I supposed all emotions of grief were gone. But one furlough while on a mission deputation trip, I walked into the kitchen of a minister's home. His wife was standing there holding a little blond-haired boy who looked very much like our son. Before I realized it, I started crying! None of us had ever met before and the poor lady didn't know what in the world she had done to cause such a scene. I was embarrassed and had to explain my strange behavior. I had just been completely ambushed by feelings which I didn't know still existed. A similar ambushing can take place in relation to resentments.

Forgiveness often needs to be reiterated. It is far better to be perfectly honest with God when we are struggling with old resentments. It is better to tell Him frankly if we are unable to surrender them and find it impossible to change our feelings. Frankly, I'm not sure we can ever change our feelings. What we can do is admit this to God, and then give Him our willingness for Him to change them.

Our prayers in this regard should be something like this, "Lord, I am sorry for my feelings of resentment and hate, but I just don't seem to be able to change them. So I give You a permit to change them. I *will* not to resent any longer. When the feelings return, I will keep turning them over to You. I don't want to keep having these feelings, and if You will give me a new set of feelings toward the offending people, I will exercise them. So I forgive completely, and ask You to change my feelings."

When we do this, and keep determining *not* to feel resentful any longer, we are surprised how quickly God can change our feelings. We should explain this to our counselees so that when old feelings ambush them, Satan will not be able to accuse them into condemnation and defeat.

I want to emphasize again how crucial It is to lead counselees to the place where they can actually pray, "Lord Jesus, by Your grace I forgive. I surrender all my desires to ever get even in any way. I relinquish them completely into Your hands." Don't underestimate the battle at this point. Counselees may say bitterly, "But I can't, I just can't forgive them. I was hurt too much." You may then need to talk something over on a deeper level; but, as soon as possible, get back to the place of prayer. You are truly wrestling with principalities and powers. Only the Holy Spirit can win the battle. So, persevere in prayer until the grace to forgive is given.

The problem with some counselees is that they have made their hatred a part of their very personalities. They have built their lives around these hatreds and find it difficult to relinquish them. I remember a young college student who shared at great length all the hurts she had received from one of her parents. She truly had a lot to resent and she used her capacity to the full. After considerable prayer along these lines, she suddenly jumped from her chair and cried out loudly, "But I can't give up my hate, I can't give it up. *It's all I've got!*" And though we talked and prayed for a long time, she did not give it up. After she graduated from college, I lost her in the passing parade of students. About fifteen years later, I was preaching in a distant city. A lady came up after the service, told me who she was, and asked if I remembered the time we prayed together about her hate. I assured her I had never forgotten her and had often wondered what happened to her. She replied with great sadness, "I want to tell you, you were right. After two divorces and a nervous breakdown, I'm beginning to realize I should have given up my hate."

Helping People Forgive Themselves

Sometimes the greatest battle is not in forgiving those who have hurt us, or in receiving God's forgiveness for our hates, but in trying to *forgive ourselves.* This is another area where we need to "pray and faint not." Here again, counselors must emphasize the will to forgive ourselves, and the commitment to continue doing this. Direct prayers should be made in this regard. Do not hesitate to ask people, "Will you right now ask God to give you the grace to forgive yourself? To abandon your strange desire to have higher standards than God does? Will you give up your right to condemn yourself? Will you ask God for the grace to never again remind Him of things He says He doesn't remember?"

When a counselee seems unable to do this, I believe counselors should exercise the authority Christ gave us, in Matthew 18:18–20. We Protestants have reacted against the Roman Catholic misuses of the confessional and the granting of absolution by priests. In doing so, we have given up one of the greatest privileges of our priesthood—being temporary assistants to the Spirit as His instruments to bring forgiveness. There are some people and some types of sin which require humans to mediate a sense of forgiveness. There are two great means of grace open to us, Holy Communion and the laying on of hands. I often use them with people who are struggling with being forgiven or forgiving themselves. I always keep the consecrated Communion elements on hand for this purpose. I have seen forgiving grace break through in miraculous ways as people partook of these sacred symbols. Again, and only with counselees' permission, I may lay hands on them. In prayer I claim the authority given to us by Jesus Himself, "Whatever you shall bind on earth shall be bound in heaven; and whatever you loose on earth shall have been loosed in heaven" (Matthew 18:18). After asking them to agree with me in prayer (v. 19), I close with "And therefore, (name), receive healing," or "Be forgiven," or "You are forgiven, in the name of the Father, Son, and Holy Spirit." If it seems appropriate, I often end the entire session with some prayers of thanksgiving for the healing God has given. If possible, counselees should join in such prayers.

Closing Words and Scheduling a Follow-up Session

After the time of prayer, before you let your counselee go, you should do two things. Schedule a definite follow-up session for not later than a week or two. We shall discuss this in our final chapter.

Then—I learned this the hard way—you should give some words of caution. This has been an emotionally draining experience. It's as if a high caliber gun has been fired, and an emotional kickback is possible. Or, it's as if something has been taken away from the counselee and they may have withdrawal symptoms. They may even experience genuine physical symptoms—a very severe headache, nausea and vomiting, diarrhea, or terrible fatigue. It is possible for a woman to start her period off schedule. If they are completely exhausted, let someone else drive them home. None of these things may happen, but it is much better to warn them of the possibility—forewarned is forearmed.

Stress the fact that their negative feelings are often unreliable and may give them a hard time for a few days or a week. Suggest they give time for those feelings to settle and more reliable and positive feelings to take their place. Also suggest they back away from further pursuing what has been prayed over, and just allow the Spirit to heal them at a deep level. Remind them that the healing of memories doesn't mean they no longer remember things. It only means that the sting and pain have been removed from these memories so that they no longer have compulsive power over their lives. Relearning and reprogramming will now be possible, and you can work together on that, beginning with the next session.

11

Healing Memories of Sexual Traumas

THE FAMOUS SOCIOLOGIST, Vance Packard, described our present moral atmosphere as a "sexual wilderness." When someone asked why he didn't use the term "sexual revolution," he replied that in a revolution people at least have some goals and know where they are going; whereas today, we are lost, wandering in a wilderness, not knowing where we are going. Every pastor and Christian counselor would confirm the accuracy of his description. In March 1983, Karl Menninger, the respected elder statesman of psychiatrists, said that in the United States incest is becoming almost as common as shoplifting. There is a sharp rise in the statistics for sexual molestation of children and teenagers, as well as for unmarried pregnancies, rape, and incest. We must add to this the rise of the gay culture. Gays are taking advantage of the breakdown of morals and the breakup of families. Many vulnerable youth, confused about their sexual identity because they have never had adequate parental models for masculinity or femininity, are being led down the path of least resistance into same-sex relationships.

All this brings to counselors an increasing number of persons who need healing from the agonizing memories of sexual traumas. Truly we live in a sex-saturated society. Those who involve themselves in the ministry of memory healing must be adequately prepared to deal with the sting and the stain of these sordid memories. It is not an easy ministry. We cannot truly help such people from a distance, protected by the armorplate of the pulpit, any more than we could lift someone out of a cesspool without getting our hands dirty.

Years ago, when I first started my present kind of ministry, a wise old counselor said to me, "Seamands, there are two topics which will always walk into your counseling room—*God and sex*. No matter how hard you try, you can't keep them out for long." It didn't take me long to discover that he was right. What took longer was to find out something even more important—*unless people come to terms with both of them, they can never be fully at peace with either one!* And in many instances this requires a deep healing of damages from past experience and a determined relearning of distorted present attitudes.

Probing Without Prying

No secrets are more carefully guarded or deeply buried in the dark cellars of the soul than sexual secrets. I am constantly amazed when people say, "I've never shared this with anyone before." I wonder how they have kept their sanity and how, at last, they have found the incredible courage to risk telling it. Here is where counselors must cultivate the art of creative listening at its highest. After long experience, some counselors develop a sixth sense that something which is sexually painful needs to be shared by the counselee. But we must be extremely careful to probe gently, to suggest, encourage, and lead *without prying*. We know what they are going to tell us, but we must not tell them we know. We must assure them it will be all right if they tell us and that we will accept them if they do or if they don't. This is done more by an attitude of spirit than by direct statements. People can sense our attitudes; they can spot a censorious spirit from a mile.

What will help bring people over the line to where they are able to share? When they can sense that *we are suffering with them.* How often I have asked a counselee why he didn't share this with his pastor or a Christian worker I knew was close by. The answer invariably is, "Oh, I just couldn't; they wouldn't understand," or, "They'd be shocked. I know what they'd say." I've had people come when I was almost certain what they needed and wanted to share. But they'd beat around the bush for an hour and never quite make it.

Watch and pray; wait and pray; listen and pray; probe and pray. But don't push and pry. It's supremely important they freely choose to share with us. In doing this they have begun the process of healing. Once they say something aloud in our presence, they can never deny it as fully to themselves again. They have offered a very important part of themselves to us that deserves our most tender and empathetic handling.

The Conflict of Contradictory Emotions

There are many reasons why sexual memories can be painful. The first is that *our sexuality is at the very heart* of *our identity*. Our masculinity or femininity is deeply wrapped up with who we are and how we view ourselves. Damage to this area is bound to deeply affect our selfesteem.

The second reason is that *sex is such a powerful emotion*. It is so strong that God's plan allows several years of growth and development before the onset of puberty. In this way our bodies and emotions become mature enough to handle these powerful feelings. One of the most terrible facts about child molestation is the awakening of such overwhelming emotions at such an early age and under such frightening conditions. It could be compared to what happens when you try to operate an extremely high voltage electrical appliance through a small extension cord. The wires overheat and eventually burn out. In a similar way, sexual molestation produces an emotional short-circuit which can cause serious sexual damage.

But perhaps the most important reason these memories are so painful is that *sexual feelings can be the most contradictory emotions we humans experience*. We need to help counselees understand their own confusion and turmoil over their sexual traumas. What they have undergone can result in their experiencing sex as an incredible combination of desire and dread, pleasure and pain, fascination and fear. In one and the same emotion we can find a contradictory combination of compulsive longing and guilty contempt. This is why unhealed sexual traumas carried into married life often produce a terrible inner conflict of wanting sex but hating it at the same time.

When Connie and her husband came for marriage counseling, I couldn't help being impressed by them. They had so much to build on—a strong and intelligent Christian faith, fulfilling jobs, and many common interests and activities they genuinely enjoyed doing together. There was only one thing they didn't enjoy doing together—making love. Well, not exactly, for the truth of the matter is that they did. It was what Tim called "Connie's weird reaction afterward" that troubled them both. In fact, the more Connie enjoyed it, the angrier she got at

Tim afterward. Connie agreed, "I just don't understand it. Sometimes I seem to go berserk. I've actually struck out at him, right after I've felt the most loving toward him."

She had read all the good Christian books on marital sex; she knew it was a gift from God, and she wasn't inhibited. After a few sessions with Connie by herself, we both began to understand her seemingly strange reactions. She had never shared it with anyone before—especially not Tim. When she was about eight years old, one of her teenage brothers began to involve her in sex play. They "never went all the way, but everything but." This had continued off and on for several years. "At first I was terrified. I didn't really understand it and felt very guilty. He kept me quiet by bribes and threats. Mother had a serious heart condition and he said if she found out about it, she might have a fatal heart attack, and I'd be the one who had killed her. So I kept mum. Later on, I just accepted it. And then . . ." Connie fell silent. I waited. "And then . . ." Silence one more. Connie hung her head and reached for more Kleenex. She did her best to turn on her automatic choke, but she just couldn't hold back the sobs *and the anger*. She got up and paced around the room. "Why that's terrible!" she cried out. "That's awful, I can't believe I could do that. Yuk! That's disgusting." I inquired very gently, "What was, Connie?" I was fairly sure I knew what she was going to say, but I was also sure that *she was the one who needed to say it*. I waited, praying silently back in the subterranean sanctuary of my soul. Finally the words came out in a hoarse, bitter voice, as if she had struck herself across the back with a whip, "I began to enjoy it." She moaned out the rest of it, "What kind of a person am I? With my own brother! I hate him for that, and yet I got so I wanted him to do it."

What was the real issue here? Why her "weird" and contradictory behavior? Where did she need the deepest healing? Of course, she needed to forgive her brother and surrender her hate for him. But the real issue was forgiving herself for getting to the place where she enjoyed it, in spite of the fact that she hated *it* and *him*.

Before we were done, we discovered a whole series of concepts/feelings which needed healing. They were all producing deep inner conflict because they were inherently contradictory and thus pushing her toward her strange love/hate sex life. She knew in her mind that sex was a good gift from God, but she was angry at Him about that too—couldn't He have thought of some other way? She liked men and was attracted to them; but she felt angry at herself for not being "strong enough" to do without them.

Most harmful of all, she loved her husband and needed the affection and joy of intercourse with him. But she was angry at herself for needing him, and therefore angriest at him whenever she showed her deepest need of him and joy in him. Sound confusing? Of course. It is. When Connie finally understood all this, she was able to forgive and be forgiven. She could then forgive her brother for being a sinner and forgive herself for being a human and begin to thank God for His gift of sex. It wasn't long before she and Tim were able to have a really fulfilling marriage.

Centering on the Real Hurt Which Needs Healing

It's so easy to be thrown off the track when dealing with people's sexual traumas. Of course, the actual sexual part is important. Remembering and sharing the specifics and their agonizing emotions is absolutely essential. But many times the mere catharsis of getting it off one's chest will not by itself bring sufficient healing and permanent change in behavior. As in Connie's story, there is often something at a much deeper level which needs greater healing, and it may be quite different from the directly sexual part of the memory. Counselors and counselees need to be very aware of the intricate intertwining of these hurts and make sure they are all dealt with in the healing process. The following three incidents bring out this truth.

• Nobody believed her. Gwen came to talk about a variety of problems. Some were her own; others involved her relationship with her husband. We discussed a great many things, including some distorted concepts of God and grace. Finally, as I had been rightly warned, sex too walked into the office. There were some problems regarding her responses during their lovemaking. These were by no means as serious as some people experience, when an unseen shutter from the past comes down and blocks the free flow of sexual feelings, but serious enough to prevent their marriage from being all they both wanted it to be.

A lot of hurt centered around something that had happened when Gwen was about eleven or twelve years old. She had gone to spend the night at the home of one of her best friends. At about two in the morning she was awakened with a start. Big Brother, who was in his late teens, had crawled in bed with her and was fondling her. Gwen pushed him away and let out a scream. Soon all the lights went on and the household was awake. Of course, Big Brother ran back into his room, pulled the covers over his head and appeared to be fast asleep. The girlfriend and her parents tried their best to calm her down, but Gwen was almost hysterical as she blurted out the story. Finally, the parents called Gwen's parents. They explained that Gwen must have had a scary nightmare and couldn't seem to get over it. It would probably be best if they'd come and take her back home for the rest of the night. Her parents arrived in a short time and Gwen went home with them.

This kind of incident is extremely common and can certainly be very terrifying to a sensitive girl of that age. It appeared to be a rather straightforward matter and the memory which needed healing quite obvious. But when we began praying about it, the real issue emerged. What was the real hurt which had caused Gwen so much pain? More than the shock and bewilderment of what Big Brother did was the fact that nobody believed her—*not even her very own mother and dad*. They too had accepted the nightmare explanation. Oh, how their words still burned and rankled in her memory—"After all, Dear, they are such a fine family and he's such a nice boy. You know he wouldn't do a thing like that. You must have had a terrible dream. We all have those sometimes and they seem so real we think they actually happened."

There is nothing more humiliating to children than to not be believed. It is one of the greatest hurts they can endure. In their eyes it's sheer injustice. They are desperately telling the truth, *but the people they want to be most truthful with are accusing them of telling lies.* Gwen felt so put down by this, so enraged. It began a whole series of unhealthy responses, particularly to her mother. Her anger also started her on the path to a picky perfectionism. So there had to be an inner healing and follow up (spiritual chemotherapy) for a kind of cancerous growth made up of injustice, sexual trauma, rage, and critical perfectionism. Thank God His Spirit is able to heal and to continue healing. Not so long ago I received this letter from Gwen:

> It's been ten years since my many visits to your office. Many times I wished I could share with you the joys and sorrows, the growing pains and victories that have happened since. A letter cannot

adequately give all that was involved in my "reprogramming." So many times I wanted to turn the clock back and never begin— that is, never start the healing. But I always was a fighter (maybe you don't remember) and the positive side of my perfectionism won over! The best part is that over the years God has used me in very much the same kind of ministry to others. We have seen the same needs everywhere, even in other parts of the world.

Hopefully, next year I will get my M.A. in counseling with a concentration in gerontology. Maybe I'll see you in my office someday—Ha! (Author's comment—not very funny!) If you ever travel in our direction, our home is yours. Our little David A. is growing up. He's precious.

Yours in Jesus,
Gwen

• Smothered by love. Larry was a minister in his twenties. Not only was he single, but he told me again and again he had no interest in women. In fact, though he lived near a beach, he said he had never had any sexual feelings toward girls. Instead, he felt attracted to masculine men. However, he had strongly repressed such feelings, especially since he had become a Christian at around age fifteen. He had tried dating young women and two of them had fallen in love with him. They had initiated the normal court-ship, with hugging and kissing. But Larry had been so uncom-fortable with this kind of intimacy that he had broken up with them. Now he had stopped dating completely—he was too afraid he could never meet a woman's demands. What brought him to me for help was an incident in the pastorate. A lonely teenage boy he befriended had begun looking to him as a father and spending a lot of time with him. Sometimes he would even stay overnight at the parsonage. Larry became very frightened by the growing strength of his homosexual feelings toward the youth and real-ized he needed to seek help before he did something which would destroy his ministry.

No one can really say for sure what causes homosexuality. It seems to be a form of learned behavior resulting from the interaction of a complex set of varied factors. However, among the more common contributing elements we often find a family pattern like Larry's—an extremely possessive, domineering mother combined with a passive or estranged father. Larry's father had openly favored his more athletic son, while being quite antagonistic to Larry and his intellectual and spiritual interests. His mother had been overprotective and overaffectionate. Larry was embarrassed as he shared with me her smother love—asking him to sit in her lap when he was a senior in college, getting into bed with him early in the mornings and hugging him, sitting too close to him while riding in the car. To be sure he did the right thing, she wouldn't let him make decisions for himself. On several occasions when he made a mistake in public, she cried and scolded him because he had "hurt her feelings." I couldn't help noting how many times Larry said disgustedly, "You know it's strange; so often she treats me more like a girlfriend would than as my mother should. She's always telling me how handsome I am and what beautiful eyes I have. And the way she holds my hand when we're in the car or walking down the street really humiliates me."

I was unable to get Larry to become aware of how truly angry he was with his mother. She had done so much for him—and he was too good a Christian to feel such anger!

And then an interesting event took place. Larry was involved in a friend's wedding. During the ceremony he had experienced some strange and overwhelming feelings. This is how he described it to me the following week. "When the couple were taking their vows, I suddenly realized I could never get married; I could never say those vows to a woman." When I asked him for the reason he gave me this fascinating reply, "Because I could never marry another woman when my mother was there watching me."

I could hardly believe my ears! Then I realized Larry was completely unaware of what he had said. Very gently and hesitantly I asked, "Larry, I didn't quite understand. Would you tell me what you said again?"

Once more he replied, "I could never marry another woman." I waited. He still didn't get it. I decided to try the playback method. So I said, "Larry, I want you to hear exactly what you are saying. Take it slowly and repeat those exact words one more time." He went over them slowly, word by word, "I . . . could . . . never . . . marry . . . another . . . " and he stopped midsentence. There was a long pause in which the silence was deafening! Then Larry began to turn red. It was as if he were a transparent glass being filled with tomato juice. The bright redness began at his neck and slowly climbed up to his face and forehead. He was so filled with rage I thought he was going to burst right then and there. We just sat in silence for quite a while, because he couldn't talk anymore. Then, we agreed on an appointment a few days hence. I gave him one simple assignment, "Larry, just allow yourself to feel all your anger against your mother; and as things come to you, write them down."

When Larry returned, he told me of three rage-filled days. As he remembered it all, the whole picture became clear. All his life his mother had used closeness, love, protection, and affection to completely possess him and get whatever she wanted. Though he was extremely angry, he was also so excited by his discoveries he could hardly get them out fast enough, "I just can't explain what's happening to me. But I can now forgive my mother and can let her go. *I can become a man and not feel guilty about it anymore.* I can live an independent life. For the first time I can imagine myself married—even sexually—to a woman!"

Then he told me he had gone to a restaurant and met a girl he had known but never really noticed before. His face was glowing. "I talked with her and enjoyed it. I was attracted to her. Her face was pretty; and when I noticed her figure, I actually got stirred up. Before this I was afraid women would manipulate me and control me, and I resented them. Now I feel free to admire them and enjoy them."

By then I was excited. "Larry, do you think you might ask her for a date?"

But Larry was ahead of me. He laughed, "Doc, I already have I've got one for tomorrow night!"

There were times of prayer in which hurts and hates were washed away. Reprogramming followed, but the change had been so tremendous that our work was easy the rest of the way. Within two years Larry met and married a fine Christian lady. Together they are serving the Lord in a most fruitful ministry. Larry writes occasionally and each letter reiterates his total healing and how happy he is in his married life.

I wish all my counseling experiences with people battling homosexuality were that dramatic and simple. They certainly are not. Some of them are the most difficult I face. They require long hours of counseling, healing, and the help of a Christian support group before genuine transformation takes place.

I have shared Larry's story to emphasize once more the main point of this chapter: when dealing with sexual matters, *make sure that you discover the real issue which needs facing and healing.* So often the sexual injuries are closely intertwined with hurts which originate from a different area. There can be no lasting healing and change until those memories are uncovered and adequately dealt with. The real issue is often the association and relationship between the two. In order to accomplish this, you need to be sensitive to the discernment of the Spirit.

• The betrayal of love. Brenda and I had spent many hours counseling together about many deep hurts inflicted on her by her family. They ranged from an abusive mother, who had once injured her so badly she required hospitalization, to a father who had tried to rape her when she was in the first grade. Our preparation completed, we began a long time of prayer for the healing of these and other stinging memories. Up to now she had described in considerable detail the physical pain she had suffered. Since she was so young, the sexual molestation was especially painful. She had talked about this aspect many times and it seemed to be the heart of the matter. But during the prayer time her voice grew louder until she was almost screaming between sobs, "Oh Mama and Daddy, how could you do that to me? I loved you so much. And I still do." The deepest pain was not physical; it was the agony of being betrayed by someone she loved. *In many sexual traumas, the key issue is the betrayal of love and trust.*

Vangy was a young mother who came for help because of various sexual maladjustments in her marriage. She had been to a secular psychiatrist who, after listening to her story, was convinced she had been sexually molested as a girl. Vangy denied it, saying she could not remember. The psychiatrist explained how the mind is capable of blocking out memories too painful to bear. However, she was not convinced and came to see me saying, "I've got to hear that from a Christian counselor before I believe it." I assured her it was perfectly possible and showed her my files on the subject. We studied in detail the story of the repressed memory of murder, told in chapter 3. After hearing her story, I agreed with the psychiatrist's judgment. In fact, I went further, since I felt she not only *could not* but also *would not* remember the details of her sexual molestation.

Her memories were interesting. In two specific instances, she could remember up to a certain point but then could go no further. The story involved an elderly man, Uncle Arthur, whom she loved dearly.

Rejected, and almost abandoned by her own parents, she felt he was the only person who really loved and cared for her. They were close friends and she remembered all sorts of wonderful things they did together. But there were two dark clouds in the blue skies of her memories. In one she remembered her upstairs bedroom. She could describe it in intricate detail—the wallpaper, the location of the furniture, her dolls. And she remembered one night when Uncle Arthur came into her bedroom and . . . Whenever she talked about this she became terribly agitated and emotional, but could remember nothing more. The other vivid picture was of something they often did together—pick blackberries. She talked in detail about the place, the woods, about filling the pails and carrying them home. But then her face grew dark and she would experience that same trembling turbulence as she tried to go on. She remembered trying to run with the pails full of berries . . . and then blank again.

After careful listening and questioning, I did something I rarely do. I told her what I felt sure was the obvious ending to each incident. I asked her to go home and spend some hours literally forcing her mind to remember what she was refusing to recall. Then she should come back the next day when I would hear the "rest of the story." She protested but finally agreed. She said she realized both her sanity and her marriage were on the brink of breakdown, unless she could come to terms with this inner turmoil.

She returned the next morning greatly perturbed. She had indeed had to force her mind to bring together the endings and the beginnings of both incidents and it was almost more than she could bear. Slowly, so slowly, she described all the details of Uncle Arthur's sex play with her. During prayer she literally relived those traumatic incidents. It was terribly painful. But there was a deeper level of agony which was the real issue. As the Lord took us back to her childhood, she sobbed it out in the voice of a little girl, "*O Uncle Arthur, why did you do that to me? You were all l had. I loved you more than anything else in the whole world. I loved you and I trusted you. How could you do that to me when I trusted you?*"

The real hurt was the betrayal of love and trust. After all the disappointments and rejections she had experienced from the important adults in her life, she had finally learned to love and trust someone. *And he too had betrayed her.* This was why her mind simply refused to put the stories together. *She did not want to have to believe this about one who she loved so much.* Certainly the sexual violation was a trauma. But her real battle was to forgive this betrayal and to allow God to restore trust in her and, also, to stop getting even with Uncle Arthur (and all men) through her relationship with her husband. We spent an unusually long time together in prayer and God answered in a remarkably deep and beautiful way. This was obvious when I received this letter:

I want to thank you for your part in my healing. It was the grand finale for me of many months of such struggle. You were God's instrument to help me possess the freedom He had promised me. And I am so enjoying my freedom. I know I have so much to learn and so does Tony, but oh, it is so great to be able to breathe fresh air after the stale foul air of the prison I was in. Freedom brings such delight to my soul. It has sort of put Tony in a state of shock—but I think he'll survive!

I guess I don't quite appreciate what my freedom means to him. After such a unique time Saturday night in our physical bonding, he gave his personal testimony in his Sunday School class the next morning. (Author's comment—I'd love to have heard that testimony!) I was not there but have been told by others he shared a lot about what's happened to me (not my past, etc.) and then ended up crying in front of everyone. Do you know, I have never seen him cry. He has not told me about it yet, but I'm sure he will. I wonder what God is doing in his life through all of this. I praise Him for His work in my life and in Tony's life. And His work through your life.

A hug and a prayer for you.

In His Love,

Vangy

We have shared together several incidents which I trust have driven home the central thrust of this chapter—to always watch for the deeper issue of which the sexual trauma is one important part. We do this by being prayerfully sensitive to the human spirit of the person sharing and to the Holy Spirit who is guiding us to all truth.

In chapter 5 I referred to Dr. James Pennebaker's research on the relationship between confession and physical health. An update on these experiments has just been published and is very relevant to our subject. In *The Lexington Herald-Leader*, Lexington, Kentucky, January 19, 1985, an article states, "Pennebaker has found that the effect of inhibiting feelings was especially striking in people who underwent traumatic sexual experiences before they were seventeen, people likely to be punished if they talked about their feelings. As a result, Pennebaker said, 'They're more prone to reporting every kind of disease imaginable—colds, flu, backaches, kidney problems, cancer.'"

How important it is that we develop the wisdom, skill, and spiritual resources to help the victims of sexual traumas find wholeness of body, mind, and spirit!

12

Follow-up, Cautions, and Conclusions

ONE OF THE chief obstacles to healing is our obsession with the immediate. The "itch for the instantaneous" pervades much of our Christian thinking. We tend to think that unless a healing is immediate, it is not of God and therefore not a "miracle." We have become impatient and frustrated with things that take time. The truth is that God Himself is going to slow down our pace, for He has no shortcuts to spiritual growth and maturity. Following the crisis of memory healing, the very important *process* of relearning and reprogramming needs to take place.

The most destructive result of repressed and unhealed memories is the way in which they have distorted our perceptions and pushed us into the wrong techniques of coping with life. Now that the painful sting has been removed from such memories, we still face the difficult task of forming new ways of relating to God, others, and ourselves. But now we are in a much better position to accomplish this. Why? Because we have a clearer comprehension of some of the forces which were previously pushing us into feelings and behavior we couldn't understand. It is true that simply having new insights will not necessarily give us a new life. But having those insights does enable us to identify more precisely the places in our personalities where we need to do the most praying and exercise the most discipline.

We need to see the whole picture. Prayer and discipline by themselves don't work for many until they have first undergone the healing of memories. In the same way, the healing prayer time by itself

won't work without the follow-up afterward. For these people, true
wholeness requires both. It would be impossible for me to exaggerate
the importance of the follow-up time for counselors and counselees.

It will be profitable to turn back to chapter 9 and review the list of
recommended books. Many of those can be very helpful in changing
and rebuilding lives. In addition to that list, I can strongly recommend
many of the books by the following authors:

A.W. Tozer	Bruce Narramore	Paul Tournier
James Dobson	Catherine Marshall	Charles Colson
C. S. Lewis	Dietrich Bonhoeffer	Norman Wright
Earl Jabay	E. Stanley Jones	Gary Collins
Larry Crabb	Charles Swindoll	

These authors have an excellent blending of biblical truth, psychological insight, and common sense. Most of us need all we can get of
these three elements if we are to change our neurotic patterns of living! Pastors and counselors should also assist people in working out
regular plans for Bible reading and memorization.

Another very valuable resource for renewing thought patterns
is found in the great hymns and Gospel songs of our evangelical
heritage. Making the effort to memorize them so they can be recalled
in the hour of temptation and struggle will prove to be very worthwhile.

Some evangelicals are prejudiced against written prayers. Yet I have
found books of prayers to be invaluable in teaching people constructive ways of praying. Among the most helpful are the prayers by Peter
and Catherine Marshall. Perhaps the finest of all is John Baillie's *A
Diary of Private Prayer.*

Many people need to follow their memory healing by developing
new relationships through participation in a small-group fellowship.
Here is where the church can function best as the healing body of
Christ. Certain wounds are so deep that there will never be complete
healing and reprogramming except in a support group which loves
and accepts us as we are, and also cares enough to confront us into
becoming what we need to be. Sometimes this is the greatest need
during follow-up time—admitting we cannot do it alone and receiving the encouragement to risk opening ourselves up to a group of
"healed helpers."

Changing Our Thought Patterns

Changing the way we think is essential. What follows is an article I give to many people who have difficulty overcoming low self-esteem and absurd, perfectionistic thought patterns. It contrasts right and wrong ways of perceiving relationships and will assist in "the process of transformation through the renewal of our minds."

THE PROCESS OF TRANSFORMATION THROUGH THE RENEWAL OF OUR MINDS

A partial list of the false, absurd, and unrealistic assumptions which contribute greatly to perfectionistic hangups and which need changing if healing is to take place.

A partial list of true, realistic, and biblical assumptions to replace the absurd ones. "Putting off the old and putting on the new" (Colossians 3:9–10) is part of the reprogramming so vital to the healing of our perfectionism.

MYSELF

1. I should be liked/approved of/loved by everybody, especially those I consider important to me.
2. I ought to be able to do anything/everything well—if I can't, it is better not to do it at all or to wait until I can.
3. I must be perfectly competent and successful in achieving before I consider myself worthwhile and before others do.
4. I really don't have control over my happiness—it is under the control of others and outside circumstances.
5. The experiences/influences of the past cannot be changed.

MYSELF and OTHERS

1. I am a worthwhile person whether I am successful in certain achievements or not.
   A. God has given His opinion of my value and worthwhileness.
      Psalm 8; Romans 5:6–8
   B. God's view on "success" is different from people's view.
      Luke 10:17–24; 1 Corinthians 1:25–31
   C. God has eliminated both comparison and competition and asks only "faithfulness" in exercising my particular gift(s).
      Luke 14:7–11; Matthew 20:1–16; 25:14–30; I Cor-

6. There is only one true/perfect solution for every problem—if I don't find it, I am sunk/lost/will be destroyed.

7. I ought to be able to make/keep everybody around me happy—if I don't, there is something wrong with me.

8. It is my responsibility to right the wrongs of the world/solve its problems/correct all injustices.

OTHERS

1. Others should take care of me/be kind to me/never frustrate me.

2. Others ought to be able to read my mind and know what I need/want without me telling them—if they can't do this, it is because they don't really like/love me.

GOD

1. God only accepts/loves me when He can approve everything I am/think/feel/say/do.

2. God may accept me as I am, but only because in the future I will never think/feel/say/do anything wrong.

3. God saves me by grace, but only maintains this relationship if I read/pray/witness/serve/do enough.

4. God holds my ultimate

inthians 12:4–27; Romans 12:6; Acts 5:29

2. I do not have to he approved /liked/loved by everyone in order to feel secure or lovable.

A. Some people can't like/love me because of their problems.
John 15:18–27; 17:14–19 Galatians 1:10; 4:12–16; 1 Peter 4:12–16; 1 John 3:11–13

B. Since I am always loved by God (regardless of how some may feel about me), I do not need to be overly concerned about the approval/disapproval of others.
John 15:9–10; 11:25–26; Romans 8; Hebrews 13:56; 1 John 4:16–19

GOD

1. God accepts/loves me even though He does not always approve of everything I do.
John 3:16–17; Romans 5:6–8; 1 John 4:7–10

2. Faith in what He has done for me (in Christ), not perfect performance, is what pleases God and puts/keeps me in a right(eous) relationship with Him.
Romans 1–5; Galatians; Hebrews 11:6

salvation in suspense—at the Great White Throne, He will judge me and then determine whether or not I will be given eternal life/heaven.

3. God, through His Holy Spirit, gives me the assurance of my salvation/eternal life/heaven now—my judgment took place on the cross. My only future judgment will be for service rewards and not for my salvation. John 3:36; 5:24; 1 Corinthians 3:10–15; 1 John 3:24; 5:6–13

Rewriting Our Autobiographies

Perhaps the most difficult task after our memories have been healed is *integrating them into our total life.* Memory healing does not mean we no longer remember our past. To begin with, this would deny the very aim we have worked so hard to achieve—remembering everything, including the most painful experiences we've tried hard to forget. Also, it would be unscriptural. The Bible doesn't tell us to forget our past in that sense. Memory healing means being delivered from the prison of past hurts. We remember, but in a different way. *We cannot change the facts we remember, but we can change their meanings and the power they have over our present way of living.* This is where follow-up counseling can be most valuable—to help people discover meaning and purpose in their lives. Too often we have taken Romans 8:28 out of its total context. We need to remember just where that great verse appears—it follows the two verses about inner healing we have quoted so often, Romans 8:26–27.

> The Spirit also helps our weakness; for we do not know how to pray as we should, but the Spirit Himself intercedes for us with groanings too deep for words; and He who searches the hearts knows what the mind of the Spirit is, because He intercedes for the saints according to the will of God.
>
> And we know that God causes all things to work together for good to those who love God, to those who are called according to His purpose.

A major part of the healing process is the discovery that God can take even the most painful of our experiences and work them out for our good and His glory. As we have said before, this does not mean God is the *Author* of everything that has happened to us. But it does mean He is the *Master* of it all. And during the follow-up sessions we help people rewrite their autobiographies by seeing and assigning new meanings to even the most painful incidents—the meanings God is going to work out through them. People who have been healed have often told me how *God is now using them to bring healing to others who have suffered similar experiences.* In effect, they have learned to say what Joseph said to his brothers, "You meant evil against me, but God meant it for good" (Genesis 50:20).

Learning How To Heal Memories on Our Own

A final word regarding the follow-up sessions. We should work with people to help them learn the basic principles of memory healing. Then they can use this form of prayer therapy with their spouse or a trusted friend. Counselors are temporary assistants to the Holy Spirit. They should aim at putting themselves out of a job as quickly as possible. Husbands or wives, friends, or small share-groups should someday take their place, and ultimately, Christians should learn to take hurtful memories directly to the Great Counselor, the Holy Spirit, and receive His healing.

Memory Healing as Preventive Medicine

Thus far we have talked about this form of inner healing as a kind of spiritual surgery. As parents, we can also learn to use it as *prayer therapy in reverse. That is, when we sense our children have been hurt by the accidents and traumas of life, we can help them open up their feelings to us and pray for their healing as a form of preventive therapy.* In this way their hurts and humiliations will not turn to hates and hits and we can keep them emotionally and spiritually healthy. Hundreds of parents have shared with me that a new sensitivity toward their children's hurts is one of the best serendipities of their own healing of memories.

Cautions and Conclusions

From the very beginning we have stressed that memory healing is *one and only one form of spiritual therapy.* I have written this book with much hesitation. My greatest fear is that some will try to use it as a gimmick, a quick and easy answer to emotional—spiritual problems. Or that they will consider it the answer for everyone. Let me say it with unbecoming intensity—THE HEALING OF MEMORIES IS NOT A CURE-ALL FOR EVERY EMOTIONAL AND SPIRITUAL HANGUP. In fact, under no circumstances should it be used with certain types of problems and personality types. It is most useful and successful with people who have severely repressed the memories of their most painful experiences and have thus tended to become closed and unable to express their true feelings about God, others, and themselves. As a result, they have then become withdrawn and unable to form close and intimate interpersonal relationships. With such persons, sometimes known as "God's Frozen Chosen," it can bring release from buried resentments, forgiveness, and the freedom to move on to genuine emotional and spiritual maturity.

However, *it should not be used with certain kinds of extremely emotional and hysteric types of people.* I have often begun counseling with people whom I felt might need healing for bad memories. However, when I asked for their written list, they have brought back great, lengthy epistles with hundreds of minor incidents described in the minutest details. These people proved not to have memories and emotions which were repressed or locked in. They had quite the opposite problem. Everything was blown way out of proportion and surrounded with all kinds of fantasy emotions. So, I have had to reverse my original plan and help such people learn *how to control undisciplined and unruly emotions which were creating havoc in their lives.* To attempt something like the healing of memories with such persons only further stirs up the uncontrolled emotions and can result in increased disequilibrium. It can literally do more harm than good. These individuals need a much more rational kind of counseling. They don't need help in contacting *unexpressed emotions;* rather they must be taught how to control *unruly emotions.* I share this in the hope that no one will make memory healing a kind of spiritual fad, or quickie emotional cure-all.

As we conclude, we discover we have come full circle. We began with mystery and we end with it. There are some things we know about healing of memories; there are some things we do not know. Certainly there have been enough positive and miraculous results in people's lives to encourage us in seeking further truth about it. There are also enough negatives to make us issue cautions. No one will ever fully fathom the mystery of memory, anymore than we will ever fully understand the mystery of God in whose image we have been created. So let us walk humbly before the Lord, asking His Holy Spirit to keep guiding us into the truth which sets us free. In the meantime, let us use the wisdom He has given us, in the spirit of Moses,. who said, "The secret things belong to the Lord our God, but the things revealed belong to us and to our sons forever, that we may observe all the words of this Law" (Deuteronomy 29:29).

FREEDOM FROM THE PERFORMANCE TRAP

Contents

To my most influential mentors
Dr. Edwin Lewis of Drew
who got me excited about the theology of grace
and
Dr. E. Stanley Jones of India
who got me excited about the Lord of grace

Preface

Early in my ministry I discovered that the experience of grace is the most therapeutic factor in emotional and spiritual healing. A doctor who works in a mental hospital in Tennessee put it this way, "Half of my patients could go home in a week if they knew they were forgiven."

The main task in counseling and inner healing is to remove the barriers to forgiveness so that people can receive grace—the gift of God's love freely offered to the undeserving and the unworthy.

Next to God's Word, prayer, and the sacrament of the Lord's Supper, the great hymns of the church rank high in healing efficacy. I have begun each chapter in this book with words from one of Charles Wesley's hymns, filled as they are with both the theology and the wonder of grace. It is fitting that on Wesley's statue in Bristol, England are inscribed the opening words of his hymn, "O Let Me Commend My Saviour to You."

My prayer is that these hymns, so precious to me in my own heritage, will bring healing grace to you.

David A. Seamands
Asbury Theological Seminary
Wilmore, Kentucky, 1988

1

The Miracle of Grace

O for a thousand tongues to sing
My great Redeemer's praise,
The glories of my God and King,
The triumphs of His grace!

Look unto Him, ye nations, own
Your God, ye fallen race;
Look and be saved through faith alone,
Be justified by grace.

AS I SAT listening to Devadas, a handsome young Indian graduate student, a story I had heard from an old-time camp meeting evangelist flashed across my mind. It was about a skeptic who told a pastor in his local community, "Your Christians seem to have just enough religion to keep them from sinning, but not enough to make them happy. They remind me of a man with a headache. It hurts him to keep it, but he doesn't want to cut off his head."

At the time I was in India serving as the pastor of a downtown, English-speaking church. My family and I had just come from almost ten years of evangelistic work in the villages where our main task had been planting new congregations and church-building among rural, uneducated people. Now we were faced with highly educated city dwellers who were plagued with the usual problems of urban and industrial life.

At the time I didn't recognize the nature of the problem being presented to me. After all, Devadas was one of the finest young adults in our congregation. A deeply committed, Spirit-filled believer from a long-standing Christian family, he lived up to his name, "servant of God." Loyal in attending every service of the church, though it meant a tiring bicycle ride of several miles, he was a thorough student of the Scriptures and a faithful witness among his jeering Hindu colleagues. If necessary, Devadas would have died *for* his Christianity—no question about that. The real question just now was why he seemed to be almost dying *from* it.

That afternoon in 1957, I hadn't the faintest idea that he was describing many of the usual characteristics of Christians caught in the meshes of the performance trap. The only thing both of us knew was that it kept him in emotional and spiritual turmoil.

For well over an hour, he shared his problems with me—his never-ending battle with *the tyranny of the oughts;* his overhanging sense of *guilt and condemnation;* a high level of *anxiety;* a sense of *low self-esteem* from constant self-belittling; denial and repression of negative emotions such as *anger or depression;* and a *legalism and scrupulosity* resulting from a damaged, oversensitive conscience.[1]

In my naiveté, it seemed obvious to me that Devadas just wasn't as *spiritual* as he ought to be. After all, I was only a decade out of seminary and filled with answers for most *every* problem. So I began to counsel him the only way I knew. Like many pastors I thought counseling was a one-to-one preaching session with a captive audience.

However, to all of my sincere questions with their implied and well-meaning suggestions, he kept giving me answers that just didn't fit my simplistic solutions.

"Brother Devadas, have you been reading your Bible regularly? If you'd increase your time spent in the Word, you would find greater peace and victory. I'm sure this would restore the joy of your salvation."

"But Pastor Seamands, I've already done that. In fact, for some time now, I've been reading an extra chapter from both the Old and New Testaments every day."

"I see. . . . Well, how is your prayer life? You remember in a recent sermon I quoted one of the great saints who said, 'Prayer is not simply the *preparation for* the battle, prayer *is* the battle.'" (I had been impressed with that and was hoping everyone else had been too.)

"Yes, Pastor. I wrote it in the margin of my Bible that morning and I have increased my prayer time. But to be perfectly honest with you, neither of these have helped much. In fact, as strange as it may sound, I seem to be somewhat worse. Something inside keeps telling me I *ought* to read even more, and I *should* pray even more. I cannot understand it, but *I never seem to be able to do quite enough. In fact, that's what seems to be the whole problem.*"

I was stumped. I believed he was telling me the truth. I knew better than to ask him about fellowship with other Christians or witnessing— I had seen his record in those areas. Somewhere in the midst of my frustration, the Holy Spirit strongly suggested, "Why don't you just shut up and listen carefully to what he is saying? You've been so anxious to impress him with your answers that you haven't really heard his questions."

For the first time having ears to listen, I actually *heard* the meaning of what he was saying. More important still, I began to *feel* his pain. "*I feel like I ought to do more. I should do more, I could do more. And I honestly try, but I never seem to do enough.*"

I later realized I had been ambushed by something quite different from the spiritual malaise that results from neglecting the regular means of grace and growth.

This unforgettable experience took place over thirty years ago. From that hand-to-hand, eyeball-to-eyeball, heart-to-heart encounter, there emerged the hazy beginnings of what in the years following would become a ministry to many hurting and disheartened Christians. These sensitive, sincere, highly motivated, and extremely hardworking people were trapped on the treadmill of spiritual performance, with no way to get off. In a sense, they were captives in a prison which was at least partially of their own making.

Performance

Devadas had said it all in his summary description. "I ought to, I should, I could, I try, but I never seem to be able to do enough." That's the inescapable bondage, the vicious circle from which there is no escape through bigger and better performance. That's the Avis button core of the curse, the horrible hub from which all the spokes emanate to hold the wheel of the treadmill in place.

While there are varying degrees of performance concentration, the syndrome itself is a kind of disease, a malignant virus at the heart of every human being. It is the ultimate lie behind myriads of ordinary lies, persuading us that every relationship in life is based on performance, that is, on what we do.

This lie insists that *everything* depends on how well we perform—

our salvation and status—our relationship with God

our sense of self-worth—our relationship with ourselves

our sense of security and belongingness—our relationship with others

our sense of achievement and success—our relationship with society around us.

Just as there are different degrees of any disease, so there are different levels of intensity in performance orientation. They vary from mild to strong, from severe to critical, from the fairly normal to the abnormal and even pathological. Performance-oriented Christians represent a wide range of despairing humanity. There are the very young in the Christian life, who are struggling to believe in a grace which just seems too good to be true. There are those who, like the Galatians, started out living by grace but now are mixing law (performance) and grace (gift). There are the perfectionists who feel sure nothing they do is ever good enough for God, others, or themselves.

Also represented are some deeply troubled persons with abnormal and even pathological symptoms, some of whom constantly battle against compulsions, like hand-washing; or obsessions, like a persuasion that they have committed the unpardonable sin; or phobias, like fear of contamination from germs. These disturbed individuals may receive some help from a Christian counselor or a book like this, but they usually require the help of psychiatrists and even special medication. In this book, I am addressing Christians who experience a more normal range of performance orientation and perfectionism. They do not display some of the extremes we have described, but they are hurting people, spiritually bound up, emotionally hung up, and relationally tied up.

I am convinced that the basic cause of some of the most disturbing emotional/spiritual problems which trouble evangelical Christians is the failure to receive and live out God's unconditional grace, and the corresponding failure to offer that grace to others. I encounter this problem in the counseling room more than any other single hangup. Dr. David Stoop, a Christian clinical psychologist in California, confirms my findings as he says, "It wasn't that I was looking for perfectionism to be a problem. It just seemed to keep cropping up as an issue with almost everyone who came to see me for counseling."[2] Unfortunately, he too counsels mostly Christians.

Pain

Before I describe some of the major problems which plague performance-bound Christians, I would like you to get the *feel* of the matter. Let me quote some statements which have come to me in letters from readers or notes from counselees. They are all cries for help and reveal some of the most painful symptoms of the disease. In these word pictures, you may identify yourself, or someone you live with. Please note the italicized phrases, since we will look at them shortly.

> I have been a struggling Christian for the past thirteen years. My problem is that *I am never at peace* and am always trying to be good—that is, *to be better. I am so afraid of making mistakes.*

> I am a college student and a believer in Christ. Your article really hit home to me. *I am always feeling that kind of anxiety, guilt, and condemnation.* These feelings invade my day-to-day thought processes. I cannot perform a task, read a book, or practice my music without *feeling I am being judged.* Several years ago I accepted Christ as my Saviour, but I feel *everything I do is not good enough for my Lord.*

> It's difficult for me to attend church anymore, because our minister stresses regular Bible reading. I want to read God's Word; but *whenever I read the Bible, I feel the Lord is "putting the whammy on me"* for what I am doing and where I am going with my life.

> That particular chapter was a picture of me exactly! Even my husband said it fit me to a tee. I have all kinds of *unrealistic expecta-*

tions. Also, *I attempt impossible performances* and try to get God's approval by keeping a lot of legalistic rules. *I thought I had to earn His love, and that caused me to almost take my life.*

I want to be used more effectively for the Lord, but *feel so unworthy and useless. I am such a failure I can't stand to live with myself.* I had such a wonderful conversion and in many ways am a "new creature in Christ." I really identified with your descriptions of *anger and resentment. It's almost like I go through a hate cycle against the people I love the most. Afterward I am so sorry and get very depressed.* I guess I'm *angriest* because I'm not having spiritual victory.

I am a missionary. God has used me to win souls. *I know all the answers,* all the Scriptures, and can quote the exact chapter and verse. But it is *all in my head. The God I serve is never pleased with me* and is certainly nothing like the gracious loving God I say I believe in—and tell others about. *Why can't I practice what I preach? I feel like a fake.*

I've come a long ways in counseling and God has made many changes in me. *I know I have to* let *go of the phony "spiritual" person I've tried to be for so many years. But I'm scared to death because I don't know who I really am and what I may turn out to be.* Is it possible to be *terrified and excited at the same time?*

I try hard to be loving, but I'm so critical and judgmental, so hard on my spouse and kids. The slightest failure on their part and I get angry and explode. Then I *feel guilty and get depressed.* My family is so loving and forgiving—but that only makes matters worse. It's almost like *a pattern that keeps repeating itself.*

It seems the harder I try, the harder I fall. When *I get exhausted and quit trying at all,* I really do feel condemned. It seems like *a pattern* of some kind.

The italicized words and sentences clearly describe the major areas of defeat and despair in the lives of Christians who have not yet fully grasped what it is to live a grace-based life. They also pinpoint the damage and pain which need to be healed before these people can enjoy a gracefull life.

- Continuous feelings of guilt, condemnation, and the judgment and disapproval of God. Again and again Christians tell me, "I feel guilty almost all the time." When I ask, "Aren't there times when you don't feel guilty, or when you have a sense of being at peace with God?" they often answer, "Not really, because then *I feel guilty for not feeling guilty!*"

Such guilt is not related to specific sinful acts or attitudes. Instead, it is a general, global sense of guilt which penetrates the entire personality somewhat as an early morning fog fills a valley. And like a fog, it varies in intensity. Some Christians live in a mild haze of divine disapproval which always surrounds them. And since they've never known anything different, they wrongly presume all Christians live that way. With others, the fog is so thick they are almost immobilized. They can hardly move in any direction or make even small decisions. They know they'll feel guilty in any case—it's "damned if you do and damned if you don't." It would be difficult to exaggerate the emotional pain and spiritual despair of such Christians.

- A sense of worthlessness, with feelings of low self-esteem and recurring inward assaults of self-belittling and even self-despising. There is so much misunderstanding regarding the term *self-esteem* it is best to clarify what we mean. The ordinary dictionary definition of *esteem* is "to value highly, have regard for; to prize or respect." When we speak of self-esteem, we mean that individuals place value on themselves as persons and consider themselves as having worth. Performance-grounded Christians do *not* feel good about themselves as persons, in spite of what they may have accomplished. However successful they may be in the eyes of others, they invariably belittle themselves— they literally tell themselves to "be little" so that they will not forget the small value they put on themselves, and their imagined insignificance in the sight of God and other people.

- A sense of phoniness and unreality, a feeling of being an empty fake, of having somehow lost touch with their real selves and not knowing who they really are. Because of the many contradictions such Christians find in their lives, they feel a loss of their own unique selfhood. There is such a chasm between *who they are* and *who they ought to be,* meaning, *who they ought to be because they are Christians,* that the pain is unbearable. They become so alienated from the self they deeply dislike that they try to deny its existence. But it keeps asserting itself to remind them of its presence. This comes out in statements such as, "I know all the answers, but they're only in my head. I don't really feel them in my heart. I tell others of Christ, but at a gut level I don't feel or live the Christian life. I'm scared to find out who I am, and terrified to let others know what I'm really like." Of course, such self contradiction drains both their desire and their power to effectively witness for Christ. Or if they do so out of a dogged determination to do their duty, they simply feel a greater sense of hypocrisy and emptiness. The saddest thing about these people is the loss of the real person, that true and unique selfhood God has given to them and planned to use for His purposes.

• Many negative emotions, especially anxiety and anger, which result in irrational fears, smoldering resentments, outbursts of rage, excessive mood swings and depression. If being accepted and loved depended on how well we performed, it's not hard to see why rage would be the inevitable consequence. We would be in a state of constant anxiety, and any failure would lead to anger at ourselves and others. This vicious circle of anger and resentment unfortunately includes anger at God, because He doesn't seem to be coming through with His promises.

These ungraced people, having little grace to give, become ungracious toward others. They have the same performance standards for other people as they do for themselves. They feel as resentful and angry against the failures of others as they do against their own shortcomings. When the pressure gets too great, they may slide into the depression which comes from frozen rage, the slow burn of resentments, and an inevitable blowup. All this leads to our final symptom.

• Difficulties with interpersonal relationships, especially where intimacy is involved. In the more shallow contacts of life, most performance-oriented people can function fairly well. Many of them are hardworking, quiet, controlled, and sometimes seem to be the "gentle Jesus, meek and mild" type. But when emotional distance lessens, when a relationship deepens and some degree of closeness is required, then many of the factors we have been describing can emerge and become disruptive, deeply affecting their ability to make and keep friends.

But it is within marriage and parenthood we see the greatest devastation. Let's face it, performance-oriented Christians are hard to live with. They are hard on themselves, hard on their spouses, and hard on their kids. Much of my marriage and family counseling involves partners of this kind. Someone has said, "Perfectionists are those who take great pains and give them to others." To which I would add, "Mostly in the neck!" It was the great Sam Shoemaker who stated, "Everyone *has* a problem, *is* a problem, or *has to live with* a problem." We could restate this, "Perfectionists have a problem, are a problem, and create a problem for those who live with them."

These are the five major symptoms of performance-orientation which need healing grace. However, there is one more important factor that must be part of this introductory chapter.

Pervasive Personality Pattern

The final two letters I quoted from, earlier in this chapter, both contain the word *pattern*. The dictionary tells us a pattern is "a design of natural or accidental origin; a composite of traits or features characteristic of an individual."[3] It is very essential we understand that the Christian who lives a performance-based life does not have an isolated problem in some hidden cupboard of his life that pops out once in a while to cause occasional emotional and spiritual upheavals. Rather, this pattern is a lifestyle, an all-inclusive way of *being*, a faulty manner of perceiving, thinking, feeling, willing, acting, reacting, and relating. This wrong way of *being* results in a wrong way of *doing*; that is, *a wrong way of coping with life and relating to people.*

The opposite of performance-orientation—a grace-based, grace-oriented life—is also a pattern of being. Such a way of life is more than a basic experience of Christ, such as conversion and the new birth, or being filled with the Spirit, or experiencing occasional times of spiritual highs. A lifestyle which becomes God's right way of *being* is lived out as the right way of *doing*—coping with life's situations and relationships. It's important that we see both the problem and the solution in this same light—as all-pervasive *wrong* and *right* ways of living life and relating to people.

This is why at the very start we must make clear there are no quick cures, no speedy solutions. Neither a miraculous Christian experience nor an instantaneous inner healing is likely to free one from the bonds of the performance trap, especially in its extreme perfectionistic forms.

No one believes more than I do in the necessity of the new birth and life in the Spirit as *the* basic ingredients of the Christian life. However, I also believe that many Christians with damaged emotions and unhealed memories need a special kind of inner healing to enable them to live truly victorious lives. All this I find to be in complete agreement with biblical principles, but I consistently warn against solutions that are more magic than miracle, and sow confusion in the hearts of hurting Christians. I spend a disproportionate amount of counseling time trying to pick up the pieces of disillusioned Christians who have unsuccessfully tried some instant cure.

I want to remind you that this warning includes the book you are now reading. Gaining a better understanding of the nature of your problem will not free you from the unhealthy and frustrating performance treadmill. As important as insight and knowledge are, they do not automatically heal or change. The notion that they do is an ancient Greek fallacy, further developed by Freud and, unfortunately, continued even by some present-day Christian psychologists. Paul unmasks this error in his crystal-clear statement, "I do not understand what I do. For what I want to do, I do not do. . . . For I have the desire to do what is good, but I cannot carry it out" (Romans 7:15, 18). Awareness and insight are of tremendous help in many ways, especially in showing us *what* we need to look for and *how* we need to pray. They also reveal those areas of our lives where we need *healing grace in order to fully live out the saving and sanctifying grace we have experienced in Christ.* While healing grace *may* at times include points of *crisis*, it will *always* be a *process* of changing our patterns of life.

From Servant to Son

This is what happened to Devadas, the young man I introduced to you at the beginning. As we began meeting together for regular counseling and prayer, we discovered several areas where there was a real deficiency of grace. Christians in India are a small minority of the total population; understandably, they sometimes feel the need to prove themselves before their non-Christian neighbors. For Devadas, this had resulted in a legalistic and joyless home life where acceptance and approval were highly conditional.

Do you remember the picture of the Elder Brother in Luke 15, who was angry when his brother came home and was met by the father's grace and a feast of celebration? "He answered his father, 'Look! All these years I've been slaving for you and never disobeyed your orders. Yet you never gave me even a young goat so I could celebrate with my friends'" (Luke 15:29). It was in this story that Devadas discovered himself, as the Holy Spirit slowly peeled away his meticulous striving and showed him a graceless and critical heart.

One Sunday I referred to John Wesley as an example in a sermon. Wesley, son of the parsonage, member of Oxford's Holy Club, an ordained Anglican clergyman and foreign missionary, was a devout seeker after personal holiness. But despite all his sacrificial service and good works, he did not find peace with God, and called himself "an almost Christian." Then on May 24, 1738 he discovered grace, while listening to someone read Luther's Preface to the Book of Romans. In Wesley's now well-known words,

> About a quarter before nine, while he was describing the change which God works in the heart through faith in Christ, I felt my heart strangely warmed. I felt I did trust in Christ, Christ alone, for salvation; and an assurance was given me, that He had taken away my sins, even mine, and saved me from the law of sin and death.

Wesley said that he became "an altogether Christian," and that whereas before he had the religion of a "servant," now he had that of a "son."

When Devadas came next to see me, he was visibly excited. "Until Sunday I never realized that I have been *literally* living up to my name—'servant of God.' I have been thinking and feeling and living not like a family member should, but like a servant does." Since everyone in India clearly understands the difference between the two, I said to him, "Devadas, let's do some role playing. You be the servant in the family and I'll be the son. Let's live out a day in their lives, from morning to bedtime, and see what the differences are." He agreed. Before long we were really into it, putting into words the wide differences between our roles.

The servant is accepted and appreciated on the basis of *what he does*, the child on the basis of *who he is*.

The servant starts the day *anxious and worried*, wondering if his work will really please his master. The child *rests in the secure love* of his family.

The servant is accepted because of his *workmanship*, the son or daughter because of a *relationship*.

The servant is accepted because of his *productivity and performance*. The child belongs because of his *position as a person*.

At the end of the day, the servant has peace of mind only if he is sure he has *proven his worth by his work. The next morning his anxiety begins again.* The child can be *secure all day, and know that tomorrow won't change his status.*

When a servant *fails, his whole position is at stake;* he might lose his job. When a child fails, he will be grieved because he has hurt his parents, and he will be corrected and disciplined. But *he is not afraid of being thrown out. His basic confidence is in belonging and being loved, and his performance does not change the stability of his position.*

Devadas and I read from Phillips' translation the thrilling words of Galatians 4:4–7,

> When the proper time came God sent His Son, born of a human mother and born under the jurisdiction of the Law, that He might redeem those who were under the authority of the Law and lead us into becoming, by adoption, true sons of God. It is because you really are His sons that God has sent the Spirit of His Son into your hearts to cry, "Father, dear Father." You, my brother, are not a servant any longer; you are a *son.* And, if you are a son, then you are certainly an heir of God through Christ.

In the weeks to come Devadas told me that every time he found himself feeling and living as a servant, he would stop and once again remind himself, saying, "Father, dear Father, *I am Your son, and I'm going to live and feel like one!*"

Through the years I have seen this miracle of grace take place in many performance-bound Christians. I dare to believe it can happen in you.

2

Barriers to Grace

Thou great mysterious God unknown,
Whose love hath gently led me on,
Even from my infant days,
Mine inmost soul expose to view,
And tell me if I ever knew
Thy justifying grace.

Whate'er obstructs Thy pardoning love,
Or sin or righteousness, remove,
Thy glory to display,
Mine heart of unbelief convince
And now absolve me from my sins,
And take them all away.

THE PERFORMANCE-BASED Christian life comes from the malignant virus of sinful pride—a pride which encourages us to build our lives upon a deadly lie. This lie claims that everything depends on what *we* do and on how well *we* perform, on *our* efforts and *our* work. We will enjoy acceptance and love if we can win them, success and status if we can earn them.

This pride extends to every area of life but is especially crucial to significant relationships, including our relationship to God (salvation), our relationship to ourselves (self-esteem), our relationship to other people (security and satisfaction from friendships, marriage, and parenthood), and our relationship to society (success and status). In other words, whether or not God loves us, or whether we can feel good about ourselves, or whether other people will like us, or whether we will be considered a success in life—all depends on how well we can perform. *Everything of importance in life is conditioned on whether we can deliver a perfect, or at least near-perfect, performance.*

Such prideful self-reliance is the very opposite of grace. I presume most Christians know by heart the common definition that grace is "the unmerited favor of God." Sometimes this is further clarified by the words, "freely bestowed upon the undeserving." Notice how the key phrases contradict what we've been describing.

Unmerited favor	vs.	Earned acceptance
Freely bestowed	vs.	Conditionally given
Undeserving receivers	vs.	Worthy achievers

By this time I can hear many of you protesting, "But that's old stuff. I know all that. Of course I believe in salvation by grace and *only* grace. Are you implying that I believe in some kind of salvation by works? Or a 'works righteousness'? I gave all that up when I accepted Christ as my Saviour, when I first became a Christian. I guess I'd have to admit I'm a lot like some of the people you described in the first chapter. But *this* couldn't possibly be the reason. Our church strongly preaches salvation by grace and I fully believe in it myself. I even witness about it to others."

I appreciate your sincerity but ask you to take a deeper look, for I've heard it too many times. You see, for almost twenty-five years it has been my privilege to counsel students and staff from Asbury College and Asbury Theological Seminary. These institutions are strongly evangelical in theology and very evangelistic in world outreach. Almost everyone who has come to me for counseling has had a sound biblical theology of grace. However, like the missionary mentioned in chapter 1, the deeper we counseled the more startled they were to discover it was "all in the head." Now it is better to have a right theology than a wrong one. But it isn't good enough. In fact it often proves a way of defending ourselves against the facts and thus failing to get in touch with the root of our problems.

Gut-Level Grace

A sound theology of grace can literally be purely *propositional* or all in the head, and not *visceral* or in the heart. We think the term *gut level* is fairly modern and realistic. But it's fascinating to remember that people in Bible times considered the stomach, the belly, as the source of deeply experienced beliefs and emotions. And so those passages which we translate with "heart," the older *King James Version* translates with "belly" and "bowels."

"Out of his belly shall flow rivers of living water" (John 7:38, KJV).

"If there be any consolation in Christ . . . any comfort . . . any bowels and mercies . . ." (Philippians 2:1, KJV).

"Yea, brother, let me have joy of thee in the Lord; refresh my bowels in the Lord" (Philemon 20, KJV).

"But whoso hath this world's good, and seeth his brother have need, and shutteth up his bowels of compassion from him, how dwelleth the love of God in Him?" (1 John 3:17, KJV)

In biblical days, the word *bowels* was used exactly as we use *gut level* now. Much more than mere emotions, it also included attitudes and actions and deeds, and was an all-pervasive way of thinking, feeling, doing, and relating. It meant that the whole personality was affected, right down to the deepest levels.

Today, many Christians have a sound biblical doctrine of grace to which they give full mental assent. It is a truth they *believe about* God, but it is not their gut-level basis of *living with* God, themselves, and others. It is *doctrinal* but not *relational*; it is believed *in* but not lived *out*.

Ted was an older seminary student who came to share some family problems with me. Typical of the many second-career men God seems to be calling into ministry these days, he was married and had teenage children. He had left a good job to obey God's call, after he and his wife experienced dramatic conversions from what he called "the fast lane of Yuppie sin." Now he commuted every weekend to pastor two rural churches. He studied hard and visited his parishioners faithfully. He forcefully preached the transforming grace of God, saw lives changed, and watched the churches grow.

Then his eldest daughter began to rebel against this new life. She changed her lifestyle—clothes, hairdo, friends, language, habits—the works, and became an embarrassment to him in the seminary community and in his pastorate. Ted was amazed at how much he was beginning to resent his daughter. He was also feeling some anger at God—how could He let this happen, when they had sacrificed so much to answer the call to service?

As we talked, I began to suggest that although God did not *cause* the situation, He did want Ted to *learn* from it, to begin to understand the pain that the Heavenly Father must have felt when Ted was living in sin. And, most of all, to understand what *love and grace* are all about. We talked and prayed together several times as Ted struggled with his feelings of anger and injustice. Slowly, he began to understand the cost of unconditional love and undeserved mercy—that God always accepts and loves us, even though He cannot approve of our behavior.

As Ted reached out to communicate grace to his daughter, he could see it was starting to make a difference in both of their lives. In our final time together, he was filled with deep emotion. "You know," he said, "I've studied about God's grace, I've believed it with all my heart, I've preached about it regularly, and seen several people wonderfully changed by it. But I can see that it's been mostly in my head. Now, God has allowed me to feel this kind of pain, because it's the only way He could shake grace loose from my head. It needed to be lowered about eighteen inches so I could experience it in my heart!"

You too may be saying, "That's exactly what I need. Like Ted, my theological and mental grasp of grace needs to penetrate into my innermost being and become gut-level grace. I want that desperately." Now if this is what you truly want, why is it so difficult? Why does it seem almost impossible to really live out grace on every level of life? Why do you cling tenaciously to patterns of performance that are totally unscriptural and that continue to make life so miserable?

At this point the easiest thing would be to go straight back to the Garden of Eden, talk about the results of the Fall and point out humanity's pride, self-centeredness, and rebellion against God. After all, isn't sin the fountainhead of this whole poisonous stream? Yes, but if we did that just now, I'm afraid it would be merely another head trip, one more interesting doctrinal excursion on a cognitive level which would not really produce change on a gut level. Unfortunately, this is what many pastors and counselors do and thereby miss the real problem—the deep-seated barriers to grace which have been implanted in many people. Of course, these barriers include ideas which operate in the conscious level of the personality. But they also include feelings, habits, attitudes and reactions, predispositions and presuppositions which have been conditioned by the memories and patterns of prior experiences and relationships. Most of these sensations operate from the deep subconscious level of the personality. They are not simply concepts or mental images. They are *feeling/concepts*, or *concept/feelings*, mental images so intertwined with emotions that each one affects the other. They need to be penetrated by the Gospel; in many instances, they require *healing grace* in addition to *a renewal of the mind*.

Cultural Barriers to Grace

In my other writings I have described how family life experiences and relationships can create in us badly distorted pictures of God.[1] In a similar way, some of the basic presumptions of a culture can affect our conceptions of grace. For most of the ideas in this section I am indebted to Ralph Satter, a graduate student in our E. Stanley Jones School of Missions and Evangelism. With his permission I am using material from his proposed doctoral thesis.[2]

Scholars who make a special study of other peoples and their cultures are called anthropologists. Their research has conclusively proved that the people of one country may have very different ways of looking at life and reality than people from another country. This distinctiveness is a *worldview*, a kind of mental map or way of looking at life which determines how a people lives. A worldview largely depends on the underlying beliefs, assumptions, and values which almost everyone takes for granted. People may not talk about them, question them, or even be aware of them. They are just "there."

In my sixteen years of missionary life in India, I was constantly running into the differences between an American and an Indian worldview which was predominantly Hindu. When I would preach on being born again, I was often misunderstood and thought to be talking about reincarnation or being born again and again and again. When the Russian leader Khrushchev visited India, he made a good impression. But later at the United Nations, he got angry, took off his shoe, and pounded the table with it. India was horrified! The Indian people associate footwear with dust and dirt, and "to slipper" someone is the greatest possible insult. And did you ever try to explain the germ theory of disease to someone who believes diseases are caused by angered spirits? Every seemingly rational argument you can use, "Germs are invisible," and "They get inside the body," only reinforces their worldview. They know the spirits are invisible and get inside the body!

A worldview is like a lens through which people see all of life. The lens in our glasses depends on the kind of refraction the optician has ground into them. In the same way, our worldview depends on the refraction of our basic ideas, ideals, and core values.

What, then, is our North American worldview? What does the Gospel look like through our cultural lens? Are there some underlying assumptions and values so deeply ingrained in the "American way of life" that they actually bend and distort the biblical understanding of salvation by grace? Are they so strong as to make it difficult for us to live by grace? Let's take a closer look at three elements of American culture which can be barriers to grace.

• Self-reliance. Most researchers would agree that self-reliance is a dominant cultural value in America. Compare, for example, an elderly American man who is dependent on his children for support with an elderly Chinese in a similar situation. The Chinese, whose society does not idealize self-reliance, is proud of his children and brags on how good they are to him. The American is ashamed and doesn't want anyone to know. Instead, he wants to boast of his independence from his children. He would rather get a loan from a bank than from a relative. He tends to apologize for bothering his friends when something breaks down.

Such self-reliance is quite contrary to grace, for grace is free for the asking; it is God-reliant, God-dependent. In the Christian life, extreme self-reliance makes us try to be our own saviors and sustainers. It's hard for Americans to think any good could come out of a dependent relationship, but that's what grace is all about. The ideal of self-sufficiency, deeply ingrained in most Americans, causes many Christians to take the very means of grace and put them on the performance treadmill. While they may use the language of grace, at a deep gut level, they live as if their salvation and security depend on how much they read or pray or give or work or witness.

• Individualism. This highly prized American value is best expressed in "doing your own thing." We are now seeing ridiculous extremes in the interpretation of the U.S. Constitution because of an excessive emphasis on individualism.

Individualism is the theme of many great American novelists, such as Ernest Hemmingway and others. In the 1985 bestseller, *Habits of the Heart: Individualism and commitment in American Life*, Robert Bellah and his colleagues glorify various aspects of American individualism that make it possible for a person to get ahead on his own initiative, in the pursuit of wealth or self-expression. Interestingly enough, even "biblical individualism" is highlighted in the book.

While Scripture gives attention to the individual, this is balanced by an emphasis on God's actions of both love and judgment upon families, communities, and nations. In the New Testament, saving grace is always relational and is found only in the fellowship of Christ and His people. There are no Lone-Ranger Christians, and the term *saints* is never in the singular. Grace is received and lived out in the community of faith. The "whosoever wills" of Scripture are balanced with "you will be saved—you and your household" (Acts 16:31).

Too many people regard religion as one more avenue for self-discovery and self-realization, rather than receiving grace, allowing Christ to reign within, and living in a grace relationship with others. Salvation is a matter of being dependently related to Christ, who said, "Apart from Me you can do nothing."

• Activism. A number of cultural anthropologists have pointed to American activism as an optimistic view of effort. "You can do/be/get anything you really want to if you work hard enough. If at first you don't succeed, try, try again." Bellah observes that the demand to make something of yourself through work is a requirement Americans put upon themselves.

Certainly, doing and obeying are stressed throughout Scripture. We *are* to be "doers" as well as "hearers" of the Word (James 1:22). All manner of good works are enjoined upon us, but never as a way of winning or earning God's approval. Christ died for us while we were powerless—still sinners—long before we could do anything to achieve our salvation (Romans 5:6–8). Redemption is a pure gift of grace and involves receiving rather than achieving. Good works are the fruit of being accepted, not the cause of it. They are our response to God's unconditional love.

But Americans regard approval, success, and status as rewards for performing well. When this value system is translated into the Christian life, salvation becomes a matter of our efforts. A cartoon picturing modern-day Pharisees was captioned, "We get our righteousness the old-fashioned way—we *earn* it!" Americans have difficulty with grace!

Satter points out that one of the best serendipities of Evangelism Explosion training is that many of the volunteers come to truly experience grace for the first time in their lives. This may *happen years after the trainees have accepted Christ as their own Saviour!*

Because many aspects of the American cultural worldview have been exported, they are now shared by other countries of the world. For example, Devadas, in my opening story, was a third-generation Christian and very westernized in his outlook. In the swiftly developing countries of the world, many people experience such barriers to grace. While we rejoice in progress, we are saddened when we see some of the same hindrances to grace developing in those nations. The American rat race needs healing, not exporting.

What About the Church?

It is possible to argue that the church, the divinely instituted body of Christ, could not possibly be part of the problem. One could point out those times and places in history where the church has greatly influenced or shaped the culture around it, often achieving tremendous triumphs over evil. For example, it is generally conceded that the Wesleyan revival of the eighteenth century saved Britain from the chaos and carnage of an upheaval like the French Revolution. Many social reforms resulted from the tenacious efforts of evangelical Christians in Parliament, from the abolishment of slavery to a law requiring the painted line found on the side of ships which limited their loads. Formerly, the greedy owners overloaded ships and many lives were lost in storms at sea.

Truly "our citizenship is in heaven" (Philippians 3:20), and we are called to "not conform any more to the pattern of this world but to be transformed," and also certainly to transform society.

Furthermore, the church is one of the very agencies of grace. Traditional Roman Catholics would go further and say it is the *only* one and that saving grace comes through their particular church. But all such ideas fail to make an important distinction. The *church*, the universal and *invisible* body of Christ, made up of all persons who believe in Him as their true Saviour and Lord, is a divine and perfect *organism*. But *the visible church as we experience it, is a very human and imperfect organization*. As such it partakes of the fallenness and imperfections of human structures.

While every genuine believer is a vital part of the invisible body, it is the visible and local church with which we are concerned at this point. We must always remember that those who make up the visible church are products of a particular culture. So it shouldn't surprise us to discover within the church certain impediments to receiving and living out grace.

- The gospel of success. American activism has clearly infected the church's idea of success. The size and design of facilities, the amount of the annual budget, steady growth in membership, and numbers in attendance—these define a successful church or ministry. The health-and-wealth gospel proclaimed by many pastors and televangelists is the most extreme example of this. The name-it-and-claim-it variety shows that Christianity can literally be absorbed by the American worldview. No wonder the church is lampooned by secular comedians as promoting a blab-it-and-grab-it religion.

To those of us who have been missionaries among the poor and oppressed, this twisted version of the Gospel is shocking. When I think of thousands of faithful Indian Christians who own no land, and are thus at the economic mercy of unbelieving neighbors, and who sacrifice for their faith and struggle just to survive, I am appalled and angered when I hear this success-by-achievement gospel that can apply only to the affluent. I heard a sermon based on the New Testament story of the Rich Young Ruler that was given an incredible conclusion. You recall how the young man refused Jesus' challenge to give away his possessions, take up his cross, and follow Him. The televangelist accurately called him a millionaire, and then commented, "The poor fool! He didn't realize it, but if he had only obeyed Jesus and sacrificed his possessions, *Jesus would have made him a billionaire!*"

Certainly, most churches do not go to such extremes. But who can deny the emphasis on activity and the pressure of programming which is the accepted routine of the weekly church calendar? Or the minister's regular call for commitment to these activities to prove the depth of our Christian experience? Gradually we accept the inference that victorious Christian living depends on how well we perform in the church program. It's not hard to understand the average pastor's frustration. His responsibility is to keep things running and to raise the money to pay the bills and meet the denominational apportionments. When he sees this not happening because of the lack of commitment of his people, he tends to make commitment the theme of many sermons. As a result the people think that commitment and performance are what Christianity is all about. A kind of faith-commitment becomes the work by which they can be justified!

All this is a far cry from the true Gospel of undeserved and unearnable grace which alone can put us into a right relationship with God so that we can be "called children of God" (1 John 3:1). *God's grace makes us worthwhile and valuable for who we are, and not because of what we successfully accomplish.* I believe the church's distorted gospel of activism and self-effort contributes greatly to the self-belittling and low sense of self-worth so many people feel. It is also a main source of guilt and shame. We are somehow made to feel guilty if we have not succeeded in every area of life—church activities, job, marriage, parenthood—or in trying to relate to someone hardly anyone can get along with. This is implied even in those situations which are obviously not our fault or under our control. One example of this is the way many churches look down on divorced persons—regardless of the cause— as if they are moral lepers.

With the success-based "oughtness" of so many churches, it is easy to consider oneself a *failure.* This is equally as true for clergy as for laity. I've seen many a young pastor break under the stress of the local and denominational performance-demand and finally leave the ministry.

• The gospel of self-reliant individualism. Another aspect of the church's life which conflicts with biblical grace is an overemphasis on *the individual Christian life apart from open grace-filled relationships with other people.* The New Testament always presumes that if we *receive* God's unconditional acceptance and grace, then we will always *give* the same kind of grace to other people. But this means that the church should provide an atmosphere where this is possible. So many churches function like one more spectator sport with little or no genuine participation in relationships. Most of us are hesitant to let people get to know us; in church, we feel we always have to "put our best spiritual foot forward" and "keep our halos on straight." When this is combined with the success emphasis, most people are afraid and ashamed to share problems or weaknesses. Some close up from the sense of, "If I'm a Christian I ought to be able to handle it myself." This too contributes to these feelings of unreality and phoniness we have described.

In spite of years faithfully attending and working in the church, many persons never experience the changes that should come from grace. Their deepest needs are not only unmet, but they are not even uncovered. The tragedy is that this kind of sterile atmosphere drives Christians into greater hiding and reinforces their emotional and spiritual problems. They join the ranks of the disillusioned and the disheartened.

• The gospel of legalism. Legalism has always been a problem for the church. The belief that salvation comes through keeping commandments and rules is as old as humankind and is the one basic falsehood behind every religious system in the world—that we can learn God's approval and love by keeping certain moral laws.

Evangelical churches and pastors believe in and proclaim a doctrine of salvation by grace through faith, and would not intentionally propagate salvation by works. But the Sunday School lessons and sermons are sometimes not heard as messages of grace. Instead, the hearers filter them through our cultural and religious worldview and distort them into a contradictory gospel—a mixed message of grace and works, unconditional love and performance-based acceptance. Like all mixed messages, this one produces confusion which results in emotional and spiritual problems.

We have looked at some of the general aspects of life which are seldom considered as possible barriers to understanding and accepting grace. Now let us turn to the greatest hindrance of all—destructive interpersonal relationships within the home and family.

3

Parental Grace— or Dysgrace

Come, Father, Son and Holy Ghost,
To whom we for our children cry:
The good desired and wanted most
Out of thy richest grace supply;
The sacred discipline be given
To train and bring them up for heaven.

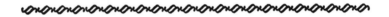

GOD USES MANY means to prepare us for our need of Christ as Saviour. One of these is *parental grace,* which is intended to be a gentle yet most effective means of grace. All through Scripture God made covenants with families. It was His intention that the children included in these covenants be brought up in the "training and instruction of the Lord" and thus be awakened to love and serve Him.

When I was a youngster, my parents often told me they had prayed for me long before I was born. I didn't like that at all. I felt it took unfair advantage of me as a little child and didn't seem to give me much choice. Later as I observed other families, I began to appreciate their prayers. Someone has reminded us that from the day we were born we were in debt—we owed for nine months room and board! This is true for all of us, but how much more for those from Christian homes!

Before we can see what a terrible barrier to grace the home can be, we need to look at it *positively*, from the viewpoint of what God intended parenting to be, in His scheme of preparatory grace.

At this point there are two ways we can go. We can look to the researched findings of psychology and the behavioral sciences (discovered truth) to provide us with the model of what a good home and proper parenting should be. Or we can look to Scripture (revealed truth) as our starting place and then later use the proven findings of developmental psychology to enlighten those principles. As an evangelical Christian, I am committed to Scripture as the primary source and the authority for judging all truth, and so we shall begin there.

Parental Grace in Jesus' Life

Let's look at the perfect family model, that which Jesus experienced. When the Son of God became incarnate in the human life of Jesus of Nazareth, none of the laws of human growth and development were suspended or violated. God could and did bypass the normal reproductive processes in what we call the Virgin Birth, but that is a misleading term. What we really mean is the Virgin Conception. As the creeds state, Jesus was "conceived by the Holy Spirit." This was certainly a supernatural act, a miracle. *But from the moment of His conception, all the regular laws of human development were in operation.* Jesus was *conceived supernaturally* but, like all other human babies, He grew in His mother's womb and was *born naturally.*

In Philippians 2:6–8, Paul describes the deep *kenosis*, the emptying or humbling involved when our Lord gave up the glories of His divine equality and kingly prerogatives. But Jesus did not give up the necessity of a human home with a mother and a father who possessed the divinely designed qualities for good parenting. God Himself built into this world a family plan, a purpose for parenting and family which reflects His own character.

The Scripture goes out of its way to picture the Virgin Mary as a *woman* of special godliness, holiness, and obedience to God (Luke 1:26–55); and Joseph as a righteous *man of* integrity, stability, and obedience to God (Matthew 1:18–25). And it portrays them as a *married couple* with high priority for the spiritual values of life. Luke tells us the natural outcome of such a home: "And the Child grew and became strong; He was filled with wisdom, and the grace of God was upon Him" (Luke 2:40). With full respect to the uniqueness and the deity of Christ, I believe we can still say that the chief instrument of God's love *at this particular time in His life* was the parental grace of Mary and Joseph. Must we not conclude from this that God the Father had carefully provided the atmosphere in which the Son's *human spirit* would find its proper identity, security, and self-esteem?

This can come about only as a human being responds during the important developmental years to unconditional acceptance, physical and emotional nurture, stability, love, and discipline. This requires parents of godly character who demonstrate righteousness, loving-kindness, and predictable graciousness. If we take the Nazareth family as our model, then we have to conclude that all deviations from that pattern in the direction of unrighteousness, instability, unloving-ness, or indiscipline, create deprivation and distortion to the foundations of personality. Such damages become barriers to grace and cause emotional and spiritual problems which often erupt later on under the stresses of the performance-conditioned life.

Luke was an amazingly careful historian, dating events as you would expect a doctor to, with clinical precision. He recorded the events at Jerusalem, in the temple with Simeon and Anna, as taking place at "the time of their purification according to the Law of Moses" (Luke 2:22). That is, when Jesus was forty days old.

"When Joseph and Mary had done everything required by the Law of the Lord, they returned to Galilee to their own town of Nazareth. And the Child grew and became strong; He was filled with wisdom, and the grace of God was upon Him" (2:39–40). The word Luke used is *paidion*, meaning "little child." It is obvious that God's grace in these early developmental years came "upon" Jesus through the nurturing grace of His parents. The channel was clearly parental grace, and we can clearly trace its results to the twelve-year-old Jesus. "And He went down to Nazareth with them and was obedient to them. . . . And Jesus grew in wisdom and stature, and in favor with God and men" (Luke 2:51–52).

This is what God intended to be the model and pattern for all parental grace. Note the five areas of parental care and the corresponding personality development so clearly presented in God's Word.

- Physical. "The child grew and became strong" (2:40). This reference is obviously to the infant Jesus. "And Jesus grew in . . . stature" (2:52) describes Him at the age of twelve. The most elemental part of parental grace is bodily nourishment and protection provided through the supply of basic needs. Though it is primarily physical, it is related to the total development of the person. Research among the famine children of Africa reveals permanent brain damage and impaired capacity for emotional expression as a result of physical deprivation. Here in America we are just beginning to understand the psychophysical consequences of underfed children from poor and deprived homes. We are also seeing what happens to those from affluent homes where tobacco, drugs, liquor, and excesses of sugar and junk foods are a regular part of their "nourishment." Either kind produces undernourished children who will suffer unhealthy consequences.

• Mental. Both Luke 2:40 and 2:52 describe Jesus as growing in wisdom. From a scriptural standpoint, this growth includes knowledge but goes much further. Wisdom is the art of reaching right ends by use of right means. It is giving to the things of God the same kind of dedication and intensity that people give to worldly affairs (Luke 16:8). Jesus' home provided the atmosphere and encouragement for full mental development; that is, a deep understanding of the Scriptures and their practical, down-to-earth application in daily living.

• Social/Relational. Jesus grew on the horizontal and interpersonal plane, "in favor with . . . men." It is obvious that Jesus had good personal relationships with other people. Being loved and cared for by parents creates a strong sense of security and belongingness which enables growing youngsters to reach out and relate to other people. The popular Gaither song expresses this truth very beautifully, "I am loved, I am loved, I can risk loving you." One of the first areas where we see the destructive effects of those deprived of parental grace is in their inability to build deep and lasting relationships with others.

• Personal/Volitional/Emotional. "Then He went down to Nazareth with them and was obedient to them" (2:51). This verse precedes the one which describes Jesus' growth and often gets left out of the list, when it is actually the foundation. Jesus had just expressed to His parents for the first time the growing realization of His true identity, by saying, "Didn't you know I had to be in My Father's house?" His parents "did not understand what He was saying to them" (2:49–50). In spite of His growing consciousness that God was His true Father, and the tension He felt because of His parents' lack of understanding, Jesus *deliberately chose to put Himself under their authority and be obedient to them.* One of the central purposes in parental grace is to teach obedience. A child needs to understand that genuine love provides limits, and that affection and discipline go together. Both are essential to healthy personality development. I have deliberately placed this just before the spiritual element. A child learning obedience and submission to the authority of parents is being prepared to surrender to the will of God. Such learning is at the heart of real maturity.

But this is not simply a matter of parents forcing obedience on their children. It is of tremendous importance to realize that the Apostle Paul carefully restated the fifth commandment in line with the spirit of the New Testament. He put part of the responsibility for the children's obedience squarely onto the attitude of the parents, so that attitude is an important manifestation of parental grace! The commands and regulations of parents need to be "in the Lord," in accordance with God's moral principles, and should be carried out in the proper spirit, so that their disciplining will not cause the children to become frustrated, exasperated, and resentful (Ephesians 6:1–4; Colossians 3:21). I shall be eternally grateful for this kind of parental grace which came to me, particularly through my father. He made it so much easier for me to believe in and surrender to my Heavenly Father.

• Spiritual/Relational. Jesus grew on the vertical plane, "in favor with God." This is the main purpose of being brought up "in the training and instruction of the Lord" (Ephesians 6:4). As John the Baptist was a forerunner of Christ, so parents too are to "prepare the way for the Lord and make straight paths for Him" (Matthew 3:3). Parental grace is intended to get the road ready for God's coming in saving grace.

Parental Dysgrace

Unfortunately, parents also have the power to strew boulders on the road and, indeed, be roadblocks instead of forerunners of saving grace.

In order to describe this side of the picture I am using the term *dysgrace,* which is the tragic distortion of grace.

The prefix *dys* has an interesting history and use in our language.[1] It comes from the middle English, *dis,* which came from the Old French, and from the Latin, *dys.* They all have their root in an ancient Greek word, *dus,* which means bad or evil. *Dys* is commonly used in medically related words when something has gone wrong, where there is *disease* (dis-ease); *dyspepsia* (disturbed digestion, indigestion); *dyslexia* (impairment of reading ability); *dystrophy* as in muscular dystrophy (deterioration and atrophy of the muscles). It is most clearly understood in the word *dysfunction* which means the disordered or impaired functioning of any system. Thus, *dysgrace* is grace which has been distorted or impaired so that it does the opposite of what it was intended to do. *Grace* is constructive; *dysgrace* is destructive. *Grace* encourages life and produces healthy personality growth; *dysgrace* impairs life and produces malignant personality growth.

What happens when parental grace becomes parental dysgrace? What results when that which God intended to be the greatest instrument of growth and development becomes an instrument of impairment and dysfunction? The very opposite takes place. Instead of helping prepare a human being for the new birth and new life with God, parental dysgrace becomes an obstacle to the new birth. Why? The foundations for interpersonal relationships are laid in the early years of childhood. Just as there is a *physical womb* in which the unborn baby's biophysical life is nourished and nurtured, so there is *an emotional and spiritual womb* in which the young child's relational life develops. An infant learns a language of relationship before it learns to speak. Prompt attention to physical needs, unconditional acceptance and affection conveyed through holding and bonding, facial expressions and tones of voice showing approval and love—all communicate messages of grace. Deprivation, neglect, conditional acceptance based on perfect performance, unpredictable affection, rejection, condemning faces and angry voices communicate the very opposite. Grace then becomes distorted and dysfunctional to the child. In later years, if ungracious words and corresponding actions are added to this early atmosphere of dysgrace, the growing child begins to live out the dysgraceful pattern of relationships he has been experiencing.

The four most basic concepts of life grow out of the interpersonal relationships we experience during our developmental years. When I refer to a concept, as I often do in all my writings, I do *not* mean a purely mental image. I mean both the mental picture and the emotional content or feelings, which surround it. Since we are whole persons, these two always go together, whether we realize it or not. So when we use the word *concepts* we are actually talking about *concept/feelings* or *feeling/concepts* which ultimately become *all-persua-sive personality patterns.* Let's look at these four life-determining concepts.

Your Concept of Self

The family is the chief source of how we see ourselves. This is so true that some have called it the "looking-glass self." At first a baby has no self-awareness. Around eighteen months of age, most children are able to distinguish themselves from others and have the rudiments of self-image. From then on their picture is enlarged until it becomes life-sized. It comes primarily from the reflections and the reactions to themselves by the persons closest to them. It is a concept/feeling about themselves. In this sense the home is like a *mirror* in which they see themselves. Their self-estimate will largely depend upon the worth, or worthlessness, reflected in the mirrors of the people who mean the most to them. Their audiovisual playbacks become the basis of how they will perceive themselves in years to come.

Jack was a young man whose friends described him as one who "had it all together." Successful in his work, happily married with an attractive family, he was well respected in both church and community. Then when he hit thirty-five things began to change—not on the outside, but within. In my counseling I long ago became aware of what I consider a kind of "young adult crisis" in the lives of many Christians. This usually takes place somewhere between the ages of twenty-six to thirty-eight. There are often several factors involved, like stresses related to marriage, parenting of children, financial needs, or relationships with parents and in-laws. However, the one which seems to bring these people for help is *the emergence, sometimes almost the eruption, of negative and destructive emotions.*These often represent the very opposite of who and what these persons think they are. This emergence is what had pushed Jack out of his comfortable life and led him to seek help. Before this he never understood my sermons on damaged emotions, and was a bit impatient with Christians who thought they needed counseling or healing.

At first Jack was embarrassed and puzzled. "All hell seems to have broken loose in my personality," he hesitantly confessed to me. I inquired about any possible physical factors. He assured me his recent, company-required checkup proved him to be "disgustingly healthy." When we surveyed possible situational factors, we came up with none. Slowly but surely it became clear—Jack seemed gripped with deep feelings of fear, insecurity, and selfdoubt. In spite of all the successful realities to the contrary, he had an overwhelming sense he was a complete failure. This was so strong that he was also being tempted by certain desires and sins quite new to him, which added to a sense of spiritual failure. It became obvious that Jack had pushed a lot of hurtful things down into the basement of his personality. As he put it, "They seem to be coming up through the furnace ducts."

From his earliest years Jack felt he was neither wanted nor loved by his parents, particularly his father. "I never felt I was accepted or loved *for myself.* Only if I didn't cause any trouble or inconvenience for them, or if I brought them recognition or pride, or they could use me to advance their reputations—only then did they act like they even wanted me, let alone loved me. For years I just bulldozed over all those feelings and worked my way to success. I wouldn't let myself look at any of this because I couldn't stand facing the truth of it."

Jack fought back the hurt and tears. As he shared a kaleidoscope of recurring painful scenes, one particularly haunted him. He was only in kindergarten, and his mother was bringing him home from the hospital after some minor surgery. He felt nauseated and weak and she was helping him into the house. Dad was outside working on the car, his head down under the hood. Without even looking up, he had said in a disgusted tone, "All right now, don't come sniveling around me. I've got important work to do."

Jack had never received the life-giving nourishment of parental grace—Acceptance, Affection, and Affirmation. Now he was suffering from a case of "emotional vitamin A deficiency." He had been a victim of parental dysgrace which had left a huge hole at the center of his being and was disrupting the most important area in his life—his relationship with God. And that leads us to the second of these life-determining concepts.

Your Concept of God

The home is like a skylight through which we glimpse our first pictures of God. We get our earliest "feltness" of God through relating with our parents. A great many of their characteristics are woven into our idea of His character, from what is *caught* as well as *taught*. Few parents realize that whatever is *permitted* in the home is both taught and caught. I spend hours and hours with adults, some of them in later life, helping them reconstruct their concept/feelings of God. Many of them have God and their parents all tangled up together. They need to get them separated before they can have a God fit to love and to live with.

While I could give scores of illustrations of horrible concepts of God which have their source in parental dysgrace, I would like us to look instead at the lifelong effect of parental grace which forms a good concept of God.

What a privilege it was to have Corrie ten Boom stay in our home for three days in 1961. She was speaking in a series of meetings at our church in Bangalore, India. (Incidentally, the things she enjoyed most were our ample supply of hot water and the thick American bath towels we provided for her!) I've never forgotten the stories she shared, as she paid tribute to the important role her home played in giving her the security and strength to withstand those terrible Holocaust prison experiences. Later I discovered she had summarized this in one of her books.

My security was assured in many ways as a child. Every night I would go to the door of my room in my nightie and call out, "Papa, I'm ready for bed." He would come to my room and pray with me before I went to sleep. I can always remember that he took time with us and would tuck the blankets around my shoulders very carefully, with his own characteristic precision. Then he would put his hand gently on my face and say, "Sleep well, Corrie . . . I love you."

I would be very, very still, because I thought that if I moved I might somehow lose the touch of his hand; I wanted to feel it until I fell asleep.

Many years later in a concentration camp in Germany, I sometimes remembered the feeling of my father's hand on my face.

When I was lying beside Betsie on a wretched, dirty mattress in that dehumanizing prison, I would say, "O Lord, let me feel Your hand upon me . . . may I creep under the shadow of Your wings."

In the midst of that suffering was my Heavenly Father's security.[2]

Your Concept of Others

Our family relationships greatly affect the way we look at and relate to other persons. Do we see them as friends, competitors, antagonists, or perhaps even enemies? Do we expect others to treat us with respect or disdain? Are they out to help or to hinder? To lift us up or to let us down?

Do we live by the Golden Rule, or do we "do unto others before they do unto us"?

The home is like a *window* through which we look at others. It affects the way we see them and the way we think they see us. What *we* think *they* think of us has a great deal to do with how we expect them to relate to us. What makes the difference is whether we have received parental grace—or dysgrace.

Dr. Ken Magid is a practicing clinical psychologist and professor who teaches physicians in a medical school. He has recently written a book called *High Risk: Children Without Conscience.*[3] His main thesis is that America is in a "bonding crisis." This means that we are raising a whole generation of children who are victims of "the unattached child syndrome." They have never been truly "bonded" with their parents and, unless this is healed and changed, they will never get close to anyone. Because of parental behavior—what we have been calling parental dysgrace—he feels these children will grow into adults who do not seem to have a conscience and who are unable to genuinely relate to other people. Dr. Magid describes them as "trust bandits," the con artists of society, pathological liars, and in some instances dangerous criminals. At the core of their lives is a deep-seated rage born of their unfulfilled needs. It seems to be locked in their souls because of the emotional abandonment they experienced as children. Dr. Magid says it's as if a voice inside them says, "I trusted you to be there and to take care of me and you weren't. It hurts so much that I will not trust anyone, ever. I must control everything—and everybody—to ward off being abandoned again."[4] His book is filled with

illustrations of many such persons so badly damaged by their homes
that they have a difficult time ever receiving or giving love to others.

I am glad that we can have a more optimistic viewpoint because of
the transforming power of Christ. Truly, "hope does not disappoint
us, because God has poured out His love into our hearts by the Holy
Spirit, whom He has given us" (Romans 5:5). But there are many
people so badly scarred by the kind of damage Dr. Magid describes
that deep healing grace is necessary to bring wholeness into their relationships with others.

Your Concept of Reality

Family is *the door* to the world. Since doors open both ways, how a
child will experience life depends largely on the parents' interpretation of what comes in and what goes out of the home. That great passage on the home, Deuteronomy 6, stresses the importance of constant
factual and moral instruction. The great principles of life are to be
discussed with and lived out before children at every opportunity;
when walking, talking, before retiring at night and upon arising in the
morning (v. 7). They are to be the lifestyle of the home, woven into
the very fabric of the family and becoming the symbols for all of life
(v. 8). They are to be written on the doorways and the gates (v. 9).
Parents are truly God's doorkeepers. Everything that goes in and out of
the home is processed by their interpretation of life.

The truth of this was borne out some years ago when several outstanding persons were asked what most affected the forming of their
moral standards for practical daily living. The majority replied it was
the family conversation at mealtime. Through our homes we receive
our concept of the world, life, reality itself, and how it all relates to
some built-in principles we will be describing later on. This is why
the *spoiled child* can have as many emotional and spiritual problems
as the *abused child*, for there is just as faulty an idea of the world and
life. Cruelty and abuse certainly distort right concepts, but so do
affection without discipline and love without limits.

Earl Jabay, chaplain at the New Jersey Neuro-Psychiatric Institute
at Princeton, has spent a lifetime working with alcoholics, drug addicts,
and neurotic patients. He says one of their main problems is an
improper view of reality and life. They think they can create a fantasy
world of their own, make their own laws, and live their own lives

accordingly. He uses this idea as titles for his books, *The God Players*, and *The Kingdom of the Self*.[5]

These are the four most important concept/feelings in our lives: those of ourselves, of God, of others, and of the world around us. And a significant part of their formation comes through the relationships we had with our parents. It remains to be seen in what way these life-determining concepts *help* or *hinder* us in living a life of grace.

4

How It All Began

My Saviour bids me come, Ah! why do I delay?
He calls the weary sinner home and yet from Him I stay.

What is it keeps me back, from which I cannot part?
Which will not let my Saviour take possession of my heart?

Some cursed thing unknown must surely lurk within;
Some idol, which I will not own, some secret bosom-sin.

Jesus, the hindrance show which I have feared to see;
Yet let me now consent to know what keeps me out of Thee.

WE'VE LOOKED AT several hindrances to grace which contribute to performance-style Christianity. Now, as we go behind these and see what causes them in the first place, we come to the heart of the problem—*sin*. According to the Bible, sin is both the *root* of what we've described as a malignant disease, and the *reason* why perfect performance can never cure it. *The heart of the problem is the problem of the heart*—fallen, diseased, and powerless to change itself.

But what's wrong with attempting perfect performance anyhow? We all want things to be perfect. The basic wrong with the attempt is that we no longer have that option. We lost it and can no longer speak of anything being truly perfect in this imperfect world. Obviously the key phrase there is "in this imperfect world." Does that mean it once was perfect? Yes, but it has fallen from the way it was, and so biblical Christians speak of a *fallen and imperfect world.* Something happened which destroyed its perfection. Does that mean life can never be fully perfect again? That's right, at least not here on this planet, and in the sense it originally was. Someday, certainly, but that will require "a new heaven and a new earth" (Revelation 21:1). Here and now, life can be perfect only in a new and different sense, in the way of God's freely given grace.

But we are getting ahead of ourselves. If we are to truly understand everything that is to follow, we must go back to the beginning. That's what Jesus did when He was questioned about the obvious difference between God's ideal plan (in this case, for marriage) and the less-than-ideal way it sometimes turns out to be in this fallen world. He said, "It was not this way from the beginning" (Matthew 19:8). Let's follow Jesus' example and go back to Creation. Interestingly enough, as I wrote this I began leafing through my copy of the *New International Version.* In turning to Genesis 1, I went back three pages too far and found myself reading these words in the Preface. "Like all translations of the Bible, *made as they are by imperfect man, this one undoubtedly falls short of its goals.* Yet we are grateful to God for the extent to which He has enabled us to realize these goals and for the strength He has given us and our colleagues to complete our task." Amazing! Not even our Bible translations can escape the consequences of a fallen and imperfect world.

The Perfect Creation

The ancient philosophers used to argue about where humans got the idea of perfection. It couldn't have come from actual observation or experience, since nothing in this world is perfect. How then did they imagine a straight line or a perfect circle, when there really were no such things? Where did such ideas come from? And so they argued back and forth.

We Christians know that the idea of the perfect comes from a *perfect* God who created a *perfect* world with *perfect* humans made in His *perfect* image. At every step of the Creation process, God declared it to be good (Genesis 1:11, 18, 21, and 24). Finally, when He had created humankind in His own image, male and female, "God saw all that He had made and it was very good" (1:31). You notice it wasn't until God created beings in His own image that He considered it *very* good.

James, in his letter, adds the important word "perfect" to describe God's created gifts. "Every good and perfect gift is from above, coming down from the Father of heavenly lights" (1:17). Think now of how completely perfect God's very good creation really was. It is described in the first two chapters of Genesis.

• God made a perfect universe governed by perfect laws— *universal perfection.* Genesis 1:1–9, 14–18 describes the creation of the heavens and earth—light, the sky, the land; the seas, vegetation; the sun, moon and planets; all living creatures with provision for their maintenance.

• God made a perfect world of plants and animals with a perfect balance between them—*ecological perfection.* Genesis 1:11–13, 20–25, and 30 describe the way God provided food and sustenance for every level of His creation.

• God made a perfect man and a perfect woman with perfect gender identity and sexual orientation—*psychophysical perfection.* "Male and female He created them" (Genesis 1:26).

• God gave them perfect personalities, modeled after His own, minds with incredible powers to learn, and emotions with a strong sense of identity and a secure self-esteem. All this was so that the man and woman would have dominion over creation—*mental, emotional, and organizational perfection.* "God blessed them and said to them, 'Be fruitful and increase in number; fill the earth and subdue it. Rule over the fish of the sea and the birds of the air and over every living creature that moves on the ground" (Genesis 1:28).

• God gave them perfect companionship with one another, modeled after the harmony of His own social nature in which Father, Son, and Holy Spirit live in perfect unity and love—*relational perfection.* This meant perfect oneness and openness, with no defenses, no guilt, shame, or inhibitions. Think of it—nothing to hide! Adam and Eve had the capacity for perfect spiritual, emotional, and physical (sexual) union (Genesis 2:18–35). Verses 24–25 imply far more than the purely physical; they infer there were no barriers of any kind—mental, spiritual, emotional, or physical. "They will become one flesh. The man and his wife were both naked, and they felt no shame."

• God gave them a perfect fellowship with Himself—*spiritual perfection.* Genesis 3:8 describes what was intended to be a beautiful and natural relation of friendship between God and humans. It is the incredible picture of the Creator-Father who walks and talks with His children. "Then the man and his wife heard the sound of the Lord God as He was walking in the garden in the cool of the day."

This was the capstone of creation. God had provided *perfect fulfillment* through His *perfect design* for all the basic needs which He Himself implanted in the human personality. His design was not only perfect, but perfectly natural in the sense that it functioned *naturally.* Every thing and every animal and every human operated perfectly within the scheme that flowed out of their created natures. No one had to work at it in order to achieve it. If they lived according to the perfect divine plan and the perfect divine principles, all would function perfectly. Psalm 8:4–6 expresses it the best:

> What is man that You are mindful of him?. . .
> You have made him a little lower than God
> And crowned him with glory and honor.
> You have made him rule over the works of Your hands;
> And put everything under his feet.

HUMANS
under
GOD
rooted in, but above
NATURE

Humans are under God, and rooted in, but above, Nature. This was the perfectly designed scheme. If the first humans would live accordingly, everything would be perfect. Ah, but that was a big *if.* And here was the one great difference between Adam and Eve and all of the creation below them. Things, plants, or animals fulfilled their purpose without having to make a choice. Their destiny had been fixed for them. But humans could accomplish their purposes only by choosing to stay *in the right relationship with their Creator*. And choice meant there was always the possibility of choosing not to do so. The various biblical words for sin express this—"crossing a line," "missing the mark," and "falling short."

The Fall

The Book of Genesis records the story of humanity's wrong choice and the terrible consequences which followed. We call it the Fall.

Humans, created to live *over and above* all other creatures, but *under* God, listened to the voice of the Evil One. Satan, one of the greatest of all the angels, had fallen from the heights of perfection, perhaps eons ago. This is described in Isaiah 14:12–15 and Luke 10:18. He desired to be as God himself, refused to accept his place, and fell to the bottom of the universe.

He sowed the deadly seeds of temptation in Adam's and Eve's minds until they began to question the goodness of God's character. They no longer saw God's loving limitation, "You must not eat from the (one) tree . . ." as the Father's gracious provision for His children to enjoy even more fully all the other trees in the garden. Instead, they were misled to perceive the limitation as the cruel prohibition of a malicious tyrant. And they chose not to accept God's word on the matter, but to do it their own way.

Even at this point there was no question of choosing good or evil, right or wrong—not in the sense, at least, in which we use those words now. Adam and Eve had only to live in childlike faith. They didn't have to make decisions of good or evil, right or wrong—they didn't even know what those words meant. Their only decision was between two opposing alternatives—to trust and obey God's word or to distrust Him and decide for themselves. Either they continued to live in a trusting, receiving relationship with God and thus to enjoy all His perfect gifts; or they refused to stay in that openhanded, obedient position, and taking matters in their own hands would begin to make decisions on the basis of what they felt was best.

Unfortunately, they rebelled against God and His way. They refused to accept the limitations of their humanity. They wanted to keep their position of being *above* nature, without being *under* God. They had perfection—being a little less than God Himself—but they wanted even more. They wanted to be *like* God, in the sense of being equal with Him (Genesis 3:4). Augustine put it this way:

> And what is the origin of our evil will but pride? For 'pride is the beginning of sin' (Ecclesiastes 10:13). And what is pride but the craving for undue exaltation? And this is undue exaltation, when the soul abandons Him to whom it ought to cleave as its end, and becomes a kind of end in itself.[1]

But when they tried to be *like* God, they not only failed to become *more* than they were, but actually became *less*. They could not achieve the glory and perfection that belongs only to God. Instead, they lost the only kind of perfection they had—a gift granted to them as beings created in God's likeness.

An Imperfect World

Because of the Fall, *imperfectness permeates the whole universe.* Try to grasp the all-inclusive losses which came about. The original and innate human perfections are gone, and we can never again regain them through our efforts, no matter how hard we try. But performance-oriented Christians find this hard to accept and go on living as if they can. "If only . . . if only we do well enough. If only someone else works harder. If only people would understand. . . . If only God would do something about it. After all, it ought to be, so it could be, it would be, if only. . . ."

In contrast to the performance *fantasy* many try to live by, let's look at what we lost in the Fall.

• We lost natural and ecological perfection. Romans 8:19–22 describes how "the whole creation" is now imperfect, groaning "as in the pains of childbirth," awaiting the day when it "will be liberated from its bondage and decay." One has but to look at the destructive list of natural evils, like earthquakes, storms, floods, tornadoes, volcanic eruptions, to see the out-of-balancedness of the natural world. *Chaos* has now entered into the *cosmos*. This doesn't mean that natural laws don't still operate; they do function, but the system is no longer perfect. One of the ways we humans still try to subdue and rule over nature is to better understand those laws, cooperate with them, and protect ourselves from natural destruction. Contemporary knowledge of ecology, weather forecasting, storm and earthquake warning, etc., is an example of trying to work with nature. However, the devastation, suffering, and death these natural evils bring are indiscriminate. They seem capricious and unjust. Insurance companies classify them as "acts of God," which is trying to explain one mystery by positing another. In counseling I have discovered that much of the anger in some Christians is because they just can't face the fact this is a fallen, imperfect, and often unfair world. They are plagued with much too high a sense of injustice, and this keeps them angry at life in general.

• We lost physical perfection. Myriads of everyday facts remind us of this painful reality—injury and suffering, disease and deformities, deterioration and death. We presume that if our first parents had not fallen, they would have passed on to their children and succeeding generations a perfect biophysical inheritance. Instead, we are all victims of a gene pool which gets increasingly imperfect, as physical, mental, and hormonal defects are passed from one generation to another. Many of these have a direct effect on our inborn temperaments and the kinds of infirmities we inherit or develop. Although these defects are not in themselves sinful, they are places of weakness which make us more vulnerable to certain temptations and thus more liable to sin. The inherited tendency toward being nervous and high-strung or toward certain types of depression are common examples of these weaknesses. One of the most difficult tasks in counseling performance-minded Christians is to help them accept their limitations and live within them.

• We lost mental perfection. We can only surmise at humankind's original mental powers. Certainly Adam's ability to instantly and intuitively class and name "each living creature" implies a kind of *direct and perfect knowledge* which we no longer possess. What he seems to have immediately apprehended comes to us only through long and laborious study.

Occasionally, in a Michelangelo or a Mozart, a Newton or an Einstein, we get a slight hint of humanity's original mental capacity. We call such a person a genius, which means we acknowledge what they have received to be a gift, and not only something they have achieved. While such rare exceptions remind us of what we lost in the Fall, we still don't mean that they are *perfect*. In the summer of 1987, newspapers carried the story of a brilliant young math student who discovered that even the great Isaac Newton had made a serious error in using the mathematical tables, following his discovery of the law of gravity. But we don't need such a spectacular proof of human imperfection. Our own daily experiences run the gamut from an embarrassing overdraft at the bank to a tragic highway death due to an error in judgment.

I am often amazed at the incredible assumptions some performance-minded and perfectionistic Christians live with. I listened to Angela tell me all the things for which she felt guilty. Her list got longer and longer, and she became very emotional as she heaped failure after failure on herself. Lines of strain showed on her face. It was obvious she was, as she put it, "living on the nub."

The more we talked, the deeper she dug herself into a quagmire of depression. I had to do something to break the melancholy spell. I leaned forward and said eagerly, "Angela, may I touch you?"

She looked startled and backed away from me. "What?"

Again I asked her, "May I touch you? You see, it's been a long time since I've seen such a divine being."

"What do you mean?"

"What I mean, Angela, is that only some kind of godlike creature could expect to do all the things you listed, let alone do them perfectly. You have absolutely divine expectations. Where did you ever get the notion that you or anyone else were expected to do all those things? What I hear you saying is you feel guilty because you can't do *everything and do it flawlessly.*"

Angela sat silent for quite a while. Then she hung her head and cried quietly.

"Do you know what I'm thinking?" she asked. "It's crazy and I'm ashamed to tell you. But this confirms what has been dawning on me lately. Somewhere a long time ago, I began to take seriously what my folks used to call me, 'Angel.' I can't believe it. I felt they expected so much of me that I began to play the part of an angel. I can't put all the blame on them—I brought a lot of this on myself, trying to feel special."

It was a Spirit-revealed moment of self-awareness which started Angela on a new pilgrimage of grace and freedom from the performance trap.

- We lost emotional perfection. There's no need to labor this point. All we have to do is to take an honest look in the mirror and see the vast array of our negative emotions—fear, worry, anger, rage, jealousy, and self-despising. Or to remember how unpredictable and uncontrollable is the range of feelings we often express, even toward those whom we love.

- We lost relational perfection. Perhaps this is the area where our emotional out-of-balancedness affects us the most. The beautiful openness and transparency which characterized Adam and Eve in Genesis 2:24–25 is gone. Now we are equipped with automatic defense mechanisms behind which we hide our true selves. We are *afraid* to bare ourselves emotionally and let ourselves be known by those close to us.

Often we are *ashamed* of our sexuality, even within marriage. Meaningful friendship, companionship, Christian fellowship, or the deeper intimacies of sexual oneness within marriage do not come about easily and naturally. They require a lot of effort—sometimes even pain. At best, they are not perfect; at worst, they can be terribly destructive.

- We lost spiritual perfection. This is the fundamental loss from which all the others come. Our *God-centeredness* has now become *self-centeredness*. What was originally a *perfectly unified and integrated self* is now *divided and imbalanced*. The human personality, once in *perfect harmony* with God, nature, others, and itself, is now *in conflict* with every one of these.

We have defaced what God created and intended to be called "son." The center has been displaced with an "I" so it spells "sin." What was perfect is fallen, bent, and broken. When you compare the thrilling beauty of Genesis 1–2 with the chilling wreckage of Genesis 3, you are struck by the terrible losses we have suffered.

No Way Back?

The worst of it is that there is no way back. "So the Lord God banished him from the Garden of Eden to work the ground from which he had been taken. After He drove the man out, He placed on the east side of the Garden of Eden cherubim and a flaming sword flashing back and forth to guard the way to the tree of life" (Genesis 3:23–24). *There is no way back to the kind of perfection the Garden of Eden represents.*

We have lost not only the perfect, but also our ability to earn, perform, or retrieve the perfect. We truly live in *Paradise Lost.* There's no way back.

But we have not lost our *memory* of paradise, or our *need or desire for* it. God left the longing for the perfect within us. This longing is one of the basic hungers which characterize humans—like the hunger for food, security, belongingness, affirmation, affection, sex, and, above all, the need to love and be loved. The drive for perfection and the perfect is a vital part of our need for God. This gnawing nostalgia for perfection is an integral part of the God-shaped blank within us which *only God (the truly perfect) can fulfill.*

There's nothing wrong with this desire for perfection. Sin enters when we, as fallen creatures, insist on *defining perfection on our own terms and seeking it in our own way.* The drive to do this is at the very core of our fallen sinfulness. This *twisted self-centered pride which is the basis of performance-based Christianity* is indicted in Scripture as a "works" salvation, or, as Paul puts it, an attempt to be "justified by the law" (Romans 3:20). Let us summarize our desire for perfection with these opposites:

A virtue becomes a vice.

An ideal is turned into an idol.

A reality becomes a counterfeit.

A gift to be received we try to achieve.

The search for excellence twists into a struggle for supremacy.

An undeserved relationship distorts into deserved oneupmanship.

The empty, open hand becomes a grasping, clenched fist.

I have gone into considerable detail to explain the biblical basis for our perverted pursuit of perfect performance. It is rooted in "original sin," and is one manifestation of it. In some Christians, however, damaged emotions are so intertwined with sins of the spirit that special healing and reprogramming are necessary. While it is true that all of us are responsible for *our own sins,* there are many people who are also *victims of other people's sins.* Sometimes it is difficult to get these two sorted out properly. Many people will never find freedom from the performance trap and all the emotional and spiritual problems that go along with it until they do. This is why the Holy Spirit (the Great Counselor) often needs the help of a temporary human assistant. This is why healing grace usually comes only with the help of a pastor, a trusted friend, or a professional counselor. We will be looking into these aspects of the problem in later chapters.

But at this point it is important to see that the roots of performance orientation are theological. If the ultimate cure is grace, then the ultimate cause of the behavior is the failure to understand, experience, and live out grace at every level of our lives. This means we must learn to give up every futile attempt to achieve right relationships by any other means than God's total plan of grace. Until we do this we are doomed to be *Christian POWs*. Prisoners of War? No. *Performance Oriented Workers* and *Prisoners of Works*.

Claire, a Modern Samson

Do you remember the lady in chapter 1 who ended her letter, "I thought I had to earn His love and that caused me to almost take my life"? She is a homemaker named Claire who in desperation had attempted to end her life. However, like many others, she admitted that she had hoped she wouldn't succeed; it was really a desperate cry for help.

Claire used a biblical picture of herself that had never occurred to me. She said that before her suicide attempt she had deeply identified with Samson in the Old Testament. Here is the picture she was referring to. "Then the Philistines seized him, gouged out his eyes, and took him down to Gaza. Binding him with bronze shackles, they set him to grinding in the prison" (Judges 16:21). Claire said she felt just like that—as if she were in a prison, strapped to a great grindstone, turning around and around, almost like a chained animal. "I felt as if I was consigned to a treadmill. Whatever I tried took me in a vicious circle. Sometimes I could keep it under control and run slowly. But usually I'd get going faster and faster, because I felt driven to keep up. That is, to feel I was doing enough. But I never was, and so never felt accepted or acceptable. I was trapped and couldn't find a way to get off. I got more and more worn out. I can understand why Samson ended up pulling the whole thing down. There didn't seem to be any way out . . . even today I wonder."

I've heard this kind of a desperate cry from many a sincere child of God who is "sick and tired of being sick and tired." That day I shared with Claire some words conveying the strongest possible assurance of hope, words that fit so well her Samson picture, and spoken by Jesus as He began His ministry in the synagogue at Nazareth.

The Spirit of the Lord is on Me,
because He has annointed Me
to preach good news to the poor.
He has sent Me to proclaim freedom for the prisoners
and recovery of sight for the blind,
to release the oppressed,
to proclaim the year of the Lord's favor
(Luke 4:18–19).

The *New English Bible* renders this, "to proclaim release for prisoners . . . to let the broken victims go free." My prayer is the good news of the Gospel of Grace—the Lord's favor—may become a reality in your life.

5

The Bad News

Sinners, turn; why will you die?
God your Saviour asks you why;
God, who did your souls retrieve,
Died Himself, that you might live.

Will you let Him die in vain?
Crucify your Lord again?
Why, you ransomed sinners, why?
Will you slight His grace, and die?

I'LL NEVER FORGET the first time I saw the Grand Canyon of Arizona. I was an MK (missionary's kid) who had seen many of the so-called wonders of the world. I had learned the hard way that the reality of sightseeing rarely lived up to the fantasy surrounding its advertising. So by the age of twelve I had already developed the practical philosophy of, "Don't get too excited about a famous sight, because it's not going to live up to your expectations."

It was in that skeptical spirit I approached the Grand Canyon in 1934. In those relatively uncommercialized days, you simply walked toward it and suddenly, there it was before you. I was shocked speechless and stood for a long time in sheer disbelief at the utter vastness of its size—the width, the breadth, the height of the chasm with that tiny ribbon of a river at the bottom—and the incredible spectrum of changing colors. It took several minutes to actually take it all in, to realize it was true. For the first time in my life the experience of something actually surpassed my expectations!

That's the picture which comes to my mind when I think of another chasm, greater even than the Grand Canyon—the chasm which exists between a perfect, holy God and imperfect, sinful human beings. It is a moral Grand Canyon and even more vast and unbridgeable. How can we get across this abyss? How can we bridge the gap? The truth is that we cannot, and this leaves us in an impossible predicament. God's Word makes it plain there is no way to negotiate a reconciliation from our side of the chasm. If it's ever to be bridged, it must be done from God's side. There is nothing we humans can do to meet the requirements of God's perfect law. Make no mistake about it— those requirements have not changed. His purpose for us is the same. He made us to live in perfect relationship with Himself and others, and He still wills our complete perfection.

Law and Love

When we talk in terms of love and law, we are not referring to do's and don'ts or a set of laws. People think immediately of the Ten Commandments, the laws of the Old Testament, or the commandments of the New. But it was Jesus Himself who told us what the law really was, as He restated an Old Testament injunction from Deuteronomy 6:5, "Love the Lord your God with all your heart and with all your soul and with all your mind. This is the first and greatest commandment. And the second is like it: Love your neighbor as yourself. All the Law and Prophets hang on these two commandments" (Matthew 22:37–40). Building upon Jesus' words, Paul wrote, "Love is the fulfillment of the law" (Romans 13:8–10). The Apostle John also emphasized love for God and others in 1 John 3:11–24, and 4:7–21. There is no doubt that the *law of love* is the center around which all the commands and prohibitions of Scripture revolve, and the principle which gives them their meaning.

To make matters even more impossible for us, God requires His law to be kept perfectly *from our hearts.* Our obedience must be *an inside job and not mere external conformity.* So it's not enough to avoid murder, adultery, or stealing, for the commandments are now highly internalized. We are required not to resent, nor to be lustful, nor to desire covetously. In the New Testament we learn that we are to love God with all our hearts, forgive people from our hearts, and do the will of God from our hearts (Matthew 22:37; 18:35; Ephesians 6:6).

This was the point behind Jesus' running battles with the Pharisees, the performance-oriented workers of His day. They kept the *letter* of the law perfectly but broke its *spirit* constantly. Jesus said to them, "You hypocrites! Isaiah was right when he prophesied about you: 'These people honor Me with their lips, but their hearts are far from Me. They worship Me in vain; their teachings are but rules taught by men'" (Matthew 15:7–9, quoting Isaiah 29:13).

When we look at God's requirements of us from the inside out, it doesn't take long to see our impossible predicament—the chasm *between His requirements and our achievements, the great gulf between the ought and the is.* In the Fall not only did we create the chasm, but we lost the power to leap across it. Now that doesn't mean we don't try, for we do. We attempt to bridge the gap in ways old and new, all equally unsuccessful.

The Sloppy Agape Way

Agape is a Greek word for love that refers to God's love or to the kind of love God puts into our hearts. Sloppy agape is a sentimentalized version of God's love which is so out of balance it excludes all the other aspects of God's nature. It is a favorite in many modern religious circles, some of which even call themselves Christian. It simply denies there is a chasm by claiming that God is so loving He overlooks our sins and failures. This sloppy agape is like a thick syrup poured into the Grand Canyon, filling it right up to the top, so that you can't see any gulf between the two sides.

Or, it may say no chasm exists because there are no real differences between good and evil, right and wrong, truth and error, sin and righteousness. There are no moral distinctions, because everything is a part of God and is therefore good. Though some things may look evil to us, this is just an illusion.

This philosophy comes in several attractive packages. There is the kind popularized by celebrities on television, or in books and expensive seminars. It is an incredible sight to see someone on a TV talk show, who you know is living by alley-cat morals, saying "I am God!" Such claims are common to the New Age Movement. Those of us who have served as missionaries in India or the Far East recognize it as an emptyheaded and Americanized version of a very *old* Hinduism or

Buddhism. There are other popular versions which reduce God to some kind of impersonal entity. Their benediction is, "May the force be with you."

Then there is a watered-down god of liberal Christians, who is so all-inclusive he is pictured as a kind of greatgrandfather in heaven, a benevolent, simpleminded deity who smiles down at his creatures and says, "That's okay, just as long as the kids are having a good time."

The Bible makes plain that God's love is holy love. The same Apostle John who tells us, "God is love" (1 John 4:16) also declares, "God is light; in Him is no darkness at all" (1 John 1:5). There are scores of references in Scripture to the "wrath of God." Since we no longer use the word *wrath* very much, let us call it the anger of God. I realize this phrase creates a major problem with some Christians, many of whom are tender, supersensitive persons with warped and fearful concepts of God. Regardless of their good mental theology, at a gut level they feel God is an omnipotent heavenly ogre out to get them, and so are terrified. This is an area where we need some balanced biblical understanding of a very important truth, so let's face it head-on.

The anger of God simply means that God's holy nature is unalterably opposed to all sin. It means God cannot overlook sin or come to terms with it by making some kind of deal. Put simply, God is against all sin, in any form, anywhere, and at any time. Sin creates a disturbance in the moral order of the world which God cannot ignore. He cannot treat good and evil alike; to do so would be to deny His own moral nature.

The anger of God does not mean what anger often means to us—a fit of temper, an unpredictable emotion, a reaction of irritated self-concern accompanied by a loss of self-control. God does not have an outburst of temper against someone because of sin and then think of ways to get even. Rather, *God's anger is His predictable, steadfast antagonism toward anything sinful or unholy.*

We become further confused if we get anger and hate mixed up, since they are not the same. Parents know this. We can be very angry at our children and love them deeply *at the same time.* In fact, good parents take it a step further, so that there are times when our very anger proves how much we do love our children. For when we truly love them, we will not tolerate anything which would harm or destroy them, either from the outside or from within. The anger of God, His holy antagonism against sin, is sure proof of His redemptive concern for His children. God loves and cares for us so deeply that He is infinitely concerned about what happens to us.

"But," someone continues to protest, "I don't understand this anger of God business—it scares me." Maybe it will help if we ask, What is the alternative to the anger of God? The alternative is not a God of love, because, as we have seen, love and anger are two sides of the same coin, and you can't have one without the other. The alternative to anger is *apathy, which would mean an apathetic God who is morally neutral and indifferent to the outcome of the battle between good and evil.* That would make him a God who sits on the moral fence of the world and says, "I don't care what happens to them. Let them sin if they want to, that's their business. I'm not going to interfere in their lives." So whenever the biblical picture of a holy God who gets angry about sin seems old-fashioned and frightening, try to imagine something a whole lot scarier—*an apathetic God who doesn't care.* Imagine what it would be like to live in a world like ours if God were personally indifferent and morally neutral. That would be a terrifying nightmare.

It is the reality of a holy God who is irreconcilably opposed to all sin that makes life tolerable in a world like ours. For this means that God cares enough to get angry when we sin, because He cares enough to want the very best for us. It means too that we know which side God is on—He has declared Himself on the side of right and righteousness. That's comforting—not scary! And it can keep us from trying to bridge the great gap between us and God by trying to change His holy nature.

The Freudian Way

We are using the name of Sigmund Freud merely as representative. He is usually considered the father of psychoanalysis, and of all psychological schools of thought which attempt to bridge the chasm by trying to change the nature of sin. This philosophy either denies there is a chasm by lowering God's standards for us, or narrows the chasm to a mere gully which is easy to jump over.

Someone has contrasted Jesus and Freud in this way. Christ says to sinners, "Go and sin no more." Freud says to them, "Go and mourn no sin." While this is obviously oversimplified, it does highlight the basic error of all who would explain the gap of guilt *merely as a matter of guilt feelings.*

Our feelings of guilt from so-called sins and failures, they say, are the result of various taboos and rules placed on our consciences by cultural and social influences. Parents, teachers, religions, the laws of our societies are among the authority sources which help form our ideas of right and wrong. They create our value systems and thus our feelings of guilt or approval. The way to get rid of those feelings is to realize that the rules come from human opinions and are quite relative. We all have different standards and these are constantly changing. There are no absolutes, they claim, no really fixed standards; since we establish them, we can also change them and thus bridge the chasm.

We see the tragic results of this philosophy in the sexual revolution of our times. Perhaps the most extreme present-day example is the change in attitude toward homosexual behavior on the part of many secular psychologists. What was once looked upon as *a sin to be avoided or a sickness to be treated* has come to be regarded as *a lifestyle to be accepted,* perhaps even *a gift to be celebrated.* The amazing fact is that this has taken place within a matter of a few years and has even affected, or should we say infected, some Christian circles. This is all the more amazing when you realize that every reference to homosexuality in Scripture is negative. It is a classic example of totally erasing the gap by eliminating the standard. It is also typical of what happens when the moral principles of God's Word are no longer considered the basis of right and wrong.

It is true that times and traditions do fashion some of the cultural norms of our conscience. There are many examples of this in the Bible itself. But the universal standards do not change. They are written into humankind.

What may be known about God is plain . . . because God made it plain to them. For since the creation of the world God's invisible qualities—His eternal power and divine nature—have been clearly seen, being understood from what has been made, *so that men are without excuse* . . . the requirements of the law are written on their hearts, their consciences also bearing witness (Romans 1:19–20; 2:15, italics added).

The Bible teaches a general revelation of some universal standards with corresponding ideas of guilt and atonement. Studies by anthro-

pologists confirm that there seems to be a universal intuition about
the gap between sinful humans and God. What various peoples do to
bridge the gap varies widely, and may be very wrong. But the basic
intuition behind the acts is very right. In one way or another they all seem
to be saying, "Without the shedding of blood [suffering] there is no
forgiveness" (Hebrews 9:22).

I saw the attempt at self-atonement in India, as I would watch a
Hindu woman use her body as a living yardstick to measure out her
length for the five-mile journey to the local temple; or watch chanting
Shiite Muslim men strike their bare chests with their open hands until
the blood came. I have also seen it in troubled Christians who come
for counseling. Some self-destruct in a respectable way through over-
work; some try to atone for their sins by the penance of inner self-
depreciation; the emotionally disturbed ones use unusual and obsessive means of self-immolation. I am always amazed at this built-in
sense of guilt and self-atonement. People may try to repress or ignore
it, but it has interesting ways of revealing itself.

Dottie was a single young adult who came for counsel. She wasn't
the least bit hesitant about sharing herself openly. I was struck by what
seemed to be an almost compulsive need to reveal the garbage of her
life in lurid detail. She was one of those modern, "liberated" Christians who feel sorry for pastors, thinking we live in a sheltered and
antiseptic world. They go out of their way to tell us about the real
world. A part of their mission is to enlighten us poor deprived souls
of the joys of their new freedom.

Dottie would pause occasionally in her x-rated recital, look at me
as if I were Exhibit A of life before the Enlightenment, and say with a
confident smile, "Now I don't want you to get any idea that I feel guilty
about this."

I must admit to a perversity which leads me to play the game with
this type, and so I would say, "Oh no, of course not. I understand—
no guilt."

Then I began to observe some body language from Dottie, as she
kept taking sheets of Kleenex from the box I always keep on a side
table. Not to wipe away tears—naturally not—since she felt no guilt;
but one by one, shredding the tissues into little pieces. The pile on the
table grew higher and higher. What fascinated me most was that she
was completely unaware of the shredding ritual. After awhile, I

decided to abandon my indirect counseling role. So I interrupted the latest chapter of her true confessions and said rather abruptly, "Excuse me, Dottie, but I don't believe what you're telling me."

"What do you mean? It's the truth, honestly."

"I believe your stories, but I don't believe your big story."

"My big story?"

"I don't believe your story about not feeling guilty about all this garbage in your life. In fact, I have the feeling your pile of guilt is as high as the mountain of Kleenex you've made on the table there."

She looked down in shocked disbelief. Obviously embarrassed, she sat silently staring at the shredded tissues. I was silent, but the Holy Spirit, whom Jesus promised would "convict the world of guilt in regard to sin," spoke loud and clear. Slowly Dottie reached for another Kleenex, and this time made proper use of it. "You're right," she sniffled. "I think I was hoping I'd not feel guilty if I was just honest about my sins. But down deep I knew better, and I knew that you knew better. I guess I was really hoping you wouldn't let me get by with it." We read together the Phillips' translation of that wonderful passage in Colossians 2:13–15 where Paul describes Christ's work on the cross.

He has forgiven you all your sins: Christ has utterly wiped out the damning evidence of broken laws and commandments which always hung over our heads, and has completely annulled it by nailing it over His own head on the cross. And then, having drawn the sting of all the powers ranged against us, He exposed them, shattered, empty and defeated, in His final glorious triumphant act!

Dottie came to understand that she didn't need to tear up either her sins or her Kleenex, or do any other unconscious acts of penance. Christ had shredded all her sin on the cross and set her free from their guilt, if she would but confess them to Him and trust what He had done for her. She discovered we can't bridge the gap by denying it exists, but only by trusting the One who bridged it as He "bore our sins in His body on the tree" (1 Peter 2:24). What a joy it was in future sessions to work with the Spirit in helping Dottie clean up her act and live as a daughter of God.

The Pharisaical Way

There is yet another unsuccessful method of trying to bridge the chasm, one often used by more legalistic Christians. Theirs is the way of obedience to a precise and codified set of rules. They use God's commandments as the main materials of the bridge. Man-made do's and don'ts are the nuts, bolts, and rivets to hold the main beams together. Very carefully they construct what appears to be a strong bridge, with their tightly knit scheme of externalized laws, rules, and regulations. The Owner's Manual which accompanies it covers every detail of the bridge. Then they swing that prefabricated bridge over the chasm and carefully, prayerfully, weld it into place. It seems to fit perfectly. Its intricate design, massive size, and inflexible quality give the appearance of immense strength. And as they walk across, they believe they have bridged the gap, and even enjoy a temporary sense of peace and security.

Prior to the coming of grace into his life, Paul constructed such a bridge. He tells about it in his Philippian letter (3:5–6), "a Hebrew of the Hebrews; in regard to the law, a Pharisee . . . as for legalistic righteousness, faultless." And, of course, it was chiefly the Pharisees of Jesus' day who had constructed such a scheme. With their 612 detailed regulations for daily living, they had honed righteousness to an exact science. The only problem was that as they kept all those rules, they missed the heart of the matter—the law of love. The fiercest display of Jesus' white-hot anger was for the Pharisees, on a day when they were more interested in keeping laws than in Jesus' healing a man with a shriveled hand (Mark 3:1–5).

Many a sincere Christian has tried to please God and bridge the gap this same way, only to discover that in God's sight it is the most displeasing way of all. It never brings lasting peace because there's always one more rule that some person or group adds to the list. Also its followers are never quite sure they really kept the law the way they should have. This is an unsafe bridge which will one day collapse in a storm.

That's what happened many years ago to a very famous bridge. Finished early in 1940, the Tacoma Narrows Bridge in Washington State was a masterpiece of engineering. A 2,800-foot suspension bridge, it provided a much-needed crossing over the waters of the Puget Sound. It cost $75 million, a staggering expenditure at the time. It attracted so much attention that a local insurance company used it as an advertising slogan. Ads reading, "As Safe As the Tacoma Bridge," helped its insurance business flourish—but only for a few months. On November 7, 1940, a high wind began blowing in the Sound, and no one knows exactly what happened next. One conjecture was that because of the unusual terrain, wind trapped in that location would actually have the effect of doubling in velocity. So the 42-mile-an-hour wind of that afternoon had the effect of 84-miles-an-hour.

Whatever the cause, the bridge began to sway slightly. That was nothing new—the media had already affectionately named the bridge "Gallopin' Gertie." But this time the swaying got steadily worse until the bridge was in a violent front-and-back oscillation like a walking caterpillar. Several terrifying incidents of high drama took place as drivers climbed out of their vehicles and crawled back on the highway bridge which was now like a washboard. Within minutes the gigantic structure splintered into pieces and crashed into the Sound. Fortunately, the only loss of life was one animal. The embarrassed insurance company had to hire anyone they could find, at ridiculously high wages, to go all over the Northwest to take down their ad—"As Safe As the Tacoma Bridge." When the bridge was finally rebuilt in 1951, the engineers gave special attention to remedy what they felt might have been the original defect, "insufficient torsional and vertical stiffness in the main girders which were only eight feet deep."[1]

Jesus ended His Sermon on the Mount with a brief parable. It was not about a bridge but it did concern construction problems. The failure of the one house resulted because its foundation had not been dug sufficiently deep into the rock. So when "the storms rose, and the winds blew and beat against that house . . . it fell with a great crash" (Matthew 7:24–27).

The Bible makes clear that any attempt to bridge the chasm by trying to keep the law, however perfectly, is doomed. The very purpose of the law is *to widen the chasm, not reduce it.*

Now we know that whatever the law says, it says to those who are under the law, so that every mouth may be silenced and the whole world held accountable to God. Therefore no one will be declared righteous in His sight by observing the law; rather, through the law we become conscious of sin (Romans 3:19–20).

The Avis Way

"We'll try harder." This motto is at the heart of the performance-minded, and describes millions of Christians, yes, genuinely reborn children of God who live daily lives of quiet desperation. Going through a seemingly endless cycle of failure, guilt, repentance, confession, forgiveness, restoration, trying something new only to be followed by another failure, more guilt, another repentance, confession, forgiveness, restoration—and so on, *ad infinitum.* Or perhaps we should say, *ad nauseum,* since they get sick and tired of the effort and a kind of spiritual disillusionment creeps over them.

This can lead to several possible serious results, one being the sheer physical and emotional exhaustion which comes from trying harder to do better. Some people living in this overloaded stress situation, crack up, and experience what is commonly called a nervous breakdown.

Others, tired of the losing battle, settle into a twilight zone of defeat and depression, ever looking for some new spiritual high which always seems to elude them. Some become angry at what appears to be their unappeasable conscience and an unpleasable God and throw faith overboard. Though it may not seem to be so on the surface, this spiritual breakaway is really worse than an emotional breakdown.

Yet others, blessed with a strong constitution and stubborn determination, hang in there, but live with various combinations of emotional and spiritual problems. They are the performance-trapped Christians of this book.

What is the basic fallacy in the Avis way? Why doesn't it ever work? *Because you can't jump across a chasm in two leaps!* You only get one chance! When God's Word says we have "all sinned and fallen short," that's exactly what it means—fallen short. If you don't make it in one leap, you miss the other side. And it doesn't make any difference whether you missed it by one foot or one hundred yards—or one inch, for that matter. When you fall short of the other side, you fall right down into the canyon.

On September 8, 1974, stunt man Evel Knievel attempted to vault Idaho's Snake River Canyon. Prior to this Knievel had achieved notoriety with his stunt riding on motorcycles. He would take off from a wooden ramp and at very high speeds sail across snarls of live rattlesnakes or lines of parked cars. He was seriously injured several times and boasted he had broken every major bone in his body except his neck. This attempt to rocket across a fearsome chasm was his most daring feat.

On that day he flashed a check for $6 million, purportedly his advance fee from the anticipated 200,000 spectators and the closed-circuit TV receipts. Actually only a few motorcycle gangs and about 15,000 people gathered at Twin Falls to watch him soar across the canyon. But his Sky Cycle never made it. Fortunately for him, the landing parachute enabled it to drift down to the river's edge. Rescue helicopters brought him back up, bruised and humiliated but not seriously injured. The 1975 *Encyclopedia Britannica Yearbook* aptly described it as "the year's most spectacular failure!"

Actually, it is a vivid illustration of humankind's most common failure—a prideful and evil attempt to cross the moral chasm and "become as God." It is doomed to failure, for Scripture assures us there's no way to make it. Because we are fallen beings, we lack the power and will always fall short. And no matter how hard or how many times we try we will always come up short and fall again. It is indeed a vicious cycle and there's no way to break out of it in our own strength.

Thank God there is a better way—His way. God's gracious provision for bridging the canyon, the way of grace, is the only answer. I can hardly wait to tell you about it.

But first we need to look at an extreme type of performance-based Christianity. It is commonly called *perfectionism, or neurotic perfectionism.* This is the most serious form of the disease. Let's see where the seeds of this sickness are sown, how it incubates and develops and some of the false cures which are proposed—solutions which do not bring answers but only become parts of the problem itself.

6

The Consequences of Dysgrace

Jesus comes with all His grace,
Comes to save a fallen race;
Object of our glorious hope,
Jesus comes to lift us up.

He hath our salvation wrought,
He our captive souls hath bought,
He hath reconciled to God,
He hath washed us in His blood.

We are now His lawful right,
Walk as children of the light;
We shall soon obtain the grace,
Pure in heart to see His face.

I BELIEVE THAT God intended parental grace to be the chief means of counteracting the Fall. However, this does *not* mean that even the best possible Christian parenting can *do away with* the Fall. The finest home cannot make a child's nature morally neutral or spiritually good, nor can it guarantee that the child will automatically choose the right. Christian parents who overload themselves with guilt need to remember something—Adam and Eve were the only people who ever had *perfect parenting* and yet they chose the wrong! We are still fallen sinners both by *nature* and by *choice*, and thus stand in need of God's saving grace. Parental grace cannot remove the *consequences* of the Fall, but it can provide the greatest *counteraction* to it. For it communicates agape love and undeserved grace in concrete and understandable terms. In fact, it operates by the same principles God used in the Incarnation. "The Word became flesh and lived for a while among us. We have *seen* His glory . . . full of grace and truth" (John 1:14). "That which was from the beginning, which we have *heard*, which we have *seen* with our *eyes*, which we have *looked at* and our *hands have touched* . . . the life *appeared; we have seen it* . . . we proclaim to you what we've *seen and heard* . . ." (1 John 1:1–3). The words I have italicized all refer to physical senses—seeing, hearing, touching. They point to concrete experiences, not abstract concepts.

A mother was trying to reassure her little girl as she put her to bed in a darkened room. "Honey, you don't need to be scared. Remember God is going to be right here with you." The little girl replied, "I know, Mama, but I need a God with skin on Him." Children don't think in abstract concepts but in concrete pictures. When my grandson heard us talk about letting Jesus live in our hearts, he looked puzzled. "But how does He get into my heart? Does He come through my belly button?" A young child's world is very physical, very literal. Ideas and mental concepts will come later. For them, words need to become flesh and blood, skin and bodies, faces and eyes which smile, feet that walk, hands that touch, arms that hug. The strongest influences on them come through real live human relationships with people they consider important, with their "significant others."

Parents are the most effective communicators of truths, values, concepts, and lifestyles, because they *incarnate them in concrete relationships.* This is the reason we have said children learn a language of relationships long before they learn to speak a single word. And this is why parental grace is so incredibly important. Through it we get our earliest experience of genuine—though imperfect—agape love. Through it we can grow up experiencing a *quality* of grace similar to what we receive from God Himself. This taste of love and grace, though partial, whets our appetite for God's perfect love and grace. More than any other single factor, it is intended to prepare us for the advent of God's saving grace in our lives. It does not guarantee our salvation, for we can still refuse to respond to God or to receive His gift. Its central purpose is to pave the way for receiving God's grace.

That's exactly why parental dysgrace is so terribly destructive. Because grace has the highest potential for *helping*, dysgrace has the highest potential for *hindering*. The greatest means of dispensing prevenient and preparatory grace can turn into the greatest means of distorting it.

The Seeds of Perfectionism

Let us now combine several important truths of Scripture with those of developmental psychology. This will help us understand some of the reasons why we become who we are. In this process we shall discover the main causes and consequences of the most extreme and painful form of performance-based living we generally call *perfectionism*.

We shall also look at some of the false ways in which people try to solve the problem.

I freely admit my indebtedness to certain scholars and writers who are generally classified as social psychologists.[1] I believe their insights come closest to those of the Bible with its central emphasis on personal relationships within family and community.

The older I grow and the more I counsel, the more I am amazed by the unfathomable mystery of human personality. There is *only One*, our Lord Himself, who "knew all men. He did not need man's testimony about man, for He knew what was in a man" (John 2:24–25). He alone who is *the Truth* knows *the truth* about the human personality. The best we can offer is *truths about the truth.* To offer more than that is to lessen the mystery and weaken our responsibility. *When we do this we take away from the fact that ultimately we are responsible before God for the choices which make us who and what we are.* It's helpful to try to explain, but we must never explain so well that *we explain away.*

Take a careful look at the chart, The Origin and Growth of a Perfectionist, scanning the whole process to get an overall picture. If you don't understand a particular section, leave it and continue to read. We are now going to break up the total figure into several parts, picture each one separately and explain it in detail.

There is a lot of confusion among Christians regarding the word *self.* That's because we use the word to convey several different meanings. Taken negatively, *self* can mean the sinful, carnal, person-centered ego, the "flesh" which Scripture indicates needs to be crucified.

```
┌─────────────────────────────────────────────────────────┐
│                 THE TRUE AND UNIQUE SELF                  │
│           (OUR POTENTIAL SELFHOOD IN CHRIST)              │
│    With inborn needs to be met for its proper development │
│                      through                              │
│                   PARENTAL GRACE                          │
│                                                           │
│     Listed in Luke 2:51-52. Physical, Mental, Emotional,  │
│     Social, Spiritual and Relational. Nourishment and     │
│     Nurture, Discipline and Instruction.                  │
└─────────────────────────────────────────────────────────┘
```

I am using *self* in the positive sense of your basic personhood, the self God intended you to be—imperishable, indestructible, and of eternal value in His sight. It is your basic human personhood, the unique you with all the possibilities for your particular personality with its talents. The God of this universe, who can't even stand to make two snowflakes alike, has designed each of us to be uniquely ourselves.

Your selfhood is what makes you to be you. In God's plan it is this potential person who, through salvation and sanctification, is to become more and more transformed into the likeness of Christ (2 Corinthians 3:18). This self is made for both earthly and eternal fellowship with God and other people.

But this self doesn't suddenly emerge. You and I were born of human parents, and from them we inherited bodies, brains, and directives about many things which have been coded into our genes. Furthermore, we were born into families which created the environment and the atmosphere in which this self would grow and develop. God designed this in such a way that we all had a whole set of needs which

BUT THESE NEEDS ARE NOT MET—PARENTAL DYSGRACE

INDIRECTLY	DIRECTLY
By deprivation of physical nourishment, emotional nurture, security, unconditional acceptance, belongingness, affection, affirmation, discipline, and instruction.	By rejection, withdrawal, ridicule, injustice, mixed messages (double binds), excessive legalism, cruelty, overcoercion, abuse (verbal, emotional, physical, or sexual).

THE ORIGINS AND GROWTH OF A PERFECTIONIST

THE TRUE AND UNIQUE SELF
(OUR POTENTIAL SELFHOOD IN CHRIST)
With inborn needs to be met for its proper development through
PARENTAL GRACE

Listed in Luke 2:51-52. Physical, Mental, Emotional, Social, Spiritual
and Relational. Nourishment and Nurture, Discipline and Instruction.

BUT THESE NEEDS ARE NOT MET—PARENTAL DYSGRACE

INDIRECTLY

By deprivation of physical
nourishment, emotional
nurture, security, unconditional
acceptance, belongingness,
affection, affirmation,
discipline, and instruction.

DIRECTLY

By rejection, withdrawal,
ridicule, injustice, mixed
messages (double binds),
excessive legalism, cruelty,
overcoercion, abuse (verbal,
emotional, physical, or sexual).

A FALSE SUPERSELF DEVELOPS

An idealized image, a fantasy and false picture of self is developed
in the attempt to get these needs filled, and thus be pleasing,
accepted, loved, and to be unique.

TO BE THIS IDEALIZED SELF NOW BECOMES THE CHIEF GOAL.
IT CONSUMES ALL EMOTIONAL AND SPIRITUAL ENERGIES.
IT IS THE SEARCH FOR GLORY.

This self gradually moves from "I'm UNIQUE," to "I'm SPECIAL" to "I'm
BETTER." My NEEDS become CLAIMS UPON OTHERS—"I'm ENTITLED TO."

THE CHIEF CHARACTERISTICS OF THE SUPERSELF ARE

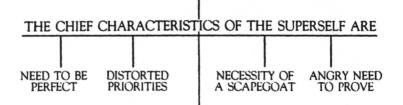

NEED TO BE
PERFECT

DISTORTED
PRIORITIES

NECESSITY OF
A SCAPEGOAT

ANGRY NEED
TO PROVE

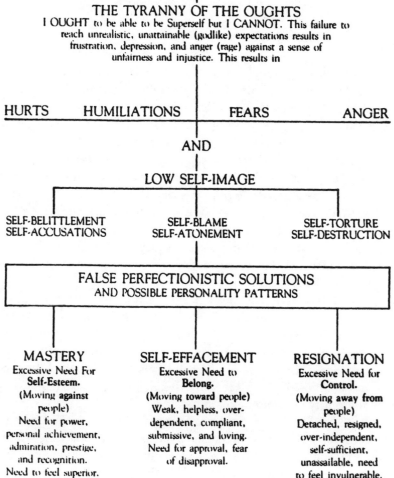

THE TYRANNY OF THE OUGHTS

I OUGHT to be able to be Superself but I CANNOT. This failure to reach unrealistic, unattainable (godlike) expectations results in frustration, depression, and anger (rage) against a sense of unfairness and injustice. This results in

| HURTS | HUMILIATIONS | FEARS | ANGER |

AND

LOW SELF-IMAGE

| SELF-BELITTLEMENT
SELF-ACCUSATIONS | SELF-BLAME
SELF-ATONEMENT | SELF-TORTURE
SELF-DESTRUCTION |

FALSE PERFECTIONISTIC SOLUTIONS
AND POSSIBLE PERSONALITY PATTERNS

MASTERY
Excessive Need For
Self-Esteem.
(Moving **against**
people)
Need for power,
personal achievement,
admiration, prestige,
and recognition.
Need to feel superior.

SELF-EFFACEMENT
Excessive Need to
Belong.
(Moving **toward** people)
Weak, helpless, over-
dependent, compliant,
submissive, and loving.
Need for approval, fear
of disapproval.

RESIGNATION
Excessive Need for
Control.
(Moving **away from**
people)
Detached, resigned,
over-independent,
self-sufficient,
unassailable, need
to feel invulnerable.

(FIGURE 1)

had to be met if we were to become the unique persons He wants us to be. These run all the way from basic physical needs for food and protection to emotional needs for security and affection. In chapter 3, we saw our model for this in the section on "Parental Grace in Jesus' Life." Our deepest needs are for personal relationships with other humans and, above all, with God. If these needs are reasonably well met, our divinely designed selves will develop with the potential of becoming whole persons.

Let us take a closer look at some of these divinely implanted needs which must be met for healthy growth and development to occur. Besides receiving food and physical care, children need to feel they are accepted, loved, and affirmed. They need a predictable, reliable sense of security and belongingness. They are made for agape-love, which includes discipline (setting limits) as well as genuine affection. And most of all, *children need an atmosphere where they feel these needs are met because of who they are and not because of what they do.*

It is in the quality of the earliest interpersonal relationships that children have their first taste of grace, or its opposite, dysgrace. It is here the good seeds of undeserved, unconditional acceptance, or the deadly seeds of conditional, performance-based acceptance are sown. Often in these early years deep-seated impressions about life are implanted which will have long-lasting effects on the way their personalities develop.

In certain kinds of homes, these needs are not met. The more obvious ones are homes where alcoholism or drug addiction make life extremely unpredictable and where children end up having to meet the needs of their parents. Or homes where physical, emotional, and verbal cruelty are common. Certainly all forms of sexual abuse (heterosexual and homosexual) are terribly damaging, since sexuality and personal identity so often develop together.

A college student shared with me that since he was a child he had been attacked by his mother. Whenever she lost her temper, she would grab him by the arm, pull him to his feet, and throw him against the wall. Once this caused a dislocation of his shoulder and he was forced to tell the doctor he had fallen from a tree. Another student tremblingly described to me the way her older brothers sexually violated her. As they took turns, the others would watch and make fun of her. Since this usually happened when both parents were away at work, she felt a lot of bitterness regarding their failure to protect her from the abuse or from the threats which silenced her. Saddest of all are those children from homes where these situations exist side by side with participation in church life and a professed commitment to biblical Christianity.

But there is also the less obvious deprivation where the growing child is robbed of emotional and spiritual nurture in more subtle ways, perhaps from a parent who outwardly goes through all the motions of caring but inwardly rejects the child. How often I have heard statements like, "My folks gave me everything I wanted—toys, clothes, money—but they never gave me love and affection. I'd trade all of that to know they really wanted me." The key factor in children feeling rejected is the emotional knowledge that they were not loved and wanted for who they were. This can take the form of long-term neglect, disinterest, or lack of discipline because parents don't care enough. Or it can come from a completely different angle. I have heard it often from children of missionaries and preachers, "I never felt that I mattered, or that they cared about me for who I was as a person. The only thing about me they were really interested in was how I would affect their spiritual reputation."

Some parents withdraw affection as a means of punishment, or employ guilt as a means of control. One lady said, "My mother was the travel agent for my guilt trips—mostly one way." Perhaps the most subtle form of conditional love is the use of mixed messages and double binds. One of Jesus' most psychologically profound statements is, "Simply let your 'Yes' be 'Yes' and your 'No,' 'No' " (Matthew 5:37). Parents who are constantly saying "Yes" and "No" at the same time create deep confusion and contradictory emotions in their children. For example, when a child asks, "Mama, may I go out and play?" the parent should not answer with a confusing, "Well, yes, go ahead, but remember I'll be here cleaning your room." It is much healthier to say, "Yes, after you clean your room (or do your homework)," or "No, I need your help today."

Do you remember some of the classic humorous double binds? You give your son two T-shirts for Christmas. When he wears one, you say to him in an injured tone, "Oh, so you didn't like the other one, eh?" Or, "I love you—even though you're stupid—or fat—or ugly—or clumsy—or even though you are a girl." Mixed messages put children in the impossible no-win position of "damned if you do and damned if you don't." This leads them to feel that nothing they can possibly do will please their parents, that there's no way to win their approval and affection.

Another area where many sincere Christian parents don't realize how much they promote an atmosphere of conditional, performance-earned acceptance is by excessive emphasis on the do's and don'ts of the Christian life. Certainly, it is the responsibility of parents to teach their children the scriptural commandments of God. They must do this both by precept—*what* they teach—and example—*how* they live. But most crucial is *the spirit in which this is done.* In Ephesians 6:4 and Colossians 3:21, Paul cautions parents not to "exasperate" or "embitter" children. Other translations expand the meaning. "Do not provoke your children to anger . . . lest they become discouraged." "Don't overcorrect . . . lest they grow up feeling inferior and frustrated."

There is an important principle involved here that we can put into a formula: R + R-R = R + R. *Rules and Regulations minus Relationships equals Resentment and Rebellion.* Rules and regulations and their enforcement by discipline must be put in the context of loving, grace-full relationships, or they will result in frustration and resentment. It is perfectly necessary and proper to enforce Christian standards and family rules by correcting and disciplining our children. But we must make it plain to them that our actions are because of *what they have done, and not because of who they are.* It's one thing to say, "We're doing this because we love you too much to let you grow up doing that." It's quite another thing to say, "You are a naughty boy," or "You are a bad girl," or "You always do things like that," or "Do you want to grow up to be like ____?" or "I don't know why we ever had you in the first place." The first is *to correct wrong behavior, to assure them that though they have broken a commandment, their relationship with you is intact.* The second is *to demean and put them down as persons and infer not only your disapproval but also your nonacceptance.* That is why legalistic and grace-less Christian homes can be emotionally destructive, even though on the surface everyone *seems to be doing the right things.*

It is not as if a child consciously decides to become a different person. The decision happens deep in the personality, below the level of awareness. If we could put it into words, it would sound something like this, "Obviously I am not accepted or loved as I am. Nothing I

A FALSE SUPERSELF DEVELOPS
An idealized image, a fantasy and false picture of self is developed in the attempt to get these needs filled, and thus be pleasing, accepted, loved, and to be unique.

TO BE THIS IDEALIZED SELF NOW BECOMES THE CHIEF GOAL.
IT CONSUMES ALL EMOTIONAL AND SPIRITUAL ENERGIES.
IT IS THE SEARCH FOR GLORY.

This self gradually moves from "I'm UNIQUE," to "I'm SPECIAL" to "I'm BETTER." My NEEDS become CLAIMS UPON OTHERS—"I'm ENTITLED TO."

---

can do seems pleasing to them. So I'd better become something else—someone else. Maybe then I'll be acceptable and lovable."

And slowly but surely, an idealized fantasy self emerges, a superself which can live up to all the expectations and demands of the parents. If this begins when the child is very young, after a while what the true self really thinks, feels, or desires is ignored, since physical, emotional, and spiritual energies are going into attaining and maintaining the superself.

All of us are afraid for others to know who we really are. This fear began when Adam and Eve hid from God behind the trees of the Garden, and from one another by a covering of fig leaves (Genesis 3: 7–8). This innate fear of revealing our real selves can intertwine with the need to become false selves. Sin is thus greatly compounded by the damaged emotions resulting from dysgrace as the pursuit of a false selfhood is an all-consuming passion. It becomes what Karen Horney so fittingly calls "the search for glory."[2]

In this process, the God-given feeling of *"I'm unique"* is twisted into *"I'm special,"* and then into *"I'm better than."* When the superself grows up, it becomes *"I'm entitled to."* Needs have been turned into *claims*—claims upon God and others. "Since I'm so special, I'm entitled to special treatment." When that special consideration is not forthcoming, the person may become angry with others and God.

In such a process, the real self is either denied or despised, and has no chance to develop. This is why such persons later will often say, "I don't really know who I am—and am afraid to find out." They sense an inner emptiness, phoniness, and a deep feeling of loneliness, and

THE CHIEF CHARACTERISTICS OF THE SUPERSELF ARE

NEED TO BE PERFECT	DISTORTED PRIORITIES	NECESSITY OF A SCAPEGOAT	ANGRY NEED TO PROVE

nothing seems to fill the void. Whatever they try is blocked by the superself and never reaches the real self. The creation of an unreal and false self is often the price of emotional survival, for there is no other way to bear the mental pain of rejection. But alienation from the true self is a terrible price to pay, and a tragic waste of personhood divinely designed "before the creation of the world" (Ephesians 1:4,11).

This is the reason why so many Christians play a comparison game and never feel like they "measure up." Instead of allowing their God-ordained self to "grow up in every way into Christ" (Ephesians 4:15), they keep trying to be super Christians, who need to be *better than* other people. The trouble with this is that they can always find another person who is still better and so the striving to be the greatest continues.

Some day this false self needs to die so that the true self may be allowed to live and to grow as it once did. In this sense, a spiritual rebirth, death, and resurrection must take place.

We come now to the four major characteristics of the superself.

• The need to be perfect. The superself is a super person who must do things perfectly. Or, at least, *ought* to be able to. The feeling is, "If I can just do and be what *they* want, *they* will accept, love, and appreciate me." The tragedy is that *they* are often persons who are never satisfied or who don't really know what they want. The superself tries harder and harder to please. The performance treadmill is now in operation with "if only" as its watchword. Such futile trying produces a deep despair in the personality that may not surface for many years.

That's the way it was with Margaret, a woman in her thirties. In spite of her dedication to Christ and a consistent devotional life, her marriage and family were being affected by her outbursts of anger and serious bouts with depression. It didn't take long to discover that she had internalized the voice of an unpleasable, perfectionistic mother until she thought it was the voice of conscience and God. Now she was her own harshest taskmaster, demanding perfection of herself, even as others had demanded it of her. Hurt, anger, and guilt kept the treadmill going. Margaret needed to face the hurts and then forgive those who had hurt her.

During one of our prayer times for the healing of some painful memories, a scene emerged which she had not shared with me. She said she had not wanted to look at it, but while we were praying, God gave her the courage to face the pain. She was just a youngster practicing for her first piano recital. She wanted to play her piece perfectly, and so she worked and worked, until the piece was memorized. At the recital, she played it perfectly. As she walked off the stage, her piano teacher grasped her elbow and said softly, "Excellent, Margaret, you played it perfectly!" She was so excited. But when she took her place beside her mother, there was a pause and then this whisper in her ear, "Your slip was showing the whole time." Margaret sobbed as she told God about this, and about many other scars. Best of all, she received grace to forgive, and also to be forgiven for the resentments she had carried for years. It was the crisis beginning to a process of changing from living under the law to living under grace.

• The need for a scapegoat. Not even the superself can be perfect. If we *have to see ourselves as perfect*, there is only one solution—we must have someone to blame it on.

We "could have, should have, would have . . . *if only.*" If only Mother hadn't done this. . . . If only Dad had done that. . . . If only brother/ sister were different. . . . If only that teacher had or hadn't. . . . If only our preacher/church would. . . . If only God had/hadn't/would. . . . If only my husband/wife/children. . . . The list is endless.

The only way superself can maintain the myth of being super is to put the responsibility for failure on somebody or something else. Even people who *seem* to put all the blame *on themselves* inwardly believe the real fault lies with those who caused them to be what they are.

This is one of the chief reasons why performance-minded and perfectionistic people are so hard to live with. Whatever happens, *blame must be placed somewhere.* This need is destructive to relationships.

• The angry need to prove oneself. I have yet to counsel a perfectionist who isn't deeply angry inside. With some people, when the anger is tapped into, it comes gushing out like an oil well. Until they experience grace at that level, the superself will remain angry, vindictive, and have to prove itself. Forgiveness is crucially important in the healing of this disease. Forgiveness—given to others and ourselves, and received from God—defuses the resentment and helps us deal with the need to prove ourselves acceptable and loved.

• The distortion of priorities and values. The superself must prove itself superior, and engages in a relentless search for an area to do so. This is where the twisted values of our sinful culture exert such pressure. The terrible overemphasis on athletics, grades, physical beauty, thinness, sexual attractiveness, fun, success (including false ideas of spiritual success), material wealth, things, clothes, cars—the list is endless—all can become the wrong centers around which the superself revolves.

Or, the superself can invert the list and then *feel superior because it doesn't seek any of these things*. The superself may do all it can to *not achieve*. It may seek the *weird and the unusual, and major on being different*.

I have stopped being surprised at *any false value, any misplaced, displaced, distorted priority which people use to show that they're different, special, and super*. When we refuse to accept and develop our real selves in their God-designed uniqueness, we pay the consequences of fashioning and developing false selves which are sometimes off the wall! Many such perfectionists cling *with incredible tenacity to* these places where they feel *different and superior*. They often tell me, "But if I gave that up I'd be ordinary, just like everyone else." I often reply, "Welcome. Join the human race!"

THE TYRANNY OF THE OUGHTS

I OUGHT to be able to be Superself but I CANNOT. This failure to reach unrealistic, unattainable (godlike) expectations results in frustration, depression, and anger (rage) against a sense of unfairness and injustice. This results in

In striving to be special, the superself receives extremely strong motivation from a driving sense of "oughtness." We *ought* to be this kind of self, but we can't quite make it. Why? Because we keep putting unreachable goals and unattainable standards before ourselves. And strangely enough, if we get near them, we will raise them even higher. Imagine a high-jumper in the Olympics. Every time they raise the bar, he clears it. Finally he jumps higher than all the rest and wins. But instead of standing on the center platform and receiving the prized gold medal, he raises the bar even higher. He tries several times, and falls with each attempt. Then he walks away dejected, feeling as if he lost the contest. Many perfectionists live this way. This sense of failure naturally produces frustration and anger against other people and often against God. As long as they live under the bondage of the performance-treadmill, they will be angry. Life will seem unfair and God will seem unjust. This will result in a range of negative feelings.

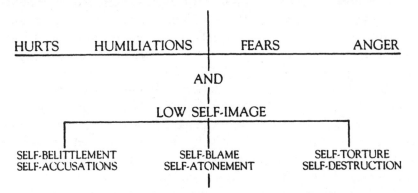

The hurts and humiliations perfectionists suffer keep their anxieties and anger churning. And not all of the anger is directed outward, for perfectionists live with a unique *combination of pride and low self-esteem.* They *always* suffer from a self-depreciation that *comes from fearful pride.* They are afraid others will discover the terrible gap between their *real selves* and their *fantasy selves* and then reject them. So they beat the public to the punch. *They reject themselves by putting themselves down before anyone else can. In this way their false pride in their superself is kept intact.*

We see this prideful self-rejection every day in perfectionistic Christians who cannot accept compliments without going out of their way to belittle their accomplishments. They must impress you with their humility and not let you catch them with their pride showing!

You can see that low self-image increases in intensity and becomes much more serious as you read from left to right. It varies from the more normal put-downs on the left to forms of self-atonement in the center—the kind A.W. Tozer described as "the penance of perpetual regret." On the right, you reach the pathological level where people inflict hurt or pain on themselves, such as picking at, or cutting the skin, or pulling out their hair.

Self-despising becomes much more pathological in the various forms of slow self-destruction—alcohol, drugs, excessive smoking, serious eating disorders like extreme overeating, anorexia, or bulimia. The ultimate is, of course, the quick self-destruction of suicide. Every reliable book on teenage suicide includes a warning about adolescents who think they have to be perfect and can't stand to live if they aren't. We have all witnessed the tragic results of this degree of self-hate, even in the lives of some who are sincerely trying to be good Christians.

In conclusion, we look at Karen Horney's classification of three *wrong solutions* to the dilemma of the perfectionist performance trap, and the possible personality patterns which can develop from them.[3] As we briefly describe them, keep in mind they are lifestyle—all-inclusive patterns of coping with life and relating to people. While they seem different from each other, they are all basically performance-based systems of living "under the law" rather than "under grace." They do not exclude one another. Persons can have some traits from more than one personality structure, but usually one type will be dominant over the others. They represent highly exaggerated and wrong ways of trying to meet the unfulfilled needs of our true selves.

• Mastery describes persons who feel an excessive need for recognition and admiration and try to win it by superior achievements in some area of life. They have to be not only good, but the best. This gives them a sense of power and domination over other people. They may indeed excel in their field of pursuit and tend to look down on those who don't. Their temptation is to reverse Christian values so they use people and love things. They exhibit qualities of hardness, craftiness, aggressive ambition, in-

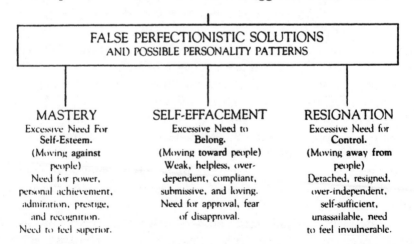

FALSE PERFECTIONISTIC SOLUTIONS
AND POSSIBLE PERSONALITY PATTERNS

MASTERY	SELF-EFFACEMENT	RESIGNATION
Excessive Need For Self-Esteem.	Excessive Need to Belong.	Excessive Need for Control.
(Moving against people)	(Moving toward people)	(Moving away from people)
Need for power, personal achievement, admiration, prestige, and recognition.	Weak, helpless, over-dependent, compliant, submissive, and loving.	Detached, resigned, over-independent, self-sufficient, unassailable, need
Need to feel superior.	Need for approval, fear of disapproval.	to feel invulnerable.

sensitivity to others' feelings, the ability to strike a hard bargain and to outmaneuver opponents. What they are saying is, "If I am strong and dominate people, they can't hurt me." It is very difficult for such damaged persons to accept love and grace and remove their masks of a false super-strong self.

• Self-effacement represents persons whose need for approval is so strong they will do anything to please people. They major in being submissive, compliant, and allowing others to make decisions. An all-absorbing "love" seems to them to be the answer to all their problems. They carry it to extremes so they never make waves or rock the boat. It's peace at any price. They rarely express an opinion or confront a person or a situation because they feel they really have nothing to contribute. This is a favorite stance for many Christians, who take this vice of excessive weakness and spiritualize it into a virtue by saying it is the way of Christian love. This is perhaps the greatest counterfeit of genuine love, which can be tough and confrontive when necessary. Self-effacing persons are really saying, "I will do anything if you'll just love me; for if you love me, then you won't hurt me."

Such persons often link up with their opposites to produce a sad and deadly combination which simply feeds one another's problems. Worst of all, it is often sanctified and blessed by some preachers and seminar leaders who misinterpret Ephesians 5:21–24 and promote this kind of destructive and neurotic relationship as if it were God's plan for marriage. It is often difficult for such Christians to receive grace, for they feel guilty and afraid and can't handle the freedom it brings.

• Resignation and detachment characterize those persons who want to be left alone. They feel if they don't get involved no one can hurt them. At any cost, they must move away from other people and not show any need for dependence. They require a lot of emotional space, and the intimate relationships of marriage may be so painful for them as to be intolerable. Many self-effacing persons who desperately need closeness and affection marry this kind of personality, because they appear to be the strong, silent type. It can become the sort of marriage where instead of complementing one another's needs, the partners drive each other into even greater extremes. It takes a lot of grace to save such a marriage, even when both partners are Christians.

In this chapter we have looked at the origin and development of the more extreme variety of performance-based Christians, perfectionists. We have also seen that any attempt to find freedom by our own efforts only leads us deeper into the mire. Let's turn now to the only solution and our only hope. God's greatest gift—grace.

7

The Good News

Jesus! the name to sinners dear,
The name to sinners given;
It scatters all their guilty fear;
It turns their hell to heaven.

O that the world might taste and see,
The riches of His grace!
The arms of love that compass me
Would all mankind embrace.

FOR SEVERAL CHAPTERS we have looked at the bad news—the moral chasm—and our utter inability to bridge it. Now let's take a look at the good news. Perhaps you've heard this good news—bad news story.

A farmer who had experienced several bad years went to see the manager of his bank.

"I've got some good news and some bad news to tell you. Which would you like to hear first?" he asked.

"Why don't you give me the bad news first and get it over with?" the banker replied.

"Okay. With the bad drought and inflation and all, I won't be able to pay anything on my mortgage this year; either on the principle or the interest."

"Well, that is pretty bad."

"It gets worse. I also won't be able to pay anything on the loan for all that machinery I bought, nor on the principle or interest."

"Wow, that is bad."

"It's worse than that. You remember I also borrowed to buy seeds and fertilizer and other supplies. Well, I can't pay anything on that either—principle or interest."

"That's awful—and that's enough! Tell me what the good news is."

"The good news," replied the farmer with a smile, "is that I intend to keep on doing business with you."

There's some rather profound theology in that story, provided we reverse the subjects. The good news of the Gospel is that in spite of our total moral bankruptcy, *God keeps on doing business with us.* Notwithstanding the hopelessness of our predicament, God has found a way to bridge the gap, restore us to a relationship with Himself, and to bring healing to the damaged areas of our personalities.

Paul exultantly exclaims, "Where sin abounded, grace did much more abound" (kjv). In the original Greek Paul uses the same root word for "abound" in both phrases. But the second time, in connection with grace, he adds the prefix *huper,* so that it literally means, "Where sin abounded, grace *superabounded.*" The Phillips version of this passage uses the imagery of the moral chasm to show that what was formerly totally impossible is now gloriously possible.

> Though sin is shown to be wide and deep, thank God His grace is wider and deeper still! The whole outlook changes—sin used to be the master of men and in the end handed them over to death; now grace is the ruling factor, with righteousness its purpose and its end the bringing of men to the eternal life of God through Jesus Christ our Lord (Romans 5:20–21).

Paul is the great Apostle of Grace. Of the 155 New Testament references to grace, 133 belong to him. Grace opens his epistles, grace closes them, and grace is the keynote of everything in between. The word *grace* is the anglicized Latin word *gratia* which was used to translate the Greek word *charis* (pronounced karis). In ordinary Greek, *charis* meant gracefulness, graciousness, favor, or kindness. It could also mean the gracious response or gratitude of someone who had received a favor.

Paul puts *charis* into the context of the good news of the Christian Gospel to mean a freely bestowed favor. As he gives it several shades of meaning, *charis* truly becomes a many-splendored thing. Paul uses it especially to refer to what God has done for us in and through Jesus Christ. You could say grace is God's love in action on our behalf, freely giving us His forgiveness, His acceptance, and His favor. It is motivated only by God's love for us and not because of any worthiness or deservedness on our part. Grace is freely given, undeserved favor. In the Christian sense, it is essentially the redeeming activity of God in Christ. Not something done only in the past, it operates also in the present, and will continue throughout the future. This means that *grace and grace alone is, and always will be, the basis of our relationship with God.* "For by grace are you saved through faith; and that not of yourselves: it is the gift of God" (Ephesians 2:8, KJV). Those words are true for the vilest and most degraded sinner; they are equally true for the ripest and shiniest saint. *This grace base will never be replaced by something else.*

The Character of Grace

If grace is freely given, undeserved favor, then it is supremely important we understand some essential facts about it.

• Grace is undeserved. Grace has nothing to do with our merit or demerit, our sinfulness or worthiness. When the Bible says grace is free, it means that God is free to show His love and mercy toward us without the slightest limitation because of our sin. The moment you even bring up the question of unworthiness and undeservedness, you cancel out the idea of grace.

Jesus never once used the word *grace*, and of all the Gospel writers John alone used it to apply to Jesus (John 1:14, 16, 17). But as the saying goes, "Why waste words?" For the entire life of Christ was a non-stop demonstration of the fact that He offered the gift of salvation to everyone, *without any regard for their worthiness.* He was a living commentary upon His own words, "I have not come to call the righteous but sinners" (Matthew 9:13; Mark 2:17; Luke 5:32). Daily He incarnated grace—love, mercy, and salvation freely offered to people whose lives had no claim on it whatsoever. In fact, this is what always insulted "righteous" people—in His day, and ever since.

In the second century, a critic of Christianity named Celsus said the idea of God loving *sinners—bad people—*was "a thing unheard of in any other religion." He was absolutely right. That's what grace is about. That's what makes it different from other religions; they offer *good* *views* and *good advice*—"Be good, straighten up your life, clean up your act, get it together, live a good life and then, of course, you can come to God. Then you will be pleasing to God and He will love you." Only the Gospel of Christ is *good news*, the incredible message of grace. As A.W. Tozer put it, "Grace is the good pleasure of God that inclines Him to bestow benefit upon the undeserving."[1]

During the Napoleanic Wars, a young, battle-weary French soldier fell asleep while on guard duty. He was court-martialed, found guilty, and sentenced to death. His widowed mother somehow arranged an audience with the Emperor Napoleon himself. Falling prostrate at his feet she begged for her son's life to be spared, explaining he was her only child and her sole means of support. Napoleon grew weary of her pleas. "Madam, your son does not deserve mercy. He deserves to die," he said coldly. To which the mother immediately replied, "Of course, sire, you are right. That's why I am asking you to show mercy on him. If he were deserving, it wouldn't be mercy." Napoleon was so touched by the logic of her statement that he pardoned the soldier.

If we were deserving, it wouldn't be grace. It is undeserved and unmerited. It is God's free gift, completely unobstructed by our sin, our guilt, and our unworthiness.

• Grace is unearnable. Not only is grace undeserved, but it is also unearnable. Many of us start out on the highway of undeserved grace saying, "Of course, God accepts me just as I am. I know I am totally undeserving and have nothing to offer Him but my sins and failures. *But from this point on, He certainly expects me to live up to certain standards of performance.*" And then, like the Galatians, many of us who began in grace quite unintentionally decide that the continuation of God's gift of grace depends on how well we perform. We subtly assume we can earn or win God's approval and fill the performance gap by works. Not works in the former sense of good deeds or hard work or payments to charitable causes—we know better than that; but in the sense of taking the very channels of grace—prayer, Bible reading, witnessing, service—and turning them into Christian works of performance. We try to change the *grace base into a performance base.* But the grace base can never be replaced by anything else. This futile attempt by so many Christians is the source of their emotional and spiritual struggles.

After many years of pastoral ministry in which it has been my privilege to counsel people of varying races and cultures, I have come to a strong conclusion that the last thing we humans surrender to God is an admission of our helplessness to save ourselves. We will give up our sins, ambitions, money, name, fame, comfort—we are willing to sacrifice and surrender them all to God. But the most difficult, costly, and last thing we will give up is *our confidence that there is something we can do which will earn us a right relationship with God.* The second stanza of the hymn, "Rock of Ages," captures our inability so beautifully.

> Could my tears forever flow,
> Could my zeal no languor know,
> These for sin could not atone;
> Thou must save, and Thou alone.
> In my hands no price I bring;
> Simply to Thy cross I cling.

Until the truth conveyed in these lines becomes a living reality, we will not understand or experience the biblical meaning of grace. The writer of Hebrews reminds us that "without faith it is impossible to please Him" (11:6). This means that God is not pleased when we attempt to substitute righteousness by achievement through performance for salvation by grace through faith. He will not allow us grace to change the terms God has set for an acceptable, pleasing relationship with Himself. "It is by grace you have been saved, through faith—and this not from yourselves, it is the gift of God—not by works, so that no one can boast" (Ephesians 2:8–9). "Not from yourselves . . . so that no one can boast" means that God will not share His glory nor allow us to claim any of the credit for our salvation. Grace is a free gift. The moment we try to pay for it, it ceases to be grace for us.

• Grace is unrepayable. Some people try to turn the gift of grace into salvation by promissory note. This is similar to the attempt to earn grace, but places more emphasis on the future. "Lord, if You will forgive me and save me, I promise I will pay You back someday."

Some people try to make this repayment through *self-atonement*, by refusing to forgive themselves for past sins or failures; or not allowing themselves to enjoy the legitimate pleasures of life, such as sex within marriage, or a fun-filled vacation.

Others attempt repayment through *self-sacrifice*. This includes different forms of asceticism, like constantly giving up this or giving away that. Or adding this or that onto their lives as a way of self-discipline. I will always remember a student named Rodney who struggled to live in grace. He had an excellent head theology of grace, but kept derailing in his day-to-day life. Every time he came to see me, the list of activities and things he gave up for the Lord was longer. One day he arrived, sat down with a sigh of relief and said, "Well, I finally gave it up." "Gave up what, Rod?" I asked. "I took my whole stereo outfit and threw it in the garbage."

I must confess my mind wasn't totally on the counseling session at that moment. We had just come off the mission field and hadn't been able to afford a stereo as yet. My teenage kids kept putting it high on our list of American "necessities." When our session was over, I rushed out to where the college garbage was gathered, but I was too late. Someone had already retrieved Rod's expensive stereo! The next time I saw Rod he had still more to add to his ascetic list.

Some try to repay God through *service*. I've counseled missionaries who sadly admitted to me that repayment had been the real motivation for their sacrificial service. Their emphasis was on all they had "given up in order to serve the Lord." But in every case they had not found joy and fulfillment in their lives. Rather, there was a kind of anger against God. They had done their best to repay Him, but He had not kept His part of the deal, in making them feel rewarded.

There is the rather direct way of *scrupulosity*, trying to repay by meticulous, punctilious, solicitous, and rigorous observance of the law—divine laws, human laws, social and cultural laws. It was his recognition of this tendency in certain Christians which led the wise Sam Shoemaker to say, "The converts of one decade can so easily become the Pharisees of the next."

"But," you are saying, "aren't we supposed to live up to God's commandments and the principles of His Word? Aren't we expected to repay God with our service and our sacrifices?" And the answer to all such questions is a firm and positive, "Yes." *The issue here is the old problem of getting the cart before the horse. We are most certainly called to respond to grace with obedience and service and sacrifice. But we are not to do these things in order to earn God's grace, win His approval, or repay Him by trying to even up the credit-debit balance sheet. We now do these things because God loves us and accepts us as we are, because He freely forgives us and restores us into His family in spite of our undeservedness and unworthiness. We do them not in order to win His love, but out of gratitude for His love. Not in order to earn His grace, but out of thankfulness for it.*

The most basic Scripture on the subject, Ephesians 2, ends with a verse which makes this crystal clear. "For we are God's workmanship, created in Christ Jesus to do good works, which God prepared in advance for us to do" (v. 10). The order of the horse and cart is very plain; we are saved not *by* good works but *for* good works. They are not the *root* of our salvation, but its *fruit*.

God's Unconditional Love

If we go back a few verses in Ephesians 2, we see the fountainhead of grace. "Because of His great love for us, God, who is rich in mercy, made us alive with Christ even when we were dead in transgressions— it is by grace you have been saved" (vv. 4-5). Grace is God's love in action toward those who do not deserve it. And this love is manifested as grace, offered us in the life and death of Christ. Hence God does not say,

I love you *because* . . .

I love you *since* . . .

I love you *forasmuch as* . . .

      or,

I will love you *if* . . .

I will love you *when* . . .

I will love you *after* . . .

I will love you *provided* . . .

I will love you *presuming* . . .

Any such statement would make His love *conditional,* would mean His love was caused by something in us—our attractiveness, our goodness, our lovableness. The reverse of this would mean there could be something in us which would stop God from loving us. *God's love for us is unconditional; it is not a love drawn from God by something good in us. It flows out of God because of His nature. God's love is an action toward us, not a reaction to us. His love depends not on what we are but on what He is. He loves because He is love.*

We can refuse the love of God, but we cannot stop Him from loving us. We can reject it and thus stop its inflow into us, but we can do nothing to stop its outflow from Him. Grace is the unconditional love of God in Christ freely given to the sinful, the undeserving, and the imperfect.

I want to emphasize the word *imperfect* for the sake of performance-oriented Christians who often ask an important question. "But what if I fail? What if I fall?"

I will always remember a turning point in the spiritual life of one of the young teenagers of our church. He had already made his personal commitment to Christ. He tried hard but, like most adolescents, was plagued by the ups and downs in his Christian life. So he often came forward to the prayer altar during the invitation time following church services. He had done so once again after a Sunday night service conducted by a visiting evangelist. I had prayed with him and now we sat talking together at the altar. His face was very sober as he shared with me his determination "to make it this time." Then he asked, "But what if I fail? What happens if I fall?"

I replied, "Steve, I've come to know you pretty well. Probably better than anyone in the church. So I think I can guarantee you one thing—*you will fail, you will fall. So what?*"

He looked up at me a bit shocked. He had expected me to reassure him, not give him a guarantee of failure. When he didn't reply, I could see he was thinking over the implications of my "So what?"

And then something seemed to dawn on him. It was almost as if the rays from a flashlight had gradually moved across his face. Very slowly he began to smile and to nod his head. "Hmmm . . . I think I see what you mean. I think I'm catching on," he said. "Of course I'm going to fail; sure I'll fall. *But that really doesn't make any difference, does it?*" And then the smile lit up his whole face.

Of course, a lot of growth followed, but that was his initial discovery of the way of grace. And his discovery—that with grace, failure doesn't make any difference—changed his life. It was a joy to watch him grow in grace. Later, he became a dispenser of grace as a pastor for eleven years, and now teaches about grace as a professor of systematic theology in a seminary. Are you wondering about my strange reply that I was sure he would fail because I knew him so well? That's because I happen to be his dad!

To ask the question, "What if I fail or fall?" is once again to attach strings to God's unconditional love and to change the nature of grace as *undeserved and unearnable favor.* If our failure could stop grace, there would never be any such thing as grace. For the ground of grace is the cross of Christ, and on the cross we were *all* judged as *total failures*. It was not a question of an occasional failure here and there. As far as our ability to bridge the moral canyon and win the approval of a holy God, *we are all total failures. In the Cross we were all examined and we all flunked completely!*

This is what the first few chapters of Romans is all about. Whether we are ethical do-gooders—the Jews—who have kept all the commandments; or whether we are out-and-out sinners who break them all—the Gentiles—makes no difference. For God in His love has provided a new basis for a right(eous) relationship with Him—free, undeserved, unmerited, unrepayable favor, graciously offered to us. That's grace. And it's ours for the receiving. That's faith. So the question of our failure or success doesn't arise. The basis of salvation is not achieving but receiving, not perfect performance but trusting faith.

"But now a righteousness from God, apart from Law, has been made known, to which the Law and the Prophets testify. This righteousness from God comes through faith in Jesus Christ to all who believe. There is no difference, for all have sinned and fall short of the glory of God, and are justified freely by His grace through the redemption that came by Christ Jesus. . . . If by grace, then it is no longer by works [performance]; if it were, grace would no longer be grace" (Romans 3:21–24; 11:6).

Grace and the Heart

The basic difficulties for performance-minded Christians do not arise from the mind—reason and logic. Merely changing their mental concept of grace will not free them from the bondage of life on the performance grindstone. Grace may begin for them as a doctrinal concept, but it must become an experience which finally saturates their emotions as well. *Grace needs to be fully realized.* According to the dictionary, realization is "the act or process of becoming real." For this to happen, grace needs to penetrate and permeate the *heart.*

There is much misunderstanding about what the Scripture means by the heart. Misguided by our everyday use of the word, we have forgotten that *in the Bible heart means every area and function of the personality.*[2] H. Wheeler Robinson, an outstanding Bible scholar, analyzed the various senses in which the Hebrew and Greek words for *heart* are used:[3]

Sense	O.T.	N.T.
Personality	257	33
Emotional State	166	19
Intellectual Activity	204	23
Volition	195	22

It is extremely important to see how the word *heart* is used to express the personality as a whole or one of the functions of personality. It represents the selfhood, the central citadel of a person where thoughts, perceptions, feelings, decisions, and actions all influence each other, and are, in turn, influenced by the other.

There are places in the Bible where *heart* shows the person *in relationship*—both good and bad. Leviticus 19:17 warns against hating "your brother in your heart." Matthew 18:35 urges, "Forgive your brother from your heart." There are several verses which describe people who honor God "with their lips but their hearts are far from" Him (Isaiah 29:13; Matthew 15:8; Mark 7:6). Here the heart is shown in the degree of intimacy—its nearness or farness. Of course, passages which command, "Love the Lord your God with all your heart" imply a strong and close relationship with Him (Deuteronomy 6:5; Matthew 22:37). It was said that early Christians were "one in heart and mind," describing a relationship where "no one claimed that any of his possessions was his own, but they shared everything they had" (Acts 4:32). Paul expressed his special relationship to the Philippians when he said, "I have you in my heart" (Philippians 1:7). And he urges them to forgive one another and to be kind and "tenderhearted to one another" (Ephesians 4:32, KJV). It would not be too much to say that the heart is the fountainhead and source of our relational life. Grace in the heart is the spring out of which flows a grace-filled life. And this means *grace must touch feelings as well as concepts.* As William Kirwan says:

> Scripture regards the emotions of the heart as of great importance. Yet the place of emotions has been misunderstood by the evangelical Christian community. At best, emotions are merely tolerated. More often, they are treated as wrong or sinful. Indeed, much Christian theology has somehow gone awry on this key matter. . . . According to the Bible emotions and feelings have a clearly defined role in the Christian frame of reference. . . .
>
> "Facts" and "feelings" are part of the same process. The brain does not separate feelings from facts or facts from feelings. There

is little distinction between the two: all feelings are psychological and neurological arousal attached to facts. . . . Nor does the Bible make a distinction between facts and feelings. . . . We deal not with facts *or* feelings, but with facts *and* feelings. . . . By seeing emotions or feelings as a key aspect of the heart we see that they are also a key part of one's being. As a key to being, they are of vital importance in the life of the Christian.[4]

Doctrinal belief in a theology of grace, as important as that is, does not change the way performance-grounded Christians live. This is not understood by a large number of persons involved in Christian service—pastors, evangelists, teachers. and counselors, and so they sincerely but mistakenly deal with problems brought to them by parishioners only on a cognitive level—preaching/teaching/admonishing. When this fails, the Christian worker—who is obviously in a position of authority over such persons—labels their problems as sin, rebellion, unbelief, disobedience, a lack of submission, self-centeredness, or the like. This only adds to the existing guilt, depression, and despair of the hurting person. I have wept over the letters, phone calls, and interviews describing such verbal bludgeoning by Christian workers in the name of Christ. I am sure God Himself weeps over these sincere but misguided efforts. Paul's words about the keepers of the Law are so fitting, "They are zealous for God, but their zeal is not based on knowledge" (Romans 10:2).

There is a better way—the all-encompassing way of grace.

- Healing grace for damaged emotions of the past
- Reconstructive grace for destructive interpersonal relationships
- Reprogramming grace for distorted personality patterns
- Recycling grace to transform cripplings into means of ministry.

In order to understand and experience this life of grace, we need to discover just how to apply this grace to the specific problems of guilt, low self-esteem, phoniness, anger, and poor personal relationships—all discussed in chapter 1.

"Wait a minute," someone protests. "I need help *right now.* As I've been reading, I've realized I need to do something about my problems, but I'm scared. *I need help just to get up the courage to face these things.*"

I've got good news for you. The same grace we've been describing can make you strong enough and brave enough to *take off your superself mask and begin to look at your real self*. For it's your real self which God loves and for which Christ died, your real self with all its sins and flaws which He has always known and never stopped loving. Feeling this at gut level gives you courage to face yourself as you truly are. I want to illustrate this with a remarkable true story that comes out of World War II.

There was a man named Stypulkowski who was a fighter in the Polish underground resistance movement from 1939 to 1944. Unfortunately, when the war ended he was in the wrong place at the wrong time and was captured by the Russian army. He and fifteen other Poles were taken to Russia to stand trial before their war crimes court. Since some Western observers were at the trials, it was necessary to get full confessions from the men in order to convict them of their supposed treason against the state. Actually, they had helped defeat the enemy with their tactics. Now, they were accused of helping the Nazis.

Prior to the trial, the men were put under rigorous interrogation to break them mentally, emotionally, and spiritually, to destroy their integrity so they would confess to anything demanded of them. Fifteen of the sixteen men broke under the grueling pressure. Only Stypulkowski didn't. And this in spite of the fact that for 69 out of 70 nights he was brutally questioned in a series of 141 interrogations. Not only did he endure them, but at one point his interrogator broke and had to be replaced. Over and over again his tormentors relentlessly examined everything he had ever done, or hadn't done—examined it for its fear and guilt content. His work, his marriage, family, children, his sex life, his church and community life, even his concept of God.

This followed weeks of a starvation diet, sleepless nights, and calculated terror. Most insidious of all were the signed confessions of his best friends, all of whom blamed him. His torturers told him his case was hopeless and as good as closed. They advised him to plead guilty so they could lessen his sentence; otherwise, it was certain death.

But Stypulkowski refused. He said he had not been a traitor and could not confess to something which was not true. He went on to plead not guilty at his trial; largely because of the foreign observers there, he was freed. Most impressive was the completely natural and unselfconscious way he witnessed to his Christian faith. He kept that faith alive by regular prayer, and every other loyalty was subordinated to his loyalty to Christ.

Oh, it was evident that he was not free from weaknesses—his accusers pointed them out to him time after time—but he was never shattered by them. The reason for his endurance was that he daily presented himself to God and to his accusers in absolute honesty. He knew he was accepted, loved of God, forgiven and cleansed. So whenever they accused him of some personal wrong, *he freely admitted it, even welcomed* it. Again and again he humbly said, "I never felt it necessary to justify myself with excuses. When they showed me I was a coward, I already knew it. When they shook their finger at me with accusations of filthy, lewd feelings, I already knew that. When they showed me a reflection of myself with all my inadequacies, I said to them, 'But gentlemen, *I am much worse than that.'* For you see, *I had learned it was unnecessary for me to justify myself. One had already done that for me—Jesus Christ!*"

Because Stypulkowski could be totally honest about himself before God, he was able to be totally honest about himself before his accusers. He could freely admit his personal failures because he knew they had all been taken care of in the Cross.

And so with all of us. When we realize that being "justified through faith, we have peace with God through our Lord Jesus Christ, through whom we have *gained access by faith into this grace in which we now stand"* (Romans 5:1), we will find the courage to face the truth about our needs, and experience healing grace.

8

Grace and Guilt

Jesus, lover of my soul,
Let me to Thy bosom fly,
While the nearer waters roll,
While the tempest still is high;
Hide me, O my Saviour, hide,
Till the storm of life is past;
Safe into the haven guide;
O receive my soul at last!

Plenteous grace with Thee is found,
Grace to cover all my sin;
Let the healing streams abound;
Make and keep me pure within.
Thou of life the fountain art;
Freely let me take of Thee:
Spring Thou up within my heart;
Rise to all eternity.

IN CHAPTER I we listed the commonest symptoms troubling Christians who are caught in the performance trap—guilt, low self-esteem, phoniness, anger, and difficulties with interpersonal relationships. It is not easy to separate these, because they are so closely interwoven in the pattern of an individual's lifestyle. To concentrate on just *one* of the problems is like trying to pull one loose strand out of a knitted garment, only to find the whole thing is unraveling.

It is this very intertwining which makes the fabric so strong and gives such persons their formidable defenses against change. I find it amazing how people will hang onto a problem, *even after they realize that it is the cause of their pain.* It's much too simple to say, "They enjoy suffering," for most of them don't. Their pain is genuine and they do not enjoy it. However, it is easier for them to hold onto something familiar, *with which they feel safe or comfortable—even though it hurts, than to let it go and face the unknown.* Change is *threatening to them;* they realize if they relinquish anything, *they will have to change their whole way of living.*

Often, during a time of deep healing prayer, the Holy Spirit draws back the curtain and the counselee will become aware of a decisive issue. It is literally as if God has put His finger on that one thread and wants their permission to remove it. But they know that if they allow Him to do that, their whole outfit will come to pieces. And how often I have heard them cry out in words similar to these, "But I can't give that up. I just can't. *It's the only thing I've got. It's the only thing that's really mine!"*

This is why, as we examine some of the various symptoms of life in the performance trap, as we look at some strands in the garment made without grace, we must again and again remind ourselves that it is an all-inclusive pattern. No one thread can be removed without affecting the overall design.

Global Guilt

Feelings of guilt, condemnation, and being disapproved by God are first on our list. This is because guilt is usually the driving force and chief motivator of such people. But exactly what is guilt? There are several meanings to the word and it will help if we sort them out. As with many other things in life, there is the good news and the bad news in regard to guilt.

The good news is that guilt is a form of mental pain; as any medical expert will tell you, pain is one of the best friends we have. It's the most valuable part of our built-in warning system. Dr. Paul Brand worked for many years among the lepers of India, and he became highly skilled in rehabilitation surgery. He would attempt to repair the disease-eaten hands of lepers so that they could earn a living after they were cured. He discovered the main problem was the fact that the lepers *felt no pain,* and so were always seriously injuring their hands or feet. After all kinds of experiments he further discovered there was no way to restore sensitivity to pain once it was destroyed, and so other means of warning had to be devised. Dr. Brand considers pain part of a brilliantly designed system and one of God's most amazing gifts to the human body. But he has also seen the other side of pain—its cruelty—as he has watched patients die in unbearable agony.

Guilt is a form of mental and emotional pain we experience when we feel responsible for doing, or not doing, something which violates our personal moral standard. In that sense, it too is a gift of God to fallen and sinful human beings, and is intended to be part of His restraining and redeeming grace. Persons who have no sense of guilt are considered abnormal. They are called sociopaths or psychopaths, and many of them are dangerous. In a sense they are moral and spiritual lepers who have lost the ability to feel the pain of guilt, even when they have violated the most basic moral standards or committed the most atrocious crimes. They are like Charlie Starkweather who in the 1950s went on a cross-country shooting spree and killed fourteen innocent victims. At his trial, when asked if he felt guilty, he replied, "No, it was just like shootin' rabbits!" He is an extreme example of someone without a conscience, without any ability to feel the pain of guilt.

But guilt can also go to the opposite extreme and become a cruel and destructive taskmaster. This is the kind of guilt so prevalent in the lives of performance-oriented Christians. For theirs is not the normal and specific feeling of guilt which comes when they have done or thought something wrong. Instead, it is a vague and generalized emotion. When I asked one counselee to describe his sense of guilt, he coined his own word to aptly describe it. "With me being guilty is a feeling of *alloverishness.*" This all-over guilt is what accounts for the *moral and spiritual drivenness* of such Christians. The constant pressure of their guilt keeps them trying to do and be more and more. Despite all the Scripture passages they know, and their many efforts to "trust and obey," they seem unable to shake off their feelings of guilt and to maintain an assurance that they are forgiven and acceptable to God. Let's try to sort out some of the reasons why these people find it so difficult to break free from the chains of guilt.

Victims of Victims

In chapter 4, while acknowledging that all human problems are the result of sin, we asked the question, "But whose sins?" One of the most basic steps in finding freedom from unnecessary guilt is to distinguish between taking responsibility for our own sins and refusing to take it for the sins done against us by other people. Research into alcoholism, wife abuse, child abuse, and sexual abuse shows there are many situations in which people are victims of victims. Unfortunately, one factor which perpetuates such generational sins "unto the children's children" is that many Christians do not break from the chains of guilt associated with them.

One of the times I have been the angriest was many years ago when a visiting evangelist preached a series of meetings for the church I was pastoring. Dolores, a sincere young woman who faithfully attended all the services, was driven by deep feelings of guilt and went to counsel with the evangelist. For the first time in her life she got up nerve enough to tell about being sexually abused by her father. It began when she was six and continued until she was nine. Finally she could bear it no longer and told her mother about it. Her mother became furious, gave her a severe beating, and accused her of deliberately "seducing" her father. With painful tears, Dolores shared the whole story with the evangelist. Then she asked what she could do to be free from the seemingly unresolvable feelings of guilt. He told her she would never get rid of those feelings "until she repented before God of her own responsibility in the matter." She was utterly shattered by his advice and came near to breaking under the newly added load of guilt.

I marvel that Dolores ever came to see me—another preacher. It's a tribute to her sheer desperation and the grace of God. And I must confess I was so angry at that evangelist I could hardly control myself. I've since learned not to be shocked at the ghastly things which pass for "Christian counseling" and "spiritual advice." It's amazing how cruel some "helpers" can be, especially in the area of heaping even greater guilt upon Christians who are just barely surviving their present load.

Can you understand the layers of guilt Dolores had to work through? Her mother accusing her of seduction; the evangelist representing the voice of God and reinforcing her mother's judgment of her. Again and again I tried to point out to her how ridiculous it was to blame a six-year-old child for seducing a grown man. But always she would come back with, "I must have done something wrong." Or, "I shouldn't have crawled up into his lap and hugged him so much." She simply could not admit how wrong both her mother and dad had been and how deeply they had hurt her. She seemed intent on holding onto the guilt. Dolores was the perfect example of so many damaged Christians. *They would rather take all the blame for what someone did to them than face the truth about the persons who did it. This is especially true when the victimizers are people they want to love and respect—like parents, important relatives, teachers, preachers, or spouses.*

A vicious and nearly unbreakable circle of guilt is set up when we hold to the guilt. There seems no way out, because there's no way for God's grace to get in. His grace enters only when we forgive those who have sinned against us. And we can't really forgive them until we admit how much they've hurt us, and then face how we feel toward them. And that's impossible as long as we keep on taking responsibility for the sins they have committed.

The verse we frequently hear quoted from the Old Testament story of Joseph, as he forgave his brothers, is "You intended to harm me, but God intended it for good" (Genesis 50:20). This is a great verse, and we rightfully emphasize the last part of the verse. But we must not overlook the first part, "You intended to harm me." Joseph squarely faced up to the evil his brothers had done. He did not minimize or excuse it. Many people today mistakenly think that forgiveness means to overlook the evils done against them; they feel they are being sweet, loving Christians. Actually, this is an exercise in unreality which keeps out the power of grace.

Furthermore, it is the Holy Spirit, the Spirit of Truth, who activates God's grace in our lives. As long as we are dishonest and untruthful in our hearts, He cannot free us from our feelings of guilt and give us lasting peace. This is why we often need a pastor, counselor, or some other temporary assistant to the Holy Spirit to help us sort out true and false guilt. Of course, it also means that when we get it sorted out, we need to take full responsibility for our own sins. With Dolores, this meant acknowledging how badly she had been hurt by the betrayal of her parents. Then she needed to forgive them, *and ask God to forgive her for resenting them for what they had done to her.* In this way true forgiveness for real guilt—*both theirs and hers*—could and did take place. It was the beginning of a new life of inner peace for Dolores.

Though the details of your story may be entirely different from hers, this process of sorting out true responsibility and actual guilt may be where you need to start your pilgrimage of grace. For in our lives, as in the life of Jesus, "grace and truth" always go together (John 1:14).

False Guilt

There are situations where we need to distinguish true from false guilt. One of the ways a child's conscience develops ideas of right and wrong is to internalize the standards of people he considers important. He wants them to approve of him, and so he gradually incorporates their values and makes them his own. This process rightly handled is the basis of a Christian home and of bringing up children in the discipline and instruction of the Lord. It is also the foundation of Christian education in Sunday School, youth group, and church. When these standards are based on Scripture, rooted in loving relationships, and reinforced by consistent example, a healthy Christian conscience will result.

But this God-designed process can also be the means of developing a damaged, supersensitive conscience which can plague Christians with an overwhelming sense of guilt. Sometimes this happens because there is an excessive emphasis on minor rules and regulations within the family or church; or when the discipline and punishment for breaking the rules is far out of proportion to their importance. Legalistic, graceless homes, churches, or communities often produce warped consciences which entrap Christians in guilt. Years ago one of my mentors told me something I have seen confirmed by a lifetime of counseling. He said, "Whenever you see excess scrupulosity, look out for emotional damage."

All this becomes even more serious when such overconscientiousness is *enforced by emotional or spiritual blackmail. That is, when guilt is used to control or manipulate people.* This blackmail can build into them a destructive sense of false guilt which can keep them on a performance treadmill for many years.

Cliff was one of the most guilt-ridden persons I've ever met. He was a spiritual workaholic with an obsession to be constantly busy for the Lord. Accompanying this was a feeling that it was impossible to relax his efforts even for a moment, because this would not be pleasing to God. He had a strange sense of always being watched. He carried an almost unbearable burden for the souls of people he contacted—their eternal destiny was his responsibility. He was sure that if he failed them, their blood would be on his hands. Several times he had been saved from the brink of emotional breakdown by some close friends who practically forced him to take a few days rest and gave him a lot of loving support. But this had actually added to his sense of guilt in the long run—God must be even more displeased and disappointed because he hadn't kept on trying.

It took a while for Cliff to stop flagellating himself and to share with me the picture of his family history. It was saturated with emotional and spiritual blackmail—as happens when none of the ordinary forms of discipline or physical punishments are employed to confront misbehavior or maintain family order. Instead, sympathy, disapproval, and guilt are used as emotional pressure points to dictate even the most insignificant family behavior. Cliff's mother carried a heavy martyr complex and used every possible means to control the family with her illnesses and nervous ailments. These required a constant round of doctors—the actual causes could never be found—to prescribe the rest and medicines which kept her going. Cliff was the eldest child who took the brunt of it, and very early got overloaded with some heavy burdens. "I felt I had to be perfect and help keep the other kids in line, because we were all poor Mother had. And I had to work extra hard to keep any load off her. After all, she was suffering enough from some terrible disease—probably a hidden cancer they couldn't locate—and from a husband who, though in front of others acted like he cared, behind the scenes was inconsiderate and worthless. A phrase we heard constantly was, 'You'll never know what I've had to put up with from your father, but that's part of a wife's duty.' All of us children presumed this to be a sexual reference."

There was also more direct spiritual blackmail, for everything had a religious connotation. To obey and please her was to obey and please God; to disobey her was to get God's frowning disapproval. By now Cliff's voice was filled with emotion. "In my mind God and Mom became the same. I see that now. And I desperately wanted to love and please them both—I mean her and God. But there was no way to love Mom. I don't think she really wanted love. She just wanted lots of sympathy for her physical sufferings, and for being married to Dad. And you couldn't please her because her needs kept changing. Poor Dad. I know now I never really saw him except through her eyes. He was actually a patient and rather wonderful guy."

Gradually Cliff began to realize it wasn't God who was always watching him. It wasn't God who kept looking over his shoulder to criticize every book he read, to question every opinion he voiced, and to disapprove of every activity or relationship in which he was involved. Yes, *it seemed like God, felt like God, sounded like God, but it wasn't. It was the voice of an unpredictable and unpleasable mother which had become internalized into his conscience.* It was so deep with Cliff that he had now joined the watchers club himself, introspecting everything about his spiritual life. When he prayed or read the Bible or witnessed, it was as if he was always watching himself praying, reading, or witnessing. Cliff reminded me of an absurd story I heard about a window cleaner on a New York skyscraper, who stepped back to look at his work! Funny? Not in Cliff's case, for there were times he almost destroyed himself by his endless introspection.

It took a long time for us to work through the many layers of Cliff's guilt. Insight into his family system helped him understand much about both himself and his parents. He needed this not so he could blame anyone, but in order to learn how to forgive and love. It also helped for us to go over a lot of the do's and don'ts together. He needed reassurance and encouragement as he learned how to vote against his own guilty feelings. This is often impossible to do on our own. *Though we may know we are right, the old voices of guilt make us feel so wrong they almost tear us to pieces.* So we must have the support of a person or a group, as one necessary step. However, the ultimate solution does not lie in just rectifying the rules, or distinguishing between God's revealed standards and internalized human opinions.

Neither does it lie in another direction—something which most counselors have had to learn the hard way. Freedom and joy would not come by my taking the place of his mother and becoming a surrogate parent or authority figure telling Cliff how to live. It's easy for Christian workers to fall into that kind of dependency trap. When this happens the cure becomes a part of the disease itself. Remember, we are only *temporary assistants* to the Holy Spirit. The ultimate goal is to help people receive their support from the body life of the church and their counseling directly from the Great Counselor, the Holy Spirit.

The deepest damage in Cliff, and many others like him who come out of such parental dysgrace, is their *unscriptural and dysgraceful concept of God.* Theirs is not the gracious God who is revealed to us in Jesus Christ. He is an unstable, unreasonable, and above all, unpleasable God whose acceptance and love we have to earn by perfect performance. Along with this, they have an unbiblical and dysgraceful concept of a right relationship with God. This naturally follows, for a wrong concept of God leads to a faulty concept of what God wants from us. And a faulty concept of what He wants from us leads to a skewed idea of how He relates to us and wants us to relate to Him. So Cliff and I worked together, allowing the Spirit to peel away several layers of distorted concepts and to heal many damaged emotions. This process reminded me of a time when a doctor informed me I needed a major operation, but that before he could operate, several secondary infections had to be cleared up.

And so it was with Cliff. He had certainly come a long way. The cruel intensity of his former feelings of guilt were gone, and he was a much more winsome witness for Christ. But he could not really get away from the overarching sense of God's disapproval. After hearing a Sunday sermon on "Resting in the Lord," he told me with a nervous laugh that his Christian life could more aptly be titled "Walking on Eggshells!" He was still living as if God's approval depended on *his* performance rather than on Christ's perfection.

In some ways, all our sorting out of real and pseudoguilt had made matters worse for him. For Christians—and please remember this is being addressed to Christians—it's not possible to solve the guilt problem for another by saying, "For this you ought to feel guilty" and "For this you don't need to feel guilty." It is not our business to condemn them for what may seem to us as a failure to live up to the demands of the law. The moment we condemn, *we are then saying we believe the opposite, that is, that we have the ability to justify ourselves by performing all the works of the law.* That is a gospel of works and not of grace. For grace is the good news that right relatedness to God no longer depends on our ability to keep the law. Rather, it depends on fully admitting we are not able to do so. Better still, we no longer need to do so. Instead, we become rightly related to God by what He has done for us in Christ. "For Christ means the end of the struggle for righteousness by the Law for everyone who believes in Him" (Romans 10:4, PH).

At this point I asked Cliff to read and reread Romans in an up-to-date translation. When we next met together, he was visibly shaken. "This business of grace is getting to me," he said, "and I must confess I'm confused. Actually my guilt seems worse, and I don't like that. But it seems to be a different kind of guilt." And then Cliff told me an interesting story. "I'm not sure I understand all this. Anyhow, recently when I was singing 'Amazing Grace,' two lines struck me afresh. 'Twas grace that taught my heart to fear, and grace my fears relieved.' I stopped singing and was thinking about the paradox in those words when very quietly inside me, it seemed that God had put His loving arms around me and was saying, 'Cliff, I accept you and love you just the way you are right now.' I've never experienced such a feeling of unconditional love. It was incredible. But immediately I felt myself getting upset, and inwardly I said to God almost angrily, *'Well, You may accept me, but I don't. After all, I have my standards!'"*

Because Cliff had expressed his thoughts out loud, he heard and understood what he had actually said. And it shocked him into the realization of what *sin, guilt, grace,* and *salvation* really mean. Sin and guilt are the *core of* the disease; grace and salvation are the *cure.* And only the Holy Spirit can ultimately bring this about within us. For while our *conscience* accuses us of violating our moral standards, or the *internalized voices of dysgrace* fill us with all kinds of false guilt, *the Holy Spirit* does not condemn us because we have failed to be good. He convicts us, says Jesus, "about sin, because men do not believe in Me" (John 16:8–9). Grace brings us to the place of *real guilt,* real guilt for our only real sin—failing to believe in Jesus Christ and trust Him for right relatedness to God. This is what happened to Cliff in that moment when he realized it was not his many sins nor his sense of badness which kept him from finding peace with God. It was *his pride, his sense of goodness.* Pride which, in an unguarded moment of honesty, had actually told God that Cliff's way of righteousness by performance was better than God's way of unconditional grace.

Grace solves the problem of guilt not in a piecemeal manner, but by giving us a whole new ground of relating to God through Christ and His cross. Grace means that God receives sinners. This is what shocked the good people of Jesus' day. "The Pharisees and the teachers of the law muttered, 'This Man welcomes sinners and eats with them'" (Luke 15:2). The Pharisees were the most morally righteous people in the land, obsessive in their devotion to keeping the Law. Yet Jesus told His disciples their righteousness must "surpass" that of the Pharisees, if they were to enter the kingdom of heaven (Matthew 5:20). What was it that distinguished the disciples from the Pharisees? It was not that the disciples were morally admirable and the Pharisees were not. Judging from the descriptions, it was quite the contrary, for the moral sins of the Pharisees were hidden, while the failures of the disciples were openly portrayed. The difference was in their relationship to Jesus. The disciples were with Jesus, joined to Him, while the Pharisees were not. The gospel of grace says this trust relationship to Christ is the only solution to the problem of guilt. For "there is now no condemnation for those who are in Christ Jesus" (Romans 8:1).

9

Grace and Emotions

And can it be that I should gain an interest in the Saviour's blood?
Died He for me, who caused His pain?
For me, who Him to death pursued?
Amazing love! how can it be
That Thou, my God, shouldst die for me?

He left His Father's throne above, so free, so infinite His grace,
Emptied Himself of all but love
And bled for Adam's helpless race!
'Tis mercy all, immense and free,
For O my God, it found out me.

No condemnation now I dread; Jesus, and all in Him, is mine!
Alive in Him, my living Head,
And clothed in righteousness divine,
Bold I approach the eternal throne,
And claim the crown through Christ, my own.

PERFORMANCE-ORIENTED CHRISTIANS generally feel low self-esteem. What do we mean by self-esteem? It is a mental image of ourselves, a collage of pictures including our *past* memories, our *present* situations, and our imaginary *futures*. All kinds of reflections, evaluations, and feelings accompany the pictures, forming a 3-D collage in living color and stereophonic sound, and generating within us certain feelings about ourselves. If those evaluations and emotions are mostly positive, we say we have a good self-image or feel good about ourselves. If they are largely negative, we say we have a bad self-image. When people come to counsel, one of the first things they share is the way they feel about themselves. Their expressions of low self-esteem range from a mild, "I don't like myself," to a vehement, "I just can't stand myself."

During World War II, a social worker helped evacuate children from London's dangerous bombing areas, taking them by bus out to the safer countryside. One day, as she lifted a four-year-old boy from the bus, she asked him, "Son, tell me your name." The lad looked up sadly and said, "Mum, I ain't nobody's nothin." Judging by their self-evaluations, that's the way many people feel about themselves.

But why is this so common among Christians? After all, it runs counter to every biblical doctrine about being adopted into God's family, becoming His children and joint heirs with Christ. If self-esteem were purely a matter of mental beliefs, Christians ought to stand taller and feel better about themselves than any other group of people. Why do so many genuinely reborn Christians suffer—and I do mean suffer—the pain of low self-esteem?

Self-Denial and Self-Worth

Many people are thoroughly confused about what it means to have a healthy Christian self-image. They've got self, self-crucifixion, self-denial, self-respect, self-esteem, self-love, self-surrender, humility, pride, and a host of other related words, mixed in a tangled mass. Perhaps we should say mess, for it certainly messes up daily Christian living.

I'm thinking of two women in midlife who came for help. Barbara felt so guilty about the fact she couldn't "get rid of herself" that every time she used the word "I" she would stop and apologize. Finally she tried to eliminate "I" from the conversation entirely. Of course, it was utterly ludicrous as well as impossible. She felt very defeated when I pointed out that this effort was not only making her more self-centered but also making me more conscious of her than ever. She had recently heard a severe sermon on "crucifying self" based on Galatians 2:20. When I asked her to slowly read the verse out loud and count the number of "I's" and "me's" on her fingers as she read, she was quite astounded to find seven of them. The most self-surrendering verse in the New Testament turns out to be the most self-filled!

The second woman, Judith, came to see that her misunderstanding of self-esteem was destroying her and her marriage. As an individual she had been denying her Godgiven gifts; and as a wife she had failed to express herself to her husband and so had become resentful toward him. Why? She was afraid of being proud and felt the only way to prevent it was to deny and crucify herself. This meant she must consider herself of little or no value, keep reminding herself of her worthlessness, and constantly belittle herself. She thought this was humility.

The phrase, "Love your neighbor as yourself," occurs in the Bible nine times; once the command regards "the alien in your land . . . to love him as yourself." This adds up to twice by Moses (Leviticus 19:18; 19:34), five times by Jesus (Matthew 19:19; 22:39; Mark 12:31, 33; Luke 10:27), twice by Paul (Romans 13:9; Galatians 5:14) and once by James (2:8). Now it is *technically* true to say that we are not actually commanded in these Scriptures to love ourselves. *But the plain inference in every one of them is that a proper kind of self-love is the normal basis of relating to others.* It's not commanded, but it is assumed. Perhaps it's not commanded because it's just presumed that the people to whom they are speaking would love themselves and therefore should make that the norm by which they evaluated their love for others. This is certainly the presupposition of Paul's advice to husbands in Ephesians 5:28–29. "In this same way, husbands ought to love their wives as their own bodies. He who loves his wife loves himself. After all, no one ever hated his own body, but he feeds and cares for it, just as Christ does the church." The Scriptures *everywhere* assume that an appropriate self-love, self-care, and self-appreciation is normal, and *nowhere* tell us to hate or neglect ourselves, or to indulge in self-depreciation.

Self-denial consists in denying not our self-worth but our self-will, and in abandoning our search for self-glory. The crucifixion of the self is our willingness to renounce our carnal, self-glorifying self and allow it to be put to death on the cross with Christ. It does not mean we renounce or belittle our God-given gifts; it does mean we surrender them to God to be used for His glory. Pride, as it is used in the Bible, is a dishonest estimate of ourselves. Paul warns against this, "For by the grace given to me I say to every one of you, Do not think of yourself more highly than you ought, but rather think of yourself with sober judgment, in accordance with the measure of faith God has given you" (Romans 12:3). Just as Paul reminds us we are saved by grace through faith and that not of ourselves, he here reminds us that God's grace and our faith will also give us an honest and accurate estimate of ourselves. In both instances, pride is excluded, because the grace and the faith are both gifts from God. As Paul so incisively asks, "For who makes you different from anyone else? What do you have that you did not receive? And if you did receive it, why do you boast as though you did not?" (1 Corinthians 4:7)

Someone once asked Corrie ten Boom how she could possibly handle all the compliments and praise that were constantly heaped upon her, without becoming proud. She said she looked at each compliment as a beautiful long-stemmed flower given to her. She smelled it for a moment and then put it into a vase with the others. Each night, just before retiring, she took the beautiful bouquet and handed it over to Jesus saying, "Thank You, Lord, for letting me smell the flowers; they all belong to You." She had discovered the secret of genuine humility.

Humility means that while I like myself and appreciate the affirmation of others, I don't need to prove my worth to God, myself, or others. Healthy Christian self-esteem rests on the firm foundation of *knowing we are accepted, loved, and appreciated by God Himself.* This generates in us a humility which is born out of gratitude for His undeserved grace and which comes from God. Feelings of inferiority, insecurity, and inadequacy do not come from God, but from Satan, as a counterfeit for true humility.

Barriers to Grace

However, as in the case of guilt, many Christians completely agree with all this and yet are still plagued by a sense of worthlessness and low self-esteem. In spite of constant efforts to memorize the right verses, think positively, and "become who they are in Christ," at a gut level they are unable to feel good about themselves. Let us look at several inner barriers to grace.

• The need to forgive ourselves. Many Christians suffer from recurring bouts of self-despising because they have not truly forgiven themselves for past moral failures. They say, "Yes, I am a Christian. I believe Christ died for my sins and so I believe God has forgiven me. But way down deep I'm spiritually kicking myself for something. I keep a slow-motion video replay of it running and end up berating and belittling myself."

We have already referred to the story of Joseph forgiving his brothers. There are several very remarkable incidents in the story. One which shows Joseph's unusual sensitivity is described in Genesis 45. Joseph, struggling with his own racking emotions, had just revealed himself to his brothers, who "were terrified at his presence." They remembered their heinous crime against him and realized he could have had them all executed. And in that tumultuous moment, Joseph could have turned in on himself and been overwhelmed by his own emotions. Instead, with an incredible insight into human nature, he realized his brothers were going to have a hard time *really believing in and accepting his forgiveness.* So he turned from any concern for himself to concern for them, wanting to help them *receive his forgiveness.* He said to them, "I am your brother, Joseph, the one you sold into Egypt! And now, *do not be distressed and do not be angry with yourselves* for selling me here, because it was to save lives that God sent me ahead of you" (Genesis 45:5, italics added). Joseph was saying, "Don't hate yourselves for what you did. Not only do I forgive you for it, but better still, God took your evil and worked it all out for good—even *your* good."

If that's what Joseph could say to his brothers, *how much more does Christ, our Elder Brother, say to all of us,* "Don't keep on being distressed and hating yourselves for some past sin. I have suffered and died for all your sins, including that one. Show that you accept My gift of forgiveness by forgiving yourselves. When you keep on despising yourselves for your sins, you are not only insulting My death on the cross, but you are also in effect declaring that *the power of your sins is greater than the power of God; that you and your sins are so powerful God cannot work them out for good. You are actually reversing God's Word to make it say,* "Where grace abounded, sin superabounded!"

This is one area where special kinds of healing prayer are often needed.[1] In this type of Christian therapy we attempt to visualize Jesus ministering to persons at the time and place of their need. This visualizing is not a creation of our human imaginations. It is always biblically based, recreating some actual metaphor of Christ, or an incident from His life as pictured in the Gospels. Let me share one woman's experience of full forgiveness through the healing of something in her past which had kept her bound.

It helped me to identify some painful memories that have blocked my growth spiritually for a long time. I had been dealing with "that sinful woman in my past" by throwing stones at her all these years. I was helped to walk back in my past in specific situations with Jesus. His response was, "Woman, where are your accusers? I don't accuse you either; go and sin no more." I am now responding to myself as Jesus would in every situation. He makes a much better Lord and Saviour than I do. . . . It has become so much easier these past few months to accept the "Saviour" side of Jesus. It's still hard to accept Him as "Lord." But I've been helped to look at my difficulty with authority figures and can see real progress of healing in that area too.

• The need to realize we don't need negative feelings anymore. Often when I ask Christians why they so obstinately hold onto their combination of past guilt and present self-disdain, they answer, "If I didn't feel that way toward myself, I'd probably fall back into open sin. I *need it to hold me in line.* There's no telling what I might do without it."

What a tragic misconception of the place of guilt and self-condemnation in the life of the Christian. There is a strong place for both in the lives of those outside Christ. That is the chief purpose of the Law in their lives—not to save them by obedience to it, but to reveal to them their sins, create within them a sense of guilty condemnation and lostness, and thus *drive them to their only hope in Christ.*

Therefore no one will be declared righteous in His sight by observing the law; rather, through the law we become conscious of sin. . . . Before this faith came, we were held prisoners by the law, locked up until faith should be revealed. So the law was put in charge to lead us to Christ that we might be justified by faith. Now that faith has come, we are no longer under the supervision of the law (Romans 3:20; Galatians 3:23–25).

Once we are in Christ, guilt, condemnation, and self-despising are no longer intended to be our chief motivators for righteous living. It will take time to change but sooner or later, love is to become the motivating force of our Christian living.

Is there then no place for the law? Has it been repealed? What does Paul mean when he says we are "not under law but under grace"?

(Romans 6:14–15) Jesus said He came to fulfill the law (Matthew 5:17); so in what sense are we Christians free from it? According to Paul we are free from its *curse* (Galatians 3:13), its *compulsive power* (Romans 7:7–9), and its *demanding rituals* (Galatians 5:1–6). *But we are not free from its moral intentions toward God, ourselves, and other people.* However, these are now fulfilled in an entirely different way, "that the righteous requirements of the law might be fully met in us, who do not live according to the sinful nature but according to the Spirit" (Romans 8:4). "Therefore, love is the fulfillment of the law" (Romans 13:10).

From a *biblical* view, Christians who hang onto guilt, condemnation, and self-belittling worthlessness are living under the curse, the sting, and the power of the law. This is so readily observable from a psychological viewpoint. The idea that fear and guilt and self-condemnation will keep us from sinning and therefore give us inner peace and joy is completely contrary to experience. Those who live that way are filled with inner turmoil and driven by strong—even strange and seemingly uncontrollable—compulsions toward the very sins they try the hardest to avoid. Why? Because guilt and self-condemnation were never intended to be the motivating force of Christian living. The underlying emotion in guilt and self-hate is *fear. And fear is actually the most self-centered of all emotions. So when we use it as an appeal to righteous living, it only makes us more self-centered and anxious. Thus it defeats its own purpose and keeps us from the goal we are trying to attain.*

Guilt and self-despising are short-term motivators, intended to shake us out of our sins and get us moving toward Christ. But they are very poor long-term motivators. They may be all right for the 100-yard dash, but the Christian life is more like the 26-mile marathon which we are to "run with perseverance" (Hebrews 12:1).

Through the years I have seen the *liberating* power of Christ. To use the words of Charles Wesley's hymn, "He breaks the power of canceled sin, He sets the prisoner free."

But I've also seen the other side of the coin—the *captivating and restraining* power of His love and grace. In another well-known hymn, Robert Robinson writes of this aspect of grace.

> O to grace how great a debtor
> Daily I'm constrained to be!
> Let Thy goodness, like a fetter,

Bind my wandering heart to Thee;
Prone to wander, Lord, I feel it,
Prone to leave the God I love,
Here's my heart, O take and seal it,
Seal it for Thy courts above.

Through the years I've observed when the chips are down, it is not guilty fear or self-condemnation that holds us steady. It is rather the visceral knowledge of God's unconditional grace and love for us. In Thomas Chalmers' phrase, it is "the expulsive power of a new affection."

Grace That Leads to Home

Evelyn's full story would fill many pages, for God had literally salvaged her out of a trash bin. Verbal, physical, and sexual abuse marked her youth. A teenage marriage to escape from home had only exchanged one set of problems for another. Soon she found herself a young divorcee trying to fill an almost insatiable need for male attention and love by going from one affair to another. And then, a Christian coworker introduced her to a warm, loving fellowship group, and she was dramatically converted. She felt God would have her finish her education. It was while a student in college that she came for counseling. In addition to the wounds of her early years, some of her own past sins had left deep scars on her life. Slowly but surely, God's saving, sanctifying, and healing grace brought remarkable changes to Evelyn's personality. The one area where she knew she must "watch and pray" the most was about her almost compulsive need for men. She realized she was, in a sense, still looking for a father.

Evelyn graduated and got a fine job as a secretary. Because she was conscientious and hard-working, she climbed the ladder and was named personal assistant to the head of the company. This meant many hours spent together at work and after hours. Although he was a married man with a family, she felt herself being drawn into an emotional closeness to him. It was never mentioned, but they both sensed what was happening.

One day, when he asked her to accompany him on a business trip, she knew down deep in her heart what this meant. She prayed and wept about it before God, but that old emptiness seemed to be drawing her into a vortex from which she couldn't escape.

On their second night out, while they were eating dinner, her boss expressed his feelings for her. She responded by telling him she felt the same way. She accepted his invitation and agreed to come to his room after the final business sessions were over. During the evening sessions, a terrific struggle took place in her. Later she wrote:

It was like a tug-of-war and I was the rope! By the time it was over, I was shaking like a leaf. Then it seemed as if a great inner peace took over. It really was "the peace that passeth understanding," because I certainly couldn't understand what I did. But as we walked out of the meeting together, I stopped and said, "Jim, I admire you more than any man I know. I want to be with you tonight so much I'm actually aching. It's my fault for leading you on. Forgive me. But you know, during the meeting I remembered something. *I remembered that a man from Kentucky told me how much God loved me, and I believed him. And I just can't go against that kind of love. It's done too much for my life and means too much to me."*

Evelyn had found the secret—the realization of God's unconditional love and undeserved grace that holds us steady in temptation. Not guilt and self-condemnation, but grace and its accompanying sense of self-worth.

Through many dangers, toils and snares
I have already come;
'Tis grace hath brought me safe thus far,
And grace will lead me home.

Did you ever notice that New Testament appeals for righteous, holy living are not *legal but relational?* Even in those passages with long lists of sins, guilt is not intended to keep the Christian in check. Almost always there is an appeal to a personal grace/love relationship. It's the same basis for commandment-keeping which Jesus gave, "If you love Me, you will obey what I command" (John 14:15). Too many Christians reverse this to mean, "If you keep all My commands, then I'll love you—maybe." Since we have the Holy Spirit living in us, the loving appeal to ethical living is powerful. How can we sin against the Spirit and risk hurting our relationship with Him?

We are told in Ephesians 4:30, "And do not *grieve* the Holy Spirit of God, with whom you were sealed for the day of redemption." And in 1 Thessalonians 5:19, *"Quench* not the Spirit" (KJV). In Ephesians 5:18,

"Do not get drunk on wine, which leads to debauchery. Instead, be filled with the Spirit." This means we are not to *substitute intoxicating spirits for the Spirit's infilling.* The appeal is not to fear/guilt/condemnation to keep us from sin, but to a love/grace/gratitude relationship with the Person of God's Spirit. It's not, "Don't break an impersonal commandment," but, "Don't harm a loving personal relationship."

The notion that we must hold onto our guilt and self-despising in order to keep from sinning, and to have motivation for Christian living, is not biblical. It is usually a hangover from a previous period in our lives, when those very emotions were forms of conditional acceptance used to "keep us in line." This carryover leads to aspects of low self-esteem which come from damaged emotions. We will consider these in our next chapter and see how grace can bring healing and wholeness.

10

Grace and Self-Esteem

O let me commend my Saviour to you,
I set my seal that Jesus is true:
Ye all may find favor who come to His call;
O come to the Saviour! His grace is for all.

Then let us submit His grace to receive,
Fall down at His feet and gladly believe:
We all are forgiven for Jesus' sake;
Our title to heaven His merits we take.

IN DECEMBER OF 1985, syndicated columnist Bob Greene wrote an article concerning a twelve-year-old boy who received a cruel card from his classmates. The card, manufactured and distributed by the Topps Chewing Gum Company, was headlined, "Most Unpopular Student Award." The boy's classmates had written his name on the card and left it on his desk. Greene had originally written about this because he felt it was wrong for a company to sell that kind of card. Topps dismissed his criticism, saying it was just a form of satire and innocent "insult humor." But the boy's teacher and school principal said it was causing him a lot of emotional damage. What amazed and impressed Greene the most was the avalanche of mail which came from his adult readers, telling of the lasting hurts they were still carrying around as a result of such "innocent" childhood incidents. Most of the people still were troubled by a sense of low self-esteem—even when they were elderly. That column was entitled, "The Pain That Never Goes Away."

The only thing in Greene's column that surprised me was his surprise. In May of 1986, I heard George Gallup, Jr. say his latest poll showed that one-third of Americans suffer from low self-esteem. He considered it to be the chief psychological malady of our day.

Let us see how we can cooperate with grace to remove the inner barriers which keep us from being healed of this painful malady.

The Deadly "I Am's"

If we are truly reborn children of God, our sense of worthlessness and low self-esteem does not come from Him—the One who called Himself the Great I Am. Instead it comes from our own deadly I am's. Let me explain.

Remember how we observed that the home is like a mirror in which we develop our self-concepts? How we come to see ourselves, and to value—or devalue—ourselves will be based largely on the evaluations of significant people in our lives. This is especially true in the early years of our development. There is no doubt there are inborn differences between children. From their very birth some children are highly sensitive and have a built-in radar that picks up the most minute details of home life. Others are born with an entirely different kind of receiving antenna which seems to screen out the static.

While these differences determine the *degree* to which children respond, there are some basic God-given needs which are the same for everyone. I am convinced that *the most serious single consequence of parental dysgrace is deeply damaged self-esteem.* Whether it has been done intentionally or unintentionally, indirectly or directly, negatively by deprivation or positively by rejection, the result is a sense of worthlessness and low self-esteem. *The perceived "You are's" of the parents become the inner "I am's" of the children.* I do not want to limit this to parents or stepparents, because other family members, neighbors, peers, teachers, and church personnel also play a major role. However, there is no doubt parents are the main ones involved. It is not that they necessarily word their rejection and say, "You are this" or "You are that." The message is given by their overall personalities, their inner and outer bearing and demeanor, by the radar they send out.

The *King James Version* of the Bible uses an old English word, *conversation*, which doesn't mean simply speaking with words, but indicates manner of life. The basic idea behind the word is the message being spoken to others by one's whole manner of living. It is this *conversation*—attitudes, actions, facial expressions, tones of voice, habitual responses, *or the lack of them*—which give us the "You are" messages which slowly but surely become the "I am's" of our lives. Long after the original people are gone—through distance, divorce, or even death—the powerful "I am's" continue to be the painful source of our self-belittling or self-despising. As Bob Greene discovered, they can literally affect us for all of life.

In my book, *Putting Away Childish Things*, I dealt with these "I am's" as childhood mottoes which cripple adult behavior, mottoes such as "Measure up," "Brave boys don't cry," and "You'll never make it." Since then, people have given me many more of these put-downs which they say helped them form a low opinion of themselves.

You've no right to feel that way.
If you can't say something nice, don't say anything.
Why do you always do things like that?
If there's a wrong way to do it, you'll find it.
What makes you so stupid? clumsy? dumb? slow? silly?
All you gotta' do is use your head once in a while.
I can't believe you did such a thing.
Why can't you be more like your sister? brother?
I hate to think of how you'll turn out.
You're going to turn out to be just like _____.
What in the world is wrong with you?
What does Jesus think about you when you do that?
God can't love naughty little boys/girls/kids.
Now *you'll* have to be the man/woman of the house.
Don't let anyone know what you're really like.
Why couldn't you have been a boy? a girl?
You were trouble before you were born.
You've been nothing but trouble since you were born.
I wish you'd never been born.
The only reason we stay together is because of you.
If I thought you were really sorry, I might forgive you.
I'm sick of you. or, You make me sick.

How could you do that after all we've done for you?
You shoulda' known better than to trust a man/woman.
Can't you do anything right?
No wonder you don't have any friends!

Notice that most of these statements are not criticisms or corrections of doing, but of being. This is extremely important in relation to our self-esteem. Psychologists who have made special studies of affirmation have come up with a formula about positive and negative strokes.

A positive stroke enhances us as persons. If it was given for *doing*—what *you did*—it's worth 1 point. If it was given for *being*—what *you are*—it's worth 10 points.

A negative stroke diminishes us as persons. If it was given for *doing*, it counts 10 points. If it was given for *being*, it counts 100 points!

My counseling experience confirms this formula. People will remember a single hurtful criticism most vividly, while tending to forget a string of compliments. And they will feel a positive or a negative statement about *what they are* much more deeply than one concerning *what they did*. Thus it's easy to see why the put-downs of *being* can be so completely shattering to our self-esteem. They hurt us not simply on the outside, for our behavior; but they pierce right into the inside of us, where the *concepts and feelings about ourselves originate.*

If these were simply isolated statements, occasionally uttered by exhausted and exasperated parents who were normally fair and loving, they would not be so harmful. But when they represent the general attitude and atmosphere of the home, the effect on self-image can be serious. Every one of them is a basic message which in one way or another says, *"You are worthless, you are bad, you are guilty, you are a failure, and you won't make it in life."* These "You are's" can become a permanent part of our "I am's"—the inner voice of our self-image—which then says, *"I am worthless, I am bad, I am guilty, I am a failure, and I won't make it in life."*

In their excellent book, *The Blessing*, Gary Smalley and John Trent maintain that our emotional and psychological makeup is such that we all need what the Bible calls "the blessing." This is the knowledge that someone in this world loves and accepts us unconditionally. Because our parents are so important to us during our formative years, we especially crave their blessing, and are hurt if we don't receive it.

Smalley and Trent detail the five biblical elements of the blessing: meaningful touch, the spoken word, the expression of high value, the description of a special future, and the application of genuine commitment.

Here, indeed, is a fine description of what we have called parental grace. Contrast this with the verbal expressions of parental dysgrace we have been describing. Or add some other parental behaviors which produce the very opposite of meaningful touch and lasting commitment. Their consequences bring with them a "curse" rather than a "blessing."

• Alcoholism. There are between 12 to 15 million alcoholics in America. Every study of the adult children of alcoholics confirms they have serious problems with low self-esteem which results in an alarmingly high percentage of them either becoming alcoholics themselves or marrying alcoholics.

• Broken homes. By the early 1990s, one-half of all the children of our country will be from homes which have been broken by divorce. In January 1988 the U.S. Government reported that one-fourth of all children in the United States were living in single-parent homes.

• Latch-key kids. The latest Harris poll reports there are 13 million kids who go home from school every day to an empty house. This is one-fourth of all American homes. The same poll reported that teachers list this as the main reason why the children are not doing well in school (CBS Evening News, September 2, 1987).

• Abuse. It is almost impossible to keep up with the rising statistics on wife battering and the physical abuse of children. Reported cases of sexual abuse of children have doubled in less than a decade.

In many instances, it is mainly verbal abuse which is so damaging to the self-estimate. The Bible is right—as we think *in our hearts* so we are. Paul uses a remarkable phrase in Ephesians 1:18, *"the eyes of your heart."* Yes, our hearts do have *eyes* by which we see ourselves from the very depths of our personality. And when we see ourselves from the perspective of destructive *I am's*, then our self-esteem is affected from the very center of our being.

All of the factors we have been describing can produce self-devaluation and self-hate which may persist even after we have become Spirit-filled Christians, so that we then feel as if God too is disapproving of us. The first step in our healing is to realize that God understands where the feelings are coming from and is as brokenhearted about it as we are. He wants to work with us in freeing us from them, for He doesn't want His children despising themselves. Truly our only hope is a whole new way of viewing ourselves through the eyes of grace.

Seven times in the Gospel of John we find Christ's great I Am's: the bread of life (6:35), the light of the world (8:12), the door (10:7), the good shepherd (10:11), the resurrection and the life (11:25), the way, the truth, and the life (14:6), and the true vine (15:1). Jesus Christ was the only one who had the right to say, "I Am," because He is indeed the great I Am, incarnate in human flesh. It was Augustine who reminded us that you and I do not have the right to say "I am," because we never simply *are*, but are always in the process of *becoming*. What a wonderfully hopeful word! By God's grace we are becoming someone different. It's high time to leave the old "I am's" far behind.

I recently received a letter from a woman who, although a Christian for many years, had struggled with low self-esteem. She wrote, "Six simple words from your book transformed my life—'how much you mean to Him.'[1] I had thought only of how much He meant to me, so it never dawned on me that I could possibly mean anything to Him. When this really got through to me, it changed my whole feeling about myself!"

God is not like some cruel or neurotic parent, who needs to put down His children. On the contrary, He takes delight in lifting up His children and helping them feel good about themselves. "Consider the incredible love that the Father has shown us in allowing us to be called 'children of God'—and that is not just what we are called, but what we *are*" (1 John 3:1, PH). "Therefore, God is not ashamed to be called their God'" (Hebrews 11:16).

It Takes an Inside Job

Our low self-worth will not be cured by something we may achieve or obtain from the outside. It has to come from the inside because the problem is so deep-rooted.

I have deliberately spent a lot of time on the destructive effects of dysgrace on self-image. Whatever its source—home, school, church, community, or culture—the consequences are a deep-rooted sense of worthlessness and self-despising. The common term we often use for this—*inferiority complex*—doesn't adequately describe the problem. When a person says, "I feel *inferior*," or "I feel *inadequate*," it's just another version of the old comparison game which puts the emphasis on *doing*. It often means inferior *to* someone because they *do it so much better*, or inadequate *for* a task. This sense of low self-esteem then is the result of not *doing* something well.

The sense of worthlessness and low self-esteem we are talking about is much more serious, because it involves a person's *being*. "*I am* worthless and unacceptable and the things I do just *reveal* to others what I really am. My failures and unacceptable behaviors simply *disclose* to people the kind of person I already know I am." Such people begin with what they think to *be an indisputable fact*—"*I am the kind of person no one could really like.*" *What they do divulges who they feel they are.* No matter what successes they achieve, or how high they climb on the ladder, or how many compliments they receive from others, they still don't feel any better about themselves. The sense of being worthless and unacceptable comes first; the low self-esteem is already in their *being, and no amount of valuable, acceptable doing will change it.*

There's no other way to explain the fact that when others point out to them obviously successful accomplishments, or very acceptable and Christian behavior, it doesn't really get through to them. They hear it but can't believe or feel it at a gut level. Instead, they refuse to accept it and actually use it to add to their self-belittling in the most ingenious ways. Do any of these sound familiar?

People are just trying to make me feel good because they feel sorry for me.

I know it's not true and he's just stringing me along. I don't want that kind of pity.

My husband only tells me I look beautiful to make me feel better. I'd rather he'd tell me the truth (this one often from beautiful women).

My wife says she's proud of me, but it's just to make me feel good (this often from the most successful men).

People say that because they don't really know me.

You probably won't feel that way about me when you get to know me better.

I don't care how many compliments I get. When you begin with a zero, it doesn't make any difference what you add on; it's still a zero.

It really wasn't me who did it, it was the Lord (a common way self-effacing perfectionistic Christians fend off compliments, after they've done anything well, such as solos, sermons, services).

I appreciate what you're telling me, but after all you're my counselor! (Freely translated means, "I know you're trying to help, but you're not telling me the truth.")

Because this deep sense of low self-worth comes from within, it can never be solved by something outside of us. And yet we try. Let's look at a couple of the ways.

• The hunt for achievement. Many feel *if only* they could achieve success in some area of their work, they would prove themselves to be worthwhile. Then they would be accepted and loved by God and others, and therefore feel better about themselves. So they work harder, perform better, and may even achieve a high measure of success, only to discover that *no amount of doing or achieving* can change how they inwardly feel about themselves. Their low self-worth simply will not allow them to accept the appropriate affirmation and encouragement. So the whole vicious cycle starts all over again and the jaws of the performance trap grip them tighter than ever.

I would not want to generalize from my own experience, but it seems to me *more men* choose this route than do women. Men are more involved in their work and naturally think they can gain status and self-esteem *by their own efforts.*

• The hunger for affection. I see *more women* trying to gain a higher sense of self-worth through affection and love given them *by others.* Unfortunately, this is as unsatisfactory as the first. As several of the quoted personal putdowns indicated, their self-doubt will not allow them to accept the affection or love offered them. It's almost impossible for them to believe anyone could love them, when they consider themselves so undesirable, with little or nothing to offer in return. Once more a vicious circle is set up which varies from their being overanxious, overdemanding, over-possessive, or overcritical, all the way to being overaffectionate and sometimes even promiscuous. While there may be periods of temporary relief, such persons often cannot maintain the relationships for which they so desperately hunger.

Healing the Source

The primary sources of damage to our self-esteem need healing, repairing, and reprogramming. This is where healing grace is required. I want to make this as practical as possible, so let me make it personal and talk to you as if we were counseling together. Here are some of the questions I would ask.

• Have you found and faced the painful places in your past which you feel are the chief sources of your low self-esteem? It is very important that you have the courage not only to honestly look at the people and incidents involved, but also to plug into the feelings which go along with them. Brain research proves conclusively that our memories store not only mental pictures from the past *but also the original emotions experienced at that time.* So when you feel you have discovered the hurts, humiliations, deprivations, or rejections, allow yourself to *feel their pain and also to feel your reactions to that pain.* This not in order to *blame others* or to *escape responsibility.* It is done so that you can honestly face up to feelings you may have buried for years.

The best way to do this is *by sharing your feelings with God and with another person in prayer.* But you cannot confess to God what you will not first admit to yourself. When you also share with another person, this brings an even deeper level of openness and honesty with both yourself and God. This kind of openness can be very painful, and feelings may arise which will shock you. But grace is never shocked, never repulsed, and never withdrawn—whatever it is faced with. It is freely given, without any reference to our goodness or badness, worthiness or unworthiness.

The greatest manifestation of grace is the Cross, and the Cross means that when *God saw us at our worst, He loved us the most.* So armed with the courage grace can bring, look squarely at the worst, the most painful, the most humiliating, the most abusive, and the most devastating put-downs of your life. *Remember* them in your mind, and *relive* them in your emotions, but don't stop there. *Relinquish* them to God in forgiving and surrendering prayer. It's doubtful you can do this by yourself, so get help from a close friend, pastor, or counselor.

• As you have faced and felt the pain, have you forgiven everyone involved? As strange as it may sound, resentment and hate keep us chained to the people and the pains of the past. Only forgiveness and love can free us from both the painful memories and the destructive evaluations of the past. Sometimes this experience of healing grace comes about in unusual ways.

Arlene struggled with an extremely low opinion of herself. Though a really fine Christian who contributed to many areas of church life, she devalued her spiritual life. Much of our counseling had centered on her mother, a deeply religious woman, a leader in her denomination, but whose overcritical and perfectionistic ways had poured out as a constant stream over Arlene. As the hurts and humiliations surfaced, so did a heavy layer of resentment she had never faced. One day she was expressing it all so realistically I just presumed it was something which continued in present relationships with her mother. So I said to her, "It sure looks to me like you need to cut the umbilical cord to your mother, and stop letting her feed you with those downgrading evaluations." Arlene looked a bit startled. "Oh, I'm sorry," she said, "I guess I didn't make it plain. My mother's been dead for over five years now."

I was embarrassed and mumbled out an apology. I noticed Arlene clammed up for the rest of the session, so inwardly I was thinking, "Boy, Seamands, you sure blew it today!"

When she came back the next time she said to me, "I realize you know I'm a nurse, but do you know where I do most of my work?"

"No, I'm afraid I don't." I was still expecting some kind of scolding for last week's boner.

"Well, I spend most of my time in the labor room helping deliver babies. I suppose I've assisted doctors cut the umbilical cord hundreds of times. So last week when you said I needed to cut the umbilical cord to my mother, it really shocked me. As I drove home, the only thing I could picture in my mind was a cord 1,000 miles long stretching all the way from here right into my mother's grave down in Florida! I actually dreamed about that crazy cord twice. You were exactly right. This week I spent a lot of time in prayer, and I found the grace to forgive her, and to ask God to forgive me for resenting and blaming her all these years. And I've been amazed—I'm not feeding on her wretched evaluations of me anymore. I am beginning to get a whole new sense of *who I am as God's daughter, and I'm learning to feed on His opinions of me. And it's beginning to feel awfully good!"*

It would be impossible to exaggerate the importance of forgiveness in this regard. Forgiveness in the *active voice*—forgiving those who have wronged and hurt us; in the *passive voice*—receiving forgiveness from God (and sometimes from others) for our wrong responses to their wrongs; and in the *reflective voice*—forgiving ourselves and refusing to continue flagellating ourselves for past sins.

The greatest barrier to receiving grace is an *unforgiving spirit.*This is especially true about the healing grace necessary to cure deep-rooted feelings of guilt, worthlessness, and self-hate. God has so created us that hidden resentments—even when we are not aware of them—create a kickback of guilt which creates a kickback of self-accusation and low self-esteem. Many times we cannot find freedom from this vicious circle because at some deep level we have not truly forgiven another.

Many people are unable to break out of this vicious circle by themselves, no matter how hard they try or how much they pray. If you are having difficulties in this area, surrender your pride and seek help from someone who can be for you a human "paraclete"—*someone called alongside to be a temporary assistant to the Holy Spirit.*

• Will you now commit yourself to daily cooperation with the Holy Spirit in giving you a new Christian self-image? Healing grace is not simply a one-time crisis gift. It may begin in a flash of insight or a very emotional high when we experience God's love and grace at a new and deeper level. *I would never belittle these spiritual highs in any way.* However, because emotions have been *badly overemphasized* in some Christian quarters, many pastors and counselors tend to *badly underemphasize* their importance. There are times when it takes a profoundly emotional experience to move a person off dead center, to loosen the mind from former mistaken perceptions, and *to actually free the will to make new decisions.* I have seen God work this way in many lives.

However, even when it *starts* that way, there is still the hard work of transformation by the renewal of the mind. Old internal *put-down I am's* are hard to break. A daily, moment-by-moment cooperation with the *instant counteractivity of the Holy Spirit is essential.* When I recently had knee surgery, I learned that the operation was only *half of the healing.* Faithfully doing the exercises given me by the physical therapist *was the equally important other half.* The same is true in the therapeutic exercises following a dynamic experience of healing grace.

In my writings I have often quoted from the best-selling book, *Psycho-Cybernetics* by Dr. Maxwell Maltz. A former plastic surgeon, he turned to counseling because he discovered that unless people change their inner picture of themselves, it won't do much good to alter their appearance. Dr. Maltz's scientific research proved that it took about twenty-one days of inwardly repeating new ideas to effect permanent changes in people's views of themselves.

I find this a confirmation of the scriptural emphasis on putting off the old and putting on the new (Ephesians 4:22–24), and the exhortation to "think on such things" (Philippians 4:8). You may want to set a three-week period in which you listen to the Holy Spirit remind you of who you really are—your true *I am* and your *I am becoming.* Then think God's thoughts about you after Him. It will bring much joy to heaven and to you!

11

Grace and Negative Feelings

Jesus, united by Thy grace,
And each to each endeared,
With confidence we seek Thy face,
And know our prayer is heard.

Help us to help each other, Lord,
Each other's cross to bear;
Let each his friendly aid afford,
And feel his brother's care.

PRESSURE IS A key element of life in the performance trap. There is the pressure of trying to live with a self we don't like, a God who seems hard to love, and others we can't get along with. Put all together, it's the *pressure of feeling caught in a trap where we are expected to live up to unrealistic and impossible demands put upon us by God, ourselves, and other people.* And, like the hamster on the treadmill, the harder we try, the faster we run; and the faster we run, the harder we have to try to keep up with the wheel. This feeling of *being trapped* generates in us some strong negative emotions which keep us emotionally disturbed and spiritually defeated.

Anger and Depression

I have yet to counsel a performance-based and perfectionistic Christian who was not at heart *an angry person.* This doesn't mean such persons are always *aware of* or *express* it openly. They often impress us as being extremely controlled or very loving. But when we get to know them better, and they open up to share their inner selves, we inevitably discover a core of anger deep within their personalities.

However, the majority of those who come for help *are* conscious of the anger, because it is a major problem in their Christian lives. They struggle with resentments and sometimes even rage, and their seemingly uncontrollable outbursts of temper are the major factor in disrupting their personal relationships at work, in church, and especially with their spouses and children. They come across as angry persons, and angriest at themselves for being the way they are. This, of course, creates a vicious circle which increases their guilt, low self-esteem, and their sense of being phony—"What if people found out what I was really like when I blow up at my wife and kids?"

I find this unresolved anger, this frozen rage, to be the chief source of the *depression* characteristic of the performance-bound person. No wonder many secular psychiatrists turn against religion when they see so many depressive patients who are scrupulous and overconscientious Christians. After all, if the ground of our right-relatedness to God is our own perfect performance, then we *ought* to be depressed and filled with feelings of angry hopelessness. For then we would truly be trapped in a no-win situation—*the ultimate injustice*—which would only add to our already existing vicious circle of negative emotions.

Thank God the ground of our relationship with Him is Christ's perfect performance for us—His perfect *life* of obedience and His perfect *death* for our sins. It is our faith in *Him*, our trusting receptivity of the gift of *His righteousness, in spite of all the sins and failures we see in ourselves*, which saves us from despair and depression. For the sake of those caught in the performance treadmill, let me assure you that this does not depend on a *perfect* repentance, or a *perfect* faith, or a *perfect* consecration on our part. George Whitefield used to say that even our *repentance* needs to be repented of. This is true about every ingredient involved in the human response to grace. Our *faith* itself needs to say to Jesus, "I do believe; help me overcome my unbelief!" (Mark 9:24) *And our surrender needs to be surrendered because it is not a perfect surrender.*

Let's look at some practical ways healing grace can deal with our anger and depression. As you read this, just imagine that you and I are talking together.

• Find and face the root sources of your anger and allow the grace of forgiveness to penetrate them. It is important that you discover who and what fill you with such anger and rage. It is not necessarily present-tense situations or persons who activate your anger. Rather, through them you are most likely tapping into the *core source* of your anger. Anger-filled persons are somewhat like telephone switchboards—through present events they plug into some past hurt and their whole system lights up. One way you can recognize this is *when your anger response is way out of proportion to the stimulus of the present situation.* Sometimes it's difficult to trace through the complex maze and find the true origin.

For both Gladys and her husband it was a second marriage. Their experiences were remarkably similar—their spouses had simply taken off with someone else and left the children with them. They had both lived as single parents for several years, had met in church, married, and now felt God had given them a wonderful second chance for a Christian family. They were very happy together and the children got along remarkably well. There was only one major problem. Gladys couldn't understand why her stepson, Mike, always seemed to rub her the wrong way. He was not a problem child and was affectionate and obedient to her. But Gladys had a strange sense of hostility toward him that resulted in her being harsh and overdemanding. Naturally it was beginning to affect the marriage and the whole family. She and her husband had communicated about it openly and she had spent many hours weeping and praying about it. We counseled together and prayed about it several times, but the mystery remained.

One day we talked about how her first husband, Ted, an alcoholic, had badly mistreated her. In the middle of the conversation she became silent. Sensing that the Great Counselor had taken over, I too kept quiet and inwardly prayed. After some time she began to express herself slowly, with long pauses in between, "I think I know what my problem is. . . . I never realized it before. . . . I see a great many of Ted's characteristics in Mike. . . . My goodness, he even looks something like him. . . has the same kind of build . . . and mannerisms. . . . I can't believe it. . . . He reminds me of him and that triggers off a lot of deeply buried hurts in me . . . and I've just realized, I don't think I've fully forgiven Ted for what he did to me." Gladys began to cry softly, "You know, I've been taking out my feelings on Mike and he's completely innocent. No wonder we were *so confused by it all*."

Now we knew *what we should be praying about*. It was a beautiful sight to see the forgiving, healing grace of the Cross cleanse away both the past source and the present stimulation for her anger. It was only a matter of time until they were enjoying a new level of loving relationships in the family.

Some good questions to ask are, *What am I really so angry about? Against whom am I actually so angry? Why does this (person/situation) make me so angry?* It's essential to face the primary roots of the problem and let grace deal with them. Hebrews 12:15 contains the heart of the matter in the form of a warning: "See to it that no one misses the grace of God and that no bitter root grows up to cause trouble and defile many." I have seen this bitter root grow in the lives of hundreds of Christians. They thought they were doing the right thing by not dwelling on the past, and so gave a kind of blanket forgiveness "to everyone who ever hurt me." And like a blanket, it covered but didn't really deal with the hurts and the hates. A bitter root was causing trouble and defiling a network of relationships. When the grace of God was applied like an axe at the root of the tree (Matthew 3:10), both the actual trouble and the diffusing defilement were taken care of.

• Face your explosive sense of injustice and allow the grace of acceptance to deactivate it. The performance-trapped and perfectionistic Christian usually feels a highly exaggerated sensitivity to anything unjust or unfair. It's like a ticking time bomb inside waiting to explode at the slightest contact with the inequities of life. Such persons often defend their angry oversensitivity by trying to turn it into a virtue. They have an insatiable need to set things right, to take up various causes, and to aggressively stand up for their rights. There is usually an unhealed wound in their past, where they were hurt or humiliated or treated unfairly, which feeds this heightened sense of injustice. Often these injustices reach all the way back into the early formative years of our lives.

Pip is the central figure of Charles Dickens' novel, *Great Expectations*, which many critics feel is his spiritual autobiography. One day after his cruel sister had humiliated him, Pip mused bitterly to himself:

My sister's bringing up had made me sensitive. In the little world in which children have their existence, whosoever brings them up, there is nothing so finely perceived and so finely felt as injustice. It may be only small injustice that the child can be exposed to; but the child is small, and its world is small, and its rocking-horse stands as many hands high, according to scale, as a big-boned Irish hunter. Within myself I had sustained, from my babyhood, a perpetual conflict with injustice. I had known, from the time when I could speak, that my sister, in her capricious and violent coercion, was unjust to me. Through all my punishments, disgraces, fasts and vigils, and other penitential performances, I had nursed this assurance.[1]

Too often, this nursed anger at injustice turns upward to be directed toward God; it is accompanied by a hidden resentment against Him. Such persons will often begin by saying they are angry at *life*. But when that is examined carefully, they realize the anger is actually against God. For as an old saying goes, "If you don't like the *design*, you don't like the *Designer*."

A dedicated Christian layman once said to me, "I've had to face the painful fact that for many years I've been angry with God. I've inwardly blamed Him for many things in my life which I felt were unfair. *I loved God, really did, I loved Him and served Him, but I didn't like Him!*" Much of this had to do with his failure to accept his personality type with his own gifts and talents. He had wasted many years "if-onlying," playing the comparison game, and angry at God because he wasn't more like a certain fellow-worker in the church. When he faced and relinquished his resentment against God, he learned not only to *accept* the personality gifts God had given him but also to *appreciate* them. Within a year God had begun to use him in a new way. People commented on the different expression on his face—less critical, more loving and caring. Slowly but surely he became a more winsome witness for Christ.

But this process involved considerable struggle, for at this point he was like all angry and depressed Christians. *They strongly feel they cannot pray—must not pray—they are too bad.* It seems as if God is disappointed and angry with them. They have lost the sense of God as loving and personal, fatherly and friendly, giving and gracious. From their emotional pit they perceive God not as the giver of unconditional love, but as one who bargains before He blesses. So while they keep on working—perhaps even harder, they stop praying in any deep sense of the word. They feel they cannot share their true selves with God, not when they have such anxiety, conflict, and depression. If they do pray, their prayers are perfunctory and unreal.

If you are caught in this kind of a trap, I have good news for you. Your hope is in looking to the Cross. There the Incarnate God voluntarily took upon Himself all the sins, the meaningless suffering, the unmerited pain and undeserved injustices of the world. There He bore all that the whole world—including *you and I*—could angrily heap upon Him. So He is not shocked by anything we may now express to Him out of our inner emotional pain and suffering. Again and again I have seen the miracle of healing grace penetrate and defuse anger, rage, and depression *when people resume talking to God in prayer.* Often those prayers begin with, "O God, it's been a long time since I've been able to talk to You. I felt I couldn't with all my feelings about You. ..." After the sound barrier is broken and communication is reestablished, healing grace begins to penetrate those negative emotions. Ultimately they experience an inflow of the love of God on a deeper level than ever before. Often this healing takes place with the help of other humans who understand and accept us *as we are*—friends, pastors, counselors, or a small group.

But the most wonderful part of all is that *God Himself lovingly works with us* to heal our hurts, defuse our hypersensitivity to injustice, and change us from *fighters into lovers, defenders into reconcilers.* His healing grace removes barriers which for so long have kept us from experiencing His sanctifying grace in our lives. We do not need to hesitate in the least to express in prayer our anger and depression, *even when it is against Him.* He has known about it long before we confess it to Him, and has continued to love us. Indeed, it is *His very grace* faithfully working in us which now enables us to both *own it and then to disown it.*

Fears and Compulsions

Some people are subject to strange and irrational fears, panic attacks, obsessive thoughts or ideas, and uncontrollable compulsions. Persons troubled by these symptoms are usually very high-strung, nervous, supersensitive, and with family tendencies toward alcoholism, depression, and emotional breakdown.

If you are identifying with this description, my first word of grace is to caution you against *assuming such problems always have a spiritual cause*. In recent years much research has been done which reveals that there are often neurological or chemical causes behind such symptoms. It is strange we evangelical Christians have no qualms about taking medicine or shots for diabetes, thyroid problems, or high blood pressure. But when it comes to matters of depression, panic attacks, and the like, we assume we must solve them *only by spiritual means*. Indeed, this in itself contributes to our unrealistic ideals and unreachable goals—"If I were really spiritual, then I would be able to handle this."

Before making such assaults on yourself, *check with a physician about any possible medical causes which may require treatment or medication*. And don't allow your superspiritual Christian friends to put a guilt trip on you for getting this kind of help. It's hard for us to imagine, but when anesthesia was first discovered, vast numbers of preachers thundered against it. Nowadays when we have to undergo an operation, we thank God for it. Remember, God made all the elements of this universe; if medication helps you live a better Christian life, then receive it too *as a gift of His grace*. Of course, this can be overdone; but the answer to *misuse* is not *disuse*, but *right use*.

Imbalanced chemistry, inadequate theology, and insufficient grace are very able to work together to exacerbate the performance/perfectionist trap. Each one feeds the other, making it difficult to know where one begins and other ends. For we know that mental patterns and spiritual outlook influence our body chemistry. *There is no more powerful medicine than grace and love.* A gut-level experience of being unconditionally accepted, forgiven, loved—God's grace—can bring about incredible miracles of change.

Pauline, a pastor's wife in her early thirties, came seeking help with the whole pattern of problems we have been describing. She had had recurring bouts with anxiety attacks since her teen years. She had a long history of being overloaded with Christian role-expectations which she felt she had to live up to. The panic attacks, lasting for a few hours or several days, terrified her, and always left her physically exhausted and deeply depressed. Within her extended family, there was alcoholism, emotional breakdown, and some traumatic deaths. Ordinarily she could control her fears, but when a panic attack struck, she was overwhelmed by the thought, "Will it happen to me?" When this happened she was unable to sleep properly; then she would feel terribly guilty because she was not trusting God. It was a no-win situation. We worked together for many hours on the terrible pressure her superspiritual self put on her. She read and reread books on grace and we spent time praying together. She would often say, "*Grace is so hard. It's so hard to let God love me.* I've been a Christian since I was twelve, but I've never really believed God loved me, the real me." Together we traced the roots of this, not just to an unpredictable, unaffectionate, and graceless home, but also to a pastor who was one of God's strict and stoical servants. She shared numberless injustices and hurt, and shed many angry tears. These were always followed by, "I'm so ashamed for you to see me *this way.*" Finally, with the barriers removed, grace broke through to the real Pauline. This is how she described it when I asked her to write it down for me.

I remember I didn't feel very much like going to my session with Dr. Seamands that morning. I was very tired. Both of the children were just getting over the chicken pox and I had slept very little the nights before. But maybe that's how it is, God can really work when we're weak, tired, and completely dependent on Him. After sharing with him I started to go down the stairs, although previously I always took the elevator. It was on that walk down the stairs God started to speak to me in a special way.

"Thank You, God, for breaking through," were the words which ran in my heart over and over again. Slowly the tears started coming, and when I got to the car the dam broke. I sat there and cried and cried as I let God reveal Himself to me, as I let Him minister to me. . . . Yes, His love was finally breaking through. I was experiencing His love as never before. In my mind, I saw Jesus with the children on His lap and I, as a child, was walking toward Him. "I want to climb on Your lap and be loved by You," were my thoughts. I was approaching Him and the disciples were scaring me away with, "He's too busy, too tired, go away." But Jesus stretched out His arms to me . . . Dare I enter His embrace? . . . Oh yes, I'll let Him love me and liberate me.

Nothing else matters anymore except God's love. He really loves me! His love penetrates, permeates my very being. Thank You, God! My heart is filled with such joy and peace. How wonderful to feel Your love. "Release me, God, from my own self-made, self-imposed prison constructed by my own wrong concepts of You. . . ."

The thought often comes to me now, that as I love my own son always, *even when he's bad* . . . I say to him, "Mommy loves you always; you don't have to be good for Mommy to love you." And that's what I hear God saying to me, "Pauline, you don't have to be good in order for Me to love you." Thank You, God, for finally breaking through. . . .

This was how grace came through to Pauline. It was the beginning of new freedom and a new physical and spiritual health. She continues to minister to others out of a grateful and grace-filled heart. Don't be misled by the dramatic crisis experience she described. That was made possible because of a long process which removed her inner barriers to grace—some of which went right back to her childhood years. How tender and beautiful of the Spirit to enable her to become a participant in the Gospel story of Jesus and the children. This brought the necessary healing from the wounds of deprivation and rejection so that she could accept God's grace. I firmly believe there is a tailor-made experience of healing grace for you too, if, like Pauline, you will *let God love you just as you are.*

Group Grace

Let me now address one of the most important but badly neglected aspects of healing grace. Many of the worst barriers to God's grace come from the dysgrace of unhealthy and destructive personal relationships in our past. Therefore many of those barriers will *be removed largely through healthy and constructive personal relationships in our present.* This is where *group grace* enters the picture.

At the very heart of the great healing passage in James 5:13–20 are these words, "Therefore confess your sins to each other and pray for each other so that you may be healed" (v. 16). Some wit has commented that many Christians and church groups have reversed that advice—they confess sins *for* each other and then pray *at* one another! In the early church, *koinonia*—a sharing, giving fellowship—was placed on a par with doctrine, prayer, worship, and the Lord's Supper (Acts 2:42). Since they did not have church buildings, they met mostly in small group gatherings in homes and other convenient places. Very open sharing and confession was made to the group which then supported the struggling person with their love and prayers. Not until the third century did the practice of private confession begin which finally resulted in the "sealing of the confessional," turning it into a strictly private matter. Thus, with a few rare exceptions, the healing power of group grace was largely lost to the church.

It was rediscovered on a large scale during the great Evangelical Revival in Britain under the Wesleys. The Methodist Church did not begin as a church but as associations of like-minded people or "societies." These were small groups of five to ten persons, led by converted laypersons, and meeting weekly in "class meetings" to study Scripture, share, and pray together. Church historians give full credit to the Spirit-anointed preaching of George Whitefield and John Wesley, and the inspiring hymns of Charles Wesley, for generating the revival. But all agree *it was the incredible power of these small groups which brought about such lasting transformation in individuals and ultimately "spread Scriptural holiness and reformed the nation."*

Unfortunately, most churches today have overlooked this great potential for changing lives, and organizations like Alcoholics Anonymous have taken it up. AA's roots can be traced back through the Oxford Movement to those early Methodist Societies. AA was founded by the famous Bill W., an alcoholic whose life had been changed through the sharing and prayer of the group meetings in an Episcopal Church. While some AA chapters today have gotten away from their Christian roots, they still use the group principles with great effectiveness.

Early in this book we described one of the saddest and costliest consequences of performance-oriented living—a sense of feeling phony, duplicitous, and alienated from our real selves. This is because such Christians let people know only their superselves. They present a *public self* to others because this is the concept of themselves they want people to believe. Actually, there are assorted *public selves presented to different people.* In this way they become so estranged from their *private self* they no longer know who and what they really are. This is one of their major sources of self-despising and inner anxiety. It keeps them feeling like hypocrites and drains their power for living and for witnessing.

Persons who live this way have literally sold their souls, their true selves, in order to gain the approval, affection, or acclaim of others. And the longer they are on the performance treadmill, the more fearful and secretive they tend to become. The only way they can get off this destructive wheel is to allow others to know their *real selves*. We all remember Socrates' famous dictum, "Know thyself." I believe the truth can better be expressed, "Let thyself be known and thou wilt know thyself."

We talk a lot about being honest with ourselves and with God. And we sincerely—sometimes desperately—try to do this in our times of Bible reading and prayer. But the kind of honesty and self-knowledge which will bring about lasting changes in our lives *almost always requires another person. It is when we disclose our true, private selves to someone else that we fully come to know ourselves for real.* Down deep we may dimly perceive the truth about our *real selves*, yet go on denying or covering it with our superselves—even in prayer. However, once we have actually put the truth into words and shared with another, it becomes increasingly difficult to continue deceiving ourselves.

Yes, it is the truth that sets us free—the truth about God and ourselves which Christ alone brings to us (John 8:32–36). And a major part of that truth about ourselves is communicated when, at cost to our false superselves, we allow others to know the truth about us. And this is where the Body Life of the Church becomes the channel of grace. It surrounds us with the trust atmosphere of our new Family of God which gives us the courage to be truly known by our brothers and sisters in Christ. Not only *known* but *loved!* This frees us from having to be someone and something we are not, since we are *accepted and loved as we are.* In this way we discover the life-transforming power of group grace.

Performance-minded and perfectionistic Christians especially need such an accepting and loving fellowship *where they can disclose their real selves without fear of disapproval and condemnation.* Trying to get out of the performance trap by *only* their own *individual* struggle is as impossible as climbing out of quicksand without a helping hand. James 5:16 infers there are some physical, emotional, and spiritual hangups which can *only* be healed when they are shared with and prayed for by other Christians.

This may begin with just one other person—a trustworthy friend, Sunday School teacher, pastor, or counselor. And there are some things which should be shared only in that confidential setting. However, *there are many of us who as soon as possible need to share and pray with a small group. There is an amazing and life-transforming power in this kind of group grace.* If you cannot find such a group, then find at least one other person—perhaps through your contacts in a Sunday School class—and *start a group by opening your life to that person.* Then let it spread to include another and another. You can usually find someone who is desperately looking for such fellowship. This transparent openness and agreed praying (Matthew 18:18–20) sets off a kind of spiritual nuclear fission which generates great power. It will explode and disintegrate those obstacles to grace in your life and allow God to set you free to live and love in the Spirit.

Recycling Grace

The ultimate purpose of grace is to prepare us for fellowship with God throughout eternity, so that we can truly worship Him and literally "enjoy Him forever." But what is the ultimate purpose of healing grace as far as our lives here on earth are concerned? It is more than salvation, sanctification, or even restoration to wholeness. His ultimate design is to take everything that has ever happened in our lives and turn it to God's purposes for good. Everything? Some of you are thinking of some unspeakably evil and painful things which either *you, or someone else, meant for evil.* Things which have left you damaged and crippled in some way—physically, mentally, emotionally, spiritually, or relationally. Some wrongs which could only be called *garbage.* Is God able to even use such things as grist for His mill and turn them for human good and His glory?

And with all the strength within me I want to say an unqualified YES! If we humans are able to build plants which can recycle garbage into usable fuel, then certainly God can do the same. The most exciting part of my ministry has been watching God do this in the lives of those who have experienced His healing grace. These people are literally the *wounded healers and the healed helpers.* God has been able to take their very *cripplings* and turn them into *blessings.*

In my mind I see a veritable parade of people, literally a "cloud of witnesses," who have experienced every kind of personal sin, evil, victimization, dysgrace, and damaged emotion you could possibly imagine. But they all experienced God's healing grace at a deep level.

Now they are ministering to other hurting people out of the very places where they were hurt the most. I'm thinking of several Christian young men who came seeking help for their struggles with homosexuality. There were hours of counseling, prayers for healing, and a long time of reprogramming which included accountability and encouragement from a small support group. They are now happily married, with families, and God has given them a special ministry to others with the same problem.

I am also remembering a large number of disheartened Christians with varying degrees of perfectionism. Legalistic, critical, and judgmental, imprisoned by worry and worthlessness, believing wrong concepts of God, and driven to find approval from God and others. Many came for help when their tightly woven system began to come apart at the seams. Some came during or just after an emotional and spiritual breakdown. Some had to be hospitalized under psychiatric care. No, there were no quick cures; it was often a lengthy, uphill struggle against well-entrenched patterns of performance-based living. But ultimately grace broke through and they became resting believers instead of restive achievers. I have likened them to persons thrashing around in the water because they felt as if they were drowning. And then finally being saved when they began believing and living out grace—*they stopped their futile efforts and trusted the water to hold them up.* Now they are expert swimmers and have a special ministry to the performance-trapped. Because they understand and know how to suffer with their struggles, God is using them to bring freedom to the imprisoned.

And then I think of all those who were victims of sexual abuse, including what is perhaps the most destructive of all, incest. In *Putting Away Childish Things*, I shared the testimony of one such victim, her remarkable healing, and how God allowed her to lead her dying father to Christ. God has used this woman in a remarkable ministry to other incest victims.

I stress all this because there are simply not enough professionally trained counselors to work with the growing numbers of damaged and hurting people. God wants to raise up a vast army of healed helpers whom He can use as His "temporary assistants to the Holy Spirit." This is the ultimate purpose of healing grace in your life—to turn you into a channel of healing grace in someone else's life. Let me share a letter from one young man God is using in this way.

I want to remind you of the first line of my journal entry a year ago today. This was about a week before you took me to the airport to send me home. 'I am at the lowest point in my life. I feel like a total failure.'

I find it hard to believe that God could change me so drastically in one year's time. This time last year I was filled with self-hatred, hopelessness, and despair. Today I can honestly say that I like myself; the future has never seemed brighter. My life is filled to overflowing with peace and joy. God's grace is my watchword. He fills up whatever is lacking in me with His grace. He is a faithful God! I know this is a permanent condition for me. I've been like this for about six months now.

This afternoon I prayed with a young man who received Christ in his heart. And tonight I shared my walk with the Lord (depression, sins, failures, and all) with a young lady to help strengthen her new-found faith in Jesus. We both got excited. God is such a faithful God. I'm just basking in His grace!

12

The Panorama of God's Grace

What shall I do my God to love,
My loving God to praise!
The length, and breadth, and height to prove,
And depth of sovereign grace.

Thy sovereign grace to all extends,
Immense and unconfined;
From age to age it never ends,
It reaches all mankind.

Throughout the world its breadth is known,
Wide as infinity,
So wide it never passed by one;
Or it had passed by me.

To RESTRICT GOD'S grace only to saving or sanctifying grace would be to miss the all-encompassing nature of God's love in action. It would be like looking at the spectacular beauty of the Matterhorn and thinking you had seen the Alps; or showing people a picture of awesome Mount Everest and telling them it was the Himalayas. Both of these peaks are outstanding for their beauty and height, but they are surrounded by a breathtaking range of mountains which serve to highlight their grandeur.

And so it is with the grace of God. Certainly there are mountain-peak experiences, but grace includes a wide diversity of "mysterious ways" in which God works "His wonders to perform." Let us look at some of the levels of the grace God reaches out toward us.

General Grace

Many sincere evangelical Christians today are running scared. They want to be truly biblical and to avoid all attempts to dilute or corrupt the Christian faith. Unfortunately, they have gone to the opposite extreme and forgotten a very important teaching of Scripture itself, that "every good and perfect gift is from above, coming down from the Father" (James 1:17). The greatest Christian thinkers and teachers, from the early church fathers through Augustine, Luther, Calvin, and Wesley, have taught that *everything* true, good, beautiful, and helpful in this world is actually a gift of God, *regardless of where it came from or how it got here.* They used many different terms for this idea, but they all linked it to God's compassion and grace for the whole world.

On the simplest level, there are the everyday gifts we all take for granted, which preserve life on this earth. "Your Father in heaven," said Jesus, "causes His sun to rise on the evil and the good, and sends rain on the righteous and the unrighteous" (Matthew 5:45). "The Lord is gracious and compassionate, slow to anger and rich in love. The Lord is good to all; He has compassion on all He has made" (Psalm 145:8–9).

On a higher level, some of the basics of human nature such as conscience, reason, and the ability to think and discover truth are gifts from God. Paul uses this idea to hold everyone responsible before God (Romans 1:19–20; 2:12–15). Of course, this *discovered truth* is not on the same level as *God's revealed truth. It cannot save us, but it is truth just the same, and has come from God.*

I get a lot of letters and calls from sincere Christians who say something like this. "Thanks for your books; they've helped me a lot. But I don't understand; it sounds like you believe in *psychology.*" I always reply, "Of course I do, and I believe in *sociology, criminology, urology, radiology, political science, mathematics, computer science, aerodynamics,* and *scores of other sources of knowledge, because I believe God is the source of all truth.*" It's just my way of trying to get them to appreciate all of God's gracious gifts, even those that might come to us through unusual channels.

The great reformer and theologian, John Calvin, wrote much about the positive merit of man's "terrestrial" culture which includes all "civil polity, domestic economy, all the mechanical arts and liberal sciences." He even referred to heathen writers, philosophers, and poets by saying,

> If we believe that the Spirit of God is the only fountain of truth, we shall neither reject nor despise the truth itself, wherever it shall appear, unless we wish to insult the Spirit of God. . . . All truth is from God, and consequently if wicked men have said anything that is true and just, we ought not to reject it, for it has come from God."[1]

What Calvin called "common grace," John Wesley included within "prevenient grace," crediting God as the author of all wisdom and understanding in mankind. But all of them really go back to Augustine, who coined the phrase, "plundering the Egyptians." This meant we Christians have a right to take the truth wherever and however God gives it to us.

The most amazing example of this is in the Bible itself. When Paul was preaching at Athens he quoted non-Christian philosophers and poets in his sermon. How many times we have all heard someone refer to those beautiful words of Scripture, "In Him we live and move and have our being" (Acts 17:28). We don't stop to realize that Paul is quoting a pagan philosopher of his day!

Why do we stress this primary and generalized idea of grace? So that we will be open to let God speak to us in any way He chooses. We do not need to be afraid of anything helpful which comes through these channels. Because God has given us the special revelation of Himself in His Word, we can test everything by Scripture. That does *not* mean we will necessarily find it in the Bible in the words we use today. Rather, our concern should be whether an idea agrees with the principles of Scripture. Anything that meets *this test* we can receive *with gratitude to God.*

Many people ask me, "Where in the Bible does it talk about inner healing or the healing of memories?" I usually reply, "It's in the same chapter which said it was okay for my daughter to have an emergency appendectomy which saved her life!"

Yes, we are thankful for each new truth, insight, invention, or discovery which comes to us from such fields as medicine, psychology, sociology, and any other branches of human knowledge. Of course, there are evil people who can use them for sinful purposes. The same airplane that carries missionaries to reach people with the Gospel can be used to drop bombs and kill them. *The answer to misuse is not disuse.* As Christians, we are *required* by God to use every gift He has given us for His glory and for human good.

Restraining Grace

If God had abandoned the creation and His creatures after the Fall by allowing the consequences of sin to have their full effects, the human race would have never survived. His love and compassion is shown in many forms of what has been called restraining grace.

Though sin has badly damaged our power of reason, God did not allow it to be destroyed. So even unsaved and unregenerate humans have this amazing gift from God—a mind which can reason, think, remember, imagine, discover, and invent. Far above and beyond all other creatures, we humans can understand the relationship between cause and effect. No, we cannot by reasoning find God or work out our own salvation. We don't even have the power to live up to the best we can reason. But God has worked through the gift of reason to help hold sin in check.

The Bible suggests that human governments which make and enforce laws are God's agents in restraining the power of evil in the world. Paul states this clearly in Romans 13:1–7 where he points out that a human ruler is "God's servant to do you good. But if you do wrong be afraid . . . for he is God's servant, an agent of wrath to bring punishment on the wrongdoer" (v. 4). Peter writes in a similar way in his first epistle (2:13–14). I remind you that they are both writing about a system we Americans would consider cruel and at times evil—the Roman Empire. But they still considered it "an agent of God" for good. I used to wonder about this until I had a most unusual missionary experience.

India became an independent nation in 1947. All of the native states joined the new government except Hyderabad State, the one in which we lived. India tried to settle the issue by every possible peaceful and diplomatic measure, but to no avail. Finally in 1948, the Indian government sent in its army and took over by force. But they were a bit too successful and captured our town a day ahead of schedule. The army then camped outside the city and waited for the new civil administration team. However, they didn't arrive until the next day. So we lived in a town of 35,000 people for 24 hours *without any government.* That night stores and houses were robbed and burned. In those days food was rationed, and the central warehouse housing the grain was looted. *I saw human nature without the restraints of enforced law and order,* and it is a sight I hope never to see again. I learned that some government, though bad, is better than no government. The country or the culture makes no difference, for exactly the same things happened during the terrible riots of the '60s in Detroit, Chicago, and Los Angeles. I now understand what those Scriptures mean and how important God's restraining grace is. Did we ever stop to thank God for His restraining grace which was at work in our lives *long before we came to know Him as our Saviour?* His restraining grace not only held us back from deeper sin, it also prevented us from being the victims of even worse evil. One of the stanzas of the hymn, "Now the Day Is Over," expresses this so beautifully.

> Comfort every sufferer
> Watching late in pain;
> Those who plan some evil,
> From their sins restrain.

In his excellent book, *The Way,*[2] Dr. E. Stanley Jones states that the earliest name for Christians was "those who belonged to the Way" (Acts 9:2; 19:23; 24:22). Of course, this refers to the way of salvation, but Dr. Jones enlarges it to also mean God's Way, the right way for everything—the way to think, feel, and act. It is the Way God has written into the nature of everything in the universe, so that life sifts down to two basic alternatives, the Way and not the Way. And the Christian way is always the right way and the unchristian way is always the wrong way.

Why is this? Because God has superimposed external laws upon us, like the Ten Commandments? No, because God has woven those laws into the fabric of the entire universe. The Way is something given; we don't produce it, we don't build it; it's just there in the nature of things. And we must come to terms with this Way and its principles, or get hurt. Thus we do not break these laws written into the nature of things; we only break ourselves on them. When we fall from a tall building, we don't *break* the law of gravity; we only *demonstrate* it when we hit the ground. And these built-in laws are manifestations of God's preventive grace; they are barriers put up at the edge of the precipice to keep us from going over. Jones quoted a surgeon who confirmed this principle. "I've discovered the kingdom of God at the end of my scalpel. It's in the tissues. The right thing morally is always the healthy thing physically."

I have used Dr. Jones' idea in my counseling ministry for many years, pointing out to people how the universe either works for us or against us. I remember a married woman who shared with me her infatuation for another man and her strong temptation to have an affair with him. She was a Christian and the Holy Spirit had been faithful in checking her impulses. But now she was beginning to rationalize and I could see it was probably only a matter of time until she yielded. Of course, she knew the biblical commandments against this, but they didn't seem to be enough to deter her. I was trying to get her to see how God's built-in moral laws operate in all our interpersonal relationships, and that the affair was doomed to futility and frustration. I kept explaining, "You can choose to go ahead with this, but the universe won't back you. You are going against it and it will go against you." After awhile she began to give in to the temptation and started down the slippery slope toward a full-blown affair. Thank God, before that took place she found herself on the verge of physical and emotional breakdown. When she came back to see me she said, "I didn't believe you when you told me, 'The universe won't back you in this.' But you were right. All sorts of things have happened to trouble me —in my body, my mind, my emotions, and my interpersonal family relationships."

She discovered what E. Stanley Jones wrote nearly a half-century before. "The word *evil* is the word *live* spelled backwards. It is life attempting to live against itself. And that can't be done . . . it is an attempt to live against the nature of reality and get away with it. It is an attempt at the impossible. The result is inevitable—breakdown and frustration."[3] This incident reminded me of an ancient proverb said to be quoted by sailors, "He who spits against the wind spits in his own face."

The Apostle Paul is the perfect scriptural illustration of this form of grace. While he was still called Saul, he was confronted by the risen Christ on the road to Damascus, "Saul, Saul, why do you persecute Me? It is hard for you to kick against the goads" (Acts 26:14). Jesus was using a common picture from ancient life. When a young ox was first yoked, it would try to kick its way out. But in doing so it only hurt itself more on a jagged spike, the goad, placed there for this very purpose. The more it kicked against the goads, the sharper the pain.

It was the goads which brought it into submission. Unfortunately, we too often have to learn the hard way, and God has built His goads of grace into all of life. First Peter 3:12 is a quote from Psalm 34:16: "The face of the Lord is against those who do evil." This "againstness" toward wrong has been written into all of life. When we understand this, we see God's anger in a completely different light. We discover God's judgment is actually a form of His mercy. We understand it as the opposite side of the coin of His love manifested in His restraining grace. It is one of the gracious ways God uses to turn us away from sin and toward Himself, in order to redeem and restore us.

Seeking Grace

Finally we come to the grace of God which seeks us for our salvation. Of course, throughout all of the various kinds of grace we have been saying God's central purpose is to bring us all to the place of repentance, faith, and new life in Christ. "He is patient with you, not wanting anyone to perish, but everyone to come to repentance" (2 Peter 3:9). So this is God's design woven into the total fabric of life. But there comes the time when we can actually sense His seeking grace at work in more specific ways.

Many of us forget that back of the familiar "We love Him because He first loved us" (1 John 4:19, KJV) is an even prior truth. We *seek* Him because He *first sought us*. Theologians throughout the ages have realized that one of the chief ways God seeks us is by creating within us a hunger to seek Him. Even we Christians, since we are human beings, tend to overlook this and become self-centered in our testimonies. John tells us in his Gospel (1:43) that "Jesus decided to leave for Galilee. Finding Philip He said to him, 'Follow Me.'" Then two verses later (1:45) he says, "Philip found Nathaniel and told him, 'We have found the One Moses wrote about . . . Jesus of Nazareth.'" What an interesting contrast. Philip claims he "found Jesus." Actually prior to this Jesus had found him! Prodding grace means God is always first on the scene long before we even think about Him. An unknown hymn writer says it best.

> I sought the Lord and afterward I knew
> He moved my soul to seek Him, seeking me.
> It was not I that found, O Saviour true,
> No, I was found of Thee.

Thou didst reach forth Thy hand and mine enfold,
I walked and sank not on the storm-vexed sea;
'Twas not so much that I on Thee took hold
As Thou, dear Lord, on me.

I find, I walk, I love, But oh, the whole of love
Is but my answer, Lord, to Thee!
For Thou wert long beforehand with my soul;
Always Thou lovedst me.[4]

We must always remember when we talk about "seeking God," or "searching for truth," or "following after light," the only reason we do any of those things is because God is already at work in our hearts prodding us with His seeking grace.

While I was preaching a Spiritual Life series at a university, a young man named Jack came to counsel with me. Like many other preachers' kids, he was rebelling against the faith of his parents and his own preteen conversion experience. He told me his story with deep shame. In his attempt to run from God he had deliberately dated a girl well known on campus for her loose morals. They had faked a signout to go to their homes for the weekend but ended up in a distant motel, spending the night together. However, what he had fantasized as a night of ecstatic pleasure turned out to be quite different. Now he felt guilty, empty and, worst of all, abandoned by God. He kept saying to me, "I just can't seem to find Him again." I kept answering, "What you really mean, Jack, is you can't get away from Him." He asked me to explain what I had said, for it was the opposite of what he felt. I opened my Bible to Psalm 139:7–8, handed it to him, and asked him to read it. He began reading as it is found in the *King James Version*. "Whither shall I go from Thy Spirit? or whither shall I flee from Thy presence? If I ascend up into heaven, Thou art there; if I make my bed. . . ." He stopped. I said, "Go on, Jack, finish it." He continued slowly, "If I make my bed in hell, behold Thou art there." I asked, "Jack, who do you think you met in that motel room?" He looked puzzled. "I don't understand. Do you mean the . . . the girl?" I replied, "No, no, Jack. I mean *God*. Don't you realize when you tried to run *from* God, you ran right smack *into* Him that night in the motel? In fact God was never nearer than then." Big tears began to trickle down his cheeks. Soon we were praying to the One who had never stopped seeking His wayward son. God's *love* had never changed, only His *strategy.* Jack learned you can *refuse* God's love, but you can't *lose* it when the Hound of Heaven is on your trail!

Sometimes God *seeks us by letting us go. Letting us go our own way and allowing us to suffer the inevitable consequences of that way in the hope that our suffering will bring us back to Him.*

In the greatest seeking chapter of Scripture, Luke 15, we see this so clearly. In the case of the Lost Sheep and the Lost Coin, there is direct action until the lost is found. But in the case of the Lost Boy (the Prodigal Son), this is not the case. The Father is silent—he does not *speak to him.* He seems inactive—he does not *stop him.* He does not *seek him* by going after him. He *seeks him by keeping quiet and letting him go into a distant country where someday a "severe famine" will occur, and he will "begin to be in need," and perhaps he will come "to his senses."*

Back in the early '70s, a young man named Andy came for help. He had reached the end of his rope, was in a deep depression, and had been contemplating suicide. As I sat and listened to his story I couldn't help thinking of Jesus' Parable of the Prodigal. In my mind I followed the parallel at every step. Andy had run away from a good home, gotten into heavy drugs, and begun to lose control of his drinking. Prior to his enrollment at Asbury College he had been living in a commune in an eastern city. The three fellows and two girls shared everything—lodging, food, and sex. But life had fallen apart. Now he was empty and fed up.

Before I realized what I was saying I blurted out, "You know, Andy, you've done everything the Prodigal did except eat the pigs' food." He looked startled and fell silent. I started to apologize, thinking I'd said the wrong thing, but the Holy Spirit was way ahead of me.

"Oh no," he said, "I just remembered . . . I've even done that!"

Now it was my turn to look startled. "What in the world do you mean?"

"Well, I attended the great Woodstock Rock Festival in '69. You remember the crowd was so huge (over 400,000) they ran out of food, and we ended up almost starving. But no one could get out to buy food. So finally helicopters flew over and dropped macrobiotic hog food in huge bundles. And we all grabbed it and ate it with our bare hands." Andy groaned out a disgusting "Yuk" as he remembered the taste.

After that there was only one incident of the parable left for Andy to make the parallel complete—the journey back to the Father's house.

Before long that part of the story had also been fulfilled! Thank God for His steadfast love and His faithful grace which reaches into every human situation. God sometimes does this by allowing sin and evil to overplay its hand. He permits it to go too far until there is a kickback of consequences. And God takes this opportunity to woo us and win us through painful grace.

Saving Grace

Finally, there is the direct action of the seeking Spirit of God upon the human spirit. At this point *all of the influences of the previous forms of grace are gathered together and the pressure of the immediate presence of God is evident in the consciousness of the person.* This is the supreme moment in the divine-human encounter. "Here I am!" says Jesus, in Revelation 3:20. "I stand at the door and knock. If anyone hears My voice and opens the door, I will go in and eat with him, and he with Me." The Holy Spirit of God is on the outside knocking and speaking. He is also within us, opening our ears so we can hear and giving us the will and the ability to respond. It is He who offers us the gift of faith so we can trust in spite of all our fears and hesitations. It is all of God's grace. Even the "faith" is "not from (y)ourselves, it is the gift of God" (Ephesians 2:8).

A great example of the pursuing grace of God is given us by John Bunyan, the author of *Pilgrim's Progress.* In another one of his writings, *Grace Abounding*, he tells of the time in his life when he was running from God. Bunyan calls these times his "flying fits." He says during those moments, when he literally fled from God, a certain verse from the Book of Isaiah would continuously come to his mind. It was so vivid and real to his memory it was as if the passage actually called out after him. "I have blotted out as a thick cloud thy transgressions, and as a cloud thy sins. Return unto Me, for I have redeemed you" (Isaiah 44:22). He writes, "This would make me stop for a while, and, as it were, look over my shoulder behind me to see if I could discern that the *God of grace would follow me with a pardon in His hand.*" What a striking picture of the pursuing grace of a loving God. Let us not think that this kind of direct initiative by God's Spirit is limited to times past. Again and again I have been astounded by it. I was when a lady shared her story with me.

Linda is now a pastor's wife, and a radiant, Spirit-filled Christian. But she did not come from that kind of background—quite the opposite. She was a battered child, abused physically and sexually by her own brothers and a stepfather. This had filled her with deep shame and low self-esteem which had plunged her deeper into sin. Finally she ran away from home and ended up at eighteen years of age in New York City. She was alone and had very few friends. One night, literally in a den of evil, she was sitting on a chair in a room. She was practically naked, and in the same room on the bed was a couple engaged in sexual intercourse. There swept over her a devastating sense of loneliness and guilt. The terrible realization of *where* she was and *who* she was and the fact *no one really cared* overwhelmed her. She suddenly realized the utter selfishness of the scene—everyone there was using each other and using her. It hit her like a thunderbolt and filled her with awful blackness, depression, and despair.

But in the midst of that situation there came (what she called) an overshadowing sense of the presence of God. The thought arose within her like an inner voice, "I love you, I always have and I always will. I really care for you and love you." She turned around, knelt at the chair, and putting her head in her hands began to sob. "O God, fill my emptiness. Please love me the way I've always wanted to be loved." That was a beginning. Within a month she underwent a dramatic conversion. She told me, "I experienced a flooding, a sense of God's complete forgiveness. And most of all, what I'd really wanted all my life—a clean heart." Reborn and restored, she got help, returned home, and was reconciled to her mother. Eventually she became the instrument through whom God reached several family members.

We have traced grace in some of its most important forms. In and through them all we cannot help but be struck by the Divine initiative. God is always first on the scene. Long before even "the creation of the world" (Ephesians 1:4) His grace had us in mind. And although Calvary occurred at a definite time and place within history, Jesus was "the Lamb that was slain from the creation of the world" (Revelation 13:8). Believe me, we have been recipients of grace (humanly speaking) for a long, long time. The way of grace is not some afterthought on God's part. It's *the* way, the *only* way God ever planned.

Ultimate Grace

This same grace will ultimately be our only basis for eternal fellowship with God in the life to come. In the final verse of the final chapter of the final book of Scripture, Revelation 22:21, John prays, "The grace of the Lord Jesus be with God's people. Amen." We can be sure every one of God's people who will worship and serve Him throughout eternity will be there for only *one reason—because they were recipients of grace—God's love freely given to the undeserving and the unworthy.* There is no other basis for entrance into the kingdom of God—here on earth or in heaven.

As a teenager, I attended many summer services held in the great holiness camp meetings of the Midwest. Sitting on the uncomfortable wooden benches, my feet touching the sawdust on the floor of the tabernacle, I listened in awe to some of the great evangelists of that day. I will always be grateful for their grace-filled messages. I remember often hearing descriptions of how it was going to be when we entered the gates of heaven. Inscribed over the arch of the entranceway, we were told, would be these words, "Whosoever will may come." But after we had entered in, if we were to look back at the gateway, we would see the words, "For by grace are you saved."

The House of the Hapsburgs had ruled the Austro-Hungarian Empire since 1273 and the family had been a major political power in Europe until the Great War of 1914–1918. The funeral of the Emperor Franz-Josef I of Austria was in November 1916.[5] It was the last of the grandiose imperial funerals to be staged.

The Hapsburgs are buried in the family crypt located in the basement of the Capucin Monastery of Vienna. On the day of the funeral, the entire court assembled in full white dress, their hats covered with ostrich plumes. A military band played somber dirges and an anthem by Haydn. The cortege wound its way down stairs illumined with flaming torches, bearing the coffin draped in the imperial colors, black and gold. Finally it reached the great iron doors of the crypt, behind which stood the Cardinal-Archbishop of Vienna, along with his entourage of high church officials.

The officer in charge of the procession was the Court Marshall. As he approached the closed door and pounded on it with the hilt of his ceremonial sword, he was following a ceremony prescribed from time immemorial. "Open!" he commanded.

"Who goes there?" intoned the Cardinal.

"We bear the remains of His Imperial and Apostolic Majesty, Franz-Josef I, by the Grace of God Emperor of Austria, King of Hungary, Defender of the Faith, Prince of Bohemia-Moravia, Grand Duke of Lombardy, Venezia, Styrgia. . . ." And so on, through the *thirty-seven titles* of the Emperor.

"We know him not," replied the Cardinal, from beyond the door. "Who goes there?"

"We bear the remains of His Majesty, Franz-Josef I, Emperor of Austria and King of Hungary"—this very abbreviated form was allowed only in dire emergencies.

"We know him not," came the Cardinal's reply again. "Who goes there?"

"We bear the body of Franz-Josef, *our brother, a sinner like us all!*"

Whereupon, the massive doors swung slowly open and Franz-Josef was borne within.

> For it is by grace you have been saved,
> through faith,
> and this not from yourselves,
> it is the gift of God.

Notes

Chapter 1
1. See my book, *Healing for Damaged Emotions*, Wheaton. Illinois: Victor Books. 1981, pp. 79–84.
2. David Stoop, *Living With a Perfectionist*, Nashville: Oliver Nelson Books, 1987, p. 13.
3. *The American Heritage Dictionary of the English Language*, Wm. Morris, Editor, New York: Houghton Mifflin Co., 1973, p. 962.

Chapter 2
1. See my book. *Healing of Memories*, Wheaton, Illinois: Victor Books, 1985, pp. 95–122.
2. Unpublished scholarly paper, *Eyes That Cannot See: American Worldview and the Distortion of Grace*, Ralph Satter, 1987.

Chapter 3
1. *The American Heritage Dictionary of the English Language*, Wm. Morris, Editor, New York: Houghton Mifflin Co., 1973, p. 407; and Appendix, p. 1514.
2. Corrie ten Boom, *In My Father's House*, Old Tappan, New Jersey: Fleming H. Revell, 1976, p. 58.
3. Ken Magid and Carole McKelvey, *High Risk Children: Children Without Conscience*, Golden, Colorado: M and M Publishers, 1987.
4. *Ibid., p.* 26.
5. Early Jabay, *The God Players* and *The Kingdom of the Self*, Grand Rapids: Zondervan Publishing House, 1969.

Chapter 4
1. Augustine, *The City of God*, Marcus Dods, Tr., in *Nicene and Post-Nicene Fathers*, book 14, vol. 2, Grand Rapids: William B. Eerdmans Publishing Company, 1983, p. 273.

Chapter 5
1. *The Encyclopedia Americana*, 1968 Edition, vol. 4, p. 532.

Chapter 6
1. Especially the writings of Karen Horney. Her books, *The Neurotic Personality of Our Time,* and *Neurosis and Human Growth*, New York: W.W. Norton Co., are classics in this field.

2. Horney, *Neurosis and Human Growth*, pp. 17–39.
3. *Ibid.*, pp. 187–290.

Chapter 7
1. A.W. Tozer, *The Knowledge of the Holy*, New York: Harper and Brothers Publishers, 1961, p. 100.
2. For a thorough discussion see William T. Kirwan, *Biblical Concepts for Christian Counseling*, Grand Rapids: Baker Book House, 1984, pp. 46–53.
3. *Ibid.*, p. 47. (Taken from Eerdman's *New Bible Dictionary*, p. 140).
4. *Ibid.*, pp. 47–51.

Chapter 9
1. For a detailed description of this form of inner healing and spiritual therapy, see my book, *Healing of Memones*, Wheaton, Illinois: Victor Books, 1985.

Chapter 10
1. See my book, *Healing for Damaged Emotions*, Wheaton, Illinois: Victor Books, 1981, p. 73.

Chapter 11
1. Charles Dickens, *Great Expectations* (Second Edition), New York: Holt and Rhinehart, 1972, p. 59.

Chapter 12
1. *The Institutes II*, ii, 15. Translated by John Allen. 2 Vols. Philadelphia Presbyterian Board of Publications, 1909, and *Commentary on Titus*, 1:12; cf. *Commentary on John*, 4:36. (Commentary on the Catholic Epistles. Translated by John Owen, Grand Rapids, William B. Eerdmans Publishing Company, 1948).
2. E. Stanley Jones, *The Way*, Nashville: Abingdon Press, 1946, pp. 19–60.
3. *Ibid.*, p. 43
4. *The United Methodist Book of Hymns*, 1964, p. 98.
5. The details of this story were given to me by Dt. Ed McKinley, Professor of History, Asbury College.